A Spirited Resistance

THE JOHNS HOPKINS UNIVERSITY STUDIES IN
HISTORICAL AND POLITICAL SCIENCE
109TH SERIES (1991)

TENSKWATAWA, "THE PROPHET"

A Spirited Resistance

>>>>>>>><<<<<<<<

THE NORTH AMERICAN INDIAN
STRUGGLE FOR UNITY,
1745–1815

Gregory Evans Dowd

The Johns Hopkins University Press
Baltimore and London

Frontispiece: Tenskwatawa, "The Prophet," by Henry Inman. Painted between 1830 and 1832, from an original by Charles Bird King painted between 1822 and 1832. The original was destroyed by fire on January 24, 1865. (*Source:*: National Portrait Gallery, NPG 82. 71, Smithsonian Institution, Washington D.C.)

The Johns Hopkins University Press
701 West 40th Street
Baltimore, Maryland 21211-2190
The Johns Hopkins Press Ltd., London

The paper used in this book meets the minimum requirements of American National Standard for Information Sciences— Permanence of Paper for Printed Library Materials, ANSI Z39.48-1984.

Library of Congress Cataloging-in-Publication Data
Dowd, Gregory Evans.
A spirited resistance : the North American Indian struggle for
unity, 1745–1815 / Gregory Evans Dowd.
p.   cm. — (The Johns Hopkins University studies in
historical and political science ; 109th ser., 4)
Includes bibliographical references (p.   ) and index.
ISBN 0-8018-4236-0
1. Indians of North America—History—18th century.
2. Indians of North America—Wars—1750–1815.   3. Nativistic
movements—United States.   4. Indians of North America—
Ethnic identity.   I. Title.   II. Series.
E77.D694   1991
973'.0497—dc20   91-16985

To my father, Victor E. Dowd,
and to my mother, Marjorie B. Dowd

Contents

Preface and Acknowledgments

> > > > > > > < < < < < < <

One hundred years ago the self-trained anthropologist James Mooney began his study of messianic movements among the American Indians, inaugurating a century of scholarly investigation of millennial movements, not only in North America but also around the globe. Mooney introduced his main subject, the "Ghost Dance" movement of the late nineteenth century, with a wide-ranging survey of earlier Native American prophets, their teachings, and, most provocatively, their influence upon one another. Since then, several scholars have given cursory treatment to the last point, but no book has taken it on as its core subject.[1]

A half century before Mooney, Francis Parkman began to conceive his own sweeping history of early America. Cited by Mooney for its description of one prophet, Parkman's *The Conspiracy of Pontiac and the Indian Uprising of 1763* investigated a series of attacks on British posts in the Great Lakes and Ohio country, now known as Pontiac's War. Though written first, the work formed the conclusion of Parkman's vast study of the colonial struggle for North America. Unlike Mooney, Parkman treated Native Americans as a regressive force, a challenge met and surmounted, more than as creative actors in their own right. Parkman nonetheless found Native America indispensable to American history.[2]

In the twentieth century, many historians of Native America have cast away Parkman's regressive Indian. With it they have thrown out both Parkman's and Mooney's impressive breadth. Employing anthropology, one branch of history has produced hundreds of regional or tribal studies, demonstrating the textured diversity of the continent's peoples and their experiences, but rendering comprehensive treatment difficult. The regional studies, moreover, allow their boundaries to be defined by Anglo-American usages, so that we have studies of New England, the South, or of a particular colony or state. These regions meant less to the Native Americans of colonial America than they do to historians and readers today.[3] Leaning on the available archival materials, another branch has studied the institutions of Indian-white relations—government, army, church, school, trade, or benevolent organization—and the policies adopted by the institutions; by the nature of its materials and orientation, this branch bends toward the East, toward Europeans and Euro-Americans, not toward American Indians themselves.[4] A third category, less abundant but probably more widely read, has tightened the focus to biography, demonstrating the choices made by individuals and their influence upon events.[5] A final branch bears mentioning; richly informative, it has produced studies not so much of Indians (or policies directed at them) as of the Europeans' perceptions of Indians.[6]

As of 1980, most studies of American Indians in the colonial and revolutionary periods sprouted from one of these branches. They have drawn the attention of some colonial and revolutionary historians who do not specialize on Native America, notably Edmund S. Morgan and Gary Nash. These two have incorporated the studies' findings into broader interpretations of American history.[7] But the limited tribal, institutional, and biographical scope of most studies has pulled American Indian history away from the broad sweep of American history, away from the misbegotten promise of Parkman. Historians of early America with other issues at heart, confronted with vast, atomized minutia, have found it difficult to comprehend a larger Native American picture. That picture, it would seem, simply could not exist.

Several historians of Native Americans in the British colonial and revolutionary periods, recognizing these limits, seeking a more panoramic vision, turned in the 1980s to the comparative method. Abandoning Parkman's Indian, recent historians have recovered and restated his promise; they have returned Native Americans to a larger, and perhaps more visible, early American drama. James Axtell has compared the encounters of Native Americans with both Jesuits and Puritans, giving a semicontinental prospect not only of policy or church but of the movement of ideas between Indian and European. Richard White has produced a fully continental study of three tribes, in effect three tribal studies linked by a common theme and demonstrating a common process. J. Leitch Wright, Jr., Daniel K. Richter, and James M. Merrell have separately taken a different tack, demonstrating that the "tribes" themselves were often multiethnic unions and that "tribal history," or the history of Indian "confederacies," can itself provide a panoramic view of Indian actions in early American history. Francis Jennings, not to be limited by past methods, has completed a three-volume study of an institution, the Covenant Chain, that was created by *both* Indians and Europeans through intensive, often brilliant, if self-interested, diplomacy. The diplomatic history of Jennings's chief subject, the Five (and later Six) Nations Iroquois, has indeed provided another outlet for those seeking something more than tribal or institutional history, as the contributors to Richter and Merrell's recent volume *Beyond the Covenant Chain* have shown. Neither strictly "tribal" nor concerned only with European institutions or with regions defined by Europeans, the new focus on intertribal relations promises a big picture with a Native American cast.[8]

This is an important shift, for it brings what is best about biography and tribal history, the acknowledgment of Indian agency, together with what is best about the institutional and policy history, a broader historical and geographic landscape. Historians have begun to realize what Mooney knew a century ago: that Native Americans acted in a world beyond the locality, that they explored ranges of possibilities and traveled widely to do so, and that they taught, learned from, and argued with each other in the process.

One of the lessons that Native Americans developed, studied, taught, and disputed between 1745 and 1815 concerned Indian identity. The lesson had small beginnings in refugee communities on Pennsylvania's Susquehanna River, but it spread widely through eastern North America, affecting Indian actions in every conflict between the Seven Years' War and the War of 1812. The lesson taught that all Indians were of a single people, separately created and required to perform special duties. Failure to fulfill these obligations had brought on a dispiriting loss of power. Given voice by prophets calling for reformation, the lesson called for action. Intertribal, indeed semicontinental, the lesson deserves a hearing by historians, for it produced a movement, a religiously charged struggle for unity. That movement drew both Indian and Euro-American opposition. That movement—its growth, hiatus, florescence, destruction, and legacy—is the subject of this book.

I follow the movement from its orgins in the turbulence surrounding the Seven Years' War (Chapters One and Two), through its submergence during and in the aftermath of the Revolutionary War (Chapters Three through Five), to its resurgence and defeat in the foreglow and intense heat of the War of 1812 (Chapters Seven through Nine). The first chapter suggests the movement's cultural moorings, the sixth briefly investigates the federal government's understanding of and efforts against it, while an afterword explores its contentious legacy and the varied shapes it took in the memories it came to inhabit.

Parts of the story have been told before. The movement produced leaders who have found rare places in standard histories of America. Most notable among these, and treated in the formative works of Parkman, Mooney, and even Henry Adams, are Pontiac and Tecumseh.[9] The careers of these leaders, however, were unusual among their peoples only for the amount of attention they have generated among writers. Long viewed as exceptionally innovative strategists and as authors of militant pan-Indianism, these two men were, I suggest, its products or, better, its adherents. They were not its creators, nor were they ever its indispensable leaders.

Histories both of "Pontiac's War" and of Tecumseh's role in the coming of the War of 1812 have posthumously rendered peculiar gifts unto the two men by keenly isolating the sacred from the profane. The two leaders, according to the current view, personify the second, secular, dimension. Pontiac and Tecumseh, both warriors, stand, negotiate, and fight as great, even pragmatic, Americans. In atavistic juxtaposition, personifying the sacred sphere, are the two major prophets, the Delaware Neolin and the Shawnee Tenskwatawa. Several works from the age of Parkman to our own day explicitly place the prophets in one camp and the war leaders in another, claiming that the Delaware Prophet "may serve as a counterpart to the famous Shawnee Prophet," that Tecumseh "took Pontiac for his model."[10]

The distinction between the sacred nativist and the secular, between the believer and the thinker, a distinction that goes far beyond that between the priest and the soldier, cannot be maintained. Perhaps the paradoxical product of Christian hostility toward native belief and of secular hostility toward belief in general, the interpretive framework should be dismantled. The prophets and the military leaders of the movement for unity drew inspiration from identical sources. Figures at opposite corners of the standard interpretation, for instance the Shawnee Prophet of the 1800s and the Ottawa Pontiac of the 1760s, shared visions and strategies, and shared them with others who will appear in this book: a Mohawk woman, Coochoochee, who lived among the Shawnees; a Delaware man, anonymous alas, who inspired a town called Kuskuski; his tribesman, Wangomend, who competed with Christians; a Cherokee war leader, Dragging Canoe, who sang war songs with Indians from afar; an Alabama Creek, Francis, who visited England; an Ottawa, the Trout, who fought alcohol abuse toward the northern tip of Michigan's mitten; Cherokee men and women, names unknown, who had visions on a low, bare, mountain in north Georgia; Sauks in Illinois, Seminoles in Florida, Senecas in New York and Pennsylvania.

The striking fact is that Native Americans themselves, unlike many of their historians, could think continentally. Many of them came to recognize commonality. Factions of them acted on that recognition, producing a movement as religious as it was political. The thesis that the movement was intertribal, that it integrated the religious and the political, and that it spanned generations does not originate with me. It was first suggested by the Shawnee Prophet himself, who in 1810 "boasted that he would follow in the footsteps of the Great Pontiac."[11] Declaring himself an heir to an Ottawa from the 1760s, whom scholars have since mistakenly isolated with Tecumseh as a pragmatist, even a nonbeliever, the prophet was doing good history on a bold scale.

Over the years of writing and revising this book I have had assistance and encouragement from many. Karen Ordahl Kupperman first introduced me to the importance of Indians in the British colonies. Entire drafts of the manuscript were read and closely criticized by Barbara Graymont, Douglas Greenberg, Martha Hodes, Allan Kulikoff and Brian R. MacDonald. Chapters and portions of chapters were examined, sometimes in the context of conference panels, by Dee Andrews, James Axtell, Jonathan Berkey, Tom Broman, John Carson, Nina Dayton, Raymond Fogelson, Jim Goodman, Suellen Hoy, Wilbur Jacobs, Francis Jennings, Thomas Kselman, Louis Masur, Mark Meyerson, Catherine Peroux, Carol Quillen, Susan Mackiewicz, Reid Mitchell, Daniel K. Richter, Daniel Rodgers, Nancy Rosenberg, Neal Salisbury, Eric Schneider, Frank Smith, Lawrence Stone, Helen Sword, Alden Vaughan, Rachel Weil, and Michael Zuckerman. Henry Tom, my editor, has gently guided the final stages of the shaping of this book. John Murrin has been the steadiest source of support and criticism; I consider myself fortunate to have been his student.

Several institutions provided financial assistance: the Department of Anthropology of the Smithsonian Institution (here I must thank William C. Sturtevant); the Newberry Library's D'Arcy McNickle Center for the History of the American Indian; and the University of Notre Dame. Princeton University provided scholarships that made my graduate study and dissertation possible. The Philadelphia Center for Early American Studies provided a generous fellowship at a crucial moment.

Earlier versions of chapters were formally presented at the Pennsylvania Historical Society, the Pennsylvania History Association, the American Society for Ethnohistory, the Philadelphia Center for Early American

Studies, the Transformation of Philadelphia Seminar, the Shelby Cullom Davis Center for Historical Studies, and the American Historical Association, and less formally at sessions of Princeton University's Americanist Group, Princeton's Graduate History Association Seminar, and the University of Notre Dame's History Seminar. In detailed ways that I now cannot recount, I benefited at these sessions from the contributions of my friends and colleagues. Portions of Chapter Eight appeared in *Critical Matrix: Princeton Working Papers in Women's Studies* 3 (1987): 1–30; portions of Chapters Two and Three in *Ethnohistory* 30 (1990): 254–278; and an expanded version of Chapter Seven in the *American Indian Quarterly* (forthcoming).

This book got its start in the basement of the Firestone Library at Princeton University. I must here thank Alfred Bush, curator of Western Americana at the Firestone, for his encouragement and help. I have also borrowed from the collections of the University of Notre Dame's Hessburgh Library, the University of Pennsylvania's Van Pelt Library, and the Powell Library of the National Museum of Natural History. I am very grateful to the staffs of the Newberry Library, particularly John Aubrey, and of the Pennsylvania Historical Society, particularly Louise Jones. I thank the efficient staff of the British Public Record Office at Kew, and the knowledgeable and helpful staffs of the Manuscript Division of the Library of Congress, the Henry E. Huntington Library, and the American Philosophical Society. The staffs of Indiana University's Glenn Black Archaeological Library, the University of Michigan's William Clements Library, the United States National Archives, the Smithsonian Institution's National Anthropological Archives, and the Library Company of Philadelphia kindly permitted me to work freely in their collections.

I have included three maps to illustrate the general locations of various towns, individuals, and events named in the text. I do not claim cartographic precision; only general accuracy. They were compiled from several sources and were drawn by my father, Victor E. Dowd with the help of Robert Loomis.[12] Finally, I thank Ada ver Loren van Themaat, for all.

Introduction

One night in 1760 the gathered people of the village of Tioga witnessed their fate in the heavens. Here, on a mountain-fringed plain beside Pennsylvania's flooding Susquehanna River, not far from the present border of New York, the villagers looked into the night sky, where two violent horses did battle in the face of the moon. Having galloped in an ascent from the east, one of the horses overpowered its western enemy. The scene left the Indians below surprised and "vexed." As they set out to discover its meaning, word of the vision swept through the villages of the valley.[1]

The people on the plain were Munsees, speakers of a dialect of the Delaware language. They inhabited one of perhaps a dozen villages that the British increasingly, though still loosely, identified as constituent parts of the Delaware "tribe," "nation," or "people."[2] They lived on the Susquehanna River, as they had for some twenty years before those celestial horses reared in the moonlight. The Tiogans had earlier come west to the Susquehanna from the Upper Delaware. Before long, most of them would again move, this time from the Susquehanna to the Upper Ohio, pushed further west by the British colonists until, eighteen years after the vision, Tioga burned under a visitation by the revolutionaries who called themselves "Americans." But looking upward in 1760, in the final North American stages of the Seven Years' War, the Tiogans, recently enemies to the British, saw a force from the east triumph in the night.[3]

The Tiogans' vision swirled out of a larger storm of nativistic visions blowing in the late eighteenth century across the Indians' Appalachian borderland with Anglo-America. With the Tiogans, other peoples saw the Anglo-American East rise as a spiritual as well as physical menace to the

Indian West. As occurred among the Tiogans, other visions would gain
acceptance not merely through the agency of a single prophet but through
the religious experiences of companies of people. This book is, in part,
about those visions, the traditions on which they were based, the traditions
that they in turn challenged, and the role they played in a movement for
Indian unity.

Not all Indians shared in or accepted word of the visions. Even as
Tiogans in enmity with British colonists spread their fearful nativistic
message, other Munsees, including Tiogans, made peace with the British,
sought their material assistance, and worked toward a policy of accommodation within an imperial system. Accommodation played a constant
counterpoint to nativism, often predictably dissonant, sometimes surprisingly harmonious. Like nativism, accommodation had adherents across the
length of the shifting and often broken Indian border with Anglo-America; it played a critical, if paradoxical, role in the formation of the pan-
Indian movement it often, though not always, opposed.

There would be a generation, roughly, between the outbreak of the
American Revolution and the signing of the Treaty of Greenville in 1795,
when advocates of both nativism and accommodation could play down
their differences, form an alliance, and advance together the cause of
Indian unity in resistance to the expansion of the states. Those twenty-odd
years saw the pan-Indian quest reach its greatest fulfillment. Militant
religion, while in something of a hiatus during those years, both provided
and continued to extend the intertribal networks upon which unity depended.

There would also be times, however—during the formative period of
the Seven Years' War and, especially, the decade that followed it, and
during the two decades that culminated in the War of 1812—when the
advocates of nativism and accommodation could not easily cooperate,
when they could not work toward the same end while understanding
things differently, and when they fought bitterly against each other, dividing their own peoples from within even as the nativist militants attempted
to unite all Indian peoples from without. During these periods, constella-
tions of individuals who possessed special knowledge of the Great Spirit—
those who came to be called "prophets" by the Anglo-Americans—rose to
provide spiritual guidance to militant followers charting the waters of
intertribal diplomacy. These prophets intensified nativism's religious dimension and generated a great deal of civil conflict, fiercely dividing
villages and even households. Their ascendance raised a paradox: commanding unity abroad, they discovered enemies at home.

Studies of individual prophets and local episodes have shed much light

on their role in "revitalizing" village or even "tribal" culture.[4] Anthony
F. C. Wallace has advanced the most powerful of theoretical formulations
regarding the rise of prophets since Max Weber launched his theory of
charismatic authority. Both scholars focus on the condition of the culture
and the personality of the prophets; however, Weber emphasizes the dramatic transformative qualities of charismatic leaders, whereas Wallace
stresses the role of the individual prophet in precipitating the "reformulation" or "revitalization" of his or her culture. According to Wallace's
theory, when an entire culture is under stress, "a single individual" may
experience dreams and visions that, if preached and accepted, mark the
"occasion of a new synthesis of values and meanings" for the culture as a
whole. Wallace studies single communities, evoking the social and, with
more emphasis, the psychological dimensions of religious movements. But
less attention has been paid, by Wallace or others, to the relationships that
prophecy forged among different Indian peoples even as the peoples re-
vitalized, or divided, from within. An exploration of the intertribal, even
diplomatic, character of prophecy in the late eighteenth and early nineteenth centuries suggests that the revitalization movements that Wallace
treats largely as discrete, if parallel, were often not only related but were
interdependent and intertwined.[5] If Wallace insists that we examine the
condition of the community as much as the personality of the prophet, I
ask that we examine many Indian communities in relation to one another—that we realize that the late eighteenth century was, until very recently, the period of North America's most widespread intertribal activity.

In shifting the focus from the village or "tribe" to intertribal relations
over a good part of the continent, striking patterns come into resolution.
Indian prophets arose not singly but in groups, and in doing so they integrated dissidents of various peoples into far-flung and often militant networks. Their followers throughout the Anglo-Indian borderlands, from
the Senecas in New York to the emerging Seminoles in Florida, were not
the disciples of single charismatic leaders alone, but were the adherents of
a broadly interconnected movement that produced many visionaries even
as it divided communities.[6] The visions of one inspired visions in others. A
prophet's ecstatic confrontation with the spirits, moreover, should be explored not so much as the critical moment in a single village's or a particular people's "revitalization," but as one of many events in the long career
of a widespread, often divisive, yet intertribal movement that shook the
local foundations of Indian government while spreading the truly radical
message that Indians were one people.

That message, often sacred in character, both drew upon and faced
challenges from the past. On the one hand, the past left to the visionaries

and their adherents the strength of traditional religious symbols—displayed in pictures, stories, dances, and songs—shared in a variety of forms throughout much of eastern Native North America. With this shared symbolic lexicon, the disciples of the vision came to an understanding of events that spanned impressive geographic, linguistic, and political barriers. The shared understanding, by peoples of widely separated regions, of symbols whose meanings sprang out of deeper understandings of the workings of the world, provided an essential principle for the pan-Indian movement of the late eighteenth and early nineteenth centuries. The principle was that the power of the British and Anglo-American invaders could be met with sacred power. The past, in other words, provided an approach to events that permitted many Indians to challenge Anglo-American expansion with a religious, militant, armed, and self-consciously "Indian" movement for thoroughgoing autonomy.

The past also, however, presented challenges. The heritage of Indian diversity and of highly localized, familial, and ethnically oriented government yielded neither easily nor completely. In fact, while nativists attempted to organize a pan-Indian movement, rival movements for centralization on a regional or "tribal" level were also underway. The problem of ethnic and regional diversity was compounded by deliberate Anglo-American efforts to keep the Indians divided and to influence Indian politics, often through the "traditional" channels of governance, that is, through the emerging "tribal" leadership.

Indians struggling for intertribal fellowship had more obstacles to confront than inherited ethnic rivalries or linguistic differences.[7] They had more to worry about than potential adversaries such as Anglo-American diplomats, traders, missionaries, or gunmen, all of whom were troubling enough. They had also to redefine, or at least to expand, the fundamentals of social and political identity. Previously characterized in the Eastern Woodlands largely by language and lineage, such identity now had to be construed in new ways. In reaching beyond both the boundaries of clan or village and the less easily defined boundaries of people, chiefdom, nation or confederacy to include all Native Americans, the seekers of Indian unity threatened to subvert both the authority of clan or village leaders and the concentrating authority of those whom the Anglo-Americans called "tribal" chiefs. In this manner, the advocates of pan-Indian unity departed from the local practices of the past, while defying local authorities who could strongly claim the past as their own.

Tensions thus arose within all levels of Indian political organization—village, clan, chiefdom, people, and confederacy—as factions divided against one another both over the manifestations of colonial power within the "tribal" councils and over the movement's attempt to circumscribe, or undermine, that power. Indians who identified with "tribal" leaders generally emphasized the interests of their particular people; these often cooperated with, although they were only rarely controlled by, the imperial powers. In the terms of this book, they were advocates of *accommodation.* Others cast their lot with the movement's militants, here termed *nativists,* holding less regard for "tribal" affiliation. Still others occupied positions between the two poles or shifted from one position to the other. Sometimes, as during the American Revolution, when there was little reason for conflict between the two positions, it was easy to occupy the center. At other times, as in the years immediately following the Seven Years' War or those culminating in the War of 1812, the center could not hold.

Within such contexts, the cost of both the nativistic movement for Indian unity and the accommodating drive for tribal centralization became internal strife. By the end of the nineteenth century's second decade, four of the peoples who inhabited the long border with Anglo-America between Lake Erie and the Gulf of Mexico, the four who are most examined in this work—Delawares, Shawnees, Cherokees, and Creeks—had paid the cost in full measure.

Because the term *nativism* has been spurned by recent scholars, let me clarify my usage. The term *nativism* discomfits some because it derives from the word *native,* which has in the past carried a host of inaccurate and even demeaning connotations. But native peoples of some of the regions that experienced colonialism, Native Americans among them, have in recent decades revived the term native, and it seems permissible to follow their lead.

There is another, related objection to the term *nativism,* one that has emerged from a scholarly debate over the nature of anticolonial religious movements. A "nativistic movement," in the language of Ralph Linton, the anthropologist who brought the term into prominence in the 1940s, is a "conscious, organized attempt on the part of a society's members to revive or perpetuate selected aspects of its culture." Linton's definition carefully recognizes that nativists concern themselves "with particular elements of culture, never with cultures as wholes," that they seek, in other words, no complete resurrection of a dead past. Nonetheless, the association of "nativism" with notions of revival or persistence, with the past rather than with the present or the future, has led some scholars to abandon the term *nativism,* feeling that it embodies, "in the word itself," the suggestion that these movements are "solely reversionary, regressive flights from the present into the past.''[8] These scholars properly object to the easy characterization of anticolonial religions as fatalistic and backward.

Nativism, however, need not suggest conservatism and regression—not if we abandon theories of cultural evolution that hold imperialist cultures as advanced and the native cultures of colonized lands as laggard. The term *nativist,* it seems to me, connotes atavism only if we accept the view that the native inhabitants of such lands were peoples at a tardy stage in a predictable process of cultural development. Once we discard that view, many of the objectionable connotations of the term go with it.

In the sense that it appears in this book, the term *nativism* has not to do with stages in time (a native past *against* a modern present) but with people in a landscape (a native adaptation to the pressures of an encroaching power). Nativists did not retreat wildly into a pristine tradition that never was, hopelessly attempting to escape a world changed by colonial powers. Rather, they identified with other native inhabitants of the continent, they self-consciously proclaimed that selected traditions and new (sometimes even imported) modes of behavior held keys to earthly and spiritual salvation, and they rejected the increasing colonial influence in native government, culture, and economy in favor of native independence. What is more, there are good reasons to employ the term *nativism* for the movement described herein, because it sought native-directed solutions, based primarily upon a cosmology composed by Native Americans, to the problem of European, and more particularly Anglo-American, ambition.

From an investigation of war, diplomacy, and ceremony among the Delawares and Shawnees in the Upper Ohio region, the Cherokees at the headwaters of the Tennessee, and the Creek peoples of the Gulf Plains, we begin to sketch the emergence of both militant Indian identity and its Native American opposition. The story cannot be entirely restricted to four peoples—Senecas, Mohawks, Ottawas, Chickasaws, Choctaws and others inevitably force their way in, as do the belligerent empire builders, impoverished backcountry yeomen, and devout missionaries from the East. But by charting the interactions of the four groups under study, particularly of the Shawnees with each of the others, we gain a view of the rough pattern of internal conflict and external cooperation, the pattern along which Indians cut their identities as they worked and dreamed in the very teeth of a new, and ultimately hostile, people.

That is the interpretation in stark strokes; a history full of people, their ideas, their passions, and their actions will follow. It is a narrative informed by the language of history and anthropology fused in the oddly named subdiscipline of ethnohistory, a close kin to what American and

European scholars of the poor tend to call the "New Cultural History."
Like both methods, this book attempts to reconstitute, through interpretations of such symbolic actions as religious rituals or public conferences, the
understandings of the historically "inarticulate." But more than the recon-
stitution of social thought and social relations is at stake here, for this work
is an effort to show that, at least among these peoples, ideas and internal
conflict played a dynamic role in diplomacy and war. The "New Cultural
History," in short, is marshaled on traditional fields.

A word of caution is in order. Despite my claim to have reconstituted
an active strand of eighteenth-century Native American thought, this is
not a history "from the Indian point of view." It is a thesis of this work that
there was no single Indian outlook but at least two major contending
viewpoints in the late eighteenth and early nineteenth centuries. If a single
perspective could be isolated, it could not find proper expression in a linear
narrative with a beginning, a middle, and an end. The main actors would
have told the story in very different languages, supported by very different
conceptions of time, space, and power than those employed here. This
study strives to render on the page those conceptions and their role in
history, but it is framed in a European-American tradition of scholarship.

That tradition has always been at its best and most dynamic when
hungry for new perspectives from which to interpret. So let me define my
task through a Cherokee legend. It tells of the Cherokee town of Gustí,
whose large council-house, or "townhouse," once stood on the banks of
the Hiwassee River, not far from what is now Kingston, Tennessee. One
night the riverbank collapsed, carrying the people and the townhouse into
the water. In later years it was said that visitors to the site could see the
townhouse dome as they gazed into the depths, and that they could hear
the muffled sounds of drumming, singing, and the pounding of dancing feet
rising garbled through the water.[9] Reading the descriptions of Indian
speeches and Native American ceremonies that have drifted into the documents recorded for the most part by outsiders is much like looking at the
townhouse and listening to the music of the Cherokees of Gustí. We have
precious few direct writings by eighteenth- and early nineteenth-century
Indians. For the most part, we sift through the writings of missionaries,
soldiers, fur traders, ethnographers, and land jobbers. While I have done
so, I have looked for the vague outlines and listened for the filtered voices,
in their muted and alien accents, of Indians who, two centuries ago,
challenged the pretensions of Anglo-America. I have, above all, strained
for the Native Americans' role in their history. I have been doubly suspicious of claims that put Europeans and Euro-Americans in control of
Indian behavior. My bias, my inclination, on approaching the sources has

been to search for the Native American provenance of the idea of Indian unity. That bias, that cut into the evidence, revealed, sadly, that the lofty idea generated internal opposition and conflict.

The thoughts and beliefs that most concern this work are about power and its relationship to ethnic identity. What follows in the opening chapter is one interpretation of one branch of Eastern Woodland Indian thinking about power. What follows that, most of the story and the rest of the book, is an interpretation of the power of that strand of Indian thought, the intertribal movement it hoped to support, and the resistance it met among American Indians, crown subjects, and republican citizens.

A Spirited Resistance

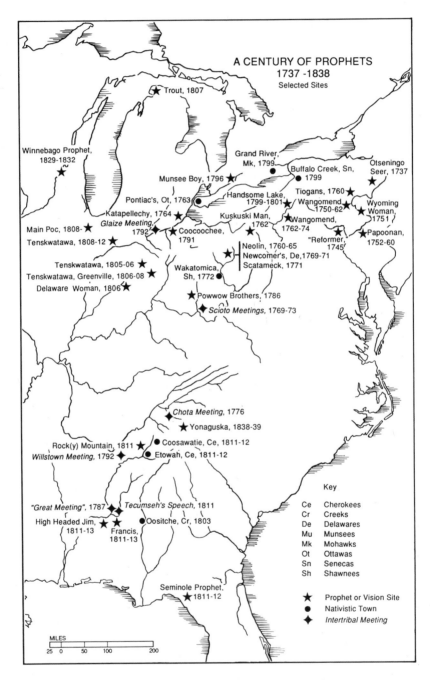

MAP I. A Century of Prophets

ONE

Power

James Kenny, an attentive dreamer, saw his hopes yield to despair. In the cool April of 1762, this serious Quaker who managed Pennsylvania's official Indian trading post at Fort Pitt dreamed an Anglo-American vision of the region's destiny: "I seen a Large Stack Yard containing many Stacks of Wheat & many of Hay being raised by great Industry on some New Rough Place that I thought could never Produce so well as it did."

From this image of vigorous productivity Kenny's dreams took a diabolical turn the following spring. One night after drifting off to sleep, he was confronted with the visage of "the Devil looking into our House, only his head put round to peep in, but on seeing me, he withdrew." In two months the dream recurred: "I dreamed two Nights ago that I happen'd to Sit down in some Strange house with some Company & instantly it was made known to me, so that I doubted it not, that the Devil sat in the Company." We will never know what exactly triggered these hellish visions, but perhaps the recent floods and renewed rumors of Indian war were involved.

A week after wrestling with one of his Satanic nightmares, Kenny verbally wrangled in the daylight with the very real Delaware warrior John Armstrong, whom the English "reconed an Ill fellow." Armstrong opposed the continued British occupation of Fort Pitt. He insisted that the garrison foreshadowed both Anglo-American settlement and the dispossession of the Indians: "The white people covets the Land & Eat them out by Inches . . . which was against the Will of God." Kenny, who believed he knew the Lord's will better than did any heathen, replied that if Arm-

strong and his people "would amend their ways leave off the Abominations they had amongst 'em & fear God, then he might Establish & increase
them, but if they resisted as they do; it was my oppinion that they would
Vanish & decay away & that the Great Creator was Angry with their
Works & would Give their Contry to Other People."

Armstrong heard Kenny out, and "acknowledged it might be so for he
belived God was Angry with them."[1] Kenny's diary betrays pleasure at this
small triumph, but Armstrong's assent was to his own interpretation of
Kenny's words, an interpretation the Indian could perceive but the Christian could not have intended. While Kenny imagined that an angry Jeho-
vah smote the Indians for their failure to recognize Him, the warrior
understood that a dissatisfied Great Spirit assaulted the Indians for their
negligence, their abominable dependence on English traders and English
rum, and their surrendering of lands to an alien people. American Indians
of the mid-eighteenth century did not have to incline toward Christianity
to believe that God was angry with them; they needed only to attend to the
words of numerous prophets and shamans who accused them of the neglect
of ritual and warned of an impending doom. While these holy men and
women absorbed some of their notions from Christian missionaries, soldiers, captives, traders, and runaway slaves—much as Armstrong absorbed
Kenny's words within his own understanding—they transformed these
imported notions into new forms, forms they included within their own
developing tradition of opposition to Anglo-American domination.

The prophets often called for the abandonment of things European, but
they did not see this, as we tend to, as a call for a collapse backward into
an actual or imagined precolonial condition. Rather, they experimented
with "new" ritual in "traditional" ways. They introduced new cultural
forms according to old processes. The peoples of the Eastern Woodlands
under study here—the Delawares, Shawnees, Cherokees, and Creeks—had
never inhabited isolated, tightly integrated cultures, however much they
might identify themselves, as peoples, against all others. Theirs were societies whose openness to innovation emerges clearly in many of the "traditional" forms most studied by historians and anthropologists.[2] Is not, for
example, the willful adoption of captured adult enemy women—itself by
now a highly studied Eastern Woodland "tradition"—an invitation to cultural innovation? And did not the traditional ceremonies originate, according to myth, in the heroic journeys of members of the communities,
highly creative acts (however they may have been inspired)? Eighteenth-
century prophets who offered new ceremonies to their people did so after
having taken such heroic journeys in conscious imitation of ancient myths,
after having embarked on traditional quests for power.

Power lay at the center of all concerns. Nothing was more important for life than power. Power meant the ability to live, to grow crops, to woo lovers, to slay animals, to defeat enemies. More esoterically, power meant the ability to heal the sick, to converse with animals, or to visit "God." But most fundamentally, power meant the ability of an individual to influence other people and other beings. Power meant successful interaction.

Power was widely distributed throughout the Indians' universe, but some things possessed more power than others. To secure power and to gain the favor of powerful beings, Indians celebrated rituals and ceremonies. To neglect ritual, conversely, was both to lose power and to incite the wrath of offended spirits. Eighteenth-century participants in the pan-Indian movement would resort frequently to ritual. The success of their movement would depend on the conviction that they could gain power through ritual and righteousness.

Throughout the Eastern Woodlands, Native Americans commonly believed that their rituals and ceremonies had once been gifts, donated by benevolent forces. According to some myths, culture heroes had received these ceremonies after crossing into other dimensions of the universe. Such passages were always dangerous and themselves demanded ritual.

According to one such Shawnee myth, recorded in the 1930s, a kindly female thunderer (or thunderbird) swept up an unloved Shawnee orphan boy and carried him off to dwell with her "people." After a time, he learned to fly about with these spiritual friends of humanity. The "thunderers would tell him not to scare people, not to make too much noise. Not to thunder too loud." It happened that the spirits decided that they had to return the boy to his original people. On doing so, they cautioned him to take sweat baths for four successive mornings, "so people won't see this lightning when you talk." The boy obeyed. He said not a word to his people until after his fourth sweat, then he told them about his visit to the upper world, and "from there on the people used him to make it rain whenever they wanted to make it rain." Having followed the prescribed rituals, the boy benefited from his passage; he could now draw the thunderers to him.[3] Had the boy ignored the thunderers' cautions, had he spoken before taking the prescribed sweats, he would not have been so fortunate. Other myths make this clear.

Several curious Cherokee warriors, James Mooney learned in the late nineteenth century, had long ago sought to enter the upper world. After a hard journey eastward, they came to the horizon's border with the sky vault, made of an immense, bowl-shaped stone that "was always swinging up and down, so that when it was up there was an open place like a door" through which the morning sun appeared. "They waited until the sun had come out and then tried to get through while the door was still open, but just as the first one was in the doorway the rock came down and crushed him."[4] Unaided by sacred power, their bravery alone could not gain them passage.

In the Shawnee version of the story, the hero had better luck; a powerful being came to his aid. He met a spiritual "grandfather," who, "knowing his errand, gave him 'medicine' to transform him into a spirit, that he might pass through the celestial courts." The hero strictly followed his grandfather's advice, learned "the mysteries of heaven and the sacred rights of worship," and returned with these gifts to his people.[5] Successful passage to and from the upper world, then, required supernatural aid and ceremony. Such travel entailed risks but could bring great rewards.

Men's Power: Weapons and Animals

It is difficult to know whether the major vertical and temporal divisions of the universe, evident in these sky-journey stories, were a matter of everyday concern for most Indians. But for hunters, the power relationships between animals and men were matters, quite literally, of consuming interest. A Cherokee story reveals the full nature of the forces that governed the relations between man and beast. It tells of a hunter who encountered a "medicine bear," a spiritual regulator of relations between hunter and prey. Anthropologists have termed such beings animal bosses, owners, guardians, or keepers. The Cherokee hunter ventured to the underworld with the powerful spirit and remained in that spirit land for a winter. As the hunter prepared to return to the Cherokees the following spring, the medicine bear predicted that it would be killed by an approaching band of hunters. But its death would be an illusion. The arriving hunters accordingly slew the bear and took its skins and fat, ritually covering its blood with leaves. They then headed homeward, accompanied by the enlightened Cherokee hunter, who turned to watch the medicine bear arise from "the leaves, shake himself, and go back to the woods."[6]

In the bear's prescience, and in its willingness to yield its skins and flesh to these Indian hunters—when it had previously displayed its ability to resist such slaughter—we find much about Indian conceptions of the hunt. English colonists and early American citizens commented on the Indian belief in animal spirituality. The spirit, the true life of any animal, resided in the heart and blood of the beast. The Shawnee Prophet told an agent in the U.S. Indian service, C. C. Trowbridge, in 1824 that the Great Spirit gave all things, even the earth itself, "a piece of his heart." A half century earlier, James Adair, an old Indian trader of long southeastern tenure, wrote that the Indians ritually abstained "from eating the Blood of any animal, as it contains the life, and spirit of the beast."[7] Thus, the bear rising out of the blood was not a literary innovation peculiar to the Cherokee myth. It was an Eastern Woodlands motif. Hunters across the continent, in fact, believed that slain animals, in the words of Ruth Underhill, "did not really die. They simply sloughed off furs or feathers and went back to their original home."[8] James Mooney suggests that each animal was allotted a "life term which can not be curtailed by violent means." If slain by a hunter, the beast would shortly be "resurrected in its proper shape from the blood drops" and would continue to live until its time was up, when its "liberated spirit" would join its kind in the afterlife.[9] This motif partly explains why animals, like the medicine bear of the myth, allowed their "clothes" and "flesh" to be taken by Indian hunters. Death on the arrow shaft lacked the frightening aspect of finality. But the animals also yielded themselves to the Indians because they received good treatment from the hunters in return.

Hunters treated animals such as beavers, deer, and eagles to extensive ceremonies at their deaths. The Indians ritually asked the spirits that guarded the beasts to forgive the killings and to encourage other animals to present themselves at the next hunt. Moreover, some hunters believed that if they had followed the proper rituals before, during, and after the hunt, the slaughtered prey, like the Cherokee's bear, would rise from the spilled blood to live again. There was, as Frank Speck notes, "no diminution in the supply of game through hunting," if the hunt was properly, and ceremoniously, conducted.[10] The prophets of the eighteenth and early nineteenth centuries, seeking to bring about a return of the diminishing game, would keep their followers mindful of this.

The Eastern Woodlands Indian hunter inhabited a mental universe divided into categories and subcategories of sacred beings. He could not live without drawing on the support of these others, and he could not gain their favor without attention to ritual. If he ignored their sacred power, he courted disaster. If he learned effective new rituals, gaining greater access to sacred powers, he approached greatness.

Throughout the eighteenth century, as chaotic misfortunes increasingly befell the Indians, it was easy to interpret these events in the light of this understanding. As disaster followed disaster, some found shame in what we might call the Indian doctrine of particular providences: "They believe their sins are the true cause of all their evils."[11] But the doctrine also produced hope. If they were the true source of their own misfortunes, if their improper behavior had brought on their troubles, then perhaps through reformation they could end them. The rub, of course, was how to reform.

Women and Power: Blood and Crops

If Indian men inhabited a universe divided into a sky world, a this world, and a nether world—a universe further subdivided into a series of categories across which one could move safely only with ritually acquired sacred power—so too did Indian women. But Eastern Woodlands women occupied a different part of that universe. Men acted in the regions of hunting and fighting; their relationship with other beings was colored by their occupation as killers—not wanton killers, but life-sustaining killers. Women cultivated foodstuffs, tended the fire, bore and nursed children, and performed various civil functions, healing roles, and other duties. Primarily they were growers—not simply nurturers but producers; their occupations and their menstrual cycles demonstrated their affinities with powerful forces different from those that aligned with men.

Worldly masculine and feminine forces had to be kept separate much of the time. In one keen manifestation of this separation, women played a very limited role in the hunting of game animals. Women and animal prey, like men and crops, stood in what Ruth Underhill has called "hopeless opposition." Men stayed away from their wives' beds when preparing for a hunt. Hunters especially avoided menstruating women. Southeastern Indian men who approached such women risked "spoiling the supposed purity and power" of their sacred bundles, pouches containing the implements with which they performed their hunting rituals. Even male shamans among twentieth-century Shawnees have kept clear of menstruating women: "Men with power can do anything, but whenever they come to a woman who is not just right, they sure are afraid of her."[12]

Indian myths relate the life-giving power of menstrual blood, a power that went to the heart of the distinction between masculine and feminine. In a Creek myth, an old woman (probably the Corn Woman) stepped over a log and "saw a drop of blood in her track. Stooping down, she carefully scraped up the dirt around the blood and carried it home." She hid the blood in an earthen jar. Soon she "discovered that the blood clot was growing. . . . In ten months it was developed into a boy."[13] A boy-spirit he was; the powerful product of a powerful woman's holy discharge held in a ceramic womb shaped by holy hands.

A Shawnee myth exposed directly the deep power of menstrual blood and its opposition to male forces. A young woman, in her menstrual seclusions, discovered a great horned serpent, a malevolent monster from the underworld. Returning to the village, she told her people about it, and the men gathered to plan an attack on the beast. During her next period, the warriors followed her to her retreat, "singing and drumming" as they went, probably to prevent their own contamination. They summoned the serpent toward a pair of crossed poles that they had laid at the lake's edge. At last, the lake churned, and the serpent surfaced to rest its head on the cross. "You are the one," exclaimed the men, but it was the young woman who struck and killed the beast with her "soiled" cloths. This was how, the myth concludes, the Shawnees discovered "of what power it is" when a woman menstruates.[14] The snake, implicitly perhaps a masculine symbol and explicitly the underworldly power whose body parts provided warriors with "great war medicine," stood in clear opposition to the power of menstrual blood, and the latter triumphed.[15]

Women's power, seated in their menstrual blood, identified them with the vital forces of the plant world. A great many Indian stories from across the fertile portions of North America linked women with plants, particularly corn.[16] The Cherokee Corn Woman, Selu, scraped corn at will from her armpits and loins. That corn fell from such bleeding scratches near the tops of her limbs reinforced the identification of corn with procreative fertility and menstrual blood. Whenever she produced corn, she secluded herself. But one day her sons followed her, discovered her secret, and decided to kill her as a witch. Selu, who was a powerful spirit, read their thoughts and gave them her word that, despite their impending crime against her, she would stay with them in the shape of corn; but they must honor her with ceremonies. In the variant recorded by Mooney, corn sprouted from the blood which marked the spot where the boys slew Selu. The Creek Corn Woman's dead body was dragged by her son around the field from which the first corn later sprang.[17]

The identification of fertile forces with women and plants intertwined with the Eastern Woodlands economy, for women cultivated foodstuffs. The soldier-adventurer Henry Timberlake probably overstated the case when he wrote that "women alone do all the laborious tasks of agriculture." Men, it appears, helped at least to clear and to harvest the fields. Using swidden-style methods, Adair noted, men would "bark the large timber, cut down the saplings and underwood, and burn them in heaps." Men also might help with the planting. This was especially true among the Creeks: "The men rarely go to war till they have helped the women plant a sufficient plenty of provisions, contrary to the usual method of warring savages." But between the planting and the harvest, women of all eastern peoples worked the fields which, barring drought, flood, blight, war, or dispossession, would provide the people with most of their food.[18]

Fields and gardens were not places for men in the Eastern Woodlands. The Shawnees taught their adopted captive, O. M. Spencer, that for men to work the soil was disgraceful. James Smith, an adopted captive among the Ohio Hurons, once spent a day working the cornfields shortly after his adoption: "When I returned to the town, the old men hearing of what I had done, chid me, and said that I was adopted in the place of a great man, and must not hoe corn like a squaw."[19] The division of labor powerfully reinforced the Indians' most profound social distinction, that between the sexes. The distinction corroborated the Eastern Woodlands conception of the universe as a complex, ordered system, in which each being had a proper place.

Yet we should not reckon without ritual, for rite could make right. Indians thought it improper for a man to work crops, yet some males could do so, such as *berdache*, nonadopted captives, and captives ritually adopted to replace a dead woman. These males occupied alternative gender roles and were not regarded as residents of the same category as hunters and warriors.[20] Ritual, more fundamentally, assured the fertility of the fields themselves. No fields could be successfully cultivated without the ceremonious supplication of the plant spirits' favor. The Corn Woman, for example, the spiritual "mother" of the Cherokees and Creeks, warned them that they must observe the Green Corn Ceremony, "for elsewhere you will find no milk whose source is inexhaustible like mine." Neglect of the ritual would be punished by famine: "If you forget to think of me, . . . but make use of me without remembering my words, I will fling among you The Desolator!"[21]

Shawnees, too, celebrated the Green Corn Ceremony, as did most Eastern Woodlands peoples. Their Spring Bread Dance was another important agricultural ceremony. Like the Cherokee Green Corn Ceremony, it kept the Shawnees in corn. Eli Ellis told an interviewer in the mid-1930s that the two mythical Shawnees who had gained both entrance to the upper world and audience with the Great Spirit returned to this world with orders to perform the Bread Dance and the War Dance. Ellis concluded, "That's the reason they have the Bread Dance. When these two fellers come down from there, they told 'em, long as they live, long as the water run, long as the world, have Bread Dance. If you quit that, it might not rain for four years."[22]

The Creek Green Corn Ceremony, or "Busk," was an elaborate affair, the importance of which a Creek described to Benjamin Hawkins in the 1790s: "It is our opinion that the origin of the Boosketau and our physics, proceeds from the goodness of [the Master of Breath]; that he communicated them in old times to the red people, and impressed it on them to follow and adhere to them, and they would be of service to them."[23] Because the ceremonies had originated as gifts of powerful spiritual forces, it followed that such gifts, if ceremonially reciprocated, might again be forthcoming. If old ceremonies had been given to the Indians by the Great Spirit, the Corn Mother, or other beings, new ceremonies might be communicated to the attentive in the future. Thus, a "traditional" sanction existed for ceremonial innovation. Not only might Indians whom scholars have called "nativists," "conservatives," or "traditionalists" have been open to change, they might have been on its very cutting edge—particularly, as in the late eighteenth century, if that edge slashed at the bonds of empire.

Ceremonies, old and new, gave Indian villagers access to spirit forces that influenced the growth of crops, while others affected the abundance of game. The people's survival depended on the cooperation of spirit forces that inhabited other quarters of the universe. Their most essential relations with other orders—with plants, animals, and the other sex—necessitated appeals to sacred power through proper ritual. Disregard for ritual meant, to the nativists, earthly disaster and punishment.

The Rites of War

Eastern Woodlands Indians had never been strangers to trade, diplomacy, and war. For generations following their first contacts with Europeans—as they fought, traded, and negotiated—they insisted on the performance of elaborate ceremonies and rituals, some new and some old, that conveyed their understanding of the principles of external relations.[24] In critical respects, the peoples believed that they stood in relation to other peoples in the same way that men and women stood in relation to all other inhabitants of the universe. Thus they treated strangers, especially enemies, with studied caution and appealed to the sacred forces for guidance, protection, and power.

Indian warriors supplicated the spirit worlds using rites that would, they hoped, give them spiritual armor, foretell their success or failure, disclose the location of the enemy and his numbers, and subdue this enemy, body and soul. They secured the favorable disposition of the spirit world both by purifying themselves with fasts, purgatives, and bathings, and by strictly obeying prohibitions against acts that would contaminate them, most notably sexual intercourse. Sexual intimacy with any woman, whether the warrior's wife or a captive enemy, constituted an abominable mixing of man in his warlike state with the life-power of a woman. The

Shawnee Prophet told American interviewer C. C. Trowbridge in 1824 that the act might literally kill a man, because active warriors "drink a great deal of a strong decoction of roots which infuse a spirit of energy & strength, and that if they enjoyed connection with their wives before counteracting the effect of this medicine by some other the consequences would be fatal to them." A half century earlier Adair reported that even the "blood-thirsty villain, Captain Jacob," a Shawnee who stood against Anglo-American expansion during the Seven Years' War, "did not attempt the virtue of his female captives, lest (as he told one of them) it should offend the Indians' God." "Generally," wrote J.C.B., a French traveler through the twilight of New France, "savages have scruples about molesting a woman prisoner, and look upon it as a crime, even when she gives her consent." Henry Rowe Schoolcraft got it right in the mid-nineteenth century, when he explained that the Indian prohibition stemmed from a warrior's "fear of offending his warlike manetos [sacred powers], and of exciting the ridicule of his companions."[25]

None of this meant, however, that women were treated gently by enemy warriors. Some saw the taking of a woman's scalp as an act of courage, not because of the resistance that she could put up, but because it demonstrated the warrior's ability to strike deep into and escape from enemy country.[26] Captured women, like men, could suffer death by torture, though the odds against such a fate were great.[27] No chivalrous respect of "noble savages" for the "weaker sex" inhibited the rape of female captives, although Indians had among their warriors their share of noble souls; the curb was the strong fear of disastrous consequences that were thought to follow the mingling of a woman's nature with the warlike state of a man, an unnatural state that had been ritually prepared.

Before an expedition, as ordinary warriors sought to gain sacred favor for their undertaking, the religious leaders of the community often attempted to divine their chances of success. Shamans might examine their sacred crystals or study the burning of a deer's tongue. A simple cooking ceremony might be performed in which the shamans placed in a kettle of boiling water one piece of meat for every warrior. When the meat was cooked, the shaman gave a piece to each man; a shortage of meat indicated casualties, a surplus meant captives and scalps.[28]

Besides divining, Indians performed mysteries designed to appropriate power from the underworld, especially from the malevolent great horned serpents, spirits with analogues across the woodlands. Native American warriors believed that their most powerful medicine bundles contained the living fragments of a slain serpent's body; these gave access to the chaotic and deadly chthonic forces. Cherokee war dancers imitated the motions of the monster and wore masks engraved with its image. Shawnee warriors paused by springs, which they understood to be the portals of the underworld, and sprinkled tobacco around them, "praying at the same time to the spirit of the spring for success on their journey and a safe return."[29]

With these and other rituals warriors reached across cosmic barriers to gain sacred power over their enemies. Trowbridge recorded the Shawnee Prophet's battle "harangue" by which shamans explicitly sought the cooperation of the underworld: "We shall conquer if we are brave. The water will wash them away, the wind will blow them down, darkness will come upon them, & the earth will cover them."[30] More than fifty years later, James Mooney found a strikingly similar Cherokee incantation. Facing the warriors after their ritual bath, the Cherokee shaman affirmed that the warriors would gain control over the enemy: "There under the earth, where the black war clubs shall be moving about like the ball sticks in the game [lacrosse], there his soul shall be, never to reappear. We cause it to be so. There under the earth the black war club (and) the black fog have come together as one. . . . We cause it to be so."[31] They sought not only to kill the enemy but also to plunge an aspect of his soul, which was itself an aspect or projection of his people's power, into a hostile arena from which there was no immediate escape.

To handle these appropriated underworldly powers safely, warriors preparing for battle ceremoniously transformed their very natures. Just as an individual returning from the thunderers' upperworld underwent several days of purification in order to prevent an abominable combination of dissimilar natures, so the man passing from the world of the villager to that of the man-killer fasted and imbibed purgatives in order to wield safely the deadly supernatural weapons he had ritually forged.[32]

James Adair wrote of the Indians' belief in the distinct opposition between war and peace: "Tradition, or the divine impression on human nature, dictates to them that man was not born in a state of war; and as they reckon they are become impure by shedding human blood, they hasten to observe the fast of three days."[33] Preparing for battle, Indian men left the vicinity of peace and, with the aid of ritual, entered that of war. After a raid they returned both to their villages and, again with ritual assistance, to the place of peace. During the fighting itself warriors sought to gain sacred power over their enemies. Enemies were beings of a different order. To defeat them, warriors once again invoked ritual.

The Indian concept of war was no simple matter. Such notions as "blood vengeance," or even "mourning-war"[34] reveal only traces of the meaning of organized Native American violence. Fighting Indians performed a complex series of ritual acts that constituted a bloody ceremony through which they rectified the spiritual order of their people. Indian warriors danced, purified themselves, and relied on charms in order to divine their chances for success, to supplicate the chthonic forces for assistance, to handle safely the deadly powers in a hostile environment, to satisfy the anguished souls of their slain kinsmen, and to send their enemies to death and a miserable afterlife. In all these actions Indians passed through or communicated across the categorical frontiers that organized their world.

Enemies, and perhaps all other peoples, stood in relation to one's own group much in the way of animals; that is, they were not full persons. Like animals they had power and commanded respect, but they stood beyond the important but permeable and shifting boundary that defined one's people. An Alabama chief within the Creek confederacy, on declaring peace in the mid-eighteenth century, told his warriors to refrain from battle in language that reveals the parallels between hunting and war: "We must ask the Spirit of Peace to prevail in purity and spotlessness among the nations which surround us. We should wage war only against wildcats, bears, wolves, and deer, and we need to support children."[35] The association of enemies with beasts appears most graphically in the story of Ben Dickinson, a Delaware warrior.

Dickinson, who had been captured in his youth and raised by the Delawares, told a more recent English captive about one of his exploits against the English colonists in the 1760s. While approaching the English frontier, Dickinson spied a colonist stalking a deer. He quickly shot and scalped the fellow, when "an old man, whom he supposed to be the father of the man he had killed, came running toward him, hallooing at him if he had killed the deer." Instead of his son, the old settler found Dickinson, who, waving the scalp, answered in English, "Yes, by G-d, and if you don't believe me here is the skin."[36] The dehumanization of the enemy is a feature shared by many, perhaps most cultures; among the Eastern Woodlands Indians it resonated in particular tones with features of a cosmology that did not elevate humanity above other creatures.

Enemies lay roughly parallel to animals in the eighteenth-century Eastern Woodlands classification: they could be killed, yet the act commanded ritual attention. When a respected Shawnee woman examined a new group of prisoners, and praised the warriors for bringing in "good meat," she spoke not in creative metaphor, but in the idiom of her people. Captain Pipe, a Delaware war leader against the Americans during the Revolution, informed the British that he would send to Detroit the women and children he had just taken prisoner: "I took some *live flesh*. . . . In a few days you will receive this *flesh*, and *find that the skin is of the same color with your*

own." In the last years of the Revolution, the Senecas marched David
Zeisberger and some of his Munsee Indian congregation to an Ottawa and
Ojibwa village. Handing the captives over, the Senecas explained to the
villagers that they "made them a gift of the whole Indian church to cook
a broth of, which," Zeisberger noted, "is an Indian war-term, and means
'We give them to you to slay.'"[37]

Before the enemy stranger entered the town, he or she had to be
purified; prisoners had to be altered to avoid a threatening confusion of
orders. The Shawnees, for example, carried sacred, elaborately decorated
"prisoner ties" into battle, which heightened their power over prisoners.[38]
With these they bound the captives' hands and necks for the rough, often
hellish journey to the Shawnee towns. Thomas Ridout's captivity narrative
vividly describes the ceremonies with which Shawnees brought him prisoner into a village. The warriors painted Ridout red, the color of success,
tied ribbons in his hair and ordered him to shake a rattle and imitate their
chants. They fired their guns and "set up the war whoop" to advise their
people of the victory. Entering the village, Ridout was struck by a woman
as he was driven toward the council house. Ridout was lucky. His captors
soon discovered that he was an English Canadian and not a Long Knife, an
enemy American citizen. But he was still a stranger and an object of
suspicion. Inside the council house, the Indians forced him once again to
sing and to shake rattles; thus purified, he was taken to his master's lodging
until he could be rescued by proper British authorities.[39]

To become a full person, to become one of the people, the captive underwent the rituals of adoption. In July 1755, at an Indian village on the
Muskingum River, about forty miles north of Fort Pitt, the resident Delawares, Caughnawagas, and Mahicans adopted the captive James Smith.
They plucked the hair from his head, bored his nose and ears, stripped him,
painted him "in various colours," and plunged him in a creek; there, he
reports, they "washed and rubbed me severely, yet I could not say that they
hurt me much." In 1742, the Cherokees adopted Antoine Bonnefoy, a
French *engagé*, in much the same manner: they stripped him, shaved his
head, painted and washed him. After that, he noted, "the way was free
before me." Bonnefoy called his condition before adoption "slavery,"
though he noted that the Cherokees treated him well.[40]

If the process of enemy adoption reveals the importance of ritual for the
crossing of boundaries, the procedure of enemy execution also involved a
concern for the ritual preservation of power. For adult men, it appears, the
odds against ritual adoption and in favor of execution were greater than
for women and children. Some men beheld their horrible destiny even
before they entered the Indian village. John Slover, who had lived among

the Miamis, Delawares, and Shawnees from his eighth to his twentieth
year, participated at age twenty-eight in Colonel William Crawford's invasion of Indian land in the Old Northwest in 1782. Delaware and Shawnee
Indians demolished Crawford's force and recaptured Slover. Approaching
a Shawnee village, the Indians seized one of Slover's two captive companions, "and having stripped him naked, blacked him with coal and water:
this was the sign of being burnt: the man seem'd to surmise it, and shed
tears." A decade later, the Chickamauga Cherokees, allies of the northwestern Indians in the war against the expansion of the United States into
the Ohio region, ceremoniously devoted William Richardson Watson to
death: "They arose and threw around his neck a broad belt of black wampum, and a bundle containing the toes of deer, in his hand by way of a
rattle. Two or three Indians placed themselves before him and as many on
each side, and began a song, . . . the poor man shaking his rattles all the
time."[41]

If the prisoner performed in the expected manner, the execution itself
took the form of a contest. Tormentors looked for the captive to do his best
to endure the tortures bravely. When an enemy party takes a Creek warrior, according to Bossu, "he expects to be burned at the stake, and he
composes his own death song. 'I fear neither death nor fire. Make me
suffer. My death will be avenged by my people.'" For as long as the victim
could, wrote Adair, "he whoops and out-braves the enemy, describing his
own martial deeds against them, and those of his nation, who he threatens
will force many of them to eat fire in revenge of his fate, as he himself had
often done to some of their relations at their cost."[42]

But it cannot have been simply a contest between the captive and his
tormentors; for the condemned victim could gain nothing but prolonged
agony for any of his momentary triumphs. No matter how brave he was in
the face of the cruelties intimately inflicted upon his person, he would still
die in agony, he would still face the buffeting blows of the war clubs in a
lonely, chaotic underworld. But if we can believe the evidence that such
contests indeed took place, then perhaps the objective of the condemned
lay also in his approach to afterlife. If the prisoner could demonstrate,
during his own immolation, that his power exceeded that of his captors,
then he would know that his sentence among the chthonic powers would
be short, for his fellows would soon liberate him in turn. His war song, in
a sense, was his very last ditch. Through it he gained the power, for himself
and for his people, to cope with the malevolent forces below and the
faggot-bearing enemies around him. This perception that torture could
reveal the enemy's power or weakness surfaces in "The Narrative of Dr.
Knight." John Knight, captured in 1782 during the demise of Colonel

Crawford's force, described in lurid detail the methodical execution of Crawford. Crawford and many other white captives taken at the battle were made to pay dearly for two atrocities committed by whites, including members of Crawford's very party, against the Ohio-area Indians: the cold-blooded murder of the Shawnee chief Cornstalk (1777) and the later slaughter of ninety unarmed Christian Delawares in the vicinity of the Moravian Indian village of Gnadenhutten (Ohio, 1782). It is worth noting that one of Crawford's officers, David Williamson, had commanded the killers at Gnadenhutten, a fact the Indians knew well.[43]

According to Knight, the village men began the torment, but the women soon joined in. For over two hours the colonel suffered the firebrands of his assailants. At one point, he begged Simon Girty, an adopted Shawnee and Loyalist who lived among and fought beside the Indians, to shoot him, but Girty declined (reportedly with a grin). For our purposes, what happened after Crawford collapsed is of greater significance: his executioners scalped him and flashed the scalp in Knight's face, declaring "that was my great captain." The next day, as a mounted Indian drove Knight before him, they passed Crawford's remains, and once again an Indian told Knight "that was my big Captain, and gave the scalp halloo."[44] The bitter irony evident in the Indians' references to the mutilated remains of Crawford as a great captain suggests that the man's defeat in battle and his behavior under torment, which included the desperate supplication to Simon Girty, revealed to the Indians the Long Knives' weaknesses.

A Cherokee legend reinforces this interpretation, recalling the first decades of the eighteenth century, when the Cherokees drove a large group of Shawnee settlers out of the Tennessee Valley. Among the war's events, recounted by Cherokee storytellers, is this: the Cherokee warrior, Tunai, overpowered a great Shawnee, pinioned the man's arms together, and drove him into the Cherokee town of Itsati, "where he was put to death by the women with such tortures that his courage broke and he begged them to kill him at once."[45] The women of Itsati demonstrated Cherokee power, power ratified in the ultimate victory over the Shawnees.

The use of torture to divine the physical and spiritual strength of the enemy complemented the more widely noted use of torture as a means of both avenging the death of a compatriot or relative and of liberating his unhappy spirit from the underworld. In each case, the Indian torturers and their Indian victims attempted to understand and to recruit the supernatural forces through ritual. As the torturers wielded their firebrands, they tested their victim's power against their own. As they scalped him and burned his remains, or threw his flesh to the dogs, they plunged his crying soul into the underworld. But in the extraordinary—perhaps only legendary—event that the victim stood resolute, jeered his tormentors, and ignored his excruciating pain, he could count on redemption; he would know that his people possessed the power to avenge his death. His torturers could expect someday to stand in his blistering skin.

The rites of war reveal much as well about Indian identity. Those who agreed with one another that they were related, that they should not kill one another, and that they could properly join together for defense, ceremony, love, and so on, defined themselves to a certain extent against other peoples. The religious nativists of the eighteenth and early nineteenth centuries would struggle as the most militant advocates of a pan-Indian identity, one that would have been alien to their forebears. Here they would meet a challenge from their rivals at home, those leaders among their peoples who worked to shore up their political authority through connections with Europeans. The nativists' rivals could call upon ethnic or clan traditions against the new intertribal identity. It must be remembered that such a move was also innovative, that "traditional" tribal identities were also in the process of development, particularly when it came to loyalties to a central tribal or confederate authority. Cherokee leaders anxious to resist pan-Indian action, for example, might call upon a loyalty to a developing Cherokee identity in their efforts to combat militant nativism. They might, in this manner, invoke and at the same time modify a "tradition" that the nativists would reject. But the nativists also had customary materials to work with as they considered the place of the rites of war in their efforts. Most important for nativists would be the understandings of power.

The Loss of Power

Ritual loomed so large in the culture of Indian war because ritual delivered the assistance of sacred powers. In preparing to enter hostile territory, Indians appealed to the underworldly forces for protection. In divining their chances for victory, warriors sought information from the spirits. In scalping and burning their captives—acts that damned the spirit of the enemy and liberated the tormented spirits of kinsmen—villagers mastered the destinies of the dead. In transforming captives into slaves or adopted kin, Indians employed rituals to permit others to live among them. Rites of passage—not just of birth, maturity, marriage, and death, but of all passages and communications from one order to another—abounded in the culture of fighting, just as they did in the cultures of hunting and planting. Among Eastern Woodlands peoples, the concern for order or, better, for the ability to master these passages and communications became acute as disorder seized the Appalachian borderlands and Gulf Plains in the eighteenth century. Among none of the peoples, however, would there emerge a consensual explanation for the disasters.

Those seeking to explain their misfortunes and disorders had much to explain. Militant, nativistic factions among many of the peoples on the Anglo-American borderlands quickly identified one source of their agonies: the prolific and aggressive people to the east. Anglo-American incursions precipitated the forced migrations of the nations from their beloved lands, and these Indians knew it. The trans-Appalachian traders distributed the whiskey and rum that destroyed the people, and these Indians knew it. The penetrating armies from the east galled their warriors, their women, and their children, and left widespread starvation by destroying Indian corn; these Indians knew that, too.

There is a broad and diverse literature that suggests that the catastrophes suffered by Indian peoples led to a decline in native spirituality, at least along traditional lines, though scholars have even employed the term *secularization* to describe the event. The primary cause of the alleged process was the failure of healers and shamans to cure and prevent the spread of disease. The death of these specialists before they had the chance to pass on their esoteric secrets to successors, it has been further argued, caused a thinning of inherited traditional wisdom. When entire communities fell before a plague or an invading army, the traditional beliefs, the "collective wisdom," fell with them.[46]

The argument deserves scrutiny. Spirituality, or religious conviction, is notoriously difficult to measure, even among societies that left behind genuine and now-public archives. Indian communities, moreover, had a greater variety of religious resources upon which to draw than the advocates of religious declension have noted. To begin with, few communities existed in utter isolation from others; they were accustomed to exchanges both of thought and of practice. The most profound of these exchanges resulted from the mourning-war complex and its attendant captivities. Young adult women—fully integrated into the culture of one people but then captured, adopted, and loved by another—would become active transmitters of culture to their children, friends, co-workers in the fields, and, in some societies, their patients. Captured children and the occasional adult male adoptee would also render permeable the lines drawn between peoples. Less profound exchanges would come about in trade, diplomacy, warfare, and more casual encounters. But all of these exchanges rendered a certain dynamism to any Indian community's belief system. Perhaps more important, they gave the Indian communities structures that, far from encouraging stasis, promoted intersocietal exchange. By capturing the intended mothers of their children from among speakers of radically different languages, communities invited change as well as exchange, however unconsciously. One result was the diffusion of notions we would call religious, such as the widely shared mourning-war complex itself. The breadth of native religious notions imparted to Indian spirituality the resilience to absorb potent shocks dealt by the forces of colonialism.

We should be careful about equating the loss of a ceremony, of a shaman, or even, horrible as it was, of entire communities as crippling blows to native spirituality as a whole. These were wrenching events, but survivors often held on. Having been raised in religious systems that were largely integrated with the patterns of daily life, yet flexible enough to incorporate notions borrowed from captives and others, the survivors could enrich their ordinary ritual repertoire with ceremonies and esoteric practices borrowed from outside of their communities, but borrowed in a traditionally sanctioned manner. They could, as their mythical forebears had, seek entry to the sky world, to obtain new ceremonies from the sacred forces in visions. This would be the path of the prophets. They could also learn from surviving neighbors, particularly as they might gather with refugees from other disasters in the creation of new communities. Cultural contact was not new to North America in the British (or for that matter Spanish) colonial period. As James Axtell puts it:

> Native groups borrowed particular beliefs, myths, culture heroes, religious artifacts, ceremonies, and even whole cults from other groups, some at considerable distances via long-established trade routes. Through this continuous process of borrowing and transfer, tribes in contiguous culture areas, such as the northeastern woodlands, came to share a large number of religious traits.

To borrow from Indian neighbors, even to incorporate Christian items into Indian ways of getting things done, did not mean to despiritualize, much less to secularize, particularly if native understandings of how things work persisted. Religious change was not apostasy, for, as Axtell notes, "purposeful change and adjustment was the only norm."[47]

Finally, and most critically, responses to the disasters that scholars have laid at the base of religious decline were not uniform; even within a village there were always a variety of possibilities. The disasters did not promote a steady, level evaporation of ancient beliefs; rather they promoted conflicts within communities over how best to cope. Thus when prophets called for a restoration of a religion "lost," their concern for the sacred may have intensified as they struck out against members of their community who sought a different method of meeting the challenge of colonialism. Prophetic declamations of spiritual loss reflect more accurately the increasing divisiveness of Native America than they do its uniform "despiritualization."

Rather than a loss of a sense of the sacred among Indians, what the disasters of colonialism brought about was a debate over the efficacy of sacred power. Those whose spirituality intensified could agree with those whose spirituality diminished that their people were, quite literally, losing ground. For some, it was apparent that the Anglo-Americans were simply more powerful and that the Indians' sacred powers had failed them. These Indians sought survival and even gain in cooperation, at least of a limited kind, with the Anglo-American or European powers. Others, in a more moderate stance, sought to decipher the secrets of Anglo-American strength, and made efforts to incorporate those secrets into their own way of living. Then there were those who understood that they had failed in their commitments to the sacred powers, particularly the Great Spirit, the remote Creator who became increasingly important, probably under the influence of Christianity. In this understanding—which itself also entailed a radical reorientation, for it meant calling into question the identity of townspeople and relatives who cooperated too fully with the Anglo-Americans—lay the central premise of the militant, pan-Indian religious movements of the late eighteenth and early nineteenth centuries.

The questioning of one's neighbors' identity often involved violent charges of witchcraft. Witches, who were effectively performers of anti-rituals, had done the most to lose their peoples the favor of the other powers of the universe, particularly the Great Spirit. Short of witchcraft, other impurities, abominations, and neglects of ritual had blocked the peoples' access to sacred power. Thus, if Indians would gather to invoke the proper rituals—and these included new rituals obtained from the sacred powers by rising generations of prophets—to reject abomination, to kill witches, and thus to purify themselves, supernatural favor would return. They would recapture sacred power. To regain their access to sacred power, Indians had to perform rituals in a state of cleanliness. They had to reject the abominations that blocked their approach to the supernatural; but first they had to expose them.

One source of impurity became obvious to many who had suffered at the hands of English-speaking traders, soldiers, and settlers. At southern Green Corn ceremonies, Adair noticed that celebrants refused to buy a ceremonial ingredient, bear's oil, from the traders because "the Indians are so prepossessed with a notion of white people being all impure and accursed, that they deem their oil as polluting on those sacred occasions."

Another Briton, who recorded his observations in the years before the Revolution, captured the Delaware Indians' sense of irony, reporting that he had "heard the Delawares, on being asked what made them more wicked than the other indians, answer, it was owing to their having been so much with the white people." In the same period, Neolin, the renowned Delaware Prophet, encouraged his followers to give up "all the Sins & Vices which the Indians have learned from the White People." Whether Neolin actually meant all white people or just the British is unclear. In fact he was apparently fond of the French. But Neolin did go further than most and planned to end, eventually, the use of all European-made trade goods. He recognized that he could not accomplish this immediately but claimed that dependence on the traders could be ended within seven years of his first vision in 1761. When the Indians, said Neolin, began to turn conscientiously away from the ways of the English, "then will the great Spirit give success to our arms; then he will give us strength to conquer our enemies, to drive them from hence."[48] Of course Neolin's very insistence that Indians abandon the English reveals the local resistance to his argument. Not all Delawares would follow him.

The beliefs of Neolin and others like him would culminate, in the early nineteenth century, in the preachings of the Shawnee Tenskwatawa and the other itinerant prophets who, from the Great Lakes to the Gulf of Mexico, joined him and his brother Tecumseh. In Neolin's generation and Tenskwatawa's, and to a surprising extent in the generation in between, these beliefs supplied the ideological core of militant Indian resistance, a resistance not only to Anglo-American expansion but also to direct Anglo-American influence in Indian government and society.

Not all Indians agreed with or could abide by these nativists' developing constructions of the Indian and the Anglo-American. In Neolin's day and even more so in Tenskwatawa's, Indian peoples throughout the trans-Appalachian borderlands found themselves polarized between the "nativistic" advocates of resistance to dependence on AngloAmerica and proponents of "accommodation" with the expansionist settlers to the east.

These conflicts reflected social divisions, and a kind of political stratification, that had emerged in the course of the Indians' dealings with Europeans. Leaders with good contacts among the Euro-American powers used their influence to consolidate power at home; sometimes, as Richard White has brilliantly detailed among the Choctaws, they did so in an arguably "traditional" manner.[49] Not surprisingly, the European and Euro-American empire builders generally recognized these strategists as tribal leaders and attempted to shore up their dominance. Having some clout with colonial powers, accommodating leaders did not share the intensity of the nativists' opposition to direct Euro-American influence. Rather, they sought benefits—not always for themselves and their kin but often more broadly for their people—from their ability to manipulate that influence.

Leaders who supported accommodation could and often did seek to defend both Indian land and formal political independence. At times, when proponents of accommodation drew arms from European opponents of the Anglo-Americans, as they did from the British during the Revolution and later from the British and the Spanish in the late 1780s and early 1790s, they won the nativists' cooperation. In these periods, although with different outlooks, accommodation and nativism worked together in the movement for Indian unity. But when the exponents of accommodation despaired of European support, as most did after 1795, when they committed themselves to cooperation with the erstwhile Anglo-American enemy, they incurred the opposition of the developing nativistic movement. While nativists sought consistently to block Anglo-American influence in Indian councils, and in that manner to prevent the sale of Indian lands, supporters of accommodation cooperated, if only reluctantly, with the Anglo-Americans.

On the critical issue of Indian identity, the seekers of accommodation often took what at first blush seems a more traditional stand than the nativists, although this pattern actually underscores their as well as the nativists' departure from the past. As William McLoughlin has demonstrated in his studies of the Cherokees, these leaders developed a largely tribal, even a national, orientation, centralizing governments and consolidating authority.[50] But the nativists expanded their identity even further, beyond the boundaries of clan and people, to include all Indians. Nativists deployed a new theory of polygenesis, stressing both the common origin of all Indians and the spiritual impurity of Anglo-Americans. To follow the Anglo-Americans' ways too closely, according to this Indian theory of the separate creation, was to violate the structure of the universe and thus to lose sacred power.

This notion, that Anglo-Americans and Indians who cooperated with them had contaminated the sources of sacred power, brings us back to the scene at which we began this chapter: the muddy clearings around Fort Pitt, in the early spring of 1763. There we left Armstrong, a Delaware warrior, as he agreed with James Kenny, a Pennsylvania Quaker, that if the Indians would "leave off the Abominations they had amongst 'em & fear God, then he might Establish & increase them, but if they resisted as they do . . . they would Vanish & decay away" for "the Great Creator was Angry with their Works."[51]

Kenny no doubt felt that he had bested a heathen, convincing him that God was angry with the Indians for their resistance to Christianity. But

within a few months, when a full-blown nativist revolt wiped out most of
Britain's garrisons in the trans-Appalachian North, when hot ball rained
from Indian muskets into the muddy works about Fort Pitt, and when
Kenny and others fled back across the Alleghenies to safety, he may have
wondered. Kenny may not have realized it, but in telling Armstrong that
the Indians should quit their evil practices, he was only suggesting to the
warrior what the nativists already believed: it was time for all Indians to
behave independently of the English, time to challenge the wisdom of
leaders who yielded too much to the colonizers, time to drive out the
invaders. The twin notions, that Indians should identify with one another
and that they should identify the British colonists with evil, notions that
would find vivid expression in the visions of prophets, did not result only
from the prophets' ecstatic spiritual journeys. They did not come blinding-
ly out of the cloudless sky or rear suddenly in the moonlight like the
celestial war horses of Tioga. They grew out of centuries of thought, and
decades of experience.

≫≫≫≫≫≫≪≪≪≪≪≪≪

TWO

The Indians' Great Awakening
1745–1775

In 1749, Captain Pierre-Joseph Céloron de Blainville, an envoy of the government of New France, undertook a claims-staking journey down the Allegheny and Ohio rivers. Céloron nailed metallic plaques, emblems of his king's claim, to stout trees. But because he knew that Upper Ohio Indians had different ideas about sovereignty, he staked the claim unceremoniously, almost on the sly. After he left, local Shawnees tore down "and trampled underfoot with contempt" the symbols of French ownership.[1] Céloron's voyage dramatized the great issue of Ohio country possession; but the journal he left does more: it provides us with a glimpse into the dynamic social and political world of the region's Indians.

Céloron described complicated interactions among Indian peoples. In early August 1749, he stopped at the village of Chiningue (Logstown), twenty miles downstream from the forks of the Ohio. Though nominally an Ohio Iroquois (or "Mingo") town, Delawares and Shawnees also peopled the village, and "besides these three nations," according to the journal "there are in the village some Iroquois from Sault St. Louis, from the Lake of Two Mountains; some Nepassingues, Abenakes, Ottawas and other nations." Filled with peoples nominally allied with the British as well as with dissidents from the nominal allies of France, the grouping, in Céloron's view, formed "a very bad village." Later that month, Céloron approached Sonioto, where the Indians displayed their lack of intimidation by firing a thousand rounds into the air as the French flotilla appeared. Sonioto, like Chiningue, was a polyglot village; predominantly Shawnee and Mingo, it had "added to it thirty men [Caughnawaga Mohawks] of the Sault St. Louis."[2]

These villages of mixed ethnicity, located on strategic paths between the Southeast, the Ohio River, and the Great Lakes, were centers of Indian trade and diplomacy. In 1752, for example, the Virginian William Trent recorded in his diary that a Cherokee embassy from the southern Appalachians had visited the Ohioan Shawnees, Delawares, and Mingos to request that they convince the English to reopen a trade in the Cherokee villages. The Cherokees, desperate for ammunition, had long been under attacks from the Creeks of the Gulf Plains. They explained to their northern hosts that if the English failed to reopen a Cherokee trade, many, even thousands, of Cherokees would be forced to retreat northward to the Ohio. Two years later, a group of Cherokees did establish a temporary settlement near the Shawnees in 1755, bringing the worlds of the Ohio and the Southeast closer together.[3]

Such relations between the Ohio country and the Southeast were not new in the mid-eighteenth century, although they would intensify in the coming years. The Ohio Shawnees had a long history of interaction with southeasterners, particularly the Creeks. The Shawnees had dwelled along the Ohio River until the Five Nations Iroquois invasion of the late 1630s, an event that signaled the beginning of a remarkable Shawnee diaspora.[4] Under strong Iroquoian attacks, the Shawnees had fled to the south and east, pretty much abandoning the Ohio country. By 1685, the scattered Shawnees were tilling the soil and hunting for white-tailed deer in Tennessee, Georgia, and Alabama, establishing close relations with Cherokees and Creeks. By 1690, other Shawnees, now at peace with the Five Nations Iroquois, inhabited eastern Pennsylvania among the Unami- and Munsee-speaking peoples who would come to be called the Delawares. Turmoil in the Southeast accompanying the colonization of the Carolinas constricted the Shawnees to widely separated enclaves in Alabama among the Creeks and in Pennsylvania among the Delawares and Iroquois.[5] The resulting close relations between Creeks and Shawnees, on the one hand, and Delawares and Shawnees, on the other, would be particularly important in the development of militant religious nativism. The far-flung networks possessed by the Shawnees provided immense opportunities for communication among borderland Indians in the mid and late eighteenth century. They also gave the Shawnees their critical influence in the militant, sixty-odd year quest for Indian unity that germinated as Céloron made his descent.

The Shawnees, though remarkable in the extent of their migrations and acquaintances, were not unique in their promotion of far-ranging alliances. What is more, like other peoples, as subsequent chapters will demonstrate, Shawnee villages often divided among themselves over the issue of war or peace with the Anglo-Americans. That qualification is important, indeed central, to the story, but, the qualification notwithstanding, the Shawnees would be among the most obvious promoters of pan-Indian action from the Seven Years' War to the age of their most famous compatriot, Tecumseh.

No people, however, not even the Shawnees, could compete in 1749 with the French when it came to Eastern Woodlands diplomacy. No event would intensify intertribal relations as would the Seven Years' War, an event for which Céloron's voyage would prove a precipitant.

The Seven Years' War and Indian Identity

The Seven Years' War involved Indians from the St. Lawrence River to the Mississippi Delta, demanding deep changes in the diplomatic relations among and the social relations within Indian peoples, changes that would shape history for a generation. Over the course of the war's active North American phase, from 1754 to 1760, Indians of the Great Lakes, the Ohio country, and even the Southeast met, both with one another and with the French, to plan for their common defense, strengthening relations and seeking the development of widespread networks along which ideas would regularly be exchanged. Those networks penetrated even such peoples allied with Britain as the Cherokees. The ideas they conducted concerned not just strategy but also identity and power.

Understandings of power, particularly those expressed in war ritual and ceremony, were traded actively among the members of the different peoples who fought shoulder to shoulder in the conflict. Early in the war, in 1755, on the eve of British Major General Edward Braddock's spectacular defeat on the Monongahela River, the French officer Daniel de Beaujeu at Fort Duquesne, now Pittsburgh, employed Indian ceremony when he sought to raise a fighting force among the Ottawas, Chippewas, Hurons, Mingos, Shawnees, and Potawatomis. He "began the Warsong and all the Indian Nations Immediately joined him except the Poutiawatomis of the Narrows [Detroit] who were silent." The Potawatomi hesitation sent the Indians into conference, and the Potawatomis, probably at the urging of the Mingos and Shawnees, marched to victory with the rest the next day. By the end of the following winter, the local Delawares and Shawnees had sent symbolic war belt after war belt to the surrounding peoples, and many responded, causing one observer to claim that the Ohioans had "caused all those Nations to chant the war [song] during the whole of the winter."⁶ Many among the Iroquois, Catawbas, Cherokees, Chickasaws, and other peoples did not join in the chorus. But factions among most Eastern Woodlands nations did, and the peoples who sang together did so in fact, not just in metaphor. As in the sharing of war belts, the singing of the war song suggests a growing identification of the peoples with one another. So it was also toward the end of the conflict in the Ohio region. In 1758, Indians from throughout the Ohio and Great Lakes countries shared in powerful ceremonies after defeating British forces under James Grant, stalling—though not frustrating—General John Forbes's and Colonel Henry Bouquet's ultimately successful campaign against Fort Duquesne. Outside the walls of the French fort the warriors of different nations dressed scalps "with feathers and painted them, then tied them on white, red, and black poles. . . . Immediately after they began to beat their drums, shake their rattles, hallow and dance."⁷

The presence of French posts, where ammunition was dispensed and where raids were often organized, drew Indians from distant regions together against a common enemy. When a band of Tiogan Delawares, three years before they saw the battle of the celestial horses with which this book opened, traveled from their eastern Appalachian slopes to Montreal, seeking assistance from the French, they kept company with Ottawas from Michigan. Also at Montreal that month were Chippewas from Lake Superior, Foxes, Sauks, Menominees, and Potawatomis, as well as a number "from a Nation so far away that no Canadian interpreter understands their language." Commerce occurred among these Indians as well as between them and the French. The exchanges were not always harmonious, but the fact of the common British enemy did make for friendships and alliances.⁸ The Seven Years' War, terribly violent though it was, opened an opportunity for the elaboration of intertribal relations. The memory of the unions shaped by alliance with France would persist long after France departed.

The departure of France from North America left the Indians more dependent than ever on the British for goods. To break that dependence without recourse to New France was for the militants the challenge of the 1760s. One strategy adopted to meet that challenge had been suggested by the extensive cooperation of Indian peoples with the armies of France and New France. New diplomatic and military ventures would have to be undertaken without the coordination provided by an imperial power, but some wondered at the possibilities of assistance from the sacred powers. Outside of but influenced by the old networks, a nativistic movement formed. It took on a strong religious dimension, one whose full range of attributes had already begun to find expression in the Susquehanna and Ohio valleys.

Northeastern Origins, 1737–1775

A nativistic movement that would last a generation to become the religious underpinning of militant pan-Indianism first developed most clearly in the polyglot communities on the Upper Susquehanna. Refugees from earlier dispossessions in New Jersey and eastern Pennsylvania, these peoples began again to fall back before the Anglo-American advance of the 1750s and 1760s. The movement accompanied refugees as they fled northwest and then west from the Susquehanna to the headwaters of the Allegheny, from whence it descended upon the Ohio country. Here it found inviting souls among the already established refugees who inhabited the polyglot villages that had been so suspicious of Céloron. Laid low during the Seven Years' War, the Indians provided the movement with deep basins of support. The Ohio River issued from mountain springs, snows, and rains. The currents of nativism issued from the reckonings of the several thousand souls, and from the many prophets who gave those souls voice.[9] Because the movement roughly coincided with British America's Christian revival, I have chosen to call it the Indians' Great Awakening. But it was not a "revival" of a religious spirit that had lain, somehow, dormant. In its most important aspect, it was an "awakening" to the idea that, despite all the boundaries defined by politics, language, kinship, and geography, Indians did indeed share much in the way of their pasts and their present. It was an awakening to the notion that Indians shared a conflict with Anglo-America, and that they, as Indians, could and must take hold of their destiny by regaining sacred power.

Between 1737 and 1775, a time of economic dislocation and much warfare in the Susquehanna and Ohio valleys, a cluster of men and women came into direct contact with the usually remote Master of Life. Styled "prophets" by the least hostile of their Christian observers and "impostors" by others, these people differed from the more common shamans or conjurers only in the level of their experience. Although their spiritual encounters may have represented departures from, or elaborations upon, more ordinary shamanistic experiences, they were not new phenomena in the mid-eighteenth century. Over a full century before, Hurons reported spiritual encounters that led them to perform new ceremonies.[10] Indian myths, moreover, are replete with similar journeys to the sky world.

In its mid-eighteenth-century manifestations prophetic nativism first

On the Susquehanna, near Owego

The Susquehanna River, between Otseningo and Tioga, sites of visions in 1737 and 1760.
(*Source*: Charles Dana, *The United States Illustrated in Views of City and Country* [New York, 1853].)

appears, mildly, in the 1737 journals of Pennsylvania's Indian agent, Conrad Weiser. Weiser found starving Shawnees and Onondaga Iroquois at the Susquehanna River town of Otseningo discussing the recent visions of "one of their seers." In "a vision of God," the seer learned that God had "driven the wild animals out of the country" in punishment for the crime of killing game for trade in alcohol. The seer convinced his listeners that if they did not stop trading skins for English rum, God would wipe them "from the earth." Weiser did not dwell on the matter; we do not learn of any ensuing reformation.[11] But by 1744, the Susquehanna Valley, increasingly populated by polyglot refugees from dispossession in the East, swelled again with prophecy.

That year, lower down the river, the Presbyterian missionary David Brainerd encountered religious nativists among the Delawares and Shawnees. He reported that "they now seem resolved to retain their pagan notions and persist in their idolatrous practices." Beset by disease, the Indians looked to the sacred powers "to find out why they were then so sickly." Among the inhabitants of one Delaware town Brainerd met "a devout and zealous reformer, or rather restorer of what he supposed was the ancient religion of the Indians." Like the seer at Otseningo, the holy man claimed that his people "were grown very degenerate and corrupt," and he emphatically denounced alcohol. But he also claimed that his people must revive what he believed were the ceremonies of their ancestors. Although the sight of the Delaware holy man stirred "images of terror" in Brainerd's mind, the shaman did not reveal any hostility toward Anglo-Americans, and Brainerd admitted that "there was something in his temper and disposition that looked more like true religion than anything I ever observed amongst other heathens."[12]

Neither Weiser's "seer" nor Brainerd's "reformer" mounted a political challenge discernible in the record. They did stand against the alcohol trade and therefore against a most visible and physical form of dependence upon Europeans. That is all. But Weiser's mission of 1737 was part of an effort to firm up an alliance between Pennsylvania and the Six Nations, an alliance that was political. The upshot of his mission and of several ensuing years of Pennsylvanian negotiation with the Six Nations did affect prophecy. The upshot was that a large group of Delawares lost their homes on the Delaware River and reluctantly migrated to new homes, under Six Nations supervision, on the Susquehanna. By the early 1750s, these and other Susquehanna Valley refugees began to demonstrate, politically and spiritually, against both Six Nations authority and Anglo-American expansion. The obvious political developments are treated as such elsewhere.[13] Let us briefly explore their religious dimension.

The first of the prophets to mount a political challenge was a young Delaware woman. Noted in 1751 by Brainerd's younger brother, John, she lived in the increasingly militant Susquehanna River town of Wyoming, which was choked with refugees. We know little of her, not even her name; indeed the Indians "seemed somewhat backward to tell" John Brainerd about her at all. But the scanty evidence is tantalizing. Her vision "was a confirmation of some revelations they had had before." She had been told by the "Great Power that they should destroy the poison from among them." The woman worried about the sickness and death of so many of her people and blamed it on that "poison," probably a witch bundle, allegedly held by "their old and principal men." The evidence, though thin, suggests a challenge to the local leadership of the town of Wyoming, a leadership bound to the powerful Six Nations Iroquois to the north and, through their cooperation, to the British colonies. Her people would attack that bondage openly and violently during the Seven Years' War.[14]

The people of this Delaware village asserted their Indian identity. They drew distinctions that separated Indians from blacks and whites. The distinctions, they felt, were God-given. Rejecting Presbyterian attempts to establish a mission among them, they explained, "God first made three men and three women, viz: the indians, the negro, and the white man." Because Europeans were produced last, "the white people ought not to think themselves better than the Indians." Moreover, the Bible was for Europeans alone; since God gave no such book "to the Indian or negro, and therefore it could not be right for them to have a book, or be any way concerned with that way of worship."[15]

This idea of the separate creation of Indians, blacks, and whites, an idea that sanctioned separate forms of worship, was widely reported in the Susquehanna and Ohio regions, where it became commonplace. On the eve of the American Revolution, it would be shared as well by the southern Indians, who described it to Anglo-Americans.[16] The notion of the separate creation gave legitimacy to the Indians' way of life. It explicitly challenged not only those Indians who had converted to Christianity but also those few who had grown too close to the Anglo-Americans. It played in harmony with the Wyoming woman's dissent from the accommodating leadership of her village. Claiming that only Indian ways could lead Indians to salvation, the theology of separation implicitly attacked Indian clients of the Anglo-Americans.

The notion had radical implications for Indian identity. Attachments to the older, local, linguistic, and lineage-oriented conceptions of one's people now competed with a decidedly innovative pan-Indianism. The notion reflected the growing cooperation of militant factions from different peoples in political efforts to unite Indians against the Anglo-American menace. It also reflected the heightening of local tensions, as Indians who rejected nativism and urged accommodation with the British found themselves accused of abomination.

The year after the younger Brainerd first encountered this separatist theology, a group of Munsee Delawares settled a new town some seventy miles up the winding Susquehanna. Munsees increasingly identified with their Unami Delaware-speaking cousins, and like many Unamis they had maintained friendly relations with the Moravians and Quakers. This particular group of Munsees displayed a marked ambivalence toward both Christianity and nativism. Its leader, Papoonan, had once been "a drunken Indian." At the age of about forty-five he "underwent a sorrowful period of reformation, including a solitary sojourn in the woods & a vision following the death of his father." Like other Indian prophets, Papoonan emerged from the vision with a message of love and reformation. He preached against the use of alcohol, as would most prophets, and he preached that the Master of Life, angered by the sins of the Indians, had met them with punishing visitations.

Unlike many of the other prophets, Papoonan refused to countenance war—a stand he may have absorbed from the Moravians and Quakers. The prophet once told a Pennsylvanian that in his heart he knew "the Quakers are Right." He and his followers remained at peace with Pennsylvania throughout the 1750s, and toward the end of the war they sought out Quakers to mediate their talks with the suspicious British authorities.

But even sincere protestations of friendship and interest in Christianity could not mask Papoonan's frustration with the social changes wrought by the Indian-Anglo trade. Recognizing the increasing importance in Indian society of access to British trade goods, Papoonan aimed his message primarily at the greedy. His own people, he worried, "grow proud & Covetous, which causes God to be Angry & to send dry & hot Summers & hard Winters, & also Sickness among the People."[17] He also aimed the message at Anglo-Americans, telling the Pennsylvania Provincial Council that their raising of the prices of manufactured goods created tensions: "You alter the price that you say you will give for our Skins, which can never be right; God cannot be pleased to see the prices of one & the same thing so often alter'd & Changed." While challenging the greed of British colonists, Papoonan, like other prophets, urged his followers to purify themselves of similar greed by "adhering to the ancient Customs & manners of their Forefathers." He and his followers resisted, for a time, Christian efforts to establish missions among them, for they were "much afraid of being seduced & [brought] off from their ways by the White People."[18]

In spite of its attempt to live in peace, Papoonan's community could not escape the massive troubles that surrounded it. Christian Frederick Post found the villagers troubled and quarrelsome in 1760. The town still existed as a native, non-Christian religious community the following year, but as Pontiac's War of 1763 embroiled the region, Papoonan, who held to the peace, lost influence. British colonial lynch mobs, having killed neutral Indians in the Paxton Massacre, forced Papoonan to flee with others to the safety of barracks under Quaker protection in Philadelphia. At the war's end, he was there numbered among the "Christian Indians." Some among his followers invited the Moravian missionaries to come among them. Others went off to join the nativistic communities that were, by then, abundant on the Upper Ohio.[19] It would not be the last failure of studied neutrality.

Further up the Susquehanna, not far from what is now New York State, Wangomend, or the Assinsink Prophet, experienced his first visions in the early 1750s, probably in 1752, the year Papoonan settled his new town. Unlike Papoonan, this Munsee showed open hostility toward the British. Indeed his message closely resembles the separatist beliefs of the Unami Delaware woman downstream at Wyoming who received her visions the previous year. The Assinsink Prophet encouraged the Indians to abandon British ways, emphatically denouncing rum drinking. He employed a chart on which "there is Heaven and a Hell and Rum and Swan hak [Europeans] and Indiens and Ride [Red] Strokes for Rum."[20] As late as 1760, his fellow villagers manifested their enmity toward the colonists when they prevented a Pennsylvania peace delegation from passing west into the Ohio country.

Wangomend, like other Susquehanna country prophets, introduced or reintroduced ceremonies in an effort to gain power. Post reported that the prophet had revived "an Old quarterly Meeting," during which the participants recited the "Dreams and Revelations everyone had from his Infancy, & what Strength and Power they had received thereby." The meeting, which lasted all day and all night, involved walking, singing, dancing, and, finally, cathartic weeping. The people of the town paid close attention to visions and dreams, not only their own but those of others. When news of the collective vision that opened this book came from Munsee Tioga, miles upstream, the Assinsink Munsees also sought to discover its meaning. Prophecy in the Susquehanna and Ohio countries was not a local affair.

Following the Seven Years' War, refugee Munsee and Unami Delawares fled the Susquehanna for the Ohio, and the Assinsink Prophet was among them.[21] There he undoubtedly encountered, if he had not done so previously, the thoroughly compatible teachings of another advocate of Indian separation from Britain, the Delaware Prophet, Neolin. The Ottawa warrior Pontiac would claim inspiration from Neolin for his siege of Detroit in 1763, and Neolin would rapidly emerge as the spiritual leader of a militant movement with political overtones. But it is important to recall that he neither invented nor was solely responsible for the spiritual quest for unity.

The Delaware Prophet, Neolin

One night in the eighteen months or so of only relative calm that followed the French evacuation of the Upper Ohio Valley, Neolin sat alone by his fire, "musing and greatly concrned about the evil ways he saw prevailing among the Indians." Strangely, a man appeared and "told him these things he was thinking of were right" and proceeded to instruct him in religion. By the fall of 1761 Neolin had gained a considerable following as he relayed the will of the Master of Life to the Delawares. Like the Assinsink Prophet, he employed a pictographic chart. Neolin drew a path from earth to heaven, along "which their forefathers use'd to assend to Hapiness." The path, however, was now blocked by a symbol "representing the White people." Along the right side of the chart were many "Strokes" representing the vices brought by Europeans. Through these strokes the Indians now "must go, ye Good Road being Stopt." Hell was also close at hand, and "there they are Led irrevocably."[22] The programs offered by the Assinsink Prophet and Neolin were identical in many particulars. Each preached strenuously against the use of rum, chief among "ye vices which ye Indians have learned from ye White people," and which each depicted on his chart as strokes through which the difficult way to heaven now led.[23]

Neolin not only drew a cosmographic distinction between Anglo-Americans and Indians, he preached a rejection of dependence on the British through the avoidance of trade, the elaboration of ritual, and the gradual (not the immediate) abandonment of European-made goods. In 1763, Delaware councils agreed to train their boys in the traditional arts of warfare, and to adopt, for seven years, a ritual diet that included the frequent consumption of an herbal emetic, after which they would be purified of the "White people's ways and Nature."[24] The ritual brewing, drinking, and vomiting of this tea became a regular feature of Ohio Valley nativism in the 1760s. Very common in the Southeast, "black drink" may have been introduced to the Delawares by their Shawnee neighbors, well connected with the Cherokees and Creeks. The practice repelled missionaries and other visitors to the Ohio country. Shawnees drank and spewed the beverage with such literal enthusiasm that one of their towns, Waka-tomica, was known to traders in the late 1760s as "vomit town."[25] Waka-tomica became a center of resistance to Anglo-American expansion and cultural influence. Here is where the Delaware Prophet took refuge, in fact, when British troops threatened to invade his hometown on the Tus-carawas River in 1764.[26]

Neolin's message clearly entailed armed resistance to Anglo-American expansion. As early as 1761, Neolin predicted that "there will be Two or Three Good Talks and then War." Neolin's words struck a chord among Indians who suffered from or looked with foreboding upon three major threats to their economies: the disappearance of game, land encroachments by settlers (now well under way on the Monongahela), and the British abandonment of customary presentations of gunpowder to the Indians. Like the seer at Otseningo, Neolin explained the exhaustion of the deer herds as the Great Spirit's punishment for the Indians' embrace of Anglo-American vices. He berated Indians for allowing the colonists to establish settlements west of the Appalachians and for the Indians' humiliating dependence: "Can ye not live without them?" And he threatened con-tinued disaster if they did not both reform and revolt: "If you suffer the English among you, you are dead men. Sickness, smallpox, and their poison will destroy you entirely."[27]

The prophet's message spread among the nations. When the French commander of Fort Chartres (Illinois) learned of the prophet late in 1763, he wrote that Neolin "has had no difficulty in convincing all his own people, and in turn all red men, that God had appeared to him." Com-mandant Neyon de Villiers was "perfectly convinced of the effect that it has had on the Potawatomi."[28] In 1764, the Wyandots of Sandusky, militants who associated closely with the Shawnees and Delawares, openly joined the crusade against the English. The combined Shawnee, Delaware, and Wyandot inhabitants of Sandusky declared that they had no fear of English numbers. Of the English they claimed that one Indian was "as good as a thousand of them, and notwithstanding they are but *Mice* in Comparison to them, they will bite as hard as *they* can." In addition to the Potawatomis, Wyandots, Shawnees, and Delawares, the prophet's message raised spirits among the Miamis, Senecas, Ottawas, Chippewas, and beyond.[29]

Many spin-off revivals occurred, just as Neolin's had spun off from the earlier Susquehanna episodes. A Delaware of Kuskuski visited Heaven in 1762. He used charts in his ministry and communicated with the Great Spirit through intermediaries, or, as James Kenny put it, through "a little God." A great chief of the Ottawas, Katapelleecy, had personal encounters with the Great Spirit in 1764. In the heart of the Six Nations country an

Onondaga received revelations critical of the Anglo-Americans and laced with separation theology on the eve of Pontiac's War.[30] With no end in sight to the British threat, these prophets, despite their many innovations, offered a solution to Indian problems that came out of Indian traditions. Reform the world through ritual; recapture sacred power. The message took hold.

Prophetic Resistance, 1760–1775

In the spring of 1763, thirteen of the British posts that stood north of the Ohio and the Potomac and west of the Susquehanna, in the heartland of religious nativism, came under devastating Indian attacks. From Senecas in New York to Chippewas in Minnesota and the Indians of Illinois, militant factions joined in a struggle to remove the British from posts so recently French. By 1765 this war, commonly known as Pontiac's War, had ended, and only four of the posts remained, most notably Detroit and Pitt.

Prophecy has long been acknowledged as having had a role in Pontiac's War, a colorful but incidental role. Generally, the prophet's message is a historian's addendum to a list of substantive causes of the war: British abuses in the trade, colonial encroachments on Indian land, Jeffrey Amherst's orders curtailing the customary dispensing of gifts to Indians, and French encouragement to the Indians.[31] A common view is that Neolin's message was a slogan employed by militants to attract warriors. Howard Peckham, calling Neolin a "psychopathic Delaware," sees the prophet as providing a justification for Pontiac's attack on the British at Detroit. Suggesting that Pontiac manipulated "the Prophet's message slightly to support his own ambitions," Peckham implies that the Ottawa leader was too sophisticated to have believed in the prophet's visions, but used prophecy to inspire his more gullible followers.[32]

Pontiac, however, portrayed himself as a true believer in the nativistic movement, and there seems little reason to doubt his claim.[33] Even addressing the Catholic French he spoke in prophetic terms. Visiting Fort Chartres in 1764 to reject de Villiers's request that he stop the war, Pontiac declared that the Master of Life "put Arms in our hands, and it is he who has ordered us to fight against this bad meat that would come and infest our lands." He warned the French not to speak of "Peace with the English," for in doing so they went "against the orders of the Master of Life."[34] Indeed, there is other evidence that Pontiac acted upon Neolin's initiative. Robert Navarre, a pro-British *habitant* who knew Pontiac at Detroit, said of Neolin's message that it "contains in blackest aspect the reason of the attack upon the English." Fort Pitt's Captain Simeon Ecuyer had it on the authority of Detroit's Major Henry Gladwyn that the Delawares and Shawnees were the "*canaille* who stir up the rest to mischief."[35]

But the extent of the prophet's influence on Pontiac or of Pontiac's influence on the war that now bears his name is less important for an understanding of Indian militancy than is the spiritual nature of militancy itself. The Delaware Prophet was not the single leader of the movement any more than was Pontiac. Both drew upon widespread beliefs in their efforts to confront the problems of 1763. The Delaware Prophet, and many other prophets who preceded and followed him, provided Indians with an explanation for their misfortunes that squared well with their traditions: Indian abominations, including cooperation with the British, caused their loss of sacred power. Construed in this manner, the disturbance could be rectified by ritual and by steadfast, united opposition to British expansion.

When the Indians failed to drive the British from Fort Detroit and Fort Pitt, when smallpox—deliberately disseminated in hospital blankets by Fort Pitt's British officers—broke out among the Ohio peoples, and when British columns marched within striking distance of Indian towns, the military unity of the Indians temporarily collapsed and the war ended. But neither prophetic nativism nor the idea of unity collapsed with it. Prophets and diplomats grew more active.

Prophecy in Defeat

Following the logic of nativism—that proper behavior could restore Indian power—it would be reasonable to expect the British victory of 1765 to have disproved prophecy and ended the Indians' Great Awakening. Neolin's followers did indeed face a crisis as they were forced to submit to Henry Bouquet's forces. Responding to the crisis in January 1765, Neolin had another vision, the last in the record. He approached veteran Indian agent George Croghan with it in April, for it required British action. Like Papoonan at the end of the Seven Years' War, Neolin requested that the British send out Quaker negotiators. The Great Spirit had recently permitted Neolin to negotiate with Britain, but only through the Quakers. Still, recovering from smallpox, without ammunition, and with a British army poised to strike their villages, the Indians were in no position to bargain. Croghan, an agent of the Pennsylvania Proprietors, suspected that his employers' political opponents in the "Quaker Party" lay behind the Indian request, and he refused it. Delaware delegates yielded to British power and signed a treaty of peace in April, but in their villages they were "in great Confusion amongst themselves and without any order in their Council," as factionalism prevailed.[36]

Such divisions plagued Indians throughout the period. Even during the war, nativists found parties of Indians ranged against them. Roman Catholic Hurons under the baptized leader, Teata, confronted militants: "We do not know what the designs of the Master of Life toward us may be. Is it He who inspires our brothers, the Ottawas to war?"[37] Mingos and Genesee Senecas sided with the militants against the wishes of the seat of Iroquois accommodation, the Onondaga Council, which eventually neutralized the militant Senecas by providing Sir William Johnson, Britain's Northern Superintendent of Indian Affairs, with Iroquois troops. And even among Neolin's people, the division between nativism and accommodation was pronounced: "The Capts and Warriors of the Delaware pay no regard to their Chiefs who advised them not to accept the Hatchet."[38]

Paradoxically, it was precisely these divisions that permitted the survival of the nativist movement for unity. Nativism depended upon its Indian opponents. Infighting extended the life of the movement. Nativists could attribute the failure of Native American arms not to British numbers, technology, or organization, but to the improper behavior of the accommodating Indians. As long as nativists faced serious opposition within their own communities, they could explain Indian defeat as the consequence of other Indians' misdeeds.

For years following the collapse of armed Indian rebellion in 1765, militant prophets continued to attract followers, and internal animosities mounted within the villages. The young people, wrote George Henry Loskiel, "began to despise the counsel of the aged, and only endeavored to get into favor with these preachers, whose followers multiplied very fast."[39] One of the best known of these "preachers" was the Assinsink Prophet, Wangomend. Wangomend had long preached that there were fundamental differences between Indians and Anglo-Americans. Like his counterparts at the Susquehanna town of Wyoming in the 1750s and like his contemporary Neolin, whom he outlasted as a prophet, he spoke of separate paths to heaven for Indians and Anglo-Americans, and he drew the paths "on the ground, showing the way for the Indians to be much more direct" than that for the Christians. God, he later said, "has created them and us for different purposes. Therefore, let us cling to our old customs and not depart from them."[40] Wangomend did not preach alone. At Goshgoshunk on the Allegheny River, where the Moravian missionary David Zeisberger encountered him in 1767, elderly women also saw the Indians' misfortunes as the result of "having changed their ancient way of living, in consequence of what the white men had told them, and this white preacher (Zeisberger,) was saying to them."[41]

Wangomend attended to a variety of voices, not only that of the Great

Spirit. One vision, which was most likely Wangomend's, suggests his concern for the depleted condition of game. While out hunting, he came across a buck that spoke to him, warning the Indians "not to have so much to do with the whites, but cherish their own customs and not to imitate the manners of the whites, else it would not go well with them."[42] Like the medicine bear of the Cherokee myth, this buck was probably the "deer master," the manitou that controlled the supply of game and made certain that hunters behaved properly.

Wangomend's erratic career lasted to the very eve of the American Revolution. For a time, after the failure of one of his prophecies to come true and in the face of a swell of Munsee conversions to the Moravian's religion in the summer of 1770, he despaired and tried to become a Moravian Christian, but within a year he abandoned the attempt, resumed his own mission, and led an intensive witch-hunt in an effort to rescue his people from abomination. As late as 1775, as the American Revolution broke out in the East, Wangomend still sought to rid his people of evil, proposing a witch-hunt at a Delaware council at Goshgoshunk.[43]

Such accusations made him many enemies, a fact that both troubled his career and made it possible, for he could only preach reformation against a convincing backdrop of corruption. We know so much of Wangomend largely because he, of all the Ohio prophets, had the most direct contact with a determined group of Moravian Brethren, a group that had attracted about one hundred, mostly Munsee, Delawares to its Ohio mission between 1769 and 1782, a significant accomplishment considering that the Delaware population at this time may have been as low as two and a half thousand.

With every twenty-fifth Delaware attending to the Moravian Brethren, and with others attending to the likes of Wangomend, Delaware fissures deepened. Nativist sentiment surfaced regularly in the two major Unami Delaware towns, Kuskuski and Newcomer's, into the early 1770s. Like other advocates of Indian separation, these nativists stressed the distinction between Indians and the eastern settlers. One, visiting the Moravian Munsees in 1771, laid out his categories of understanding before Zeisberger. Christianity, the nativist said, was "for the white people. . . . God has made different kinds of men and has made each kind for a different purpose." The Indian clearly worried that to worship in the Christian manner was to violate the cosmic order. Another Indian, claiming to be a literate ex-Christian, told his townspeople "that he has read the Bible from beginning to end and that it is not written in it that the Indians should live like white people, or that they should change their lives." The nativists of

Kuskuski never threatened the mission with violence, but they worried at its success and sought to convince the Christian converts to return to the nativist fold. One nativistic "new preacher" used images of Anglo-American society as the symbols of danger to Indians, declaring that the Moravians sought to have the Indians "transported as slaves, where they would be harnessed to the plough, and whipped to work."[44]

A prophet at Delaware Newcomer's town, so named by the English for its leader, not only accused the Moravians of plotting to enslave the Delawares but claimed that worse catastrophes awaited all the people if Moravian successes continued: in three and a half years "there would be a terrible flood . . . and until then nothing which they would plant would grow." Drawing on Indian traditions that regarded fasts as a means of rectifying disorders caused by an improper mixing of categories, this prophet recommended a diet of only corn and water for four months to forestall the disaster.[45]

The people of Newcomer's town pondered these developments in the midst of a terrible epidemic. Some of them had sought answers in the faith of the Moravians, others joined the Moravians seeking powers to supplement their own beliefs, but still others shunned the Christians as they intensified their efforts to rectify the disturbances that had left them so vulnerable to harm. As the sickness persisted, the village council hit upon a solution that may well have been proposed by its famous resident, Neolin. Drawing upon their ideas about the power of fasts to enable humans to cross into other dimensions, the council decided to raise two boys as prophets. For two years the children would receive daily emetics, and they would eat only corn and water. After this preparation, "they would become very spiritualized and have many visions, revelations and dreams, they would even possess a special spirit and strength." Whether any boys underwent this preparation is not known, but the idea was not completely new. Eight years before, Neolin had proposed a variant: all the boys were to "Live intirely on dry'd Meat & a Sort of Bitter Drink made of Roots & Plants & Water." Now, in 1770, the town council, by underfeeding two of the village children, sought to create prophets to help them meet future disasters.[46]

The drive for purity so vividly represented by the regular purges and fasts that the nativists endured found expression in another form of purge, the witch-hunt. Witches and witch bundles, or "poison," became chief objects of nativistic wrath as Indians felt a loss of power to resist disease, want, and Anglo-American expansion. Indians saw witches as inherently evil beings who enjoyed killing; to discover witches and "poison" among them would be to understand their calamities. In 1772, a council at Kuskus-ki suspected that one of the Moravian Indians possessed such a bundle, the "strong poison by which many Indians are killed."[47]

Although the witchcraft accusations against Indians well connected with the colonists resulted in little violence during the early 1770s, they did contribute to growing divisions within the villages of the Unamis and Munsees. While nativists urged unity in the face of the Anglo-American threat, Delaware councils divided. The nativistic Indians of Newcomer's town squared off against a faction led by the accommodation-minded Delaware war captain, Chief White Eyes.[48] This fracture among the Dela-wares would prevent the Shawnees and Mingos from obtaining much Delaware support in their attempts to prevent the Anglo-American cap-ture of Kentucky during what has come to be called "Lord Dunmore's War," after the royal governor of aggressive Virginia.

The Scioto Conferences and Dunmore's War, 1767–1775

Currents of nativism ran as deeply among the Shawnees as they did among the Delawares. Because there were no Christian missionaries settled among them, however, we have fewer records. This emptiness is itself revealing, for Moravians, Presbyterians, and Baptists all attempted to preach to this militant people but were not allowed. Instead, the Shawnees welcomed the preaching of Delaware nativists, even after Neolin's powers had waned.

One of these Delaware prophets, Scattameck, became a vessel for the sacred at Newcomer's town in 1771. Like previous visionaries, he strongly recommended that the Indians drink "Beson (medicinal herbs and roots), in order to cleanse themselves from sin." Two other Delaware "preachers" supported Scattameck. The Shawnees "received the tidings with joy and sent the message on to the Delamattenoos [Miamis]." According to Zeis-berger, Scattameck claimed that adherence to the ritual would bring the Indians a good crop even if "they planted but little." Zeisberger held this teaching responsible for a famine among the Shawnees, but the Indians apparently saw the matter differently. Despite their hunger, the missionary noted, "the idea continues and has not been recalled . . . the matter re-mains unchanged."[49]

Scattameck, following the other prophets, invoked the doctrine of In-dian separateness. During one vision he learned that Europeans and Indians did not share the path to salvation, that the son of the Great Spirit desired that Indians "should come to him by another way than that used by the white people."[50] This separatist notion, although informed by the Christian notion of salvation as a coming to God, nonetheless was clearly and consciously anti-Christian, and it continued to resonate among nativists.

The Baptist minister David Jones found his mission to the five Shawnee towns in 1772 and 1773 mired in thick Shawnee nativism. During these early childhood years of the great future nativist, Tecumseh, Jones encountered an enthusiasm to match his own. After he entered the village of Chillicothe, Shawnees brought Jones to Red Hawk, from whom Jones requested permission to preach. Red Hawk refused in separatist terms, arguing that Indians should live and worship in their own manner: "When God, who first made us all, prescribed our way of living, he allowed the white people to live one way, and Indians another way."[51] Jones failed to gather a Shawnee audience.

The Baptist noticed that the Indians entertained suspicions that his object was to promote their enslavement, that "the white people had sent me as a spy." The Shawnees' rumors were not far off the mark, for Jones actually was reporting on the land for speculators. David Zeisberger, who had no designs on Indian land, was shocked by reports of Jones's views on the subject. Jones openly criticized Indians for allowing the land to "lay waste," he accused them of being a "lazy people," and he declared that "in a few years the land would be taken from the Indians by the whites." If the customarily hospitable Indians needed any excuse, Jones had supplied it, and they sent him packing; but not without first sending spirits against him, and perhaps having some fun at his expense. Three Shawnees, wearing spiritually endowed masks, accosted the missionary; according to Jones, "the foremost stooped down by a tree and took sight as if he designed to shoot at me: but I could see that he only had a pole in his hand."[52]

Even Zeisberger, certainly more discreet and less self-interested than Jones, the missionary-land agent, became an object of the Shawnees' suspicion. Attempting to preach to them in 1773, he was discouraged by Chief Gischenatsi of Wakatomica, where ritual vomiting continued. Europeans, argued the headman, "always profess to have great wisdom and understanding from above, at the same time, they deceive us at will, for they regard us as fools." The spiritual wisdom and justice of such seemingly good British subjects as Zeisberger, the chief argued, was merely a scheme to "deceive the Indians, to defraud them of their lands."[53] He turned Zeisberger away.

Among the Mingos, the Iroquois inhabitants of the Upper Ohio region and close allies of the Shawnees and Delawares, the story was much the same. At Dyonosongohta, not far downstream from the village where, a generation later, the Seneca Handsome Lake would have his visions, Zeisberger heard an Indian insist that the "Indians are men, even as are the whites, but God has created them differently." When Zeisberger asked the Indian if he had heard that God had come to earth as a human and died on the cross, the Seneca Mingo quipped, "then the Indians are certainly not guilty of His death, as the whites are."[54] Christian doctrine must have struck nativists as odd. It provided them with more evidence of the abomination of whites: here were a people who admitted to having killed their God. Toward the end of the eighteenth century, Quaker missionaries would hear Senecas of the same region express similar sentiments.

The nativist conviction that Indians were one people under God, at least equal to but quite different from Anglo-Americans, had serious diplomatic consequences. It certainly provided a measure of unity during Pontiac's War, and it continued to influence Indians even beyond their defeat in that struggle. For militants who sought to oppose Anglo-American expansion with armed resistance, it provided justification in their struggles against leaders who cooperated with the British. It also gave an opportunity, through cooperation with the militants of other Indian peoples, to nullify the authority of leading advocates of accommodation. The popularity of the doctrine meant that dissenters from one village or people could find a ready home among the nativists of another.

Stirred by the promise of sacred power, but conscious of their earthly need for numbers, militant Shawnees sent messengers out to surrounding peoples. They took tentative steps close on the heels of Pontiac's War, inviting the Great Lakes area Indians to a "general congress" at one of their villages in 1767. Determined to defend their lands, Shawnee and Mingo nativists continued to insist on their independence from the "protection" of the Six Nations Iroquois, a powerful people who were well connected with the British, and who had British support in their dubious claim to lands in the Ohio country and beyond. Of the supposed Iroquois sovereignty over the Ohio country and its inhabitants, Red Hawk declared in 1770 that "their power extends no further with us." Angry at the Iroquois-British Treaty of Fort Stanwix in 1768, which ceded Shawnee hunting ground south of the Ohio to Britain, Red Hawk and others sought to raise an anti-British Indian confederacy.[55] Although Shawnees directed much of their anger at the Six Nations "for giving up so much of the Country to the English without asking their Consent," they had the support of many Iroquoian Mingos, who also had long hunted in the Kentucky country.[56] Beginning in 1769, militant Shawnees joined by the "Delawares and other Northern Tribes," courted the Cherokees and the Creeks far to the south, as they had during the Seven Years' War and Pontiac's War. In February 1769, some Cherokees and Creeks agreed to visit the "very large Council House" that the Shawnees had just built on the Scioto. The Shawnees also invited the Indians who remained in pockets along the Susque-hanna to come live with them in the Ohio country, "where they have Lands for them which the Six Nations can not Sell to the English." The Treaty of Fort Stanwix had put a final end to serious Six Nations' claims to leadership over the Ohioans, whose nativists now considered the Six Nations councillors as "Slaves of the White People."[57]

British official correspondence in the period betrays a fear that the mili-tants might accomplish their objective, forming a new, militant confeder-acy. In 1770, when the British learned that the Shawnees and Delawares had recruited Cherokees and Creeks as participants in another pan-Indian conference held that year at Shawnee villages in the Scioto Valley, they doubted that the Indians could actually form a general confederacy, but worried about the matter nonetheless. Indeed the British commander of American forces, Thomas Gage, considered the prospect "a very danger-ous Event."[58]

The Scioto conference achieved a notable success. Although it did not have the power to end the desultory hostilities that had long simmered between the Cherokees and the peoples of the Great Lakes and Illinois, the conference stood strongly in favor of such a peace. George Croghan ob-served that "all the Western tribes over the Lakes, and about Lake Michi-gan, as well as the Ouabache [Wabash] Indians had unanimously agreed to make peace with the Cherokees and other Southern Indians." British Southern Superintendent of Indian Affairs John Stuart later learned that some Cherokees had accepted a "painted Hatchet" from the "Shawanese, Delawares, and other Tribes of the Western Confederacy."[59]

The possibility of Shawnee-Cherokee cooperation was undergirded by a fact of which the British were well aware: both the Shawnees and the Cherokees hunted in the Kentucky lands "ceded" by the Six Nations to Great Britain. John Stuart, learning that the Shawnees had revealed the extent of the cession to the Cherokees, was relieved to learn that most Cherokees would not believe it was true, "for I had never mentioned it to them." But notwithstanding Stuart's misleading silence, interregional Indian diplomacy intensified, and it caused alarm among the English. Traders, fearing property losses in an uprising, countermanded their orders for supplies and prepared to flee Cherokee country while they awaited the Scioto conference's results. British General Thomas Gage recognized that the Shawnees, if successful in recruiting the southern nations to militancy, would completely isolate the Six Nations (and with them the most influen-tial Briton among the northern Indians, Sir William Johnson), "against whom they have been much exasperated, on account of the Boundary Treaty, held at Fort Stanwix." Stuart, Johnson's counterpart in the South, complained that his job among the southern Indians would be easier if the Shawnees, whom he wryly called "the Northern and Western Gentry," would stay out of the Southeast. Even religious notions may have circulated with the Indian diplomats, for it was in 1770 that the Cherokees first voiced the theology of separation. Bargaining for a good price in a land cession to Britain, the accommodationist Attakullaculla may have borrowed the phrase from the militants when he declared that "There are three Great Beings above, one who has the Charge of the White, one of the Red, and one of the Black people." Although the Indians' Great Being gave them the land, "the white people seem to drive us from it."[60]

In 1771, the Shawnees repeated their previous year's efforts with another conference at Scioto. That year ceremonial belts, strings of beads, symbolic war hatchets, and dried scalps circulated between the Ohio country and the Southeast as Shawnees and Mingos exchanged proposed strategies with militants among the Creeks and Cherokees. Such widespread militancy encouraged dissident Cherokees to speak out against the recent Cherokee land cession made with Stuart at the Treaty of Lochaber (October 1770). Although the cession was carried out, Cherokee militants continued to develop their plans for a broad-based opposition to Anglo-American expansion. In the cession's wake, militants, joined by the northerners, created such disturbances among the Cherokees that prudent traders fled to the South Carolina settlements, "where Pannick Spread with amazing Rapidity."[61]

The efforts on the part of Indians of the Ohio country, particularly the Shawnees, to "establish what they call a general Peace," threatened the English with the prospect of another major Indian war. Rumors of proposed attacks on the English mingled with reports that "the Rogue Mankiller," a leading Cherokee militant, had recently led a party of Cherokees against a small British party near the confluence of the Mississippi and Ohio, killing the colonists, and taking the last man, an African-American slave, alive. On the party's return to the Cherokee towns, it presented the nation with the scalps, but the Cherokees were not prepared formally to go to war and rejected the offer. They continued to be divided over their policy toward Anglo-America. Such divisions similarly plagued both the Creeks, who awaited messages from the Northern Shawnees, and the northern Indians themselves, particularly the Mingos, who remained angry at their Six Nations kinfolk for the Stanwix cession.[62]

The militants labored to form their confederacy well into the year 1773. General Gage, who thought them "ingenious and Sound Politicians," noted that the Six Nations had failed to stop the Shawnee "Contrivers" of "a general Union of all the Western & Southern Nations."[63] But militant unity remained limited; the results of their efforts fell short of the militants' expectations. By 1773, the militants had not consolidated enough authority to meet the threat posed by the Anglo-American settlement of Kentucky. To gather members from many nations together to discuss pan-Indian resistance was not to form a union; they had yet to win over key village councils. Since 1767 many Delaware chiefs, particularly White Eyes, had advocated the avoidance of confrontation with the Anglo-Americans. Tensions increased in many Delaware towns. White Eyes left the nativistic Newcomer's town and set up his own village to avoid daily strife. Croghan wrote that many chiefs, some even among the Shawnees, opposed the confederacy and "has Tould thire Warrers that itt wold End in there Ruin Butt the Worrars Say they May as well Dey Like Men as be Kicked about Like Doggs."[64] Such division added urgency to the militants' quest for support among other Indian peoples, but it imposed clear limits upon their efforts to organize on a grand scale.

The test came in 1773, when white frontiersmen slew the Shawnee wife and children of the Mingo chief, Logan. No militant himself, Logan retaliated, and other Shawnees and Mingos joined in the fray. These border incidents triggered Dunmore's War (1773–1774), the central issue of which soon became the British claim to Kentucky. Militant Shawnees and Mingos, protesting not merely the murders but also the invasion of their lands by hunters and squatters, won the support of some Delawares, Wyandots, Miamis, Ottawas, and even a party of Cherokees,[65] but they had substantial support from no nation. Suffering from want, and not wishing to become embroiled in another Pontiac's War, most Indian councils held the peace. Lacking numbers, the militants still attempted to resist the British conquest of Kentucky. They persisted in their calls for assistance, but they could count only on the justice of their cause and the sacred powers that could be invoked through ritual.

Explaining the matter to British agent and once-adopted Shawnee Alexander McKee in March 1774, a Shawnee pointed to the Virginians' new settlements. "We have had many disagreeable Dreams this winter about this matter, and what we have seen and been witnesses to since we came here seems to confirm our fears." The British colonies had clearly intended war. To resist, the militants could only put a hearty trust in ritual. Shortly after their narrow but critical defeat at Point Pleasant, in what is now West Virginia, Zeisberger learned that the Indians had prepared for the battle with "the warrior beson, which they use when going to war, in order that they may be successful." Another medicine, probably a sacred bundle, was "thought to be capable of preserving them from arrow and ball." According to Zeisberger, the bearer of the bundle was killed in the battle, but neither "disagreeable dreams" nor militant nativism died with him.[66]

The serious failure of both ritual and pan-Indianism in Dunmore's War did not kill the idea of Indian unity and the networks that supported it. McKee had noted in 1774 that the plan for unity "had been on foot for many years," and it was not surrendered. Throughout 1774 and 1775, militant northerners and southerners exchanged delegations.[67] Northern nativists could still attribute their defeat in Dunmore's War to the misconduct of those among their own people who had not defended their lands. But more important to the survival of militancy was the opening presented by events across the Alleghenies in the British colonies. With the American Revolution, the nativists' English-speaking enemies divided against themselves, providing the militants with an opportunity to cooperate with leaders who favored the British in a new struggle against the Anglo-American settlers. Breeches within many Indian communities temporarily closed, religious nativism became submerged beneath a broader movement against Anglo-America, and the largest, most unified Native American effort the continent would ever see erupted with the American Revolution.

≻ ≻ ≻ ≻ ≻ ≻ ≺ ≺ ≺ ≺ ≺ ≺ ≺

THREE

Revolutionary Alliances

1775–1783

W hile a distant Congress debated independence in May 1776, a party of militant Shawnees, Mohawks, and Ottawas traveled from the Great Lakes to the southern reaches of the Appalachian Mountains to urge the Cherokees to assist them in war. A witness to the councils at the "Beloved Town" of Chota on the Little Tennessee River, the British deputy Henry Stuart, described the militant Indians' activities in a remarkable letter.[1]

At that Chota meeting a Shawnee speaker, once a renowned "French partisan," unrolled a huge belt of wampum. Roughly nine feet by six inches, the darkly beaded piece had been "strewed over with vermilion, red trade paint." No Indian observer—indeed in the eighteenth century few white observers—would have mistaken the significance of this war belt, this symbolic "hatchet." The call to arms was not lost on the Cherokees; they had seen it many times in recent years.

The Shawnee supported his call with a series of arguments. First, he spoke of the aggressions of the "Virginians," as the white intruders were called. The Shawnees, he sadly reminded the Cherokees, "from being a great nation, were [now] reduced to a handful." They had once "possessed lands almost to the seashore," and like them, all "red people who were once masters of the whole country [now] hardly possessed ground enough to stand on." Among the Virginians, he continued, "it was plain there was an intention to extirpate them, and that he thought it better to die like men than to dwindle away by inches." It was an argument characteristic of the eighteenth-century militants: Indians shared a history of trouble with the Anglo-Americans; they should thus share in the struggle against them.

The Shawnee expanded his argument. The Indians, fighting together, would not fight alone. The Shawnee told the Cherokees that "the French, who seemed long dead, were now alive again, that they had supplied them plentifully with ammunition, arms and provisions, and that they promised to assist them against the Virginians." Whether the Shawnee had substituted the French for the British at Detroit, or whether he referred only to the *habitants* of the Great Lakes, the Illinois region, and the Louisiana country is unclear, but he was not alone in his talk about the resurgence of New France. This hope for a revival of the French counterweight to the British Empire, a hope earlier widespread among the Great Lakes Indians during Pontiac's War, may represent a modified form of nativism, a peculiar millennialism that could accommodate European goods and assistance, but not European control. In a more familiar vein, and in a bow to nativist sentiment, the Shawnee also suggested that the Indians would receive aid from a greater power than France, for "their cause was just and . . . he hoped the Great Being who governs everything would favour their cause."

He then ended his speech by reminding the Cherokees that they had accepted a Shawnee hatchet "six years ago [1770]." If he intended to criticize them for their lack of support during the late war with Virginia, he did not make it explicit. He did, however, call upon them to seize the hatchet and "use it immediately." Meanwhile, he promised to "carry their talks through every nation to the southward."

When the Shawnee finished speaking, Dragging Canoe, the rising Cherokee leader of a growing militant faction, accepted the northern belt, symbolically accepting the idea of a Cherokee alliance with the northerners. Dragging Canoe's agreement surprised no one. For over a year, since Richard Henderson's disputed private and (even from an Anglo-American viewpoint) illegal "purchase" of extensive Cherokee lands at Sycamore Shoals in March 1775, Dragging Canoe had promised to resist with arms Anglo-American expansion into Cherokee lands. His challenge to the Henderson purchase meant a challenge to the authority of the important Cherokee signers of the deal, who included his own father, Attakullaculla, and two great warriors, Oconostota and the Raven. Dragging Canoe thus threatened to divide the Cherokees into two camps: one militant and insurgent, the other neutralist and under the present leadership. In the northern Indian embassy, the dissident Dragging Canoe found allies for both his challenge to Cherokee authority and his resistance to white intruders on Cherokee lands.[2]

Toward the end of the conference, a head man of the Overhills Cherokee town of Chilhowee, who had himself once lived among the Mohawks,
"rose up to take the belt from Ciu Canacina [Dragging Canoe]." Further
exhibiting the understanding of ceremony shared by these northerners and
southerners, he sang "the warsong and all the Northern Indians joined in
the chorus. Almost all the young warriors from the different parts of the
nation followed his example."

While the militants, members of peoples from across the Eastern Woodlands, expressed their solidarity in song, the "principal chiefs of the Cherokees, who were averse to the measure" and who had signed the Henderson agreement, "sat down dejected and silent." These leaders of Cherokee
accommodation recognized their loss of authority. The Anglo-American
traders and officials with whom they had bargained, and on whom they
relied for goods to distribute among their people, had divided against
themselves. Though neither the British nor the colonists had yet asked the
Indians to choose sides, the British had earlier provided Dragging Canoe
with three thousand pounds of gunpowder;[3] here were northern militants
suggesting how to use it. The militants possessed the initiative, the allies,
the matériel, and the just cause they needed to make a convincing case for
war against the aggressive Anglo-Americans. As the party of neutral accommodation, headed by Attakullaculla, Oconostota, and the Raven, listened to the warriors sing the northerners' war song, it knew that it was
hearing a vote of no confidence. It did not openly oppose war, but its
silence spoke nonetheless. The Cherokee militants had thus come rapidly
to power, but only amid division and doubt.

Two themes emerge from Henry Stuart's letter: first, the amplification
of native calls for a pan-Indian alliance, which meant that by the late
eighteenth century the idea of united Indian resistance to settler expansion
had taken hold among the Eastern Woodlands peoples. These calls continued to elicit mixed responses in Indian communities; villages often
divided from within while their militants united with members of other
and often distant towns and peoples. But as warfare escalated, leaders of
accommodation saw an opportunity in the Revolution to regain influence
and to restore harmony among their peoples. While remaining allied with
Britain, they would ally with the nativists, and oppose the United States.

Second, the letter suggests the currency of militant religious notions.
The religious nativism of the 1750s and 1760s, which had so brilliantly
accented the militants' language, became partially eclipsed during the
Revolution by the exigencies of cooperation between advocates of nativism and those of pro-British accommodation. But however muted religious
nativism became, this was no period of despiritualization.

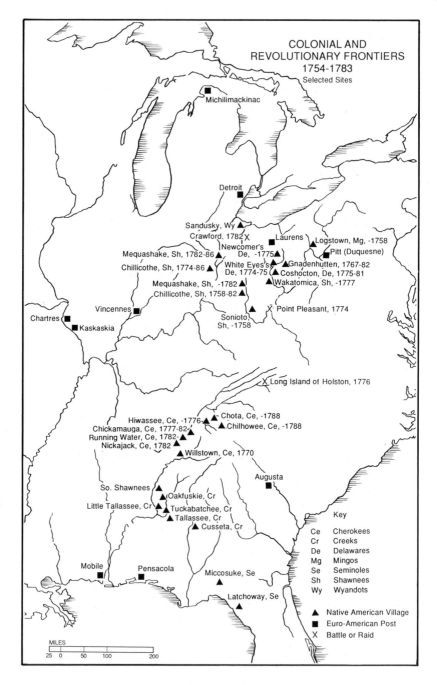

COLONIAL AND
REVOLUTIONARY FRONTIERS
1754-1783
Selected Sites

Michilimackinac

Detroit

Sandusky, Wy ▲
Crawford, 1782 X   Laurens   Logstown, Mg, -1758
                          Newcomer's   Pitt (Duquesne)
Mequashake, Sh, 1782-86 ▲   De, -1775 ▲
Chillicothe, Sh, 1774-86 ▲   White Eyes's ▲ ▲Gnadenhutten, 1767-82
                          De, 1774-75 ▲Coshocton, De, 1775-81
Mequashake, Sh, -1782 ▲   ▲Wakatomica, Sh, -1777
Chillicothe, Sh, 1758-82 ▲

Vincennes   ▲   X Point Pleasant, 1774
Chartres   Sonioto,
   Kaskaskia   Sh, -1758

                             X Long Island of Holston, 1776

                  Hiwassee, Ce, -1776 ▲   ▲ Chota, Ce, -1788
         Chickamauga, Ce, 1777-82 ▲▲   ▲Chilhowee, Ce, -1788
         Running Water, Ce, 1782 ▲
         Nickajack, Ce, 1782 ▲
                          ▲ Willstown, Ce, 1770

                                        Augusta
      So. Shawnees ▲
                  ▲ Oakfuskie, Cr
Little Tallassee, Cr ▲▲
                  ▲ Tuckabatchee, Cr   Key
                  ▲ Tallassee, Cr
                     ▲ Cusseta, Cr   Ce   Cherokees
                                            Cr   Creeks
                                            De   Delawares
                                            Mg   Mingos
  Mobile   Pensacola   Se   Seminoles
                         Miccosuke, Se   Sh   Shawnees
                         ▲   Wy   Wyandots

                         Latchoway, Se   ▲   Native American Village
                         ▲   ■   Euro-American Post
                                            X   Battle or Raid

MILES
25 0   50   100   200

MAP 2. Colonial and Revolutionary Frontiers

Pan-Indianism and Division, 1775–1777

Although the Indian quest for unity intensified during the Revolution, Shawnee embassies to the Cherokees and other southern Indians did not represent radical innovations in 1776. The Shawnees had a long history of contact with the Indians of the South. Relations were eased by the presence among the Creeks of a Shawnee ethnic minority, the Southern Shawnees, descendants of seventeenth- and eighteenth-century migrants, who maintained the language and other recognizable aspects of the northern culture. Throughout the Seven Years' War, a militant Cherokee faction had concerted efforts with these Southern Shawnees and their militant Upper Creek allies, as well as with the French-allied Shawnees of the Ohio country. The Northern Shawnees had more than kinship at their disposal, they had also personal contacts, having attempted to bring the southerners into the confederacy that they had sought to form on the eve of Dunmore's War.[4] While the Shawnees and Mingos suffered blows during that fiasco, militant Creeks continued to join the Shawnees in efforts to convince all southern Indians that alliances should be formed against the British colonies.[5]

The Shawnee militants persisted in their search for Indian unity because the threats to their lands and livelihoods did not cease with the withdrawal of Dunmore's forces from the Ohio country, because indeed these threats became all the more frightening with the possibility of unrestrained Virginian expansion, and because Shawnees found increasing encouragement from the surrounding Indian peoples. A Shawnee hostage, taken by Dunmore to guarantee the peace, escaped from Virginia to his people in the summer of 1775. He brought news about the radical changes in the East and the threatening implications that they held for the Indians. The "People of Virginia were all determined upon War with the Indians except the Governor [Dunmore] who was for peace but was obliged to fly on board of a ship to save his own life." After receiving the news, "several of the Indians were employed in Conjuring the whole night."[6]

That same summer, according to "Adopted Shawanese" James Rogers, the Chippewas, Ottawas, and Wyandots, with the "French and English at Detroit," strongly advised the Shawnees against treating with the Anglo-Americans. Such advice fueled the militants' hopes, and the Shawnees spent the summer "Constantly Counseling." One visitor, struck by the mood in the villages, reported that the Shawnee "Women all seemed very uneasy in Expectations that there would be War."[7] He did not report what they feared more: precipitous actions on the part of their own men or invasion on the part of the Long Knives, as the Anglo-Americans had come to be called.

What was new in revolutionary years was not, then, the visit of the Shawnees to the Cherokees, which had become routine in recent years, or the idea of Indian unity against the Anglo-American threat, which had roots at least as deep as the Seven Years' War. The new element was the widening support upon which militants seemed able to draw. The support had already been indicated by the northern Indians' and Britons' warnings to the Shawnees not to treat with the Anglo-Americans, but it was now strikingly confirmed by Cherokee actions during and following the Chota conference of May 1776.

The acceptance of the war belt and the singing of the war song by Dragging Canoe and the warriors who backed him were ritually sanctioned actions; a cynical undertaking of the commitments implied in these actions could, in the Indian view, bring punishment upon the participants' peoples. When Dragging Canoe accepted the belt and was supported by "Almost all of the young warriors," the old and now ignored Cherokee leadership knew that the militants meant business, and the Cherokees committed themselves to the quest for Indian unity in a war against the Anglo-Americans.

To honor their commitments and to forward their strategies, a Cherokee party carried the northern Indians' "Talks and war Tokens" to the Creek country, while thirteen Cherokees joined four Shawnees in a trip to the Ohio and Great Lakes countries. Along the way, the latter party killed two Kentucky men and captured three women of the Galloway and Boone families. Alarmed Kentuckians mounted a two-day pursuit, which ended in a shooting fight, the rescue of the women, and the deaths of two of the Shawnees.[8] The bloodlettings marked the first instances, during the revolutionary era, of Cherokee and Shawnee cooperation in battle. Over the next eighteen years, militant Cherokees and Shawnees would fight beside each other, often in alliance with other Indians from either the South or the North, sometimes in alliance with both. Over the next eighteen years, the militant Cherokee-Shawnee connection, so falteringly forged over the course of the two decades preceding the Revolution, became a critical link in the militants' chain across the Eastern Woodlands. Once considered inveterate enemies,[9] militant Cherokees and Shawnees had come by the early years of the American Revolution to recognize a new kinship in the face of a common enemy.

While the Cherokee delegation met with militants in the North, its countrymen waged a war to the south. Early in the summer of 1776, small parties of Cherokees punished the Virginia, North Carolina, South Carolina, and Georgia borderlands. Mustering on a more impressive scale began in July, as Dragging Canoe led 150 warriors against the Virginians who had taken over the Watauga Valley. The Wataugan intruders made formal their claim to the lands at the Henderson purchase, a deal recognized as illegal by colonial authorities and as wicked by Dragging Canoe and the militants. Forewarned, the Wataugans met and repulsed the Cherokees at the battle of Long Island on Holston (July 20, 1776).[10]

Determined to throw the newcomers back, the Cherokees planned more powerful incursions. In the Overhills Cherokee Towns, six hundred warriors planned to attack the Wataugans and Virginians, to drive the recently arrived Anglo-Americans from what is now northeastern Tennessee, and "to take away negroes, horses, and to kill all kinds of cattle, sheep, &c." Again, the settlers were forewarned, this time by Jaret Williams, whose report also conveyed the precarious condition of the Cherokees. Declaring that "they are well stocked with bows and arrows," which the Cherokees apparently intended to use in killing animals alone, Williams's report suggests that they desperately needed ammunition, which the British were slow to supply, despite Cherokee successes in keeping "several thousands of Rebels on the Frontier from going down to Charleston to join their Army in opposition to General Clinton."[11]

Cherokee shortages of firepower led to the disasters of 1776. Between mid-July and the end of October, the yeoman militia of the borderlands launched four expeditions against the Cherokees—all remarkable in the record of Anglo-American irregular war during the Revolution. After months of destruction, Oconostota, Attakullaculla, and the Raven, the old leaders of the nation, sued for peace.[12] As British deputy David Taitt wrote to the loyalist governor of eastern Florida, "The want of assistance and being in the utmost distress for Provision has drove the Cherokees to take this step."[13]

The Americans had overpowered the Cherokees, destroying most of their crops, goods, and homes by the fall of 1776. The British superintendent wrote to his superior that the Cherokees were "distressed disarmed and flying into every nation for protection."[14] Unlike the Senecas and Shawnees, who would recover from similar drubbings in 1779 by obtaining British support at nearby Niagara and Detroit, the Cherokees were far more exposed to Anglo-American wrath and far less proximate to British supplies. This distance from the British, which both denied to the Cherokees the firepower they would need to repel American invasions and reduced their ability to recover from famine, destroyed any hope among accommodating Cherokees, who had been reluctant to fight in the first place, that an alliance with Britain could serve their needs. Threatened and outgunned, the Cherokee party of accommodation came to terms with the Anglo-Americans. From 1777 on, powerful Cherokee factions within the nation rejected any policy of militant resistance to the new republic.

Cherokee leaders who were recognized as legitimate by the United States came to terms with the states of South Carolina and Georgia in the Treaty of DeWitt's Corner on May 20, 1777. Cherokee negotiators ceded lands along the Savannah and Saluda rivers in northwestern South Carolina. They later marked agreements with Virginia and North Carolina in the Treaty of Long Island on Holston, July 20, 1777, in which they also ceded lands, this time in the area of northeastern Tennessee. In effect, the treaties ratified the current Anglo-American occupation of the now officially ceded ground.[15] But the negotiations met dissent. To many Cherokees, the agreements seemed to sanction uncontrolled Anglo-American expansion. Cherokee militants refused to abide by them. A Cherokee secessionist movement gave birth to the new and short-lived tribe, the Chickamaugas.

Chickamauga Resilience

Dragging Canoe led the opposition. Earlier that spring, he had organized with militants to secede from the nation and remove west from the Little Tennessee and Hiwassee valleys to the Tennessee River valley proper. Most of the militants came from the Overhills section of the Cherokees. Remaining hostile to the United States and retaining their connections with the Southern Shawnees, these militants became known to Anglo-Americans as the "Chickamaugas." Calling themselves *Ani-Yunwiya* or "the Real People," the secessionists, whom John Stuart thought comprised the "far greater number" of Cherokees, called into question the legitimacy of the treaty party.[16] Breaking so profoundly from their accommodating countrymen, they chose a fine country in which to align themselves with other peoples.

The first Chickamauga settlements took their Anglo-American name from the Chickamauga Creek, which flows north and west into the Tennessee River from what is now northern Georgia. John McDonald, a deputy in the British Indian Department, had already established himself on the creek, with a small store at the site of an old Creek settlement, some two miles from the Tennessee River. There Dragging Canoe made his town. The Chickamaugas planted about ten other towns on both sides of the Tennessee.[17]

From their new settlements, the Chickamaugas could communicate quickly with militants among the Upper Creeks to the immediate south, and with their British allies further below in Mobile and Pensacola. These connections permitted the persistence of Chickamauga militancy and overcame the problem of isolation from British supplies. In March 1778, a delegation of Chickamauga Cherokees left British Pensacola "firmly attached to His Majesty," after Southern Indian Superintendent John Stuart had put his department to great expense outfitting them.[18] By the end of the year, about a thousand Cherokee warriors could be found among the militants.

The resilience of the southern arrangements became manifest in 1779. While Chickamaugas scoured the valleys of east Tennessee and Kentucky, Colonel Evan Shelby and Colonel John Montgomery led their Virginia and North Carolina militias against the almost undefended towns in April 1779. They razed eleven towns and plundered the British commissary. Unlike the 1776 raids against the original Cherokee towns, however, these attacks did not bring the victims to terms. Instead, the Chickamaugas sought more aid from the British, drew supplies from the newly British-occupied posts at Augusta and Savannah, and established new towns in more defensible positions nearby. They remained both hostile to American expansion and "exceedingly well disposed" toward the British.[19]

They also remained "well disposed" to the northern militants. In 1779, groups of northerners joined the Chickamauga settlements, while parties of Cherokee militants joined Shawnee settlements in the North. A war captain named Shawnee Warrior took command of a party at the Chickamauga town of Running Water. "Renegade" Cherokees could be found fighting in the North beside Shawnees, Miamis, and Wyandots from this period until the battle of Fallen Timbers in 1794.[20] Some would, after the turn of the nineteenth century, join the nativistic followers of the Shawnee Prophet, brother of Tecumseh.

Continued Chickamauga militancy and connections with the Indians of the North encouraged the Upper Creek militants, just to the Chickamaugas' south, to break with the neutralists among their own countrymen and to take arms against the Anglo-Americans. At first, the Creeks had "declined to act with" the Cherokees. But Emistisiguo, a firm ally of the British and a man who had long resisted the militants' attempts to launch a united Indian war against the southern British colonies, began, with the Revolution, to see possibilities for the success of a British-supplied Indian alliance. Under the new circumstances Emistisiguo considered the strength of a pan-Indian union armed with British firepower. In November 1776, he wrote to John Stuart that "if the red warriors to the northward would hold a red stick against the Virginians there, I would hold one against them here."[21]

But the Creeks, like the Cherokees, were divided among themselves over the issue. In Upper Creek villages, where Emistisiguo exercised influence, where his erstwhile militant opponents had long agitated against Anglo-American settlement, and where the Southern Shawnee minority largely dwelled, sentiment generally resolved upon British alliance and a war against the Americans. British agents and traders, such as Lachlan McGillivray, had good political credit in this section of the Creek confederacy. In the Upper Creek towns of Oakfuskie and Tallassee, however, neutralists prevailed.[22] The Oakfuskies and Tallassees sought to maintain the long-standing Creek policy of staying clear of conflicts among whites. So too with most Lower Creek villages, early on. The rebels' extraordinary success against the Cherokees in the late summer and early autumn of 1776 struck even the militant Upper Creeks "with such a Panic," that they demanded that the British support them with troops before they would raid the Americans. The Oakfuskies, Tallassees, and the Lower Creeks, meanwhile, treated with the Americans.[23]

A third group of Creek origin, but clearly emerging in this period as a separate entity, stood solidly against the Anglo-Americans. These "Seminoles" allied with the British in their own interests. Cowkeeper, headman of the Latchoway Seminoles, notified the British officers that while the Seminoles would fight both to defend their land and to reduce "The Rebel Enemies of our Great King & Protector," they would also keep "whatever Horses or Slaves or Cattle we take" as their own.[24]

Continued Chickamauga resistance to the north, the new Seminole resistance to the southeast, and British victories in South Carolina and Georgia combined with the threat of Anglo-American expansion to bring most Creeks over to the British-Indian alliance by 1779.[25] Between the early fighting and the spring of 1779, when the Upper Creeks became firmly committed, Chickamaugas, sometimes accompanied by "Northern Indians," visited Creek villages and British posts in the Creek country to encourage them to join the movement. They argued that it was only a temporary shortage of manpower that kept the Georgians from taking their lands, and they "upbraided" the Creeks for not having assisted them when the Americans attacked the Cherokee nation in 1776. "Their spirited speeches," John Stuart wrote following a conference in January 1778, "had a good effect." That spring, Upper Creeks attacked the Anglo-American borderlands. By the spring of 1779, Chickamaugas and Upper Creeks jointly raided the Carolina and Georgia frontiers.[26]

The Fiasco of 1779

Shawnee messengers among the Creeks returned northward with Creek militants and messages of cooperation in the winter of 1778–79. At British Fort Vincennes, on the Wabash River, the Shawnees urged the Illinois and Wabash peoples to give up any traditional feelings of hostility toward the southern nations. One speaker "produced a long white belt sent by the Great Chief of the Creeks" in order that all "Indians might know the design of the Creeks, vizt., to be in friendship with them and at war with the Virginians—that by that belt they open'd a road which should be kept free and open that a child might walk safely in it." A day after receiving the "road belt," a grateful Piankashaw declared that "the Great Spirit certainly had compassion on the Indians, since he brought them together in peace." He passed the belt to the Miamis, who accepted it, promising to forward it to the Ottawas. A symbolic union was promised from the Gulf of Mexico to the shores of the Great Lakes. The possibilities for cooperation seemed rich.[27]

Hoping to capitalize on the movement, Henry Hamilton, the British commander at Vincennes, prepared to "concert a general invasion of the Frontiers." Hamilton laid plans with the several nations to harass the "Virginians" in a broad attack "by the Chickisaws Cherokees Shawanese Delawares etc. from the Southward—By the Mingoes Miamis Wyndots and Senicas from the Northward, and from the Poutwattamies Ottawas Chippawas and Hurons of the Lakes toward Kaskaskias." Already, he noted, there had been "Accounts of a considerable number of Southern Indians being assembled on the Cherokee [Tennessee] River who are designed to come this way." He believed that the year would soon see "the greatest Number of Savages on the Frontiers that has ever been known."

To forward his plans with the Indians, Hamilton had sent Edward Hazle on a mission from Vincennes to Pensacola. Hazle traveled with Kissingua, an "Acute Resolute and Artful" Indian of Ottawa and Miami parentage who "Speaks most Languages." The two were to invite the southern Indians to meet that spring at either Vincennes or the mouth of the Tennessee River. Kissingua spent the spring and summer among the Cherokees and the Creeks. At the Creek town of Tallassee in July, Kissingua "convened the Neighboring Chiefs, acquainted them of the unanimity subsisting in the whole Northern District and of their determination to assist His Majesty's troops in the reduction of the Rebels." British officials in the South reported that his talks were well received.

Kissingua traveled at least partly in the capacity of an agent—perhaps ally is a better word—of the British. But while Kissingua was venturing

southward, Hamilton learned of autonomous southern plans that re-
sembled his own. The southerners, including the Chickasaws, Cherokees,
Choctaws, and Creeks, planned to send four parties northward against
Americans in the Ohio drainage: "one towards Kaskaskias to attack the
Rebels there, another to go up the Ohio to assist the Shawanese, a third to
come to this place to make peace with the Ouabash Indians and drive the
Americans out of their Country, and the fourth to remain at the mouth of
the Cherakee [Tennessee] river to intercept any boats coming up the
Mississippi or going down the Ohio." Thus, in 1779, southern Indians,
northern Indians, and the British hoped to orchestrate a coordinated strike
against the Anglo-American intruders. For years they had strengthened
their bonds; now they prepared united actions.[28]

The Indians' and Hamilton's plans for a massive 1779 campaign collapsed, however, after Americans under George Rogers Clark, who had
taken Kaskaskia and Cahokia the previous year (Americans had also captured Vincennes, but the British had retaken it), captured Vincennes once
again and intercepted a shipment of supplies destined for the Indians. One
of Clark's chief objectives in his daring Vincennes campaign was to prevent the planned Indian council from being held at the mouth of the Tennessee River. Despite the rugged conditions and the numerical inferiority
of his force, Clark determined to halt the advance of Indian-British plans.
As he put it in a letter to Patrick Henry, "the Case is Desperate but Sr we
must Either Quit the Cuntrey or attack Mr. Hamilton."[29] Clark and his
followers crossed the wooded, wintry, sodden landscape of southern Illinois, coming upon Vincennes by surprise in February. The British, not
knowing Clark's limited strength, surrendered, disastrously throwing the
grand plans awry. Deprived of their supplies and temporarily divided by
Clark's successes at Vincennes and elsewhere on the Wabash, the Indians
could not plan their assault.

Recovery, 1779–1781

If Clark's strike upset a program for pan-Indian action on an expansive
scale, and if it even precipitated a brief defection of Illinois and Indiana
country Indians to the Americans,[30] Indians nonetheless over the next
several years adopted and realized more modest plans for unity. Through
a fascinating pattern of cooperation, the Shawnees and Chickamauga
Cherokees kept alive their militant networks, networks that drew together
peoples as distant from one another as the Creeks near the Gulf of Mexico
and the Chippewas of the Great Lakes.

In 1779, Chickamauga Cherokees and Shawnees exchanged delegations—they might be thought of as consulates—in order to further understanding and cooperation. The cohabitation provided Shawnees and Cherokees with translators who could assist in planning. It schooled individuals in ways to traverse the increasingly dangerous terrain that separated the two peoples (Kentucky had a population of some eight thousand European- and African-Americans by 1782). Most important, it expanded the intertribal networks of support, much needed in the wake of the many Anglo-American raids.[31]

Cooperation on a semicontinental scale continued into the spring of 1781, when a delegation of Delawares, Cherokees, and Shawnees met with Major Arrent de Peyster at Detroit, seeking arms and provisions. One of the speakers at the ensuing conference, the Swan, a "Chief of the Cherokees," had self-consciously adopted the role of middleman between the northern and southern Indians. Addressing de Peyster, the Swan said, "My business with the Shawnees (amongst whom I reside at present) is to support the general League of Friendship" between the British and the Indians. He held up a belt of wampum, which he claimed to have first "rec'd four years ago from Gov'r Hamilton." Back then he had "communicated the contents of it to the Southern Nations." The Swan suggested that the "good effects" of the communication "begin already to be felt as they [the southern Indians] have commenced Hostilities against the Enemy."[32] A Cherokee consul to the Shawnees thus told the British commander at Detroit, in the heartland of the Ottawas, Wyandots, and Chippewas, of the actions of Creek Indians near Pensacola.

In other words, between 1779 and 1781, most of the Indians between the lakes and the gulf had united in their opposition to the United States. Although there were no massive, coordinated strikes involving large parties from all the peoples, northern Indian expeditions were often accompanied by small Chickamauga parties, and southern raids featured combined Southern and Northern Shawnee, Chickamauga, and Creek forces. Such cooperation, backed by English supplies, made possible the remarkable military success of Indians in the American Revolution. While the king's armies surrendered in the East in 1781, Native Americans everywhere north of the Creek country had regained considerable power, if not the military initiative. Between Yorktown and the fall of 1782, Anglo-American settlements from Tennessee through Pennsylvania saw some of the heaviest raiding ever.[33] Even the Peace of Paris, as a future chapter will demonstrate, did little to dissipate Indian unity. From the final years of the Revolution through the critical engagements of 1794, the Indians of the trans-Appalachian borderlands trained their guns with more consistency, more unity, and more consequence than did any other Indians in the history of the United States.

Cooperation between militant nativists and advocates of accommodation with Britain provided the foundation for this unprecedented—if not uninterrupted—unity. From 1776 to 1794 Indians who had once counted only on sacred power to combat Anglo-American expansion now found allies among Indians who counted more on firepower. During this period, while ammunition and other critical goods could be had from European powers that also opposed American expansion—in the North from Britain, and in the South from Britain until 1783 and from Spain and Spanish-commissioned British traders thereafter—nativists and many of the advocates of accommodation entered into a marriage of martial convenience.

Eclipsed Nativism, 1775–1783

King George's servants in the Indian country had deeply ambivalent feelings about the persistent ceremonialism of the Indians, but in the presence of their woodland allies they willingly took part: speaking in imitation of Indian oratory, dressing in accoutrements of Indian design—some of it made possible by the cloth, metal, and porcelain products of Europe—and even dancing to the sacred music that shaped warriors from the forms of peaceful Indian men. In their reports to their superiors, they excused their behavior as essential to good relations. Indians, in their view, had to be humored to be won over. At times, however, Britons appear to have been won over themselves by the power of rituals they may never have understood. Instead of Anglicizing Indians through the dispensing of clothing, food, war matériel and alcohol, British agents occasionally feared their own attraction to Indian ways. The best of them, like the Girtys, Matthew Elliot, Alexander Cameron, and Alexander McKee, put the fear behind them.[34]

Imagine the thoughts of a Great Lakes–area warrior, about thirty-five years old, once a young follower of Neolin or Pontiac, as he watched Detroit's British officer, Lieutenant Governor Henry Hamilton, dance among his allies in the late 1770s. Within memory—and the detailed memory of these participants in a nonliterate culture was widely respected by colonials who knew them—the British posts of Detroit, Niagara, and Pitt had been the stubborn objects of nativist assault. Now two of those posts provided the Indians with both arms and armed allies. The warrior might nurse an old suspicion of the redcoat, but more likely he would accept his old enemy's conversion as a triumph. Now his own people were united, for the most part, against the menace to the east; now his own villagers found support not only among those who understood his tongue, but also among distant Indians to the south. Now these united Indians together fought the true enemy who had engrossed the lands just south of the Ohio River and who had begun to menace the river's northern banks.

Perhaps the near unanimity of the trans-Appalachian struggle against the United States explains the partial eclipse, in the documents at least, of religious nativism, which had always been directed as much against Indians at home as against the enemy abroad. No charismatic religious leaders gained sway over immense polyglot followings during the Revolution. As British agents in the South and North provided Native American warriors with firepower, radical quests for sacred power, with all their potential for internal divisiveness, may have seemed redundant.

But the eclipse was not total, and in its penumbra we can see that Indian beliefs in their separation from whites and in their own ways of gaining power continued to develop. This was no period of widespread despiritualization. Indians continued to perform their rituals, to attend to their shamans, and to deploy symbols laden with Indian understandings of power. Indians seeking sacred power celebrated ceremonies throughout the American Revolution; traditional notions of how power was gained and lost persisted. Christianity among Indians, only an imprecise reverse indicator of the strength or weakness of traditional Indian spirituality, was in marked retreat. Forms of religious nativism that proscribed specified Christian modes of behavior were strong in the North and apparent among the Cherokees, though they had not yet made an impressive appearance among the Creeks, but then, neither had Christianity. The Creeks remained committed to their ceremonies, and therefore to their traditional understandings of power. The persistence and resilience of Creek ceremonialism, along with the extensive relations that the Creeks maintained with other Native Americans to the north, would provide for the Creek embrace and adaptation of northern religious nativism in the future.

Among the Upper Creek allies of the British, the Green Corn Ceremony, also called the "Busk" (from *boskita* or *poskita*), retained its central position in the culture. So important was the Green Corn Ceremony to Creek conceptions of power that Creeks would not neglect it even if its celebration interfered with what the British deemed sound military strategy. In the summer of 1778, for example, the Creek ceremonial calendar conflicted with the British strategic calendar, and the former won out. The Indians, who had suffered poor harvests for two years, delayed their raids until they had completed the eight-day ceremony. British Indian agent John Stuart, attempting to concert redcoat, loyalist, and Creek raids, found "No Indian being willing to go out on any Expedition until the Feast was over: being precluded by their Religion, the Use of Corn, or Pulse of any kind, before the offering of the first fruits." By the following year, the British Indian agents had adapted to Creek scruples, and wrote optimistically of the warriors that they would go out against the enemy, "as soon as the Busk or green Corn Feast is over, which will be in the course of this month."[35]

Enduring Creek spirituality also surfaces in descriptions of Creek conjurers. Shortly before the Revolution, in 1772 and 1774, David Taitt and William Bartram independently affirmed the importance of Creek conjurers. One conjurer would soon rise to become a powerful leader of the Creeks. His name, Efau Haujo, was more generally recorded in a direct translation, Mad Dog. The translation loses the connotations of loyalty (dog) and spirited, martial enthusiasm (mad). Mad Dog, no "mad dog" in an English sense, was highly regarded by his people. In 1772, Taitt found Mad Dog working against a proposal to allow the traders to bring their cattle among the Creeks. If the traders disliked the Indian "method of living," the Creek argued, "they may return to their own Country again." While involved in this debate, Mad Dog also attempted to perform a spiritual feat that Taitt properly found remarkable.

Six months before Taitt's arrival, a Creek from Tuckabatchee had been killed and scalped by a Choctaw war party. The victim's wife, Mad Dog's sister, saw her dead husband "sometimes in the night," when he "keeps about the Square and hot house." The woman and Mad Dog believed that "if they make the Physick strong Enough, and take proper care," the departed one would make a public appearance. While Taitt visited the town, he saw the people fast and "dance every night on purpose to bring back" the late warrior. Some of the inhabitants, however, were not scrupulous enough; the headman of the town broke his fast, which "spoild the Physick" and prevented the dead warrior's return.[36] The incident stands as a reminder that the failure of the sacred powers could be as well attributed to the vices of the people as to the impotence of ritual.

Two years later Bartram encountered a greatly respected Seminole conjurer who was "acknowledged by the Indians to have communion with powerful invisible beings or spirits." The shaman, no foe of European goods, intimidated the British trader M'Latche into extending him credit. Bartram noted that among the Creeks in general, conjurers had "great influence in state, particularly in military affairs." They could "predict the result of an expedition," and had such influence that "they have been known frequently to stop, and turn back an army, when within a day's journey of the enemy."[37]

The Cherokee story is much the same. In Cherokee country, conjurers also held considerable prestige as the war approached. In 1774 the British agent Alexander Cameron witnessed the influence of one conjurer, the Big Sawney, whose rituals brought victory to his town in the rugged Cherokee sport, "ball play." Ball play was openly acknowledged by Cherokees to have strong parallels with warfare.[38] The Cherokees bet heavily on the game; for many it was serious business. That April, Cameron noted, Cherokees gambled boldly; he saw "whole towns returning home in their Buffs." One town "carried off every Prize," which was "judged by all to be owing to the Great Gift of Big Sawney's Conjuration."[39]

It seems likely, given the affinities of the ball play with Cherokee warfare, that the Cherokee conjurers continued to work with warriors. It is certain that warriors themselves performed rituals to secure power during the Revolution. Cherokee warriors joined the northern visitors in a "war song," for example, at the Chota conference of 1776. During the war, perhaps in an effort to gauge the strength of their white Tennessean enemies, the Cherokees burned at least one prisoner.[40]

Cherokee and Creek ceremonialism, though resilient and persistent, was and had always been open; it did not prevent the southerners from adopting new beliefs and modifying old ones. While Ohioan and Great Lakes Indians developed a militant nativism that combined a strong ritual approach with new notions about Indian identity, many Indians of the South also attended to the sacred powers while thinking about themselves in new ways.

After the initial defeats of the Cherokees in 1776, for example, and shortly after the secession of the more militant factions under Dragging Canoe, the Cherokee leader Old Tassel used the nativistic argument of the separate creation to defend his people's ways. Old Tassel had not joined the secession, but he did remain popular with the secessionists. His later murder by whites would provoke a united Cherokee retaliation in 1788. In 1777, Old Tassel defied Anglo-American demands for land and promises of schools and missions. The Great Spirit, he said, "has given you many advantages, but he has not created us to be your slaves. We are a separate people!"[41] Other Cherokees could see in the theology of separation reason for Indian unity; Old Tassel limited his use of it to defend his people and their religion from Christianity.

It is revealing that Anglo-American talk of directing cultural change through Christian instruction provoked Old Tassel's near-nativistic remarks. Nativist sentiment emerged most clearly in the face of systematic threats to native control over cultural change. In the Cherokee-Creek Southeast, such threats only rarely had come in the form of missions. To be sure, Spanish Franciscans had long maintained influential missions from coastal South Carolina to Florida's panhandle, but these had been finally destroyed by Anglo-Creek raids early in the eighteenth century. French Catholics brought some Alabama Creeks to the cross, but left little mark when they withdrew. A few other missionaries, Moravians, Anglicans (including "Methodist" John Wesley), and Presbyterians, had ventured among the Cherokees and Creeks, but their missions had thus far been short-lived and entirely unsuccessful.[42]

To the north, however, the kinds of evangelical pressures that provoked Old Tassel's declaration of Indian identity were more abundantly felt. Christian missionaries and lay Europeans had made small but significant inroads against older Indian religion for over a century preceding the Revolution. Groups of Wyandots, Ottawas, and Caughnawaga Mohawks had been Roman Catholic since the seventeenth century. Among the Delawares in the late 1760s and early 1770s, Moravians "gathered a harvest" of almost one hundred Indian souls in the towns of Schönbrunn, Salem, and Gnadenhutten, all on the Tuscarawas River, a tributary of the Muskingum and Ohio rivers.[43] Competition from missionaries encouraged Shawnee and Delaware militants to sharpen a precise nativism that had yet to divide Cherokees and Creeks.

That nativism has been examined in some detail. Suffice it to say here that the leading northern missionary, David Zeisberger, continued to struggle with nativism. In 1777, the Delaware council at Coshocton, the center of that faction of Delawares who remained strongly influenced by Americans during the first five years of the Revolution, ordered the Moravian mission town of Schönbrunn to relocate to a site closer at hand. When Zeisberger obliged, a nativistic faction threatened to replace the abandoned Schönbrunn meeting house with another more "convenient for offering sacrifices." These and other nativistic Delawares, numerous in the Unami division, regularly demonstrated that they were "enemies of the gospel." Zeisberger often encountered Delawares who had decided that if "in the land of the Indians the gospel is preached, it must cease."[44] As the Revolution developed, and as it drew more and more Indians to oppose the United States, Zeisberger's converts returned to "the old heathenish customs and usages."[45] A nativistic upsurge threw the Moravians on the defensive, as neutrality evaporated, as warfare engulfed the North, and as the Indian movement for unity came closest to achieving fulfillment.

≫ ≫ ≫ ≫ ≫ ≫ ≫ ≪ ≪ ≪ ≪ ≪ ≪ ≪

FOUR

Neutrality, A World Too Narrow

1775–1781

O nly one group of Upper Ohio country Indians would hold out for friendship with the emerging republic for most of the Revolutionary War: the inhabitants of the polyglot cluster of villages surrounding Coshocton. All others had taken arms against the United States by the fall of 1777. Established as the opening shots of the Revolution were fired in the East, Coshocton with its environs became a refuge for Indians of the region who sought to stand apart from the widespread pattern of hostility toward the Anglo-American rebels. Although the village leaders, who favored neutrality, were Unami-speaking Delawares, Coshocton also sheltered Munsee Delawares and Shawnees. Coshocton's Shawnees, members of a people often portrayed as adamantly militant, reveal that forces other than simple tribal or ethnic loyalty were at work in dividing Indians during the early years of the American republic's expansion. Instead of joining close relatives in battle against the United States, these nonmilitant Shawnees had decided to dwell among a like-minded faction of Delawares.

The movement for pan-Indian unity was cut against such factions. It cannot be fully understood without some inquiry into the opinions, policies, and failures of Indians who stood against it. The Shawnees and Delawares of Coshocton did just that. While north and south of the Ohio River religiously minded nativists joined supply-minded advocates of accommodation in an alliance with Great Britain, the Coshocton villagers sought peace with the United States. Alone in the Upper Ohio between 1777 and 1779, they were not alone on the continent; factions among the Six Nations, Catawbas, Cherokees, Creeks, Chickasaws, Potawatomis, Pianka-shaws, and others also sought cooperation, tolerance, and harmony with the Anglo-American settlers. Like the Coshoctons, many of these peoples would ultimately meet bitter disappointment.

Because of the proximity to Coshocton of Moravian missions, of an active American frontier garrison at Fort Pitt, of the British garrison at Detroit, and of Britain's agents operating along Lake Erie, we have good records concerning such divisions in the Ohio country during the revolutionary era. The history of Coshocton reveals not only the complex divisiveness of Indian politics and diplomacy but also the intractable difficulties, often anchored stubbornly in the thickening sediments of Anglo-American hatred, that borderland Indians faced when they looked to the east for peace.

Shawnee Divisions, 1775

If ethnicity alone determined Indian allegiance in the American Revolution, Shawnees would not have dwelt among the Coshocton Delawares. Though few in number, Shawnees had already gained a reputation both for their violent defense of their lands and for their energetic efforts toward Indian unity, a reputation that would become fixed in the person of Tecumseh, only a child in the war-torn 1770s. At the beginning of the decade, for example, the commander of Britain's North American forces had commented that the "Plan formed by the Shawnese, of uniting the Nations in one general Confederacy," was "a Sensible Scheme, and dangerous to us."[1] But if Shawnees did stand at the center of the movement for unity, they did not stand united. Ethnicity does not sufficiently explain action; Shawnee tribal identity was and had always been weak. Indeed, there were several groupings of Shawnees: the Chillicothe, Piqua, Kispoko, and Mequashake "bands," or clusters of related villages. These rarely achieved harmonious concert. Like other peoples, the Shawnees also suffered from contingent divisions, stemming partly from the recent defeat in Dunmore's War but going back far beyond that conflict. It did not surprise the Shawnees that some of their number packed up and carried their belongings to neutral Coshocton.

The American Revolution aggravated the existing Shawnee lesions. As rumors of the Revolution trickled into Indian country, so did rumors that the Shawnee hostages taken by Virginia during Dunmore's War had been murdered. Shawnee militants, demanding satisfaction for the reported killings, found their calls for war encouraged by other militant northerners from among the Ottawas, Chippewas, and Wyandots. This support gave them hope that the isolation that had bedeviled them in Dunmore's War would end with intertribal alliance. In the fall of 1775, parties of Shawnee warriors, largely from the Chillicothe and Piqua divisions, undertook hostilities against the Virginians, raiding the new Long Knife settlements on the Kanawha River. By October, militants who had never reconciled themselves to defeat in Dunmore's War joined a "party of Different Nations gone to Observe the Settlement on Kentucke."[2] The following year, militant Shawnees played a key role in the northern Indian embassy to the Cherokees.

While militant Shawnees raided Anglo-American settlements and encouraged the southeastern Indians to rise, other Shawnees, drawn largely from the Mequashake band but also from the divided Kispokos, sought to maintain peaceful relations with the Long Knives in the wake of the Dunmore's War fiasco. These Shawnee neutralists had an influential leader in Cornstalk, a man who had opposed militancy in Dunmore's War but who had nonetheless organized the Shawnee defense against the invading Virginians. After the defeat of the Shawnees in the months following the battle of Point Pleasant (1774), Cornstalk again raised the banner of neutrality. Few Shawnees could deny he had the interests of his people at heart, and he rallied a considerable following.

But it was not easy. Iroquoian Mingos criticized the neutral Shawnees in the summer of 1775 for "cowardly making the Peace; & called them big knife People." Cornstalk notified the Americans that many Piqua Shawnees agreed with the Mingos' assessment and were resuming hostilities against the Kentuckians. In September, the "Grenadier Squaw," Cornstalk's sister and a wealthy woman with her own close connections to the Anglo-Americans, informed the American agent, Richard Butler, that many Shawnees are "not yet Reconciled to the white People & that they are stirred up by many Windots & Mingoes." She added of the Shawnees that "there is a Devision Among ym Selves."[3]

Nor did the Americans give Shawnee neutralists strong arguments to work with in forwarding their policies. At the Pittsburgh Treaty Council of October 1775, delegates of the Continental Congress met with those of the Shawnees, Ottawas, Delawares, and Six Nations. All that the Shawnees secured at the conference was the promise that the Ohio River should stand as the permanent boundary between the northern Indians and the Anglo-Americans. For militants, the promise was only a promise, and it ratified the Anglo-American seizure of Kentucky. The congressional delegation did not, by the resulting treaty, recognize any *Shawnee* claims to land; it merely recognized *Indian* rights to Ohio lands. This might have satisfied the militants had they not been aware of the congressional interpretation. They knew that by Indian, the Congress meant Six Nations and Wyandot.[4] In the American view, following British-Iroquoian precedent, Shawnees and Delawares held Ohio lands only by Iroquoian permission.

Moreover, the commissioners still pressured the Shawnees to deliver "prisoners" taken in Dunmore's and previous wars. Cornstalk claimed that he had already complied with these conditions; that, at Lord Dunmore's insistence, he had sent the white captives of the Shawnees back to "see their Relations." It was true, he conceded, that many of the released captives had come back to the Shawnees "of their Own Accord," but these were now "as free as our selves." He could try to induce them to "go and see their Relations" again, but he knew they would refuse. Cornstalk could not force them and asked the Americans to yield the point.[5]

The commisioners of the Continental Congress would have none of Cornstalk's reasoning, and neutralists among the Six Nations and Delawares refused to support the Shawnee leader on the issue. Instead, they agreed with the congressional delegates that the Shawnees should live up to their earlier commitment to Dunmore and send back the "white Indians" from among them. When the commissioners informed the Shawnees that their portion of the treaty present would be withheld until they gave a suitable answer, the Shawnee neutralist Nimwha promised to comply with the demand of Congress.[6] As always in recent years, his people desperately needed goods.

Both open recognition of their need for European goods and resignation to their loss of Kentucky marked the neutralists among the Shawnees. They sought trade with Anglo-Americans and a boundary against white settlement at the Ohio. Still recovering from Dunmore's War, particularly from the loss of trade during that war, they attended to Cornstalk's and Nimwha's arguments for peace, arguments supported by the work of leading members of the Shawnees' close neighbors, the Coshocton-area Delawares.

Accommodation in Coshocton, 1775–1779

The Delaware leaders who consistently advocated good relations with the United States were White Eyes and Killbuck. They lived near the cluster of Moravian mission towns of Schönbrunn, Gnadenhutten, and Salem. Neither had converted to Christianity, but the most outspoken neutralist, White Eyes, consistently opposed nativists who threatened the missions.[7] White Eyes had been proposing a Delaware partnership with Anglo-America since 1773. This accommodationist, who had set up his own village in order to escape conflict with the nativists of Newcomer's town, had nonetheless helped persuade the leadership of that town to remain neutral during Dunmore's War. Though no Christian, he had declared to Quakers in 1773—in words very different from nativist, separatist theology—that because "we two Brothers the Delawares & the Quakers were brought up together" in Pennsylvania, "it is our Saviour's Mind they should be of one Religion."[8]

His position gained strength among the leaders of the very people he had so recently separated from, in part because even the nativists had a certain fondness and respect for Quakers, as Neolin had indicated when considering surrender in 1765. The civil chief Netawatwees (or Newcomer) of Newcomer's town himself came around to White Eyes' position after witnessing the nativists' loss in Dunmore's War, pledging to Moravian missionaries in 1775 that the Delawares intended to "accept the word of God as being the truth, as they might learn from the believing Indians whom they had before them as sufficient example." Netawatwees still implied, even in this profession of intention to convert, that Indians had no need of white missionaries, that "believing Indians" could do the work of God. He had not completely abandoned the suspicion of missionaries that he had expressed only a year earlier, when he had accused the Moravians of harboring witches. But by the winter of 1775–76, the Delaware movement toward accommodation with Anglo-Americans had gained strength, and the missionaries noted that individuals who were once the Christians' "bitter enemies and would [neither] hear nor know anything of God's Word [are] now showing themselves very obliging and confidential toward us."[9]

It does not seem to have been God's Word, however, that the neutralist leaders were truly after, at least not Zeisberger's version of it. Zeisberger, who was no one's fool, had long attributed any favor shown the missionaries by the Unami Delaware chiefs more to politics than to sincere spiritual seeking. He would not change his mind during the Revolution. In 1781 he reflected on these earlier years in his diary, noting that the Unami leaders, a group that had included White Eyes, Netawatwees, Killbuck, and Pipe, had sought "to involve us with themselves, especially in their chief things and councils, for they thought hereby best to have access to our Indians." Unami leaders professing a desire to become members of the church had actually, according to Zeisberger, sought "to become masters of it." Even so, he concluded, "many of them were our good friends."[10] The last pair of observations were not contradictory; they embodied neutralist Delaware policy. The Coshocton Indians sought friendship, goods, and technological expertise from the missionaries and the Anglo-Americans, but they did not want to sacrifice their independence. Nor did they

THE REVEREND DAVID ZEISBERGER

Zeisberger, missionary to the Ohio Indians on the eve of and during the American Revolution, opposed Indian prophets and provided information on British and northern Indian movements to the Americans at Pittsburgh. (*Source:* John Heckewelder, *A Narrative of the United Brethren among the Delaware and Mohegan Indians* [Philadelphia, 1820].)

want to lose contact with relatives who had joined the Christian missions. Familial love and the ties of kinship played a role in Coshocton politics, as they always had. The Coshoctons' goals surfaced most plainly in the maneuverings of White Eyes, by 1775 the acknowledged leader of the neutralists.

White Eyes had two aims for his people. First, he sought to gain Congress's recognition of Delaware possession of lands north of the Ohio. Second, he sought Anglo-American instruction. He sought both landed autonomy and active economic cooperation under the direction of white teachers. Once achieved, the two ends would bring security of title and the benefits, as he saw them, of an economy productive of material goods. They would also win back the Christian neophytes, or at least provide for their continued place among the Delawares.

In July 1775, White Eyes reminded the Americans that Lord Dunmore had offered to secure a "Grant from the King for the lands claimed by the Delawares." At the same time, he sought to league with the new Congress. His people would be better off "living as White People do under their Laws and Protection," a protection, he hoped, that would establish the Delawares' possession of their land. Unfortunately for White Eyes, Dunmore had fled Virginia; the Revolution had effectively nullified any promises the royal governor had made. In White Eyes' effort to gain Anglo-American recognition of Delaware lands, he now had to push his claims before the newly appointed commissioners of the revolutionary government.[11] From the start, he pushed against strong forces.

The revolutionary Americans, even when pressed to keep Indian war parties off their borders, would not ratify any treaty that implied Delaware possession. They did not wish to offend the still largely neutral Six Nations, on whose spurious claim to much of the trans-Appalachian west many of the colonial purchases had been made, including, for example, the Kentucky cession disputed by the Shawnees in Dunmore's War. American support for the Six Nations' claims to the Ohio country, against those of the Shawnees and Delawares, hindered attempts by the Shawnee neutralist Cornstalk and the Delaware neutralist White Eyes to increase support for their peaceful policies.[12] If White Eyes' hopes for American recognition of Delaware possessions went unsatisfied in the early years of the war, his desire for economic acculturation ran up against even more formidable barriers.

The neutralist vision of economic and technological transformation unfolds suggestively in a set of documents from the negotiations of the treaty council at Fort Pitt, September 1778. According to the terms of the treaty, negotiated largely by White Eyes, the Delawares of the village of

Coshocton and the neutral Mequashake Shawnees should "become the same people." In strong opposition to nativist notions of the separateness of Anglo-Americans and Indians, White Eyes desired that "young men" of Coshocton and the United States "may be made acquainted with one another & that there may be no distinction between them." The representatives of Congress promised to send schoolmasters to the Coshoctons to teach their children.[13] The most radical American suggestion, never implemented by Congress, guaranteed the Delawares' possession of all their claimed lands and suggested, audaciously, that the Ohio Indians still in friendship with the United States might "form a state whereof the Delaware Nation shall be the head, and have a representation in Congress: Provided, nothing in this article to be considered as conclusive until it meets with the approbation of Congress." It is inconceivable that such a proposal was accepted, in good faith, by even the most broad-minded of the commissioners, but it certainly illustrates the lengths American agents were willing to run and the lies they were willing to spin in order to achieve Delaware neutrality.[14]

Neutral Delaware leaders Killbuck and White Eyes were serious enough about peace with the United States to send three of their loved ones—George White Eyes (White Eyes' eight-year-old son), John Killbuck (Killbuck's sixteen-year-old son), and Thomas (Killbuck's eighteen-year-old half brother)—deep into Anglo-America, to Princeton, New Jersey, to live in the home of Indian agent Colonel George Morgan. There they attended the local schools, including the college.[15]

More indicative of his willingness to cooperate with the United States was White Eyes' intention to have an American garrison established near Coshocton to protect his people against the rising opposition of his militant Indian neighbors. The fort was to provide the Coshoctons with "Provisions and Ammunition," as well as with protection.[16] This did not mean military alliance. The Delawares were not ready to combine their request for a fort with a pledge to give active support to the Americans, at least not in 1778.

Agents of the United States, however, sought to enlist the Delaware warriors. In January 1779, an apparently altered version of the treaty of 1778 was read to the Delawares, who immediately challenged one very important article. The Delawares objected to what they heard, claiming that Anglo-American scribes had inserted into the treaty a provision committing Coshocton to active support for the United States. Killbuck, learning of the written article early in 1779, said bluntly that it had been "wrote down false."[17] What he and White Eyes had agreed to, he recalled, was to "pilot the Army" toward the enemy, and to send White Eyes forward to meet the enemy in a spirit of negotiation.[18] Killbuck's memory is supported by the fact that this was precisely the role that White Eyes had played during Dunmore's War, just four years earlier, when he marched before Dunmore's Virginians to encourage the Shawnees and Mingos to come to terms. For the time being, the Delawares gained their point.

The American promise to build a fort as both a supply base and a possible defensive haven for the Delawares and an American plan for the capture of Detroit combined to produce Fort Laurens, an isolated, poorly supplied garrison that failed to secure any of its intended ends. Harsh Indian raids prevented the Congress from undertaking an assault on Detroit, and poverty prevented the Americans from adequately supplying the little garrison or, through it, the Indians. So ragged was the American army at Fort Laurens that when its commander warned the Delawares to support American actions lest they suffer the enmity of the United States, the Indians met his threat with "a General Laugh."[19]

Supplies

Laughter can be deep testimony, and at Fort Laurens it spoke of an important reason for the eventual demise of Delaware and Shawnee neutrality: the United States failed to supply the Delawares in the late 1770s with the goods they needed to survive. Colonel George Morgan believed in 1776 that Indian friendship could be bought, but he feared that the British were able to supply the Indians with goods "at a price greatly inferior to those exacted by our Traders." Two years later, Edward Hand, then commander of Pittsburgh, desperately requested that "If there is not a possibility of obtaining lead, I wish we might be indulged with a cargo of bows and arrows, as our people are not yet expert enough at the sling to kill Indians with pebbles."[20] No lead for Hand's army meant no lead for Hand's Indian neighbors.

The lack of supplies debilitated the neutralist Delawares. In Philadelphia in May 1779, a delegation of Coshoctons reminded Congress that the United States had promised to establish a trade, supplying the Delawares with goods, "School Masters and Mistresses," craftsmen, and "Husbandmen to instruct the Youth of their Nation in useful Arts." It reminded Congress that at every treaty the promise had been renewed, "without ever having been complied with in any degree, whereby the said Delaware Nation have become poor & naked."[21]

Congress itself, however, remained too poor and its own troops too naked to send goods to the Indians. The members also doubted that "the People in the Back Counties" would allow an Indian supply train to pass unmolested, "so violent are the Prejudices against the Indians." Even the

Delaware carrot of certain land cessions failed to raise the necessary supplies. American officials stalled with the excuse that England stole the goods at sea and with the promise that France would soon wrest the seas from Britain, but nothing could be done at the moment. The Indians left Philadelphia with light loads and heavy concerns, but not without reminding Congress that the time might soon come when Coshocton would turn to the British. From Pittsburgh, as the winter of 1779–80 approached, Colonel Broadhead sent the same message to General Washington: "If no provision is made for these naked wretches they will be compelled to submit to the Enemy and to be employed by them or perish." He remained doubtful of Coshocton friendship the following spring, for he still lacked goods.[22]

Britain, meanwhile, did its best to keep the other northern Indians in cloth, powder, and ball. The British knew they had the advantage in Indian relations. General Frederick Haldimand wrote Major Arrent de Peyster in 1780 that "the Indians in general, wish to protract the War." Added to the danger of Anglo-American settlement, Indians generally favored the British because "it is impossible they can draw resources from the Rebels & they absolutely depend upon us for every Blanket they are covered with.[23] Game remained scarce, trade was disrupted by war, and winters in the Ohio country could be fierce. The Indians needed blankets. It was a simple need, but if it could not be met in trade with the Anglo-Americans it had to be met somehow. Even for Indians who distrusted militant nativists, who put no faith in pan-Indianism, British supplies were *one* reason to take arms against the Anglo-Americans.

Although the British on the Great Lakes possessed greater material resources than did the Americans in the Upper Ohio country, they too could encounter difficulties in supplying the Indians. When a load of poor muskets was sent to Detroit in 1781, the frustrated Commander wrote Quebec that he needed good rifles; these muskets were so shoddy that the warriors turned them immediately over to women, for use as pot trammels. Ammunition was also in short store, leaving the Indians "greatly displeas'd with the small allowance they receive."[24] But British assistance was better than nothing, and Indians continued to demand it.

They did so particularly in the wake of American raids. In the South, the raids of 1776 had driven the Cherokee nation proper to neutrality, but in the North, circumstances differed, and American raids only increased Indian hostilities. The Senecas suffered from the most serious northern invasions in 1779. The Shawnees were greatly exposed to Kentucky raiders and suffered three invasions: Colonel John Bowman's raid in May 1779, which destroyed the town of Chillicothe; and George Rogers Clark's invasions of August 1780 and November 1782, each of which destroyed several militant Shawnee villages. Clark's raids, conducted when the growing season was well under way, not only destroyed the Indians' stores but deprived them of their next season's food. Far from crushing Shawnee or Seneca militancy, however, the raids actually strengthened it. The raids may have accomplished the objective of delaying Shawnee incursions into Kentucky, but they resulted in few Shawnee or Seneca warriors' deaths. Also, unlike the Cherokees of 1776, the Shawnees could retreat for assistance and protection to Detroit or to the villages of other militants, and the Senecas could retreat to Niagara. As a result, the raids did not force militants among either people into neutrality. If anything, they fed Shawnee militancy by forcing the displaced Indians to rely on support from the British and the militant northern nations.[25]

Murdering Neutrality, 1777–1779

For all its importance, the availability of British supplies did not by itself induce neutrality-minded Indians to join militants in the late years of the Revolution. Equally important was the murderous hatred for Indians that had developed during years of warfare among the inhabitants of western Pennsylvania, Maryland, and Virginia. Hatred became as established an article of backcountry commerce as was Indian land, and though not uncontested by Indians or by American individuals, it combined with a land hunger to inspire a series of killings that ruined the Coshoctons' chances for accommodation with the United States. As early as March 1777, George Morgan of Fort Pitt worried that his neighboring citizens were ready and anxious "to massacre our known [Indian] friends at their hunting camps as well as Messengers on Business to me." The reason for the hostility, he noted, was partly vengeance, but coupled with it was an expressed "ardent desire for an Indian War, on account of the fine Lands those poor people possess."[26]

Later that year, several murders seriously eroded Ohioan Indian neutrality. In September, a party of neutral Senecas on its way to the annual autumn treaty at Pittsburgh came under rebel fire. Morgan found it necessary to have the Indian delegates bunk in his personal quarters. The "horrid murders" of Indians prevented a treaty council from taking place that month. They also turned many Senecas against the Americans.[27]

The horrid murders were mere preliminaries to the first decisive act, the murder of Cornstalk, the leading Shawnee exponent of neutrality. By the time of his assassination, many of his people had already rejected his neutralist arguments. Shawnee parties had struck Anglo-American settlements in Virginia and Kentucky throughout the early years of the war, and the militia garrison of Fort Randolph, a Virginian outpost on the site of Point Pleasant, grew deeply embittered against the Shawnees.

On September 19, Fort Randolph's commander, Matthew Arbuckle, took two Shawnees prisoner. They were not hostages; Arbuckle did not notify the Shawnees of any demands that could be met for their release. Eight days later, Cornstalk's son arrived, demanding to know why the two men had been taken. Arbuckle had him seized. By November 7, "satisfied the Shawanese are all our enemies," Arbuckle had taken prisoner two more visiting Shawnee chiefs, the once-nativist Red Hawk and the neutralist Cornstalk himself. Cornstalk's detention sent ripples of concern throughout the Ohio country. Zeisberger reported to the Americans that the act jeopardized negotiations with the neutral Coshocton Delawares, who now feared for the safety of their envoys to Fort Pitt.

Fort Randolph, meanwhile, lost a soldier to an Indian raid outside its walls. In revenge, the garrison turned its guns on the unarmed prisoners within, murdering Cornstalk, Red Hawk, and all their fellows. Denunciations of Virginian treachery accompanied news of the act throughout the Indian villages of the North. The erstwhile Shawnee neutralist Nimwha became at once an enemy of the United States. He would later both capture Daniel Boone and lead a withering assault on American Fort Laurens. General Hand wrote east that if there had been any chance for peace with the Shawnees, "it is now Vanished." In the murders' wake, remaining neutrals among the Mingos and Senecas had taken up the war club; of the Coshocton Delawares, Hand remained uncertain.[28]

American officials struggled to maintain neutralist factions among the Shawnees and Delawares at Coshocton. A month after the murders, Hand wrote to Patrick Henry that he knew "it would be vain for me to bring the perpetrators of this horrid act to justice," but by April, several Anglo-Americans stood trial for the crimes at the Rockbridge County Court. It is almost needless to say that all were acquitted; no citizen would testify against them.[29]

While the frontier citizens and their militia commanders supported the murderers with their silence, Colonel George Morgan tried, in an address to some assembled Shawnee chiefs, to place the blame on the Mingos and Wyandots who, he asserted, "came and kill'd some of our People near the Fort [Randolph] whilst yours were in there on purpose to have them hurt." He and the Virginia officials tried to reassure the Shawnees that the killers would be brought to justice.[30] No doubt the promise sounded hollow in Shawnee ears.

Another series of killings compounded the effect on the Delawares of

Cornstalk's murder. In February 1778, General Hand left Fort Pitt with five hundred militia in order to destroy a cache of British arms on the Cuyahoga River. Spring flooding hampered their march, but before abandoning it the patriots found and killed six Delawares at Beaver Creek. The victims of the five hundred Americans consisted of an old man and a woman from the Unamis, and three women and a boy from the Munsees. The outrage profoundly deranged Delaware neutrality. The Coshocton council sent word to the Americans that it had lost credibility among its neighbors. It had long boasted among the northern nations of the advantages of peace. In return, complained a member of the council, the Americans drove "the Tomahawk in my head, of which the others will be glad and mock at me."[31] A faction of sixty warriors under one Captain James renounced neutrality and hurried to Detroit. There, after presenting the British, Miamis, and Chippewas with two scalps, Captain James stood before the Chippewas, Ottawas, Hurons, Potawatomis, and Miamis to sing "the War song, on that Belt you have given me." He made it clear that he spoke only for the Delawares who accompanied him: "I cannot say anything for the rest of the nation."[32] As the cluster of villages centered around Coshocton had divided from the rest of the Delawares, so had the Coshoctons splintered once again.

White Eyes and Killbuck remained opposed to war, despite the grave episode. They argued among their people that war against the white settlers simply could not be won. Unlike most northerners, they believed that even the combined forces of the northern Indians and the British could not overpower prolific, expansionist, and armed Americans. White Eyes and Killbuck accordingly allowed the Beaver Creek affair to pass and worked to tighten their relations with the United States. White Eyes even guided General Lachlan McIntosh on an expedition down the north bank of the Ohio River. The ultimate, unrealized purpose of the expedition was to establish a series of posts along the "Great Trail," which ran between Detroit and Fort Pitt.[33] McIntosh completed only two posts, Fort McIntosh, at the junction of the Beaver and the Ohio, and Fort Laurens, about fifty miles further west along the Great Trail.

White Eyes, as we have seen, had no intention of fighting beside the Americans, but he was willing to guide them, to allow them to establish posts within Delaware territory, and to negotiate for them with their Indian enemies, if possible. He was also willing to carry messages over the dangerous terrain between the two new posts and Fort Pitt. Performing a like service for the Americans in November 1778, the neutralist met his death. The Americans, fearing the effect of the news on Coshocton, announced that he had died of smallpox. George Morgan, much later, related that he had been bushwhacked by American militiamen. Given the tenor of feeling, Morgan's story rings true, and so it is most generally given.[34]

White Eyes rode horseback at the time of the killing, at least that is suggested by the full saddlebag, saddlecloth, saddle, and bridle listed among his personal belongings. The "Inventory of Sundry Movables" taken after his death discloses a mixture of European and Delaware goods fit for a leader interested in Anglo-American ways. With his pair of scarlet "Breeches" he carried a buckskin pair of pants, buckskin leggings, and two breech cloths. With his four jackets (one of them scarlet, silk, and laced with gold trimmings) were a fur cap and a beaver hat. He hunted and fought with a rifle, walked in shoes (he had three pairs), sported buckles and a silver medal etched with the portrait of George III, warmed himself in one of his two green coats, painted his face, smoked from a pipe-tomahawk, treated with a belt of wampum in his hand, and saw the world (or perhaps only his close work) through the lenses of his spectacles.[35] By frontier standards—both sides of the frontier—he had been traveling well clothed. His possessions indicate not only his material dependence on Western goods, but also the importance, economically, of his position as a broker with the Americans. If he could get goods from them, he could pass them on to his people.

Despite the cover-up of White Eyes' murder, Delaware-American relations continued to sour in the heat of other murders and murderous plots throughout 1779. In June, Colonel Broadhead informed his Indian "Brothers" at Pittsburgh that "some wicked person" in the neighborhood had mortally wounded a Delaware whom Broadhead professed to love "as my Son." Broadhead, by his own account, found the best care available for the victim and attempted to discover "the Villain that hurt him but because it was done in the Dark I could not find him out." Later that summer, Delawares returning from cordial but ultimately insubstantial conferences with the Continental Congress had to take "an unexpected & circuitous Route" to avoid ambush by Indian-haters among the Delawares' Pennsylvanian allies.[36] By the end of 1779, the murders had driven many, but not all, Coshocton Delawares and Shawnees into the arms of the militants, and the erstwhile neutral ground disintegrated in civil conflict.

Polarization and Realignment, 1779–1781

The Coshocton-area Delawares, led by White Eyes and Killbuck, and the neutral factions of Shawnees, led by Cornstalk and Nimwha, had kept the peace in the early years. By 1777, the Coshocton Delawares had gathered into their village and its environs 400 of the 500 Unami Delaware "Fighting

Men," 20 of the 90 Munsee Delaware warriors, and after Cornstalk's murder, 50 of the 300-odd Shawnee gunmen, most of them Mequashakes. Coshocton, the bastion of neutrality, thus contained some 470 neutralist men, and, we can assume, their families. If men of fighting age constitute a fourth or a fifth of the entire population, greater Coshocton probably supported some 2,000 people: a respectable size for a community on either side of the frontier.

Militant Delawares and Shawnees constituted, at the beginning of the war, a slight minority of the combined Delaware and Shawnee populations. One hundred Unami Delaware gunmen had migrated west, as fighting broke out, to join up with the militant Wyandots and Miamis; about 70 Munsee fighters had placed themselves among both the militant Unamis and the Mingos; and most of the 250 Shawnee warriors remaining in the Upper Ohio region had also sided with the militants.[37] Over the course of the war, these militants would see their own numbers rise at the expense of their Coshocton compatriots, as escalating disaffection from the Americans propelled erstwhile neutralists away from the Pennsylvania and Virginia frontier. But until the completion of neutralist alienation from the United States, militant attitudes toward Coshocton heated.

The differences among the Ohio Indians reached their emotional peak in 1779, a year in which the Coshocton Delawares came to actual blows with their anti-American kinsmen. The year would see one of the few instances, since the Seven Years' War, of Upper Ohio country Indians firing at each other in battle. This abandonment of neutrality by Killbuck and his followers would represent no community consensus; it would tear at divisions within the shrinking Coshocton community. Things would go so badly for the Coshoctons over the next two years that by early 1781 most of them would recoil from the policy of friendship with the rebels and would join their kinsmen in a war against the United States.

As 1779 opened, shortly after news of White Eyes' death reached Coshocton, villagers expressed their commitment to neutrality. They opposed proposals for military alliance with the United States. Although in the year's early months the Delawares would not fight for the Americans, they did, like the neighboring Moravian mission towns, render valuable assistance to the garrison at Fort Laurens in two significant ways. First, they warned the garrisons at Laurens and Pittsburgh that a concerted Indian force, including some Shawnees and Delawares, had gathered at Detroit to plan an assault on Laurens. Along the same lines, they informed Pittsburgh of the progress of the siege of Fort Laurens once it had begun. Second, they helped to raise that siege, persuading, in a series of councils that ended around March 12, 1779, the enemies of the United States to depart. It was after these meetings, after most of the attackers had already withdrawn, that reinforcements relieved the wretched garrison. Morgan credited the Coshocton Delawares with having "saved Fort Laurens."[38]

In the process of winning accolades from an American commander, Killbuck—now, after White Eyes' death and Pipe's withdrawal, Coshocton's most important voice—incurred the wrath of the northern Indians. Killbuck found it impossible to maintain a friendly neutrality with both the United States and its northwestern enemies. The Ohio militants had earlier expressed their anger at the Coshocton Delawares for blocking "the Path of the Warriors going against the Rebels." Unable to carry out their raids, the warriors had returned to Detroit "with tears in their eyes." These northerners, Killbuck had complained to the Americans, "mock, and make all the Game of me they Can."[39] Now at Fort Laurens he once again blocked the path, and the northerners, including a growing number of Delawares, publicly berated him for it. By midspring, Killbuck considered drastic action, perhaps to respond to the jabs of his militant neighbors. A party of Coshocton Delawares under Killbuck would fight for the Americans.

Broadhead, learning of the Coshocton leader's sentiments in May, wrote excitedly to John Heckewelder that the Mingo, Wyandot, and Shawnee enemies of the United States would soon "consider the Delaware Indian allies as no contemptible foe, which added to the fast connection between them and us must and surely will end in their final extirpation." His next sentence, however, reveals that his new allies did not all share his optimism: "I sincerely wish our allies the Delawares may make themselves easy and no longer remain in a state of such apprehension."[40]

Toward the end of June, pro-American Coshoctons crossed the Rubicon, shedding the blood of their militant relatives. A young Delaware, Nonowland (George Wilson), scouted for twenty militiamen in a raid toward the Seneca country, encountering a party of Senecas and Munsees. Nonowland joined in the fighting himself, and his party took a Munsee Delaware scalp. When the warriors returned with the expedition to Pittsburgh, they presented the hair to visiting Coshocton delegates. These carried the scalp back toward their village, still a home to neutral Munsees. Coshocton had only recently lost a warrior to the Indian-haters on the white frontier. Now one of its number had killed someone closely connected to some of its inhabitants. Killbuck's support for Nonowland's act earned him the militant Munsees' enduring disgust.[41]

Nevertheless, on July 12, Killbuck and the Coshocton Council pledged to become firm allies of the United States. Soon another Indian scalp came in with a party of Delawares and Americans, and on August 11, 1779, 8 of the Coshocton warriors joined Broadhead's 628 men in an attack on the western flank of the Seneca Nation. The 8 Coshoctons marched with 15 rangers in the advanced guard. They had only one actual skirmish: with a group of 30 to 40 Indians descending the Allegheny in seven canoes. The incident served only to give the main body of Senecas time to flee before the army's approach. Broadhead reached the abandoned Seneca towns, destroyed eight of them, and put houses and corn to the torch, forcing the Seneca refugees into greater reliance on Britain.[42] In response, northern Indian opposition to Coshocton mounted.

In October, an assembly of "Chiefs and Principal Warriors" from the Mingos, Hurons, Delawares, and Shawnees gathered at the Upper Shawnee village on the Mad River to disown the Coshoctons, for "they have help'd to shed the Blood of our friends to Northward." The gathering asked British agents to send "as many troops as you can spare if only to protect our Women & Children, while we harass the Enemy." Revealing his own sense of identity with other Indians, including even his Coshocton opponents, a militant speaker declared against the erstwhile neutral community: "We hope to see a day that those injuries will not pass with impunity even from those of our own Colour."[43]

At this point, barely 10 Coshoctons had actually undertaken hostilities against their kinsmen and neighbors to the north and west. In mid-September 1779, on Broadhead's return to Pittsburgh, 30 more Coshoctons (including some Mequashake Shawnees) sought to accompany the Americans in arms. But Broadhead lacked the supplies with which to pay them, and he had to turn them away. They returned to Coshocton, poorly armed and clothed. Their town lay open to enemy strikes.[44]

Broadhead's inability to secure supplies continued throughout 1780. Without any goods, he could barely maintain a defensive posture at Pittsburgh, much less supply warriors for an expedition against Detroit. When abandoning Fort Laurens in the summer of 1779, he had promised the Coshoctons that he would reestablish the fort to protect them. By the fall of 1780, it was clear that he could not do so. The intervening year brought about other changes that, as far as most Delawares were concerned, gave the lie to American promises. In 1779, for one thing, Congress had guaranteed the Delawares possession of the land (without informing the Six Nations), but that very year, Anglo-American hunters crossed the Ohio, drumming the woods with shot and consuming the game. Second, at the time of Broadhead's expedition of 1779, it had appeared likely that the Americans would crush the Indian militants to the north and west. By 1780, it was clear that the militants were stronger and more vigorous than ever.[45] The Coshocton people had risked their reputations among their strengthening kinsmen and had gained little thereby. By early 1781, a faction opposing Killbuck seized control, and Coshocton policy turned abruptly about.

Broadhead got word of the coup in January. He absorbed the depressing news that the reliable Killbuck not only no longer led the Coshoctons, but now sought to live with the Moravians and was considering "becoming a Christian." The deposed leader, Broadhead learned, felt isolated and did not believe that either Broadhead "or the Council of Cooshockung [were] at any loss about me." Killbuck persisted in his personal alliance with the United States, turning further against his own people. He kept Broadhead abreast of Delaware plans, for he still had sources. He informed Broadhead, through the neighboring Moravian missionaries, that the Coshoctons were launching expeditions against the Wheeling and Pittsburgh regions. The Coshocton Council, meanwhile, did everything it could to "blacken the Character of Killbuck," because he "is a Friend to the States."[46]

Broadhead, contemplating the destruction of the town, sent orders from Pittsburgh that "any Friends" among the Coshoctons should "remove hither without loss of time & remain under our protection." Near the garrison at Pittsburgh, he knew, "their daily transaction will be seen and known." The refugees who followed his order encountered not only suspicion but hatred among the citizens. Broadhead's local critics openly admitted as much, calling the refugees the "objects of the peoples jealousy and aversion." The Continental Congress and the army were wrong, the locals believed, to expect Indians to be of service to the United States; far better to kill them: "With all due respect to that honorable body [Congress] while they were bestowing commissions on savages the state of Pennsylvania judged right by offering a bounty on their scalps." The critics got more personal, charging Broadhead with both employing an Indian "harlot" and trading with the Indians, using goods from the commissary.[47]

It was in this wrathful season that Broadhead decided to undertake a rapid strike against his ally, the Coshocton Delaware community. It stands as a mark of Killbuck's thorough alienation from his own people that Broadhead secured his and his followers' assistance. On April 7, 1781, Broadhead and his 150 Continentals descended the Ohio to Wheeling, where the militia doubled his force. The combined 300, guided by pro-American Coshocton refugee warriors, advanced northward to overwhelm and raze Coshocton.

If Killbuck had any remaining illusions about the militia's attitudes toward Indians, they may have been exposed when the invaders summarily executed fifteen captured Coshocton warriors. And if that was not enough,

American Martin Wetzel murdered an enemy envoy who had been promised safe conduct, while five neutral Moravian Indians who had been visiting fled homeward under militia fire. But Killbuck and his loyal followers now had no choice but to risk it with the Americans, lest they incur a heavy penalty from the northern Indians. Under the unsteady protection of the United States, he and his warriors returned with the Continentals to Fort Pitt.

Like most of the American expeditions against Native American villages during the Revolution, Broadhead's attack had harassed, injured, and dispossessed the Coshoctons, but it did little to interfere with their new militancy. The Coshoctons fled, "half naked," to Sandusky, where they were taken in by militant Delawares and Wyandots and where they were supplied by the British.[48] From there, they joined in the heavy raids of 1781, the most alarming attacks yet witnessed by the Anglo-American inhabitants of the revolutionary frontier.[49]

"Two Angry Spirits"

Among the targets of northern Indian raiding was the Moravian mission. Three hundred warriors from the Wyandot, Delaware, Shawnee, Ottawa, and Chippewa nations arrived in the Moravian towns in mid-August 1781. The pro-British, accommodationist Wyandot "Half King," Pomoacan, and the recently defected Delaware war leader, Pipe, led the warriors in the company of Matthew Elliot, a Loyalist with good Shawnee connections. Despite the participation of Elliot and some *habitants*, the Indians displayed hearty nativistic behavior.

Soon after their arrival in the Moravian towns, Pomoacan, appropriating nativistic usages, spoke to the gathered inhabitants. Pomoacan claimed to fear that two dangers threatened the Moravians' Indian followers. Living on the frontier between the northern Indians on the one side and the Anglo-Americans on the other, the Moravian Indians lived in physical danger. Adopting the ways of Christians, the Moravian Indians also lived in spiritual danger. He spoke in what may not have been metaphorical terms. Outlining the precariousness of the Moravian position, he said, "Two powerful and mighty spirits or gods are standing and opening wide their jaws toward each other to swallow, and between the two angry spirits, who thus open their jaws, are you placed."

The northern Indians captured the missionaries and delivered them to the British at Detroit. They spared the inhabitants, but plundered the homes, threatened the leaders, and killed much of the livestock, "not only from hunger, but from caprice." Zeisberger derived one accidental benefit from the damage the nativists did to his possessions, for among the items scorched by the militants were diaries, letters, and "other writings." Of these he later recalled, "yet were we glad that they fell into the flames and not into strange hands."[50] He evidently thought they would have supplied interesting reading for a British commandant concerned about spies, a role the missionaries had, in fact, adopted.

During the war's first years, the Moravians had become closely associated with pro-American Coshocton. Coshocton's leaders had provided the Moravians with Delaware Indian protection against northern Indian and nativist abuse, while the Moravians had provided the leaders at Coshocton with a conduit for discussions with the Continentals. In one letter to Colonel George Morgan, Zeisberger had enclosed a message from White Eyes, adding that Morgan should "be cautious enough that it may not be known among the [Delaware] people . . . why these Messengers who know nothing of the matter themselves, come to the Fort—for White Eyes and I are blamed & accused before the Governor at Detroit for giving you Intelligence."[51] These accusations, Zeisberger knew, were true.

The erstwhile pacifistic missionaries sounded the call to arms. In July 1777, Zeisberger requested of General Edward Hand that "an Army might soon come out." This, he believed, would "be the only Method to get a Peace settled among the Nations." Zeisberger later gave Morgan his "opinion that there will be no Peace & the Nations will not be quiet until they are subdued & Detroit is taken." Brother John Heckewelder also tendered military advice to the Americans, revealing the best method of subduing Indian populations. It was useless, the ex-pacifist argued, to destroy Indian towns if the inhabitants had already secured and hidden their corn. Informing the Americans that John Bowman's 1779 invasion of the Shawnee towns had accomplished little because the Indians had quickly rebuilt their homes and replanted their crops, he noted that no peace could be had unless "a campaign is made before the corn is ripe."[52] He did not have to point out that striking at Indian corn meant striking at both combatants and noncombatants. Heckewelder and Zeisberger may have themselves been noncombatants, but they had become partisans in a war, partisans of the Americans and the enemies of the majority of borderland Indians.

Zeisberger personally played an important role in the defense of Fort Laurens in 1779, when he slipped information to the garrison of Indian and Loyalist plans to take the fort. He also sent word to the defenders of Pittsburgh that the secret token employed by neutral Indians to gain passage into that fortified town had been discovered by the rebels' enemies.

Another Moravian Christian, the Indian Joshua Styles, worked as a spy for the Americans from 1779 until his discovery by the British in 1781. In keeping with nativist opposition to clients of the Americans, Delaware and Shawnee nativists would execute Styles as a witch in 1805. Zeisberger had supported his revolutionary-era activities.[53]

Continental officers acknowledged the missionaries' contribution to the war effort. Indian agent George Morgan considered Zeisberger's "advice & assistance as the most particular favour to me & as the greatest service to the United States." Colonel Daniel Broadhead agreed that he depended on the Moravians, including their congregation of "intelligent Indians," for information about British and hostile Indian movements in the North.[54]

Although with sharply different emotions, the Indians of the North, including the majority that was at war with the United States, also acknowledged the Moravian role. They had begun planning as early as March 1777 to capture the missionaries and carry them to Detroit.[55] Those plans had been frustrated by Delawares White Eyes and Killbuck, who protected the missionaries. But by 1781, with White Eyes dead and Killbuck out of power, with Coshocton in ruins, and with most Coshoctons now joining the war against the United States, the mission lay exposed to the northern Indians.

Although Moravian cooperation with the Americans was the main reason for both the capture of the ministers and the disruption of the Moravian Indian towns in that late summer of 1781, the nativistic hostility of many of the northerners toward the Christian communities also played a role. An example of the kind of threat these communities held for traditionalists is evident in the story of the Indian convert Deborah, who had joined the Christian community at Schönbrunn in 1773, when her own son had accused her of making deadly witchcraft against his child. Zeisberger noted that the accusation was "perhaps one of the reasons for her coming to the Congregation." Although she found protection among the Moravians and passed their scrupulous examinations, the outside Indians never gave up their suspicions. These were reinforced when, upon her death late in 1780, "a small heathen idol was found among her effects, that is a Beson, such as old women have among the savages, in which they cherish the confidence that, so long as they have it, they will suffer no want."[56] The suspicion that the Moravians harbored witches, a suspicion nurtured by such incidents, had plagued the mission throughout its history.

Indian opponents of the Christian mission, despite their seizure of the ministers in 1781, did not deliver the heaviest blow to the mission; that came from the rebels the mission had done so much to protect. In the most gruesome assault on neutrals in the Coshocton area, eighty to ninety Long

Knives under Colonel David Williamson coldly and methodically killed the inhabitants of two Moravian towns, Salem and Gnadenhutten, in March 1782. In all, the militiamen murdered ninety-six unarmed men, women, and children, whom they had gathered at Gnadenhutten. Most of the victims were Munsees, some Unamis, possibly a few were not Delawares but Shawnees. So shameful was the action that, over a century later, a most-partisan advocate of United States expansion, the scholarly Theodore Roosevelt, concluded his narrative of the event with a condemnation of Williamson and his party: "It is impossible not to regret that fate failed to send some strong war party of savages across the path of these inhuman cowards, to inflict on them the punishment they so richly deserved."⁵⁷

Williamson's attack was no spontaneous outbreak of frontier frenzy. Almost a year before, three hundred militiamen had planned an assault on the Moravians. Colonel John Gibson of Fort Pitt had opposed that earlier scheme, writing to Governor Thomas Jefferson of Virginia, "The Moravians have always given us the most convincing proofs of their attachment to the cause of America, by always giving us intelligence of every party that came against the frontiers; & on the late expedition they furnished Col. Broadhead & his party with a large quantity of provisions when they were starving."⁵⁸ But by 1782, with the missionaries themselves captive in Detroit, and with the Pennsylvania, Maryland, and Virginia back countries reeling under effective Indian assaults, American affection for the Moravian Indians of Ohio, who had done them such service, had vanished.

The depth of backcountry hostility for all Indians was not lost on the few Coshocton Delawares who had, following Killbuck, allied with the Americans and sought refuge at Fort Pitt. When Captain Williamson and his band returned from their genocidal mission, they proceeded to kill members of Killbuck's party.⁵⁹ Most escaped, but the American cause among the Delawares, already lost, had reached its pitiful epilogue. Congress's inability to supply necessities and the intensified Indian-hating on the Anglo-American side of the frontier had combined with the strength of the northern militants and the attractiveness of the British alliance to finish the Coshoctons' experiment in peace with the new nation.

The massacres had also ended the most energetic phase of the Moravian mission in the Ohio country. Not for another sixteen years would the remarkably able missionaries gain a stable Indian congregation south of Lake Erie. Fortunately for the missionaries themselves, they had been held captive near Detroit when news of the bloodletting reached them. The British, recognizing that the massacre would also kill Moravian Indian sympathies with the American cause, allowed the missionaries and the remnant of their congregation of converts to settle near Detroit; eventually they settled in Ontario.[60] These Christian Indians and their missionaries, who had taken great risks for the United States, found ultimate asylum in the land of the Loyalists.

Killbuck himself survived the militia's fury and remained at Fort Pitt until 1785; on no day, Zeisberger later reported, could Killbuck be "sure of his life, on account of the militia." In the late 1780s, with enemies among the whites and among the northern Indians, this poor advocate of accommodation with Anglo-America joined the Moravian community in Loyalist Upper Canada. There he lived under the threat of Indian retaliation. His story is emblematic of the hopelessness of Ohioan Indian cooperation with the United States between the outbreak of the Revolution and the final defeat of the Ohioan militants in 1794. Grasping that hopelessness is important to any understanding of the widespread success of pan-Indian diplomacy both during the Revolutionary War and in the decade that followed its formal end. Both neutrality and cooperation with the United States had been and would continue to be ruled out, in most instances, by the intensity of hatred and the conflict over land along the frontier. Indian conflict with the new nation would become the norm. In missionary David Zeisberger's words, as good for the neutral Coshoctons as for the Moravian Indians, the world between the militants and Anglo-Americans had grown "already too narrow."[61]

Results of Gnadenhutten

The murders at Gnadenhutten contributed to the nativist cause. The missionaries had been long suspected of aiding the Americans and harboring witches. Now they were accused, by some, of having actually "called the white people," the militia, to Gnadenhutten. Surviving Moravian Indians of the Ohio country found it difficult to keep the new faith. The militant northerners sent many of the survivors to live with the Shawnees. Their new hosts made it clear that "no word of God should again be heard in the Indian land." Unami Delaware warriors in the Shawnee towns insisted that the Christian Indians "accept heathenism and live as they lived."[62]

The calamity at Gnadenhutten triggered an Indian revival, not only of nativistic argument but also of that practice that had been suppressed by cooperation with the British: the ritual torture of prisoners. Major de Peyster wrote from Detroit that the Gnadenhutten killings, "at the time the Indians were almost wean'd from it, have awaken'd their old custom of putting prisoners to the most severe tortures."[63] British reports of the torturing of American prisoners suggest that it was not a clear revival of the old ritual, but that a new element had entered into the practice: that of punishing an individual enemy for his personal involvement in a punishable act.

The initial victims of the revival were members of the Sandusky Expedition, one of the last land operations of the Revolutionary War. This company of some four hundred volunteers, under the command of Colonel William Crawford and Colonel David Williamson, had planned to destroy the Indian bases at Sandusky. Indians had reason to hate both commanders. They knew Crawford for his destruction of a Mingo town toward the end of Dunmore's War and Williamson for his leadership in the Gnadenhutten atrocity. As the volunteers made their way through Ohio, cocky militiamen announced their intent "to extermenate the whole Wiandott Tribe." They did so "not only by words but even by exposing Effegies which they left hanging by the heels in every camp."[64]

The aspiring conquerors, however, met total defeat in a two-day battle near Sandusky on June 4 and 5, 1782. The Shawnees and Delawares followed their victory, pushing "their retaliation to great lengths," by lingering over the immolation of prisoners, some of whom, according to British agent Alexander McKee, were "known to them to be perpetrators" of the Gnadenhutten massacre. Zeisberger, who kept in touch with his Indian friends scattered among the Shawnees, also noted early in 1783 that the Shawnee fires consumed any prisoners believed to have taken part in the Gnadenhutten killings. "As soon as it is known that any prisoner had part in that affair, he is forthwith bound, tortured, and burnt."[65]

In their efforts to cooperate with the British and in their desire for British ransom and arms, northern Indians had suppressed this most violent expression of their traditional war ceremonialism. But the revival of the torture of captives, a form that would persist throughout the 1780s and into the early 1790s, did not mean revolt against Britain. Nativists still cooperated with both the pro-British mediators among their own people and with the British themselves. They would continue to do so even after the British withdrew from the war in 1783.

Determined to put a stop to white settlement, nativists and those who favored accommodation would work together in the 1780s and early 1790s to pressure British officials in the North for supplies. They would also maintain their ties with the southern Indians. Until 1794, advocates of accommodation with European powers, who counted on obtaining firepower in the North from Britain and in the South from Spain, continued their cooperation with nativists, who sought sacred power from ceremony.

Not until after the Americans' victories in 1794 would an explicitly nativistic movement shake the frontiers. But even that movement would draw strength from the networks that Indians had worked so hard to maintain between the outbreak of revolutionary violence in 1775 and the defeat, in 1794, of this phase of the Indian quest for unity.

≫ ≫ ≫ ≫ ≫ ≫ ≪ ≪ ≪ ≪ ≪ ≪ ≪

FIVE

A Spirit of Unity

1783–1794

Two names dominate Native American history in the 1780s and 1790s: Alexander McGillivray of the Creeks and Joseph Brant of the Mohawks. The two men appear, in much historical writing, as Europeans in Indian garb, as statesmen who thought beyond their tribally minded people toward an expansive, even nationalistic, vision of Indian unity.[1] Although the view is, at bottom, unfounded—for the idea of unity had solid Indian roots by 1783—there is much in legend and fact to lend it apparent support. The two men invite comparison and contrast with the two most celebrated nativistic advocates of unity, Pontiac of the 1760s and Tecumseh of the early nineteenth century.

Both Brant and McGillivray had widely used British names; Pontiac and Tecumseh are known to us in transposed Algonquian. Pontiac and Tecumseh supported nativistic movements for unity; religious nativism has little to do with our picture of Brant and McGillivray. Indeed, while nativists displayed open hostility toward the ascendancy of European culture, even as they assimilated elements of it, Brant and McGillivray sought actively and self-consciously to gain fluency in the ways of the newcomers. Brant in legend and McGillivray in fact descended from European and Indian ancestors. Both men held black slaves. Both read English. Both drew pay and held commissions from the British forces in the American Revolution. Brant worshiped at the Anglican altar; McGillivray could write in the Anglo-American idiom of republican virtue, although he despised republicans. Brant sailed twice to England; McGillivray spent years in Charleston schools. For historians seeking European influences in Indian political thought, Brant and McGillivray furnish ample evidence. But it is a mistake to portray the European tones of their thought so deeply that the Indian values are overshadowed.

Unlike Pontiac and Tecumseh, who owed their prominence largely to their reputations as speakers and warriors, Brant and McGillivray owed their rise to their skills as mediators between European powers, the United States, and the Indians. But despite this role and despite their training, both men retained their Indian identity. Like Pontiac and Tecumseh, they remained dedicated to preserving political autonomy and economic security for their people. They strove persistently to defend Indian land. Their methods could embrace both a striving for widespread Indian unity and an insistence upon a steady European supply of goods. They adopted this strategy as Indians. As we have seen, this combination of Indian union and European alliance was no radical innovation demanding peculiar genius; it had a respectable tenure among the Indians by the end of the Revolution.

To understand the history of the Indian struggle for unity between the Revolution and the age of Tecumseh, it is necessary to focus not on individuals—on McGillivray in Alabama or Brant on the shores of Lakes Erie and Ontario—but on the Indian people and ideas that surrounded the two, binding the two together. From 1783 to 1794, Shawnees and Chickamauga Cherokees maintained steady communications between the northern and southern Indians. Tens of thousands of Indians, most of them illiterate, non-Christian, and only marginally conversant in Anglo-American ways, shared a vision of pan-Indian cooperation with the more Anglicized McGillivray and Brant. For some, resistance to Anglo-American expansion depended on trade with the British, either through the British posts on the Great Lakes or through the weak Spanish stations in the Floridas and Louisiana. These Native Americans were close in spirit to McGillivray and Brant, and they derived their strategies from long, often cooperative dealings with Europeans. For others, spiritually distant from the two, notions of religious nativism permeated the idea of Indian unity. While Brant and McGillivray depended more on the first tradition than the second, both traditions existed quite independently of the two adroit politicians.

The two traditions, which had become mutually tolerant during the Revolution, remained so until the mid-1790s. Militant, religious nativists praised the Great Spirit while passing their more accommodating fellows European-made ammunition. The cooperation of nativism and accommodation rested upon a dual means to a mutual end: the united Indian defense of both land and political autonomy. This contingent compatibility pro-

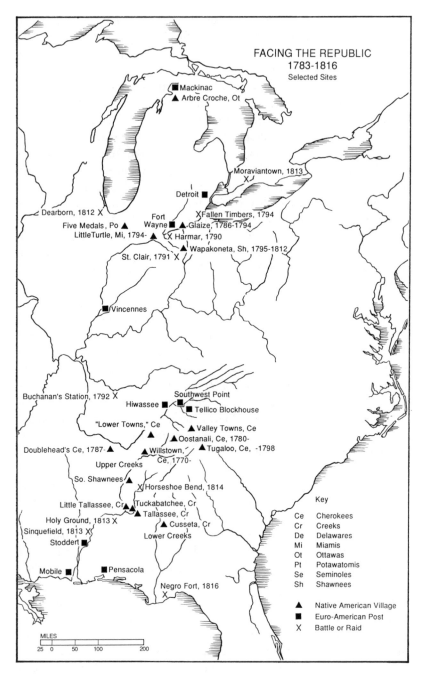

FACING THE REPUBLIC
1783-1816
Selected Sites

■ Mackinac
▲ Arbre Croche, Ot

Moraviantown, 1813
X

Detroit ■

Dearborn, 1812 X

Fort
Five Medals, Po ▲   Wayne ■ ▲ Glaize, 1786-1794
LittleTurtle, Mi, 1794- ▲   X Harmar, 1790
▲ Wapakoneta, Sh, 1795-1812
St. Clair, 1791 X

X Fallen Timbers, 1794

■ Vincennes

Buchanan's Station, 1792 X   Southwest Point
Hiwassee ■ ◄ ■ Tellico Blockhouse

"Lower Towns," Ce   ▲ Valley Towns, Ce
▲   ▲ Oostanali, Ce, 1780-
Doublehead's Ce, 1787- ▲   ▲ Tugaloo, Ce, -1798
▲ Willstown,
Upper Creeks   Ce, 1770-

So. Shawnees ▲
X Horseshoe Bend, 1814

Little Tallassee, Cr ▲ Tuckabatchee, Cr
▲ Tallassee, Cr
Holy Ground, 1813 X   ▲ Cusseta, Cr
Sinquefield, 1813 X   Lower Creeks
Stoddert ■

Mobile ■   ■ Pensacola

Negro Fort, 1816
X

Key

Ce	Cherokees
Cr	Creeks
De	Delawares
Mi	Miamis
Ot	Ottawas
Pt	Potawatomis
Se	Seminoles
Sh	Shawnees

▲   Native American Village
■   Euro-American Post
X   Battle or Raid

MILES
25 0   50   100   200

MAP 3. Facing the Republic

duced the most united, independent Indian resistance in North American history. The resistance would crumble under the pounding of American arms in 1794, but not without leaving a powerful legacy to Tecumseh, the Shawnee Prophet, the Red Stick Creeks, and their contemporaries.

The Truce of Paris, 1783

The end of the War of Independence briefly reduced the violence of the borderland war that had really begun in 1774, but it did nothing to calm the Indians' apprehensions of continued American expansion. Word of the preliminary agreement, foreshadowing the Treaty of Paris, reached the Indians in the fall of 1782. It gave them nothing. The proposed boundary line left the Indians "Thunder Struck at the appearance of an accommodation So far short of their Expectation." Northern Indians vented their disgust with Britain in a nativistic insult: "It was an act of cruelty and injustice that Christians *only* were capable of doing, that the Indians were incapable of acting so." Southern Creek and Cherokee Indians called the news a "Virginia Lie," but when it proved true, they showed their frustration with Great Britain. McGillivray, writing in the name of the "Chiefs of the Creek, Chickasaw and Cherokee Nations," decried the Treaty of Paris for its disregard of the Indians. The combined peoples protested that "as we were not partys, so we are determined to pay no attention to the Manner in which the British Negotiators has drawn out the Lines." With apparent sarcasm, he added that the Indians had done nothing to give the British king any claim to their lands, "unless fighting by the side of his soldiers in the day of battle and Spilling our best blood in the Service of his Nation can be deemed so."[2]

Chickamauga activity in the service of pan-Indian unity hardly faltered with the suspension of British-American hostilities. In March 1783, fifty Chickamaugas traveled toward Detroit to request British assistance against "the Rebels." Along the way, they rested at Shawnee villages. Throughout the spring of 1783, other militant Cherokee bands, who had resided for some years with the Shawnees and Mingos in the Ohio country, disregarded a British "Proclamation of Peace" and went out against the Anglo-Americans. Joined by their militant northern comrades, they harassed the new republic's borders.[3] These resident Cherokees provided their Shawnee hosts with mediators useful in future Shawnee diplomacy in the South. Militant Shawnee diplomats sent "war hatchets" westward and southward in early 1784. They asked the Chickamaugas to join them the following spring in convening a pan-Indian council at Chickamauga Town. The Shawnees promised to visit all "the red people, and make everything straight and strong." They then proceeded further south to the Creek country.[4]

Among the Creeks they must have felt at home. There they had relatives, the Southern Shawnees, members of the Creek confederacy. They also encountered a sympathetic desire for widespread Indian alliances. Our best source on Creek politics in this period, McGillivray himself, saw Indian unity as an extension of strategies employed by the Indians during the Revolution; he felt unity would be strongest when backed by European supplies. McGillivray wrote to the commander of Spanish Pensacola, Arturo O'Neil, that by allowing British traders to work among the Creeks, Spain kept "up the formidable Indian Confederacy of the late war against the Americans," which "must always be a great check on the States in preventing their ambitious designs of possessing themselves of all the western Countrys." The Creek leader understood that his requests for Spanish assistance paralleled the efforts of the northerners among the British: "While these [southern] Nations Continue to receive the Same Support of Trade and Encouragement through the Floridas as the English Nation afford the Northern Indians from Canada the Indians will never Solicit the Friendship or the Alliance of the Americans." The Spanish agreed, permitting an effective, well-supplied British company to work the Spanish Gulf in violation of the Spanish Empire's regular practice, hoping, at McGillivray's urging, to maintain a Native American buffer against the United States. Demonstrating that he could think intertribally, McGillivray cooperated in the extension of the British company's trade to the Chickamaugas.[5]

These Creek, Chickamauga, and Shawnee maneuvers alarmed the Americans. In the fall of 1785, American agents feared that McGillivray had effectively designed "a dangerous confederacy between the several Indian nations, [and] the Spaniards and British agents, with whom he is connected." The Americans worried that the explosive mixture of their own "disorderly citizens," the Indians' militant alliances, and the Europeans' monarchical machinations would detonate with furious effect.[6]

By the end of 1785, Chickamauga Cherokees and militant Creeks had renewed their connections and secured European supplies. Militant Shawnees had also repaired networks with both their confederates in the North and their relatives in the South, still drawing supplies from British posts and traders. No state of full-scale war existed between any of these peoples and the United States, but deep resentment over American claims to Indian lands made true peace unlikely in the winter of 1785–86.

Killing the Neutrals

Militants ignored the Paris Treaty that had ignored them, and warfare resumed after 1786, to continue with vigor until 1794. Factions among all peoples opposed the renewal of war but they failed to maintain that opposition beyond 1788, and that failure meant a consolidation of militancy. The failure resulted from a pattern of forces and events strikingly similar to those that had destroyed the neutrality of predominantly Delaware Coshocton in the late years of the American Revolution. Peace factions willing to sign treaties to placate the United States found themselves offended and alarmed by Anglo-American violence. The republic's citizens, coveting their Indian neighbors' lands, managed to alienate most of the republic's Indian supporters, leaving the militants with the initiative in Indian councils.

Among the Shawnees, a neutralist leader, Malunthy, arose in the late Cornstalk's band, the Mequashake Shawnees. Supported by few of his people, he marked the "Treaty of the Mouth of Miami" in January 1786. This doubtful commitment was ignored by most Shawnees, particularly those outside the Mequashake band. Shawnee parties, in alliance with a "banditte of desperadoes under the name of Mingoes and Cherokees," raided the frontier as Shawnee militants argued north and south for a continuation of the war.[7]

Facing these raids, Kentuckians lashed back with poor discrimination. It is perhaps more fitting than ironic that they ravaged towns belonging for the most part to the Mequashake neutrals. The Kentuckians, riding into the towns at harvest time in 1786, found them abandoned. In an episode that reveals the occasional warmth of personal relations across a frontier too often brutal, a Kentucky volunteer had deserted, sped off, and warned the Indians of the army's approach. Only Malunthy, waving in one hand the disputed treaty and in the other "the thirteen stripes," met the troops—who killed him.[8]

Malunthy's fate and the fate of the smoldering Mequashake villages became lessons in the course of unity. By the end of 1786, the northern Indians were ready to declare that "any cession of our lands should be made in the most public manner, and by the united voice of the confederacy." The northern Indian manifesto insisted that the Americans restrain all surveyors "from crossing the Ohio." Participants in this council included members of the Six Nations, Wyandots, Delawares, Shawnees, Ottawas, Chippewas, Potawatomis, Miamis, "Wabash Confederates," and, not incidentally, the militant Chickamauga Cherokees.[9]

Cherokees faced far more powerful divisions over the question of resistance to Anglo-Americans than did the Shawnees in the early 1780s. The most significant division separated the Chickamauga militants from the Cherokees proper.[10] The Cherokee neutralists, under the leadership in the 1780s of Old Tassel, found themselves under intense pressure to cede lands to a group of backcountry citizens, and very effective fighters, attempting to form a new state to be called Franklin. Phony treaties between Franklin and various Cherokee chiefs, followed by raids and counterraids, marred relations, but Tassel consistently turned to Congress in his efforts to resist Franklin's threat to Cherokee lands. When militia invaded in 1788, the unarmed Tassel met them at the town of Chilhowee and attempted to negotiate. Militia officer John Kirk, who had recently lost eleven relatives to militant Indian raids, and who now styled himself a "Captain of the Bloody Rangers," was in no talking mood. Wielding a tomahawk, Kirk killed Tassel.[11] The killing convinced any remaining neutralists among the Cherokees of the futility of negotiations with either the Franklinites or Congress.[12] During the summer and fall of 1788, the neutralist Cherokees joined their militant Chickamauga kin in a united war against the Americans.

The bizarre pattern of American aggression against the most moderate of Indians also shaped attitudes in the Creek country. Creeks emerged from the Revolution strongly divided over their policy toward the new states. One cluster of factions favored military alliances with both Spain and the militant Indians to the north, while another favored accommodation with both Georgia and the United States. Two prominent Creeks who had stood for good relations with the United States during the Revolution continued to do so: the "Tallassee King" (an Upper Creek, also known as the "Tame King") of the town of Tallassee and the "Fat King" of the Lower Creek town of Cusseta. To accommodate the Georgians following the Treaty of Paris, the two leaders signed away extensive lands in "treaties" of 1783 and 1785. They did so against the wishes of many Upper and Lower Creeks. The rising leader McGillivray repudiated the cessions. McGillivray and his anti-American party claimed that all Creeks possessed the disputed lands equally with the Tallassees and Cussetas; chiefs of the latter towns thus had no right to dispose of those lands without the consent of the entire Creek confederacy.[13]

To illustrate the point, militants attacked the Fat King's property, burning his house, killing his cattle, and destroying his family's garden. Across the Tallapoosa River from the neutralist-led town of Tallassee, at the village of Tuckabatchee, representatives from ninety-eight Creek settlements met in the spring of 1785 to denounce the Georgia deals. In the

Hopthole Mico,
or the Tallassee King of the Creeks

This important Creek leader leaned toward the United States between the outbreak of the Revolution and 1788, when he aligned with his erstwhile foe, Alexander McGillivray. The print is from a sketch by John Trumbull, and appeared in
Trumbull's autobiography. It was executed when the chief visited New York with
McGillivray in 1790. (*Source:* National Anthropological Archives, Negative No.
1169-L-4, Smithsonian Institution, Washington, D.C.)

coming years, the militant Creeks repeatedly notified the state legislature that Tallassee King and Fat King "have no authority to cede lands."[14]

Georgia resorted to desperate measures. At first, these seemed innocent enough. Georgia's commissioners requested that a council be held with the Creeks at Shoulderbone Creek on October 15, 1786. Once again, of Creek chiefs of stature, only the Tallassee King and Fat King, who was not willing to be intimidated by Creek actions already taken against him, appeared. This time, however, the Georgians had no wish to settle for a treaty with the two leaders alone. They sought to force the Creeks into sending a full representation. They took the Tallassee King, Fat King, and their followers hostage. Armed Georgians confined the neutralist Creeks, setting one warrior free to bring Georgia's demands to the Creek council. Georgia demanded that Creeks accept the disputed cessions as valid. Georgia required the Creeks to return all the booty they had taken in raids against the state. Georgia insisted that the Creeks give "satisfaction for all the murders that they committed on their citizens last summer." Most important, Georgia demanded that Mad Dog, "King and Chief of the whole nation," come to negotiations.[15] But the Georgians blundered, injuring their only friends. Mad Dog, McGillivray, and the Creek Council called the bluff. Of the hostage neutralists, the militants claimed that "their detention gives no Concern to us & their friends [the Americans] are Welcome to keep them as long as they chuse." By spring, Georgia released all Creek hostages without achieving a single demand.[16]

The hostage incident at Shoulderbone Creek forced the neutralists to reconsider their relationship with the Americans. Georgia Commissioner James White visited the Creeks at Coweta as the freed hostages returned to their villages. He had the good fortune to attend a "general congress" of the nation. Unfortunately for White, none of the Indians present, not even the very "men who had ceded the lands to the Georgians," would support Georgia's claims. When a Creek headman asked the Tallassees and Cussetas to give their opinions of the disputed treaties, the neutralists "sat immobile like sentenced criminals." The Georgian "urged them to speak, but they did not wish to answer anything."[17]

Neutralist efforts evaporated entirely in June 1787. Seeking vengeance for the recent slaying of two whites by Upper Creeks, Georgians lashed back at the first Creeks they could reach, killing thirteen of the Fat King's Cusseta townsmen. The accommodationist Fat King now insisted that Georgia execute "an equal number" of its citizens as the price of peace. Governor George Mathews refused, and Cusseta joined with the militants in war.[18] Ironically, that war advanced the cause of American unity more than it did Indian unity, for Georgia, seeking aid from other states, rapidly supported the ratification of the new federal constitution.

Like the militia at Gnadenhutten and Pittsburgh in 1782, the Kentuckians at Mequashake in 1786, and the Franklinites at Chilhowee in 1788, the Georgians had, in a sense very real to the Cussetas, killed their best friends among their Indian neighbors. The Americans' killing of neutralist supporters among the Delawares, Shawnees, Cherokees, and Creeks between 1782 and 1788 brought unprecedented opportunities to Indian militants. For years, the militant factions among the borderland peoples had been forging alliances with one another. Now militant sentiment rose, and internal divisions healed as the bonds between the borderland Indian peoples strengthened. As the United States left the confederation behind, the new constitutional government faced the specter of a pan-Indian war supported by European arms. As Richard Butler, American superintendent of Indian affairs in the Northern Department, wrote in 1787, the Indians "have laboured exceedingly to form a general confederacy among themselves from North to South in order to become formidable, and as far as they are capable of being bound to each other I believe they are." Butler understood that this development boded for "a general war, *with European supplies and friends*," that would "give a severe shock to our frontier."[19]

The healing of the Indians' internal differences, a cauterization of wounds under the heat of American attacks, coincided with the laborings of pan-Indian militants. The American killing of neutralists temporarily kept the United States from exploiting Indian divisions. In later years, the federal government would successfully exploit such divisions by working effectively with "agency" or "annuity" chiefs. But as the federal government came into being between 1787 and 1789, a remarkable unity of purpose bound borderland Indians from the Gulf of Mexico to the Great Lakes.

1783–1790: Persistent Spirituality

As during the American Revolution, the cooperation of nativist and accommodationist muted religious nativism, but religious expression, often tinged with nativist sentiment, did find its way into the historical record. From the beginning of the period, when Indians first learned to their horror of the Treaty of Paris, many, nativists among them, responded to the crisis in sacred terms.

One group of Ohioan Shawnees, accompanied by Cherokees, asked the Six Nations to support their resistance, declaring that the land the British had ceded to the Americans was the "Gift of the Great God who made all things to us." A Cherokee in another quarter, Chief Tassel, bargained with Americans, with some success, at the Treaty of Hopewell in 1785, announcing that "I am made of this earth, on which the great man above placed me, to possess it. . . . This land we are now on, is the land we were fighting for, during the late contest, and the great man made it for us to subsist upon."[20] Neither statement is strictly nativist, but both convey the traditional sense of order, the reluctance to violate place, that nativism drew upon. At the very least, they indicate the continued importance of Indian spirituality.

Led in part by so Anglicized an individual as McGillivray, few such sentiments entered formal negotiations in the Creek country. McGillivray was no nativist. But McGillivray's influence went only as deep as his support in the nation. He had a strong ally in Mad Dog, a sometime militant with a strong traditional claim to Creek leadership. Like McGillivray, Mad Dog vigorously opposed the Anglo-American advance. But he could do so in nativist terms. While young McGillivray had been in an English school in Charleston in the early 1770s, Mad Dog, leader of the town of Tuckabatchee, had been conjuring and arguing in council against allowing British traders to bring their cattle into the towns. By the spring of 1786 Mad Dog presided, perhaps as chief speaker, over a Creek national council. In a culture in which heredity played only a part in the selection of leaders, in which prestige counted as well, Mad Dog's record as a traditional shaman did not cost him leadership. His ally McGillivray considered the "Famous Mad Dog" the most important of Creek "Chiefs of Consideration."[21]

Mad Dog, like Pontiac before him or Tecumseh in later years, countenanced cooperation with European powers who would supply arms. The Spanish considered him "very friendly." Arturo O'Neil once gave him "four hundred pounds of Powder and eight hundred of Balls of Trade, so that he and his warriors may defend themselves from Bears and other fierce Animals," by which, perhaps following Indian usage, he meant Americans.[22] Mad Dog welcomed Spanish assistance, and in McGillivray he found an able intermediary. McGillivray, too young to gain the position of peace chief and too poor a warrior to take that avenue to leadership, found in Mad Dog traditional sanction for his own prominence in Creek affairs.

It is not certain that Mad Dog continued to act as a shaman in the 1780s, but the Creeks in general expressed deep religious sentiments. William Bartram reported at the end of the decade that the Creeks and Cherokees would "judge any man to be out of his reason that should doubt of" the immortality of the soul. He noted that while these Indians differed from Christians in attributing a "spirit or soul" to each animal, their belief in "rewards and punishments in a future state" compared very roughly with Christian belief. Far from being despiritualized by their encounters with Europeans, the Creeks and Cherokees continued to "relate [an] abundance of stories of men that have been dead or thought dead for many hours and days, who have revived again, giving an account of their transit to and from the world of souls. . . . And these people have always returned to life with doctrines and admonitions tending to encourage and enforce virtue and morality."[23] These spiritual travelers clearly resembled, in stark outline, both the historical prophets and the mythological travelers to the sky world. This "abundance of stories" provided the models for the Creek, Seminole, and Cherokee prophets of the early nineteenth century.

Other reports confirm the strength of Creek ceremonialism in the 1780s and early 1790s. American traveler John Pope, independently of Bartram, concluded that the Creeks displayed scrupulous religiosity. French adventurer Louis Le Clerc de Milford, among the Creeks throughout much of the 1780s, later reported their dedication to the Green Corn Ceremony, at which the shaman "kindles the new fire and administers the new war medicine."[24] As during the Revolution, Creek warriors and counselors adjusted their activities around this central ritual in the Creek calendar, believing that it worked to secure sacred power for the peoples of the confederacy. Even the worldly McGillivray seems to have accepted its importance. Writing to O'Neil, he once reported that only after the towns had finished the rite would they respond to Georgia's aggressions. In unconscious agreement, Benjamin Fishbourne of Georgia wrote from Fort Augusta that he believed war would follow the ceremony. Two years later, McGillivray called the period following the Green Corn Ceremony the "fittest time to meet" with American commissioners for a treaty.[25] Creek sacred power would then be at its height.

Much then remained of Creek rituals of power, even beneath the avowedly Machiavellian—a term he understood—leadership of McGillivray. His reference to the Italian thinker came on the eve of his most controversial mission: the negotiation of a treaty with the United States in New York. There, in the summer of 1790, he signed the first treaty to be ratified by the U. S. Senate. It was an inauspicious beginning. Georgia objected to the treaty, for though it included a Creek cession of disputed lands already settled by Georgians (who would, in any case, have been very difficult for the Creeks to dislodge), it did not recognize Georgia's claims in full, leaving the Creeks with the hope of federal support and Georgia with but half a loaf. Nor were all Creeks convinced that the treaty was in their interests, for certain articles suggested foul play. The treaty had several secret provisions. These gave McGillivray and his chief followers federal commissions and salaries, the sums of which rumors exaggerated. Spanish officers and British traders, additionally, feared the loss of their Creek allies, and worked against the arrangement with the United States, while militant Indians feared it was a surrender. Under such pressures, McGillivray soon symbolically broke with the Treaty of New York, although he never repudiated it openly. After accepting and distributing the first installment on the American salaries, he sent word to the United States that he would accept no more, and he never allowed the boundary of the ceded lands to be surveyed. McGillivray learned that he had strayed too far from Creek wishes. In diplomacy as in religion, though it may have disagreed with his Charleston education, McGillivray attended to the beliefs and wishes of his followers. By 1792, he and the Creeks had drifted back toward cooperation with the militants.[26]

Far to the north, Shawnees also looked to the spirit worlds for assistance, and like the Creeks, they adhered to their Green Corn Ceremony.[27] But more striking among the Shawnees was the warrior society described by their young captive, Mary Moore. Captured in 1784, the girl encountered "a sort of association called the 'Powwow Brothers.'" The all-male society met frequently and secretly. In that year, the society related to the village a terrifying encounter with the Great Spirit, an encounter that resembled the more intensely nativistic visions of earlier and later periods.

While the warriors met in their cabin, the Great Spirit appeared. Oddly, he remained a small presence, at first "not larger than a man's hand." Then he grew until he "got to be the size of a boy twelve years old." The little presence, the Creator, declared his anger with the Indians "for forsaking the ways of their fathers. In former times, their paths were marked with the tracks of men and dogs; now only with the tracks of horses. They were more proud, and less kind."[28] Bewailing the Indians' departure from proper ways, the vision reverberated with nativist thought. Such internal criticism reflected changes in Shawnee society, changes brought about not so much by uniform "despiritualization" as by an intensified conflict between nativists, who self-consciously sought to raise religious sensibilities in defense of Indian autonomy, and proponents of accommodation, who sought more material forms of power. This conflict was muted but not stifled by the great possibilities of cooperation in the 1780s and 1790s. Early in the latter decade, while Shawnees continued to correspond with militant Creek and Cherokee warriors to the south, and while they firmed up their confederacy in the Northwest, shamans among the Shawnees would amplify their nativistic message.

Unity at the Glaize, 1792

On September 30, 1792, two Shawnees and two Miamis stood amid a council of the gathered Indian nations at a watered plain, the Glaize, near what is now Defiance, Ohio. The four Indians walked silently among the seated representatives, pausing to present "the end of a Calumet to each Person . . . which they smoked." The ceremony took some time, for the nations attending included "Delawares, Shawnees, Miamis, Chippewas, Ottawas, Hurons, Munseys, Conoys, Mohikons, Potawatomies, Cherokees, Creeks, Sacs, Reynards," and "Mingoes of the Glaize." When all had smoked, Messquakenoe, or Painted Pole, the Shawnee speaker, rose to admonish the multitude to listen attentively.[29]

The Glaize provided a perfect setting for the council. Recently settled by refugees from American attacks in southern Ohio, the Glaize became, according to its historian, Helen Hornbeck Tanner, the "headquarters for the militant Indian Confederacy protesting American advance northwest of the Ohio River." Like the Susquehanna region of the 1740s and the Upper Ohio of the 1760s, the Glaize sheltered about two thousand refugees of different Indian peoples facing similar problems. Such regions became fertile seedbeds for pan-Indian sentiment.[30]

Painted Pole opened the conference with strong expressions of unity, tinged with religious meaning: "This is the day which the great Spirit has appointed." Drawing on developing notions of Indian identity and separateness from white people, the Shawnee stressed that the meeting was for "the good of all nations of our colour." On the second day of the conference, he emphasized the strength of the western confederacy. Holding strings of wampum he said, "All these Speeches in my hands, are from different nations, assuring us of their support." He explained that the Cherokee and Creek delegates had "come in consequence of our Speeches, to assure us their Nations will unite with us." The Indian confederacy, centered north of the Ohio, would in turn send messengers to "the Southern & Western Nations" to inform them of its strength.

A Delaware rose, giving Painted Pole a strong second. His name was Buckongahelas. He had been urging resistance to Anglo-American territorial expansion since the early years of the Revolution. "Don't think because the Shawanoes only have spoken to you, that it was their sentiments alone, they have spoken with the sentiments of all the Nations." The gathered Indians, he added, were "animated by one Mind, one Head, one Heart." Five days later, Painted Pole recited recent American attempts to break the Delawares and Wyandots from the confederacy, "that we might not act as one Man." But the good peoples had put the American "Speeches at their backs and we then united as one Nation."[31]

Painted Pole had reason to speak with such confidence. Remarkable unity had been achieved. We have already seen that pan-Indian sentiment had for a generation produced meetings of northerners and southerners. With the collaboration of neutralists with militants in the late 1780s, the pace of diplomacy between the Great Lakes and the Gulf of Mexico accelerated. One such meeting took place in the Creek nation. The "great Meeting," at the Creek town of Little Tallassee in May 1787 included "chiefs of the Iroquois, Hurons, Mohacks, Oneidas & Shawnise, on the part of the Northern Confederacy." Chickamaugas also attended. The Indians agreed to unite their armies "for a general defense against all Invaders of Indian rights," and to meet again in November.[32]

Cooperative military ventures attended by members of different nations abound in the record of the late 1780s. American settlers in the Cumberland region stood as particular targets for joint Creek, Cherokee, and Shawnee expeditions. American boats on the Tennessee and Cumberland rivers became especially vulnerable.[33] Cherokees and Shawnees struck together at Americans in the Northwest and at American vessels on the Ohio.[34]

In 1792, the year of the meeting at the Glaize, Chickamaugas, Creeks, and Shawnees launched their most concerted efforts. Shawnees took the initiative in these actions. Following the northerners' defeat of Arthur St. Clair in November 1791, Shawnees sent emissaries southward. The previous history of Shawnee relations with southern peoples virtually guaranteed that the emissaries would find the nations hospitable. American David Craig reported in March 1792 that "some Shawnees are settled" at the Chickamauga town of Running Water on the Tennessee River, a "common crossing place for the Creeks." The same was true at Nickajack, also on the Tennessee. Farther south, among the Creeks, the Shawnee emissaries would still find a resting place with the Southern Shawnees.[35]

The emissaries traveled through the Chickamauga and Creek towns in 1792. They invoked the names of both the late Chickamauga leader Dragging Canoe and of the still living and active Alexander McGillivray in their efforts to form alliances. They threatened that "they should consider all Indians their enemies who did not join them." They promised to wage "war with the American States, as long as any of them should live." The southerners received them well. At the Chickamauga towns of Running

Water and Lookout Mountain, Creeks joined Shawnee and Chickamauga residents in scalp dances as they ritually prepared to attack the encroaching settlers of Cumberland. Even the Spanish indicated their favorable inclination toward, indeed privately claimed credit for, the Indians' "defensive confederation."[36]

Long before the Shawnees finished their mission, David Craig had become convinced that the Chickamaugas and Creeks "will join the Shawanese in a war." Receiving Craig's warning, the southwestern territorial governor, William Blount, agreed that his frontiers were imperiled. The American secretary of war, Henry Knox, who had long hoped to confine his army's activities to the Old Northwest, found it "really painful to reflect, after all our efforts for peace with the southern Indians, that affairs in that quarter are so critical. It would seem from representations, that a few more sparks would light up a pretty general flame."[37] Throughout the summer and fall of 1792—as the Shawnees returned northward with southern emissaries to hearten northern confederates at the Glaize—Shawnee, Chickamauga, and Creek warriors invaded the Cumberland settlements.[38]

Nativism at the Glaize, 1792

Painted Pole thus opened the Glaize meeting against a background of cooperation among Indians from the Great Lakes to the Gulf of Mexico. The Shawnee speaker found the prospect of continued pan-Indian concert so pleasing that he pointed to the southern delegates four times in the course of his speeches. Creek and Cherokee participation meant more than assistance for the northerners in their efforts to throw back the Americans, it meant also the returning favor of the Great Spirit. The Indians, Painted Pole argued, had recaptured sacred power.

On October 7, he offered an interpretation of events, an interpretation that he considered the belief of "all the Nations as far as the setting of the Sun, as well as to the Southern deputies." Referring to the confederacy's recent victories over American armies, the Shawnee attributed Indian successes "to the great Spirit who governs all things and who looks on us with as much or perhaps more compassion than those of a fairer complexion."

Painted Pole did not limit his nativism to the notion that the Master of Life favored the Indians. He also attacked the American diplomats' promises to "civilize" the Indians. His people had learned, from papers captured during a recent battle, that the Americans intended to drive away enemy Indians, and to transform the cultures of those Indians who cooperated with them. Americans would force Indian men to take "Hoes in their hands to plant corn," and would "make them labour like their beasts, their

oxen & their Packhorses." These American attempts both to alter traditional economic arrangements and to enslave the Indians failed, the Shawnee argued, because the "Great Spirit," favoring Indian goals, "was good
enough to assist us, to throw them on their backs."[39]

The Indians had first thrown the Americans "on their backs" at the
nearby Miami towns in October 1790, in their victory over Josiah Harmar.
Receiving news of General Harmar's advance, Shawnee warriors under
Blue Jacket and Miamis under Little Turtle had drawn support from Delawares, Potawatomis, Chippewas, and Ottawas. It "is astonishing," wrote
a British observer as the Indians rallied, "with what spirit and alacrity the
Indians at this place, prepare to go to the assistance of their friends." In
two engagements on October 19 and October 22, the Indians cast the
American forces into confusion, killing or capturing 108 soldiers, costing
the Americans 500 horses, and forcing the invaders to retreat.[40]

Harmar's defeat profoundly disturbed the western borders of the
United States. Anglo-American settlements in western Pennsylvania,
western Virginia, Kentucky, and the Cumberland reeled under new Indian
assaults while the settlers, already suspicious of the conflict "between their
interest, and those of the marine states," grew indignant at the ineffec-
tiveness of the newly constituted government.[41]

American forces seemed even less effective the following year, when
the Indians once again threw the soldiers "on their backs." The northerners' extraordinary defeat of General Arthur St. Clair would remain
throughout the republic's history as the most lethal battle for U.S. soldiers
fighting American Indians. The commander himself, a seasoned veteran of
the struggle against Britain, called it "as warm and as unfortunate an
action as almost any that has been fought."[42] St. Clair's 1,400 troops advanced twenty-nine miles north of Fort Jefferson, the American post deep-
est in Indian Country. On November 4, a half hour before sunrise, a
smaller force of Indians struck the already wakened camp. Miamis, Shawnees, Delawares, Potawatomis, Ottawas, Chippewas, Wyandots, Mingos,
and Cherokees quickly shattered American resistance. The soldiers broke
ranks, threw away their arms, and ran a treacherous marathon to the safety
of Fort Jefferson, which the survivors reached that evening. Not 500 of
these were unharmed. Of the remaining, 630 soldiers were killed, captured, or missing, the rest wounded. Casualties amounted to well over half
of St. Clair's force. Not one of the expedition's targets had been destroyed,
unless one counts the 20-odd Indian dead and the 40 wounded.[43]

Immediately following the battle, the warriors cleared and established
a "large painted Encampment between one Quarter & half mile in
Length" in which to celebrate their victory. They stripped and painted "all

the small saplings" with "Hieroglyphicks." The "General colour was red," signaling victory and life.[44] Oliver Spencer, a captive among the Shawnees during this period, more fully describes the importance of spirituality to the fighting northerners in the wake of St. Clair's defeat. The Shawnees of Spencer's and neighboring villages found religious guidance in Coocoochee, a Mohawk woman who dwelt among them. They consulted her "before going on any important war expedition." Her neighbors esteemed her most for her "powerful incantations and her influence with the good spirits." In 1792, about fifty Shawnee warriors consulted Coocoochee about what success would come of their expedition. The woman entered her cabin, performed her incantations with "a low humming sound of the voice," and returned "with a countenance unusually animated," assuring the warriors of victory.

Coocoochee not only divined, she also preached in the language of nativism. She decried the arrival of the Europeans, "their increasing strength and power, their insatiable avarice, and their continuing encroachments on the red men." She feared that the Indians "were no longer powerful." Not only had they been "reduced by diseases," but they had been "thinned by civil wars." To explain these misfortunes, Coocoochee "spoke of the anger of the Great Spirit against the red men, especially those of her own nation, nearly all of whom had perished." Although Spencer did not record any direct claim by Coocoochee that the Great Spirit's anger stemmed from the Indians' willful association with Anglo-Americans, such an interpretation is suggested by her singling out of "her own people," the Mohawks, as special objects of the Great Spirit's wrath. She may have identified the Mohawks with Brant, who moved in these years toward compromise and negotiation with the Americans.[45]

Spencer heard another venerated Shawnee explicitly connect the Indians' loss of sacred power to Indian misdeeds. This speaker also attributed the revival of the Indians' martial prowess to an advent of sacred power: "Their late victories over the whites, particularly their signal defeat of St. Clair, were evidences of the returning favor of the Great Spirit." Notably, the annual Green Corn Ceremony provided the setting for this expression of nativism.[46]

A Stockbridge Indian and an accommodationist, Captain Hendrick Aupaumut visited the Glaize to attend the meetings in 1792. He discovered powerful sentiments against treating with the United States. Militants told Aupaumut, himself a literate Congregationalist, that American proposals to "civilize" the Indians held little attraction in the wakes of the Americans' late murders of neutrals. And even if the Indians were to trust the federal government, they knew of tensions within the republic; they knew of the capital's inability to control the frontier: "they urge that the United States could not govern the hostile Big Knives—and that they the Big Knives, will always have war with the Indians." Aupaumut also noted the strength of ceremonialism among the confederates. When the Shawnees held "a great frolick, according to the old Custom" that August, Delawares, Miamis, and "outcast Cherokees" attended.[47]

To the south, Cherokees and Chickamaugas understood northern nativism. A few months before the Glaize meeting, the Cherokee Little Nephew requested, in the language of separatist theology, that the United States remove white trespassers from Cherokee lands. Although he would not go so far as those who argued that different gods had made whites and Indians, he did claim that the one Creator made the Indians first, and that they had "raised the whites."[48]

Richard Justice, a Chickamauga conjuror, meanwhile, led the militants in ceremonies at Lookout Mountain. When two of the war leaders, Turtle at Home and the Glass, returned to the Chickamauga towns with several scalps, "Richard Justice and the Glass took the scalp of the man and tore it with their hands and teeth, . . . as did, also, the warriors generally, with all the forms, gestures, and declarations, of a war dance." At about the same time, Dragging Canoe's brother returned from the northern Indian confederacy, bringing with him a captive white child, symbolic of northern cooperation with the Chickamaugas. One week later, the militant Cherokees prepared to appeal to the sacred powers for aid with the Eagle Tail Dance.[49]

Militant ceremonialism, so evident among the Shawnees and strongly suggestive among the Chickamaugas, pervaded the Creeks. For example, at the heart of the Busk, the most important Creek ceremony, lay a strongly nativistic element. The "new fire," symbolic of both the presence of the Great Spirit and of annual regeneration, had to be kindled by traditional methods—the flint and steel of the Europeans seeming impure. The drinking and vomiting of black drink, practices that had spread from the southeast to the Delawares in the mid-eighteenth century, continued among the Creeks in the 1790s. Described as having "an appearance of a religious nature," the ceremony purified the bodies and minds of chiefs assembling for council and transformed the nature of warriors.[50]

Creeks continued especially to invoke sacred powers through war ceremonies during this turbulent period. In their war bundles, or "War Medicine," Milford wrote, "They have such faith . . . that it would be difficult for a Grand War Chief to turn his army to account if the warriors were deprived of it." In 1792, John Pope recorded Creek notions regarding battle deaths. Creek Warriors, he wrote, avoided the "Ghosts of their departed

Heroes who have unfortunately lost their Scalps or remain unburied." These ghosts, unavenged, were "refused Admittance to the Mansions of Bliss," and they would forever wander "in the dreary Caverns of the Wilderness."[51]

The strength of ceremonialism contributed to the formation of a non-traditional but nonetheless nativistic Indian identity. The intensification of diplomacy and military cooperation among the peoples encouraged both the exchange of religious notions and the mutual recognition of cultural similarities among emissaries and hosts. The emerging Indian identity, combined with the successes scored by cooperative military ventures, supported the militants' hopes for pan-Indian struggle against the Americans. Painted Pole vividly expressed those hopes when he claimed, at the Glaize in 1792, that the Great Spirit favored the Indians once more.

Pan-Indian Action: Willstown and Buchanan's Station, 1792

On the very day that Painted Pole opened the meeting at the Glaize, a combined force of Creeks, Cherokees, and Shawnees descended upon Buchanan's Station, not far from Nashville. Plans for the raid had materialized in a council at Willstown, a Chickamauga community along a tributary of the Coosa River, the waters of which flowed from Chickamauga country south through the Creek nation into the Alabama River and from thence to the Gulf of Mexico at Mobile. Also along the Coosa, between Willstown to the north and the predominantly militant Upper Creek villages to the south, lay the seat of the Southern Shawnees. Under the leadership of Black Dog, these Shawnee members of the Creek confederacy had recently welcomed Northern Shawnee emissaries and now prepared to accompany them in war. They secured the support of most of the Upper Creek towns and a few of the Lower.[52]

Having smoked with the Creeks, the Shawnee delegation departed for the Chickamauga Council at Willstown. Before their arrival, the Chickamauga militant, Little White Owl, who had fought beside northerners at St. Clair's defeat, requested that the Cherokees proper (the Overhills and Valley towns) send him a northern Indian war pipe that had been given to the Cherokees years before. Perhaps this was the "hatchet" that had passed to the Cherokees in 1770. Little White Owl learned that Cherokee neutralists had destroyed the ceremonial object. He had a pipecarver fashion a replica, for he needed something "to show to the Northwards."[53]

This insistence on ceremony suited the atmosphere of the ensuing conference, which had been scheduled to coincide with the Chickamauga Green Corn Ceremony. Three entire nights of dancing interspersed the talks. During one of these dances the warriors made ritual attack on the United States. Four hundred to five hundred gunmen—armed, painted black, and stripped to their breech cloths in the cool autumn night— danced a "war dance around the flag of the United States," during which "many of them fired balls through the flag."[54]

Having finished the arrangements, the militants attacked Buchanan's Station. Territorial Governor William Blount estimated the size of the force at some four to five hundred Creeks, two hundred Chickamaugas and Cherokees, and thirty to forty Shawnees. The expedition stood as a tribute to Indian cooperation, a union of Indians from Ohio to Alabama. But it also demonstrated the seriousness of the Cherokees' reemerged internal divisions, for while youthful Cherokee warriors joined their Chickamauga cousins, Cherokee leaders in the older parts of the nation betrayed them and exposed them to danger by warning Blount of the attack.[55]

Meeting a prepared foe, the Indians met defeat. They had hoped, after taking the station, to drive the settlers from Nashville and then turn to Powell's Valley. Instead, they not only failed to destroy the post, but saw their Chickamauga leader, John Watts, seriously wounded, and fifteen of their number, including a chief named "Shawnee Warrior," killed.[56]

Damaging though this defeat was to the Indian cause, the effort against Nashville demonstrates the importance of Shawnee communication with the Creeks and Chickamaugas in the late 1780s and early 1790s, a communication that influenced the future militant Shawnee actions under Tecumseh and the Shawnee Prophet. In the fall of 1792, when the militants mounted their siege of Buchanan's Station, and when the confederated nations north of the Ohio met at the Glaize, Tecumseh was about twenty-four years old; Lalawethika, later to be called Tenskwatawa, the Shawnee Prophet, was about seventeen. Both had already seen the Shawnees come to occupy a critical position in the advocacy of pan-Indian union. Judging from the extensive Shawnee intercourse with the Creeks and the Cherokees, the two youths must have been well schooled in notions of pan-Indianism. They must also have been exposed to notions of religious nativism, of the separate creation, and of sacred power. When, in another dozen years, the two began to emerge from the obscurity of youth to prominence in the old Northwest, they could draw on a familiar idiom in their argument for pan-Indian unity.

Defeat, 1792–1795

Despite the thrashing of the intertribal forces at Buchanan's Station, the movement for unity continued. Following the meeting at the Glaize, Painted Pole himself journeyed south to raise spirits among the Cherokees and, if possible, the Chickasaws. He remained among the southerners for two or three years. Perhaps he accompanied the Shawnees who, in the fall of 1793, convinced the Creeks to maintain the "Union in defense of their Land." Such Shawnee missions to the Creeks worried federal agents, one of whom offered to any Creek warrior "a horse-load of goods for each" Shawnee emissary kidnapped and brought to him, "or half as much for their scalp." It may be a measure of Shawnee-Creek cooperation that the agent had no takers.[57] Creeks and Chickamaugas, in turn, toured the North with their own messages of war. In mid-June 1793, the Indians described themselves in a message to the British governor of Upper Canada, John G. Simcoe, as members of "the Confederated Nations as far south as the Muskogees and as far North as the Lakes."

Militants committed to pan-Indian unity interfered with the diplomatic maneuverings of Joseph Brant in 1793. Brant was no opponent of unity, but he did seek both to insure that Mohawks were preeminent and that peace was made from strength; he argued that peace should be settled with the United States while the Indians still retained the military initiative. He proposed to the Indian confederates that they yield some lands north of the Ohio to the United States. In contact with Americans, Brant thought he had good reason to believe that the plan would meet with American approval if he could persuade the Indians to adopt it. But while brokering talks between American agents and militant Indians, his proposal was derailed by the arrival of a militant Creek delegation. The southern support convinced northern militants to hold out for the Ohio River boundary. Brant called the Creek presence the "sole cause of the abrupt termination of the negociation for peace."[58] When the American commissioners would not yield to the militant Indians' demands for an Ohio boundary, negotiations ended. The "Indian American Confederacy," in a message that included Cherokee "signatories," sent a request for arms to the British. The Indians also, in Shawnee Captain Johnny's words, looked "up to the Great God who is a Witness to all that passes here for his pity and his help."[59]

But the greatest confederate achievements had already been accomplished. The years following the Glaize meeting brought an end to the union of northern and southern Indians. Tecumseh would later endeavor to unite the peoples, but he would not equal the successes of less widely known Shawnee, Cherokee, and Creek ambassadors of the 1780s and 1790s. Most significant, he would not gain any influential Cherokee support.

The achievements of the early 1790s were undone, in part, by distant events. The new French Republic waged a war with England and Spain that strained European military resources in America. The Creeks, who depended on Spanish assistance and British trade, felt the disruptions acutely. By the summer of 1794, the Spanish attempted to convince the Creeks and Chickamaugas to "suspend all hostilities."[60] The Creeks had also lost McGillivray. This valuable broker with European powers died on February 17, 1793. Mad Dog remained at the head of the nation. Georgia, meanwhile, threatened the borderlands with new incursions.[61] More ominous, a pro-American faction among Chickasaws in what is now western Tennessee threatened the Upper Creeks with war. That contest never got beyond a few desultory raids, but the challenge to unity raised considerable concern.[62] Despite these difficulties, Creeks continued to attack the Cumberland region, only coming to terms with the Americans after their northern allies abandoned the struggle.[63]

American victories at the Chickamauga towns along the Tennessee River effectively put an end to Chickamauga militancy in 1794. Major James Ore and 550 Cumberland and Kentucky militia mounted an assault on two Chickamauga towns, Nickajack and Running Water. Surprising Nickajack on September 13, the Americans killed 70 Indians, most of them men. After the usual burning of cabins and crops, the expedition attacked the hastily abandoned town of Running Water, which it also destroyed. Coinciding with both the news of Indian defeats in the North and the Spanish withdrawal of aid, these raids brought the Chickamaugas to terms. John Watts, the leader at Willstown, met with Chief Hanging Maw and 400 warriors to sign the Tellico Blockhouse Treaty. He also urged the Chickamaugas to return to the Cherokee fold.[64] Although Cherokees remained strongly divided over the issue of accommodation with the United States, Chickamauga militancy had ended. Never again would the northern and Creek militants find strong allies among the Cherokees. The effective collapse of Cherokee militancy reduced prospects for pan-Indianism along the Eastern Woodland borderlands.

The Cherokees had little choice. Kentucky boasted a large enough population to gain statehood in 1792, Tennessee in 1796. These dense outgrowths of American settlement interfered with Shawnee-Cherokee communication. Neither could Cherokees easily retain their far-flung connections with the Spanish on the Gulf of Mexico and the British on the Great Lakes. The collapse of Cherokee militancy followed the more temporary but no less serious collapse of Indian resistance in the North.

In August 1794, Anthony Wayne's "legion" of 3,000 soldiers successfully broke Indian resistance. Armed with good artillery and cavalry, the legion opposed 1,300 warriors (some reports have it as low as 400) on August 20, 1794. While awaiting Wayne, the Indians had appealed to the sacred powers. Their spies had informed them that the legion would strike on August 18. In ritual anticipation, the warriors began "a strict fast" on the day before the expected battle. Unfortunately, the Indians' sources proved wrong. Wayne did not show, and the gunmen fasted a second full day. When their scouts reported no movement on the third day, many of the warriors rose "from their ambush in order to take some refreshment." Wayne had the good luck to strike the half-starved warriors when their force was divided at the Battle of Fallen Timbers.[65]

Although the Americans probably suffered casualties roughly equal to those of the Indians, they clearly held the victory.[66] The legion not only took the field, but took it permanently, establishing another in a chain of American posts that now ran from Cincinnati on the Ohio to Fort Wayne (Indiana) at the headwaters of the Maumee. The troops destroyed the surrounding countryside, including the extensive Indian settlements to the east at the Glaize. By spring, the Indians were "truly" starving and depended on their American enemies for food.[67]

The Indians' failure to stop Wayne marked the destruction not only of foodstuffs but of Indian hopes for British support. Although a volunteer force of perhaps two hundred French- and English-speaking Canadians had actually fought beside the Indians, they had no official recognition. With the Indians, they were turned away from British Fort Miami as they fled to its gates following the action. The British officials refused to commit themselves at this unfortunate turn, leaving the Indians "much dejected." British agent Alexander McKee recognized that the confederated peoples had "lost all hopes of the interference of the government" of Upper Canada.[68]

As the Creeks and Cherokees had lost Spanish aid in the South, so the northerners had lost British support. Soon, Jay's Treaty confirmed the loss and prompted British evacuation to Ontario. Starving, disarmed, and undoubtedly weary of twenty years of war, the northern Indians came to terms with Wayne in the Treaty of Greenville, signed over the course of the summer of 1795. The treaty marks the end not only of the war but of the twenty-year cooperation of militant nativists with Indians who trusted more in European technology than in Indian ritual, more in firepower than in sacred power. This end of cooperation became manifest in serious divisions not only among the peoples, but within them. In the coming years, certain features of the Greenville Treaty would irritate these divisions.

The treaty granted the United States sixteen "squares," of various sizes, for the establishment and maintenance of posts. It gave the United States extensive lands in southern Indiana and Illinois along the Ohio and the Wabash. Most significant, it placed in American hands all lands south and east of a line running down the Cuyahoga and Tuscarawas rivers in northeast Ohio, then westward across Ohio to the headwaters of the Miami and Fort Recovery at the headwaters of the Wabash, finally in a straight line roughly south to a spot opposite the mouth of the Kentucky River on the Ohio. This provision of the treaty, in other words, gave the Americans all of southern, central, and eastern Ohio. The Indians were left with the northwestern corner of what is now the state.

The treaty also formally institutionalized federal influence within tribal government through the creation of an annuity system. The United States promised annual payments of one thousand dollars to the Wyandot, Delaware, Shawnee, Miami, Ottawa, Chippewa, and Potawatomi "tribes"; the less numerous Kickapoo, Wea, Eel River, Piankashaw, and Kaskaskia peoples would receive "the Amount of Five Hundred Dollars each Tribe." Given to Indian leaders to distribute among their people, the annuities gave the Americans a permanent lever within a tribal power structure formalized in concurrence with federal agents.

The treaty declared an American commitment to the cultural transformation of the Indians. It inaugurated the American "civilizing" mission among the northerners, suggesting that if any tribe (meaning any recognized tribal leader) so desired, the annuity could be paid in the form of "domestic animals, Implements of Husbandry & other utensils convenient for them, and in consideration to useful artificers who may reside with or near them & be employed for their benefit." The provision fed the cause of neutrality and undermined the revolutionary-era alliance of nativism and accommodation among the defeated Indians. Abetted by American payments and convinced of the overwhelming and unchecked strength of the Americans, advocates of cultural and political accommodation with the United States gained strength among the northerners. The two most notable for our purposes among these, the Shawnee Black Hoof and the Miami Little Turtle, both signed the treaty.[69]

It is especially significant that Little Turtle came around to signing the document, for his embrace of the United States would provide an important foil for the rise of militant nativism in the next decade. In the shorter term, it is equally significant that the erstwhile enemy of the United States did not act alone. The treaty cannot be seen as a neutralist coup, for even such former militants as the Shawnees Painted Pole and Blue Jacket, and the Delaware Buckongahelas agreed to the terms. Resistance had been broken, the confederacy had fallen apart. American officials cultivated clients among native leaders.

For much of the next decade, the dream of pan-Indian union seemed dead. The resistance that had been pursued so vigorously since the 1750s seemed shattered—but for a decade at most. When the movement for unified resistance revived in 1805, it rose in the form of a nativism no longer muted by alliance with the advocates of accommodation.

The movement, for which the Shawnee Prophet and his brother Tecumseh would become the most famous exponents, received an important legacy of ideas and strategies from earlier pan-Indian efforts. Since before Pontiac, since the 1740s, when the early prophets received visions in the refugee villages along the Susquehanna, hundreds of Indians had maintained and extended networks of diplomatic and military relations, argued for pan-Indian union, redefined Indian identity, and preached the redemption of their people through the recapturing of sacred power. Once more would the fruit of their labor feed Indian resistance along the entire breadth of the Indian-American borderlands.

SIX

>>>>>>> < < < < < < <

Republican Interlude

A new order emerged in the trans-Appalachian borderlands following the defeat of pan-Indianism in the mid-1790s. Through Jay's
Treaty (1794) with Britain, which like other European-American treaties
ignored Indian possessions, the United States secured the military posts
within its territorial claims. In the Treaty of San Lorenzo (1795), Spain
recognized the American claim to lands at the core of the Creek confederacy. The influence of Britain and Spain in North America, visibly in retreat
at these treaty tables, receded still farther as truly devastating wars deranged Europe. As European power in Indian country ebbed through
diplomatic channels, American power flowed aggressively to replace it. It
flowed directly into Indian councils, where it found considerable Native
American tolerance, if not support.

Indians believing in the need for the conscious adaptation of European
ways, many of whom had been once, when armed from Europe, willing to
league with nativists against the United States, now sought to come to
terms with the republic. American agents, paid by the federal government,
worked closely with these Indian leaders. Their combined efforts promoted a mission of "civilization." Rapidly among the Cherokees but with less
success among the Creeks, Shawnees, and Delawares, the "plan of civilization," supported by the federal government and by several churches,
became rooted in tribal government.

Among all the involved peoples, however, including the republic's citizens, the civilizing mission met a thicket of difficulties. The Anglo-Ameri-

can brambles grew not only from the opposition of citizens interested in Indian lands, but also out of an intellectual seedbed sown with incompatible crops, as many scholars have shown. An essential motivation of the mission, the assumed superiority of Anglo-American culture, entangled it from the start, for the missionaries' conviction of their religious and cultural superiority alienated the targeted peoples. This was as true of non-religious agents as it was of the religious missionaries.

The secular employees of the mission, moreover, underestimated the obstacles that spread across their path, a failing that led them into tactical contradictions. Once they undertook the mission, they never adequately reconciled their aims with their methods. In what one scholar calls a "lapse in logic," these Americans sought to make good citizens out of the Indians, but employed coercion, cajolery, and deception to do so.[1] The agents were under great pressure from American governments—territorial, state, and federal—to accomplish their task, with the understanding that it would increase the land available to the republic. Governments and missionaries alike claimed that if Indian men abandoned hunting and took up the plow, they could live well, and on less land. The surplus lands would then come up for grabs. In practice the process inverted. Pressured by their land-hungry countrymen, American agents among the Indians obtained land cessions from impoverished Indians even before the successful conversion of Indian men into yeomen farmers. To justify the inversion, the mission's proponents came to argue that by restricting Indian land they restricted Indian hunting and thereby compelled Indian men to farm. The American acquisition of Indian land perversely took on a philanthropic guise; taking became giving.[2]

As early a professional historian of the era as Henry Adams noticed the moral contradictions within the civilizing mission. Adams discovered that although President Thomas Jefferson had advocated the establishment of an Indian farming class, he had sought to do so through the manipulation of Indian debt. In Adams's words, Jefferson "deliberately ordered his Indian agents to tempt the tribal chiefs into debt in order to oblige them to sell the tribal lands, which did not belong to them, but to their tribes."[3] Jefferson, that indebted foe of debt, attempted to create an independent Indian yeomanry by driving Indian leaders into the red. This contradiction, between Federal efforts to "improve" Indian economies on the one hand, while both increasing Indian indebtedness and decreasing Indian landholding on the other, placed the civilizing mission precariously upon a badly fissured foundation. The contradiction, with the others, had to be sustained; the federal government had to meet world opinion with a policy of benevolence while also meeting its citizens' desire for land.[4]

The dense undergrowth of the Indians' recent history lay violent hazards in the way of the "plan of civilization," and the most vital and stubborn of the strands took the form of prophetic nativism. Between 1795 and 1815, individual prophets and groups of Indians claiming supernatural inspiration posed direct challenges to those leaders who advocated political and even cultural accommodation to the power of the United States. Insurgent nativists drew upon their histories of intertribal cooperation. They looked to their shared beliefs in the ritual demands of power. Turning to the spirits as well as to their intertribal comrades, they attempted to rally support against those tribal leaders who ceded land to the Americans. Prophetic parties of Shawnees, Delawares, Creeks, and many others actually broke with their accommodating countrymen to prepare an intertribal, Indian union against the expansion of the United States, an effort that eventually merged with the War of 1812.

The federal agents and their fellow citizens were loath to recognize the power of prophetic nativism. They had a different explanation for Indian activity in these decades. They explained the nativists' successes by asserting, on slender evidence, that the British manipulated the prophets. So pervasive was this thesis that one ex-president and two future presidents held to it during the decade that ended in 1815. Viewed against the background of the civilizing mission, the thesis has curious ramifications.

Thomas Jefferson, writing John Adams from Monticello on the eve of the War of 1812, described the Shawnee Prophet, Tenskwatawa, as "more rogue than fool, if to be a rogue is not the greatest of all follies." Jefferson did not reveal to Adams that in 1807 he had ordered Indiana's territorial governor, William Henry Harrison, to "gain over the prophet, who no doubt is a scoundrel and only needs his price." Instead, and inexactly, Jefferson recalled to Adams that his administration left the Shawnee alone, "till the English thought him worth corruption, and found him corruptible."[5]

In Jefferson's view, which was not uncommon, Indians could be bought. Among some of Jefferson's contemporaries the belief stemmed from the notion that "savages," residing outside of civil society, could not be expected to possess public spirit, or civic virtue; among others, it was a more general understanding of human frailty in the face of monarchical power. Indian nations, in either case, without the requisite virtue, were thus subject to bribery by greater powers like Britain. The notion litters the correspondence of two prominent young republicans, soon to emerge as national heroes and later as presidents from opposing parties, William Henry Harrison and Andrew Jackson.

Harrison's correspondence from Indiana in the years that led to the War of 1812 is replete with the claim that "this said Prophet is an engine set to work by the British for some bad purpose." With monotonous repetition Harrison invoked the conviction that "the Prophet is a tool of British fears or British avarice, designed for the purpose of forming a combination of the Indians, which in case of war between that power and the United States may assist them in the defence of Canada."[6]

Harrison's mechanistic view of British relations with the prophet was convenient, for it provided a sense of urgency to his acquisitions, for the United States, of Indian land. Harrison justified the acquisitions by arranging them through the tribes' proper, that is the federally recognized, delegates. Indian claims against these leaders represented British, anti-republican machinations. Ironically, Harrison never recognized that the favors he showered upon compliant chiefs implicated him in the very corruption with which he charged Britain and Native America. Instead, he willfully bribed individual leaders into selling their people's lands while arguing with dense redundancy that Britain lay behind Indian hostility to the United States.

With less evidence at his disposal than that held by Harrison, for British agents did operate on Harrison's borders, Andrew Jackson portrayed the southern Indians, far removed from the British posts, as the automatic agents of British will. In letters to his wife he wrote that "ruthless savages" had been driven to "horrid deeds, by the infernal engines of British policy." Before Congress declared war on Britain, Jackson accused the government of Upper Canada of inciting a Creek attack on Tennessee through Tecumseh and his brother, "the tool of England." Because the impoverished, revolution-racked Spanish empire, reeling under the foreign occupation of its mother country, seemed incapable of furnishing Indians with arms from the weak garrisons in the Floridas, because the United States now possessed Louisiana, and because the British traders among the South's Indians openly supported the Americans—even after war with Britain broke out—Jackson in Tennessee was forced to strain his view to Canada to spy his British menace.[7]

The origins of the prophetic movement that would later complicate the War of 1812 lay not, despite contemporary republican declarations, in British conspiracy. They lay instead in the history of eighteenth-century militant nativism, in the intratribal conflicts that followed the collapse of general militancy in 1794, and in the continued American pressure for Native American land. The prophetic movement grew out of a religious tradition, a tradition fertilized by the Indians' discontent over their dependence upon an encroaching power. The movement grew around an established lattice of intertribal relations, and though it never achieved the breadth or complexity of earlier militancy, it raised ecstatic hopes during the last, broadly intertribal armed struggle in the Eastern Woodlands.

The Collapse of Trade

Indians had plenty of cause for discontent. Even in the brief intervals in which their lands and lives were not immediately at risk, Indians faced a complex welter of difficulties following the American victories of the mid-1790s. Those hunters who could obtain furs and skins found American trade goods difficult to come by and English trade goods either expensive or in short supply. In the last years of the eighteenth century, the European fashion demands for peltry diminished; with the Napoleonic Wars, the market shut down completely. Traders could not supply their Indian clients with goods, except at very high prices to be paid in pelts and hides, the animal bearers of which were, in turn, in short supply.[8]

Compounding the bad market for furs, in other words, was the continued pressure on the already overhunted stocks of game. In the South, from the Red River in Louisiana to the Oconee River in Georgia, officials complained in the first decade of the nineteenth century that pelts were few and "worthless." A decade earlier, it was reported in Michigan that "there is but little Beaver killed on any of the Rivers between this and the Mississippi." Of the eastern tribes, the writer continued, only the "Menominees, Sacs, and Renards brought in deerskins and raccoons, and in some years a great quantity of bears," but many of these pelts came from west of the Mississippi. Fort Wayne, the main entrept for the Shawnees, Delawares, Wyandots, Potawatomis, and Miamis, recorded its largest harvest of deerskins for the years between 1804 and 1810 in 1807. Almost seventeen hundred doeskins were traded by the summer of that year. The Indians received the equivalent in goods, or in reduction on their credit, of forty-four cents for each deerskin. Doeskins were not alone, but they amounted to the most important item in the trade. The receipts that they and the other items brought, spread among the thousands of Indians depending on the agency, could not have amounted to much. By 1810, the Great Lakes region showed very poor returns in the fur trade; by 1812, deerskins could not be traded on a profitable basis east of the Mississippi.[9]

The crisis in the hunting economy gave hope and argument to federal advocates of the civilizing mission. It also gave hope to seekers of Indian lands. As Indian indebtedness to traders and federal agencies grew, officials urged tribal leaders to sell their lands, both to remove the debt and to purchase the stock and the agricultural implements necessary for a transition to civility. The chief American agent among the southern Indians,

Benjamin Hawkins, mindful to make the argument only in response to Indian complaints of "the scarcity of game" and of the American "withdrawing of presents," advised Creek leaders both "to sell some of their waste lands to meet the present and future wants" and "to give the plan devised for their civilization a fair trial among the young and middle aged." While pressing the Creeks to cede lands, Hawkins promised both a good initial price, further annuity payments, and assistance in "civilization."[10]

The same arguments that Hawkins employed to express the benevolent intentions of the seekers of Creek lands found Senate approval in the text of a treaty made by William Henry Harrison with the Delawares. In its preamble, the 1804 treaty stated that the Delawares had found the Greenville annuities insufficient "to supply them with the articles which . . . afford the means of introducing amongst them the arts of civilized life." The Indians, the treaty asserted, were "convinced that the extensiveness of the country they possess" only gave "opportunity to their hunting parties to ramble to a great distance from their towns." To obtain the needed material goods and to restrict the rambles of their hunters, the text continued, the Delawares relinquished a portion of their claim to lands east of the Wabash. In compensation, the United States agreed to pay the Delawares "an additional annuity of three hundred dollars, which is to be exclusively appropriated to the purpose of ameliorating their condition and promoting their civilization."[11]

Six years and as many northwestern land cessions later, Harrison again linked land cessions to the civilizing mission, but with less benevolent intent. He reported to the secretary of war that, with Jefferson, he thought intensified American colonization north of the Ohio was the "best and cheapest mode of controuling the tribes, who were most exposed to the intrigues of the British." To achieve that end, "the extinguishment of the Indian Title was pushed to the extent it has been, . . . so to curtail their hunting grounds, as to force them to change their mode of life, and thereby to render them less warlike, and entirely dependent upon us." So much, then, for the development of an independent Indian yeomanry.[12]

Indian dependency—the American control of the Indian tribes through conscious economic manipulation—had become the manifest goal of the government's civilizing mission, a goal Americans justified in view of the threat posed by the Indians' dependence upon Britain. Unfortunately for the orderly vision of management conceived by the likes of Jefferson, Harrison, Hawkins, and a host of others, the Indians did not conform to the republican vision. Instead, they discovered American intentions to deprive them of land and liberty; so Harrison, at any rate, believed as he regretted that American goals had not "been so secretly kept as to escape their own or the sagacity of their British friends."[13] By 1810 Harrison's treaties had met with four years of opposition, much of it led either by the most-renowned opponents of Indian dependency, Tecumseh and his visionary brother, the Shawnee Prophet, or by their less-known, yet abundant, allies.

SEVEN

〉〉〉〉〉〉〉〈〈〈〈〈〈〈

Renewing Sacred Power
in the North

In 1794, when the United States brought down the militant bridges—
those long diplomatic spans joining Seminoles of the Gulf to Chippewas
of the Great Lakes—the collapsing fragments did not descend gracefully
into ethnic or tribal heaps. But the federal government would have had it
that way. In vain did the United States try to organize peoples beset with
internal struggles into clear administrative units. Federal agents attempted
to rationalize their control through the cooperation of men they identified
as tribal leaders, but these accommodating leaders had their own aims, and
they divided against one another as they faced increasing nativist defiance.
The nativists, meanwhile, recalled their spirited efforts toward intertribal
union, and they despised the leaders of accommodation for allowing the
United States to exercise political, economic, and cultural authority over
the Indians. They denounced the annuities that funneled wealth through
tribal leaders willing to sell Indian land. They contemplated the renewal
of an intertribal resistance movement that, they hoped, would overarch
the merely tribal factions recognized by the United States. Through all of
these postures, attitudes, and actions, the nativists attended to prophets.

Throughout the Great Lakes and what little remained to Indians of the
Ohio Valley, prophets arose, challenging Indians to reflect upon their
ways. In 1796, at a town of Munsee Delawares in Ontario, a young boy's
"apparition" encouraged the Munsees to celebrate "a great festival." The
child "reproached them" for having neglected ceremony and urged them
to revive ritual and "make it good," so that "calamity may be turned from

123

them." Three years later, across Lake Erie at the Seneca town of Buffalo Creek, a young girl's dreams compelled her to oppose the civilizing mission inaugurated among the Senecas by the Quakers. The "Devil," she warned, "was in all white people alike . . . , the Quakers were doing no good among them, but otherwise, and it was not right for their Children to learn to read and write." Her dream led Senecas to hold councils within their towns on the subject of the Quaker presence. The town that hosted the Quakers decided to ignore the girl's admonitions and allow the Friends to remain. But as Anthony F. C. Wallace finds in his study of Seneca "revitalization," other Seneca visionaries sounded similar alarms.[1]

While Seneca and Munsee villagers pondered the rise of local prophets, a Mohawk on Ontario's Grand River received word from the Great Spirit that the white-dog sacrifice, still in practice among the Senecas, should be renewed among all Iroquois nations. Word spread to the largely Christian Oneida Iroquois in New York, where a non-Christian Oneida rose to preach against hard liquor, and where a faction openly resumed what it termed the old forms of worship, including the white-dog ceremony.[2]

The most profound of the Iroquois episodes began in the late spring of 1799, when a heavy-drinking Seneca warrior, Handsome Lake, experienced visions that eventually led him to advocate serious moral and social reform. Wallace, in his elegant study of the movement, divides Handsome Lake's visions and preachments into two series: "the First, or Apocalyptic, Gospel" (1799–1801) and "the Second, or Social Gospel" (1801–14).[3] Handsome Lake's first set of visions and teachings conforms to the pattern of northwestern prophecy, so well, in fact, as to suggest an unstudied depth of common understanding, and thus, of communication, among the different peoples. This "First Gospel" fits neatly within the tradition of militant nativism, a tradition represented in the 1760s by, among others, the Delaware Prophet, Neolin, and in the 1800s by the Shawnee Prophet, Tenskwatawa. The latter, who though not the sole author of a "new religion," would become the most important Native American prophet of the early nineteenth century. At the risk of collapsing a half century into a single ritual moment, at the risk of violating linear conceptions of time that themselves run counter to predominant Native American modes, let me describe continuities that join the prophets of the 1760s both to the peaceful Handsome Lake of the turn of the nineteenth century and to the quickly ensuing messianism of Tenskwatawa and his militant allies.

An acute sense of their peoples' abominations seized Neolin, Handsome Lake, and Tenskwatawa immediately before each of their visions. Neolin sat by his fire in 1760, "greatly concrned" about his people's "evil ways." In 1799, Handsome Lake, who feared that he was "evil and loathsome," fell

THE OPEN DOOR KNOWN AS THE PROPHET,
BROTHER OF TECUMSEH

One of several prominent prophets in the Old Northwest, Tenskwatawa is here
portrayed almost twenty years after the military defeat of the movement he
supported. He lost the closed right eye early in life. Painted by George Catlin, oil
on canvas, 1830. (*Source:* National Art Gallery, 1985.66.279, Smithsonian Institution, Washington, D.C., Gift of Mrs. Joseph Harrison, Jr.)

"upon his bed sick and behold he was in a trance for nearly the space of an hour." Tenskwatawa, working among diseased Delawares and Shawnees on the White River (Indiana) in 1805, collapsed "with a deep and awful sense of his sins."[4]

Neolin and Handsome Lake, in their first visions, both met, at the doors of their dwellings, strangers who instructed them in religion. This does not seem to have happened to Tenskwatawa. Instead, Tenskwatawa's vision brought him directly on the same dazzling journey undertaken by Neolin and Handsome Lake in each of their subsequent, but by no means secondary, dreams. In "his great distress," Tenskwatawa "appeared to be travelling along a road, and came to where it forked—the right hand way he was informed led to happiness and the left to misery." Along the path of unhappiness moved "vast crowds" toward many different houses of punishment. He saw "great multitudes in each of the houses, under different degrees of judgement and misery." Several years earlier, Handsome Lake had journeyed to a similar fork, where "the spirits of the dead" were divided. "The narrow road," he found, "leads to the pleasant lands of the Creator and the wide and rough road leads to the great lodge of the punisher." Four decades before these visions, Indians reported that Neolin had discovered a fork, but in his visions there were two wide roads to hell and a difficult path to paradise.[5]

Both Handsome Lake and Tenskwatawa saw the same punishment inflicted upon the departed spirits of drunkards. In Tenskwatawa's vision, the drunkard was offered "a cup of liquor resembling melted lead; if he refused to drink it he [the tormenter] would urge him, saying: Come, drink—you used to love whiskey. And upon drinking it, his bowels were seized with an exquisite burning." Handsome Lake's drama of the inferno included a large cast of sinners whose torments approximated their misdeeds; first among them staggered the sot in his scorching cups. We do not know that Neolin had seen such suffering; we do know that he and his fellow prophets forbade the drinking of rum, an evil practice he associated with Anglo-America.[6]

Much as the Christians supplied the alcoholic ticket to hell, popular Christianity supplied much powerful imagery for these three prophets' descriptions of the place. Neolin, Handsome Lake, and Tenskwatawa all saw raging fires along the dreaded path, frighteningly evocative of the Christian inferno. As scholars have shown, there is no clear evidence that Indians had traditionally believed in an afterlife of punishment for earthly wrongdoing. Evildoers in some versions of the traditional Eastern Woodlands otherworld suffered intense isolation and loneliness; they could not dwell among their loved ones and families, who inhabited a bountiful paradise. But evil ones did not suffer direct, painful torment after their deaths. They may have experienced a fate more akin to that prophesied by "the Trout." This Ottawa, a spokesman for "the first man created by the Great Spirit," probably Tenskwatawa, warned his people in 1807 that "no Indian must ever sell rum to Indians. It makes him Rich, But when he dies, He becomes very wretched. You bury him with all his wealth, And he goes along the path of the Dead. They fall from him, He Stops to take them up, And they become dust. He at last arrives almost at the place of rest. And then Crumbles into dust himself."[7] In his attitudes toward rum, the Trout spoke with the eighteenth- and early nineteenth-century prophets, but in his descriptions of the afterlife, he differed from Neolin, Handsome Lake, and even Tenskwatawa, whose mouthpiece he claimed to be and whose hellish visions sported clear Christian influence. The Trout's view more closely resembled an older view than did those of the other visionaries.[8]

If the major prophets' hells display obvious Christian lineage, their heavens, again quite similar to one another, seem more deeply rooted in Native America. Neolin had to climb to heaven over a difficult mountain, aided by both ritual baths and stylized spiritual instructions. At the top he saw three attractive villages. Approaching one of these, he was guided to the Master of Life by a "handsome man, clothed all in white." The first thing the Master did was to order Neolin to sit on a "hat all bordered with gold." The hat, in all likelihood, represented the vices Indians had received from the Anglo-Americans. Even in the seventeenth century hats covered Europeans in native iconography.[9] In 1786 hats symbolized the citizens of the United States when the Shawnees and Delawares declared war, announcing to their western Indian neighbors that they would "destroy all the men wearing hats . . . who seem to be leagued against us to drive us away from the lands which the Master of Life has given to us."[10] In 1807 the Trout insisted that Indians not wear hats, that they avoid symbolic contamination. Neolin, then, under instructions from the Master of Life and in the Master's own abode, sat upon the emblem of Anglo-America. The gold trim, a nice touch, could only represent the characteristic that Indians most often associated with English-speaking colonists.

Handsome Lake also had to ascend a narrow path, but once in paradise, he was enveloped in the "fragrant odors of the flowers along the road." Images of loving relations overwhelmed him. His departed son, grandson, and niece—even his departed dog (truly a non-Christian concept)—greeted him in a richly inhabited land filled with "the most marvelous and beautiful things." Like the Delaware Prophet's spiritual escort, the Seneca's guide had fabulous clothes, this time of "a clear Sky Colour." Tenskwatawa left us less of his vision of heaven, but we know that the road to

paradise "was all interspersed with flowers of delicious smell." He
glimpsed heaven as a house "where everything was beautiful, sweet, and
pleasant."[11]

As the seers shared visions of heaven and hell, so they shared the call for
the deliberate renewal of ritual. The prophets of the mid-eighteenth century, including Neolin, gave ceremony a central place in their teachings.
Handsome Lake's first visions fell immediately on the heels of several
Iroquoian calls for an intensification of ceremony, and he soon added his
voice. The Great Spirit encouraged the Senecas to perform the white-dog
sacrifice as a "preventative against the Sickness," and to dance only the
"worship dance," a performance that had not yet been desecrated by
liquor. Tenskwatawa's visions came likewise about a year after a great
"feast of love and union" in the fall of 1804, at which the Indians "danced
and rejoiced before the Great Spirit and proposed to revive the religion of
their ancestors." Tenskwatawa's ceremonies, like those of his contemporary Handsome Lake, and like those of the Assinsink Munsees of 1760,
would involve public confessions, trembling, and cathartic weeping.[12]

The emphasis on the renewal of ritual, and the self-conscious selection
of certain old rituals, reflected the notion that Indian suffering stemmed
from Indian spiritual failure. The whites were not simply more powerful;
the Indians had lost power through neglect and abomination. If Indians did
not recapture the favor of sacred powers through spiritual reformation, the
prophets warned, worse lay ahead; if, on the other hand, they practiced as
they should, a dramatic change in fortune awaited them.

The apocalyptic teachings of the early nineteenth-century prophets
bore the two faces of doom and glory. A Delaware woman who had visions
in 1806 warned that if the Big House Ceremony were not celebrated with
care, a whirlwind would soon wipe out the people completely. The Trout
thought the world "broken," that it "declines." The Indians to the west of
the Ottawas would soon all "fall off and die," unless they sent deputies to
be instructed in ritual. Handsome Lake warned of a "visitation of Sickness" if his teachings were neglected. But the fear induced by such threats
was offset by the hope that came with prophetic promises. The Trout
believed that, through the power of a war-club dance, the Ottawas and
Chippewas would "distroy every white man in america." Tenskwatawa's
first visions also contained such notions, shaped in traditional myth. He
encountered a crab, a common "earth diver" in Native American creation
stories, a being that brought up the muck from which the earth was made.
The Great Spirit promised the Shawnee Prophet that if the Indians abided
by his teachings, the crab would "turn over the land so that the white

people are covered." Later Tenskwatawa indicated that Anglo-Americans were not in danger as long as they left the prophet's town at Greenville, Ohio, alone. But if the United States attempted to meet his prophecy with force, "if the white people would go to war, they would be destroyed by a day of judgement," or, according to another source, "there will be an End to the World."[13]

On the eve of the War of 1812, prophecy in the North, despite its innovations, belonged to a developing tradition as old as the peoples' elders. Nativists had previously expressed that tradition most vigorously between 1745 and 1775, especially after 1760. They had continued to invoke it, though often in the shadow of cooperation with Great Britain, during the long wars of the 1770s through 1790s. They did so as participants in a broad movement: challenging tribal boundaries, altering Indian identity, inventing a strategy of resistance against Anglo-American expansion.

In none of these periods did the nativists seek to turn back the clock. The nativists' own innovations, innovations that would have been as apparent to them as they are to us, give the lie to any notion that they sought simply to revive a dead past. It was not the material or even the ceremonial inventory that they sought to revive, but the process through which strength was gained. The nativists invented and borrowed, but they did so in a manner that seemed sanctioned by tradition. Whatever changes had been introduced by the visionaries were, as Wallace notes for Handsome Lake's villagers during his first set of teachings, "not upsetting to a people who were prepared for such progressive revelation by the customary usages."[14]

The prophets' adherence to indigenous processes of religious change permits us to define them as nativists, for they sought native solutions to the catastrophe of colonialism. That their visions precipitated religious innovations, even borrowings from Christianity, is not in itself indicative of Indian apostasy. The myths teach that the Great Spirit, in times of trouble, calls upon some of his creatures to carry new ceremony to the people. Indians expected, anticipated, and actively sought such visions. "Traditional" Eastern Woodlands cultures did not set themselves in opposition to change; indeed, the main story in the colonial period is that of adaptation. But for nativists, acceptable changes were to come about through traditionally sanctioned means. By 1800, one of the requisites for such sanction was Indian control. Nativism meant, in this context, not the conservation of a current tradition, or revitalization of a dead or dying culture, but independence of, and resistance to, direct intervention by the American republic.

Prophecy, Trade, and Dependency

In the 1760s, the Delaware Prophet had claimed that a resumption of proper ritual would allow the Indians to live independently of the Anglo-Americans. He had argued that the Great Spirit would reward righteous Indians with abundant game if they reduced their dependence upon the colonists. The game had been withdrawn, in fact, because the Indians had been "given up to evil." Perhaps no Indian ever pushed the same argument as emphatically as did the Trout in 1807, when he spoke for the Shawnee Prophet. Reciting a vision reminiscent of other prophets' dreams in earlier decades, this Ottawa described the Great Spirit opening celestial doors to reveal game animals. The beasts behind the first door represented "the Animals that are now on the Earth." Indian misdeeds—"killing them too young, And giving their meat to the whites"—had stunted and emaciated the creatures. So had the ancient Indian practice of anointing hair and skin with the fat of big game. But opening the second door, the Great Spirit revealed "a Bear and a Deer extremely fat, and of a very Extraordinary size." These represented the animals of the creation. They may also have been the spiritual "animal guardians" of Indian myth.[15]

Indian misdeeds, the Trout learned, had not only enfeebled the game, they had reduced its abundance: "My Children. You complain that the animals of the Forest are few and Scattered. How should it be otherwise? You destroy them yourselves for their skin only, and leave their bodies to rot, or give the Best pieces to the Whites. I am displeased when I see this, and take them back to the earth. That they may not come to you again." Moravian missionaries understood the Shawnee Prophet to speak in the same idiom two years earlier. The Great Spirit "had shown him the deer were half a tree's length under the ground and that these would soon appear again on earth if the Indians did what he told them to do, and then there would be an abundance of deer once more."[16]

The Trout and Tenskwatawa knew that the Indians' gross overhunting of game for the peltry trade had led to a decline in deer stocks. To hunters the Trout addressed a warning not to kill "more animals than are necessary to feed and Clothe you." Indians, he urged, should not rely upon the whites' cloth but should wear only "Skins, or Leather of your own Dressing." Tenskwatawa seems to have been less strict on this score, arguing that trade was permissible as long as it was on terms that the Indians deemed just. He proposed that a one-for-one trade be instituted: one shirt for one raccoon skin and one blanket for one deerskin.[17] The call for such a trade, impossible given the Indians' complete lack of influence on an overseas market deranged by the Napoleonic Wars, stood as much as an open challenge to Anglo-American economic authority as did the Trout's call for a total refusal to trade. But Tenskwatawa sought isolation far less than he sought to free Indians from the outside control that, in his view, was ensnaring the Indians of the borderlands not only through trade but also through the annuity system and the "civilizing" mission.

Internal Divisions over the "Plan of Civilization"

By the winter of 1805–6, when the Shawnee Prophet began to prophesy, four men had secured recognition by the United States as the leaders of their tribes in what are now Ohio and Indiana. Each of these men had earlier built distinguished military careers in the wars against the Anglo-Americans; each of them had ended those wars by signing the Treaty of Greenville. Their military reputations gave them widespread support among their peoples; their cooperation with the United States following the wars gave them the confidence of American officialdom. They had fashioned themselves, by 1804, into the chief conduits for the passage of the U.S. annuities to Indians. Little Turtle of the Miamis, Black Hoof of the Shawnees, the Tahre of the Wyandots, and Five Medals of the Potawatomis were the four; of these, Little Turtle and Black Hoof have a central place in this narrative as useful foils for the nativist movement. Annuity chiefs, in fact, provided the anvil upon which the prophets forged this early nineteenth-century phase of the struggle for Indian unity.

During the first decade of the nineteenth century, Little Turtle gathered a great deal of power in the Old Northwest. His influence was so strong that Secretary of War Henry Dearborn informed Harrison that "the neighboring Indians are . . . extremely jealous of the Little Turtle."[18] His influence may have resulted, in part, from his success in winning an unusually large annuity for the Miamis at the Treaty of Greenville, a feat he accomplished by insisting that the Eel River Indians were a separate tribe, confederated under his authority. Partly too, he basked in the former glory of his reportedly brilliant leadership in the victories over Harmar (1790) and St. Clair (1791). In general, however, he retained power through his effective management of the Miami annuity, his refusal to indulge in luxuries for himself, his generosity toward his Miami people, and his hospitality to whites. Once in power, he handled himself with such skill that animosities toward him often worked in his favor, for the federal agents opposed "those jealousies" with "all the fair means in our power."[19] All fair means tended to translate, on this particular frontier, into all means fair or foul. This was demonstrated in the Miami leader's partnership with William Wells, the federal government's agent at Fort Wayne.

Wells, who knew several Indian languages as a result of his childhood captivity among the northerners, worked closely with Little Turtle in attempting to manage Indian-American relations in his quarter; so closely, in fact, that by 1809 charges of misconduct led to his demotion from agent to translator. This demotion, despite his impressive skills and connections, makes little sense when viewed in the light of accusations, leveled in 1807, that he had mistranslated speeches to advance his own and Little Turtle's interests. Whatever the logic of his superiors, he was suspected in 1809 of both deliberately exaggerating the Shawnee Prophet's friendship for the British and, more seriously as far as the federal government was concerned, of embezzling Delaware annuities.[20]

Wells and Little Turtle had also interfered with the federal and Quaker effort to "civilize" the Shawnees. They intended to prevent rival neighboring leaders, including Black Hoof, from rising to prominence in relations with the federal government. Throughout the first decade of the nineteenth century, Little Turtle had managed to secure annuities for his Miamis at almost every cession of land, often by challenging the claims of other peoples. He wanted no contenders to threaten his hold on the disposition of land, which he was coming to view as a precious, transferable commodity.

But in his efforts against the Shawnee annuity chief, Little Turtle misspent energies that he might have devoted against those who would become more serious opponents: those who hoped to prevent land from ever being traded as a commodity again. For the true threat to Little Turtle came not from his accommodating rivals but from the resurgence of militant, pan-Indian nativism under the direction of prophets. Not until the Shawnee Prophet threw down the gauntlet by settling among the Miamis in 1808 would Little Turtle and Wells move strongly against him, and even then, it would be Wells, not Little Turtle, who would attempt to deal the telling blows. So hostile would Wells become to Tenskwatawa by 1809 that, when groups of famine-stricken nativists appeared begging at Vincennes, Wells suggested that Harrison "starve all." Wells would later boast, in the summer of 1811, "Yes sir I would of destroyed this scoundrel 4 years ago had I not of been prevented by my superiors," but the written record suggests it was a little more like two or three "years ago."[21] By 1809, to be sure, Wells and Little Turtle would begin to combat resurgent, militant nativism. Previous to that, they directed their main efforts against rivals of their own ilk.

Black Hoof, Little Turtle's rival among the faction of Shawnees eager to work out an accommodation with the United States, also dispensed government annuities. Like the Miami leader, Black Hoof carried a good

CA-TA-HE-CAS-SA-SA-BLACK HOOF,
PRINCIPAL CHIEF OF THE SHAWNEES

Shawnee leader in wars against the United States to 1795, he signed the Greenville
Treaty, opposed the nativist movement, and, after the War of 1812, stood unsuc-
cessfully against Shawnee Removal. From an 1830 lithograph made for Thomas L.
McKenney, printed in his *History of the Indian Tribes of North America* [Plates]
(Philadelphia, 187–?). (*Source:* National Anthropological Archives, Negative No.
45, 113-E, Smithsonian Institution, Washington, D.C.)

record as a warrior. An elderly but active man in the early nineteenth century, he reportedly had been among those who surprised Braddock in 1755; it is certain that he had fought valorously in the wars of the 1780s and 1790s.[22] Balancing these youthful military achievements was his elderly posture of warmth for the Americans. The point on which the balance between youth and age rested came in 1795, after devastating northwestern defeats, when Black Hoof put his mark on the Greenville cession. For the next two decades, he cooperated with the federal government.

Black Hoof's training may have prepared him for work as a broker between Native and Anglo-America. He was of the Mequashake Shawnees, whose community had produced Cornstalk and Malunthy, the great advocates of neutrality in the 1770s and 1780s, men who had met not only disappointment but death at Anglo-American hands. The band was, like other communities, a divided one. It had produced its share of militants, as it would produce Seekaboo, a nativist prophet who would soon play a critical role in spreading the militant movement to the South. But among the Shawnees, the Mequashakes had the strongest tradition of negotiation, a tradition Black Hoof had adopted in 1795.[23]

Little Turtle and Black Hoof did not simply cede land, accept annuities, and redistribute the proceeds among their people. They too had designs for the future. To carry them out, they actively cooperated with the Quaker bearers of the civilizing mission. These missionaries of religion and culture sought to establish "demonstration farms" and, through their example, to persuade both Indian men to abandon the hunt for the fields and Indian women to abandon the fields for domestic pursuits, most notably the spinning of cloth. The Friends received limited federal support and cooperation. In 1804—in accordance with an agreement among Quaker delegates, Little Turtle, and the Potawatomi Five Medals—Quaker Philip Dennis planted his twenty-acre farm about forty miles southwest of Fort Wayne, on rich soil beside the Wabash. There, argued Little Turtle, both the Potawatomis and the Miamis could benefit by observing Dennis' progress, but Dennis was clearly in Miami territory.[24]

In 1807, Black Hoof likewise allowed the Quaker William Kirk to set up a demonstration farm near the Shawnee town of Wapakoneta, within reach of the Wyandots at Sandusky. Black Hoof's support enabled Kirk to enclose one hundred acres of land and to plant a full two hundred acres in corn. By April 1808, Kirk reported progress: several of the Shawnees operated private farms; the people as a whole possessed "a good stock of Cattle and Hogs." The Wyandots' "improvements," he claimed, were similar. A year later Indian agent John Johnson noted that Black Hoof's people had both a sawmill and a gristmill under construction; many lived in log houses with chimneys; their village, overall, bore "the marks of industry."[25] Despite these developments and despite petitions on Kirk's behalf, the war department, apparently because of Kirk's poor record keeping, withdrew its support from the mission in late 1808.[26] It is worth noting that Little Turtle and Wells, seeking to put down potential rivals, had stood against Kirk's arrangement with the Shawnees and Wyandots, but they may not have had a role in his difficulties with Washington. The brief history of Kirk's agency demonstrated, and this is the critical point, that the Quakers, the federal government, the Indian agents, and the government chiefs—all the main advocates of accommodation in the Old Northwest—were seriously divided, often for the most petty of reasons, while a strong nativist movement rose to challenge their scattered projects.

The Quaker missionaries faced troubles more difficult to negotiate than factionalism among the forces of accommodation. For one thing, they had underestimated the difficulties of their mission. For example, they clearly intended to alter the sexual division of labor among their Indian observers. Philip Dennis actively attempted to dissuade the young women who "wished to work in preparing the ground and in tending the corn." He hired a white woman to teach them spinning and knitting instead. The Quakers argued against all Indian tradition that women "are less then Men, they are not as strong as Men, they are not as able to endure fatigue and toil as men." Women should "be employed in our houses, to keep them clean, to sew, knit, and weave; to dress food for themselves and [their] families."[27] Such an arrangement practically reversed the current production arrangements among Indians, for the men obtained clothing through hunting and trade, while women raised the crops and vegetables. Quite apart from cosmological consequences Indians would fear in such a transformation, the material demands of the Quaker proposal were enormous. Among the Indians, men had little knowledge of fieldwork; women held such knowledge in abundance. If carried out, the proposed gender revolution might have resulted in a dangerous drain of horticultural skills, of which women alone possessed the full range.

Even proponents of accommodation could, therefore, support the role reversal with little more than words. When the Quakers arrived, Little Turtle claimed that he "and some others of my brother Chiefs have been endeavouring to turn the minds of our People [men] towards the Cultivation of the Earth," but he admitted no success.[28] The Quakers would not do much better among the Shawnees or Miamis as the War of 1812 approached. The Shawnee Prophet, who emerged as the chief opponent of the civilizing mission, clearly preferred traditional gender roles to those sponsored by the Quakers. According to William Wells, the prophet declared Kirk to be a "Master" imposed on the Indians by the president, "from which circumstance it was Evident that the President intended making women of the Indians—but when the Indians was all united they would be respected by the President as men."[29] The Prophet's concern with the civilizing mission and the gender revolution it entailed grew out of both the very earthly grounds that it robbed Indians of their political independence and the cosmological proposition that it robbed Indians of the favor of sacred powers. He and other opponents of the mission directed their most searing attacks at its Indian sponsors, whom they believed were undermining the strength of the Indian peoples.

In 1805, shortly after his first visions, the Shawnee Prophet challenged directly the authority of both the Shawnee Black Hoof and the Delaware Indian leadership. The prophet spoke openly against those "chiefs who were very wicked, would not believe, and tried to keep the people from believing, and encouraged them on in their former wicked ways." Black Hoof, the prophet's strong opponent, maintained the loyalties of many Shawnees despite the prophet's vigorous denunciations. To give the Prophet independence of Black Hoof and his followers, as well as to challenge the Greenville Treaty upon which Black Hoof's authority partially rested, "the Great Spirit told" Tenskwatawa "to separate from these wicked chiefs and their people," and to establish a town at Greenville, "where the peace was concluded with the Americans; and there [to] Make provision to receive and instruct all from the different tribes that were willing to be good."[30]

A realignment of Indian loyalties resulted. While Black Hoof and Little Turtle each worked against the other and lobbied with their particular American allies to secure influence with the federal government, Tenskwatawa sought intertribal support for both a rebellion against these government chiefs and a posture of defiance toward American expansion. Tenskwatawa's effort was thus against both domestic and foreign authority. The moment for domestic success, moreover, was opportune. His Indian opponents, as we have seen, were divided against themselves.

The Witch-Hunts

The nativists' struggle for the control of Indian councils manifested itself most violently in the Shawnee Prophet's witch-hunt, a hunt for witches who bear little resemblance to those of Christian lore or British colonial society: the first accused were often powerful men. Opposition to witchcraft, a long-standing feature of nativism, lay at the center, not the periphery, of the Shawnee Prophet's code. Tenskwatawa began preaching, one source has it, on the death of Pengahshega (Change of Feathers), a powerful Shawnee opponent of witches. What is more, similar witch-hunts and accusations had bedeviled Indian communities during the nativistic upheavals of the 1750s, 1760s, and early 1770s.[31]

Tenskwatawa claimed that the Great Spirit had given him the power to discover witches, even among powerful leaders of the community. To find the guilty parties, the prophet stood the villagers in a circle about him, and "after a great many ceremonies," he pointed to the evil beings. Tenskwatawa's witch-hunt initially hit the Delawares with the greatest severity. The prophet had been living among the Delawares when he experienced his first visions. By the late winter of 1805–6, strong parties of Delawares sought "to destroy all the reputed witches, . . . as well as those who had poison among them. They resolved to use fire to bring about the confessions of those whom the Schawano would accuse." All of the known condemned Delawares had close ties with the Americans and with the civilizing mission. Two of the condemned were chiefs: Tedapachsit and Hackingpomska, and they had both signed the Greenville Treaty of 1795 and had ceded land to the United States at the Delaware Treaty of 1804, agreeing that the new annuities would be "exclusively appropriated to the purpose of ameliorating their condition and promoting their civilization." Tedapachsit had openly supported the activities of Christian missionaries. Hackingpomska, though taken prisoner, was not executed, perhaps because he yielded for the moment to the growing opposition to the white missions, joining a Delaware Council in favoring native prophets over American ministers. An old woman, baptized by the Moravians, also fell victim to the charge; so did the Indian "Brother Joshua," who not only had converted to Christianity but who had been an active spy for the United States during the American Revolution, as the militants had then suspected.[32] Tenskwatawa's Delaware targets accepted, even cultivated, direct American intervention in Indian government, religion, and society. For such evil they had to die.

By midsummer, internal Delaware opposition to the killings led many to recoil from the witch-hunt and to turn their suspicions against the hunters, leaving the Delawares deeply divided over killings that had so clearly reflected political and cultural conflict. As one Moravian missionary put it while he fled Delaware country, "The Indians hate each other with a bitter hatred, which may flame forth at the slightest provocation."[33] This hatred was not tribal. Delaware followers of a Shawnee attacked their Delaware leaders.

Among the Shawnees, two of Black Hoof's followers, accused of using "bad Medisin," lost their lives to the prophet's assassins in the spring of 1807. Not surprisingly, in view of the nativists' hostility toward leaders who cooperated with the Americans, Tenskwatawa had even discovered Black Hoof to be a witch, along with chiefs Black Snake and Butler. None of these was killed, but it is worth noting that the three supported the federally sponsored Quaker mission.[34]

Recriminations between Black Hoof's and the prophet's parties flew so furiously that the federal government temporarily treated the nativist movement as a strictly internal Shawnee affair. In early August 1807, while anti-British passions boiled in the United States over the H.M.S. *Leopard*'s attack on the U.S.S. *Chesapeake*, President Jefferson declined to relate Indian matters to British naval policy. With "respect to the Prophet," he informed his secretary of war, "if those who are in danger from him [i.e., the chiefs] would settle it their own way, it would be their affair. but we should do nothing towards it." Nothing, in Jefferson's curious usage, meant a little judicious peddling of influence: "The best conduct we can pursue to countervail these movements among the Indians is to confirm our friends by redoubled acts of justice and favor."[35]

Throughout 1807, beating against the winds of continued federal favor for annuity chiefs, the nativists' notions slipped deeper into the Upper Great Lakes region. In the spring, when Michigan Territorial Governor William Hull advertised the intent of the government to purchase some lands from the Ottawas, Tenskwatawa's messianic Ottawa ally, the Trout, launched his more stringent brand of nativism, though he did so in the Shawnee's name. By September, Michigan's traders felt the first force of the Ottawa revival. "All the Ottawas from L'arbre au Croche," wrote one merchant, "adhere strictly to the Shawney Prophets advice they do not wear Hats Drink or Conjure." These Ottawas planned on spending the autumn at the prophet's town and refused liquor even when offered it free of charge. The traders lamented, "Rum is a Drug [on the market]. . . . Indians do not purchase One Galln per month."[36]

By the spring of 1808, when the prophet gathered his followers for a move to the Wabash River, near Tippecanoe Creek, on lands claimed by the Miamis, the Miami chief Little Turtle finally took serious notice of the prophet. With the Potawatomi Five Medals, Little Turtle threatened to kill Tenskwatawa if he made the proposed move. In response Tenskwatawa loudly condemned all government chiefs who had "sold all the Indian land to the United States" and who had asked the president to "appoint masters over them to make them work."[37]

If the nativists opposed the accommodating chiefs for their advocacy of the civilizing mission and for their role in land sales, it was the latter role they most vocally condemned. Between 1804 and the end of 1808 the governors of the Indiana and Michigan territories had negotiated a half dozen treaties with the annuity chiefs. According to these treaties, the United States had obtained a large chunk of southeastern Michigan, large cessions in southern Indiana and Illinois, and most of the land that had been left to the Indians in Ohio. The United States had also gained the right to build and use a road through a portion of what remained of Indian territory. Washington paid for these grants with increased annuities, to be distributed through certain recognized Indian leaders. To opponents of the annuity chiefs, the payments reeked of bribery.[38]

Fort Wayne and Tecumseh

In 1809, the annuity chiefs unwittingly and negligently galvanized the nativists with another land cession. The affair began in the summer of 1809, when the secretary of war wrote Harrison that he could proceed with his desire to purchase more lands along the Wabash, but only if the governor was certain that the undertaking "will excite no disagreeable apprehension and produce no undesirable effects before It shall be made." Harrison proceeded to negotiate with the Delaware, Potowatomi, Miami, and Eel River Indians, making separate treaties with the Weas and Kickapoos later that year. The main text agreed to, the Treaty of Fort Wayne, ceded over two and one half million acres to the United States, for about two cents an acre—a high price in Indian treaties, but still a massively unequal exchange.[39]

The Treaty of Fort Wayne has long been recognized as a milestone on the road to the battle of Tippecanoe. From this period forward in histories of the West on the eve of the War of 1812, Tenskwatawa's brother, Tecumseh, fashions and leads the pan-Indian movement. Reginald Horsman sees the treaty as consolidating the opposition movement under Tecumseh. R. David Edmunds argues that while the Shawnee Prophet led the movement until 1809, with this treaty the more practical aspects of Indian resistance took precedence over the religious, allowing the more pragmatic Tecumseh to gain ascendancy over the prophet. Edmunds powerfully demonstrates Tenskwatawa's earlier leadership, but both scholars agree that following the Treaty of Fort Wayne, it was Tecumseh who, in Horsman's words, "transformed a religious revival into an attempt at Indian unity."[40]

The prophet, however, lost no power following the treaty; he still led the nativists from his headquarters at Tippecanoe. His preaching, as we have seen, had always exhibited both the political overtones and material concerns that political and social historians seek to grasp and find worth grasping. Like Tecumseh, Tenskwatawa spoke out vigorously against both the Fort Wayne cession and the Indians who had agreed to it. In the spring and summer of 1810, half a year after the signing of the treaty, the Prophet informed a discovered American spy that his people were "much exasperated at the cession of Lands made last winter" and that they had "agreed that the Tract on the N. west side of the Wabash should not be surveyed." His disciples followed up this declaration by successfully opposing a surveying party in September.[41]

Tecumseh, meanwhile, spoke out against the government chiefs long targeted by Tenskwatawa. In August 1810 Tecumseh informed Harrison that he intended "to level all distinctions to destroy the village chiefs by whom all mischief is done; it is they who sell our land to the Americans." He asked Harrison to repudiate the Fort Wayne treaty, for the annuity chiefs "had no right" to sell the claim. He did not threaten Harrison with war; rather he threatened "to kill all the chiefs who sold you this land." By retaining the American claim, Tecumseh warned, "you will have a hand in killing them."[42] Tecumseh, like the prophet, was still less openly hostile to the United States than he was to its allies among Indian leaders.

Tenskwatawa and Tecumseh both objected to annuities. The prophet refused a salt annuity in July 1810. Tecumseh, in a direct confrontation with Harrison at Vincennes later that summer, clearly equated the annuities with the loss of land: "By taking presents from you, you will hereafter say that with them you purchased another piece of land from us," and further: "When you speak of annuities I look at the land, and pity the women and children."[43] On the issues of land cessions, annuities, and internal authority, the two brothers stood together in the years between Fort Wayne and the battle of Tippecanoe. The two were, as the evidence suggests, of much the same mind.

It is on the subject of Indian unity that scholars and tale-spinners alike have most emphasized the particular wisdom of Tecumseh. Even here, although he was an energetic ambassador and a man of martial distinction, Tecumseh, like his brother, was more participant in than progenitor of the movement we associate with his name. Tecumseh drew on both the nativist vision of his brother and the broader dreams and practical legacies of two generations of militants.

In his speech to Harrison that August, Tecumseh argued, as had Ohioan and Great Lakes Country militants for at least three decades, that "all the lands in the western country was the common property of all the tribes." No land could be sold without the consent of all. To establish the principle, he intended, as had others, to unite the tribes in a movement against American expansion. The prophet also argued that "no sale was good unless made by all the Tribes," and he welcomed Indians of all tribes to join in his spiritual revival, his rebellion against the authority of annuity chiefs, his rejection of Christianity, and his defense of Indian lands.[44]

To support his intertribal call, the Shawnee Prophet had at his disposal a concept of Indian identity that had been developing since at least the middle of the eighteenth century, a concept embodied in the notion of the separate creation of whites and Indians. The notion did not lead directly to nativism; it was so widespread that even such federally recognized chiefs as Black Hoof and the Wyandot Tahre expressed the view at the turn of the nineteenth century.[45] But government chiefs could never turn it to their advantage with the dexterity of the nativists, for in its logical conclusion, the doctrine meant an Indian rejection of American control.

In 1805 the Presbyterian missionary, James Hughes, found the Wyandots divided over their concepts of the creation. Some believed in a single Great Spirit, others held "that there are two Gods, one the creator of the white people, and the other of the Indians, whom they call the Warrior." The Shawnee Prophet believed something akin to the latter notion, as he told C. C. Trowbridge in 1824. He recalled that at the creation "The Great Spirit then opened a door, and looking down they saw a white man seated upon the ground. . . . The Great Spirit told them that this white man was not made by himself but by another spirit who made & governed the whites & over whom he had no controul." The Trout, the Ottawa spokesman for the nativist movement, further defined the Americans (he distinguished, as had the Ottawa Pontiac before him, between the Anglo-Americans whose seaboard polities thrust aggressively westward and the less expansionist Canadians) as creatures of the "Evil Spirit" from "Scum of the great water."[46]

The separate, even evil, nature of American citizens emerged also in Indian interpretations of Christianity. As in the mid-eighteenth century, some Indians turned Christianity against Christians to demonstrate the depth of the missionaries' abomination. In crucifying Jesus, these argued, Europeans had killed their own God. During the first, more militantly anti-Christian phase of Handsome Lake's mission, his half-brother Cornplanter, who "liked some ways of the white people," told the Quaker missionary Henry Simmons, "it was the white people who kill'd our Saviour." Simmons countered, "it was the Jews," and then tried to drive the point home by dragging out the already hackneyed argument that Indians were members of the lost tribes of Israel: "Indians were their descendants, for many of their habits were Semilar to the Jews, in former days." We don't know what Cornplanter made of that contention—perhaps he was simply at a loss for words—but twentieth-century practition-

ers of the Handsome Lake Religion have made no mention of it and consider the crucifixion a deed performed by whites. They have learned that
the Seneca Prophet, in his early visions, met Jesus, who described himself
as "a man upon the earth who was slain by his own people." Jesus had
ordered Handsome Lake to "tell your people that they will become lost
when they follow the ways of the white people."

Nativistic northwesterners leaned more heavily on the argument. Responding to a Moravian missionary in 1806, one of Tenskwatawa's followers said of the crucifixion, "Granted that what you say is true, He did not
die in Indian land but among the white people." In 1810 Tecumseh himself,
revealing his own concerns for things spiritual, asked Harrison in the same
pointed terms, "How can we have confidence in the white people[?] when
Jesus Christ came upon the earth you kill'd and nail'd him on a cross."[47]
Given the Shawnee's nativistic assumptions, it was a logical question.

If, as the Shawnee Prophet said, Americans were unchangeably inimical
to Indians, if "the Great Spirit did not mean that the white and red people
should live near each other" because whites "poison'd the land,"[48] and if
all Indians came from a common creation different from that of others,
then it only made sense that Indians should unite against the American
threat. In emphasizing their separation, Indians gave spiritual sanction to
Native American unity.

Intertribal, Prophetic Nativism

Tecumseh has captured a more prominent place in American history than
any Indian of his day, arguably of any day. His advocacy of a union of
Indians in defense of their lands has won him praise as a "Shawnee Warrior-Statesman" in the title of a children's biography and as "The Greatest
Indian" in the estimation of biographer and historian Alvin Josephy. Glenn
Tucker's biography of the Shawnee leader credits him with devising the
Shawnee Prophet's religion as a means of achieving unity: "Such an amal-
gam could have been the product only of a mind rich in knowledge, firm
in purpose and supple in understanding—the sort of mind that was dis-
closed in Tecumseh's speeches."[49] R. David Edmunds rightly rejects that
particular interpretation; yet even this best biographer of the brothers sees
something quintessentially un-Indian about Tecumseh's endeavor: "Americans have always been fascinated with Tecumseh's attempts to unify the
tribes. His struggles seemed logical to whites because it was what *they*
would have done. His plans reflect a white solution to the Indians' problems. Unfortunately, they were much less appealing to the Indians. . . .
Tecumseh may have dreamed of a pan-Indian union, but most of his fol-

lowers remained a tribal people. They still saw the world from a tribal perspective."[50]

Tecumseh did *not*, however, significantly differ from his followers in culture or in vision; nor was it tribalism that blocked his success. He certainly stood out as an expert organizer, warrior, and an indefatigable traveler, although many others from the revolutionary era and the two decades that followed it could rival him even in those talents. In his hopes and in his vision, moreover, he stood with, not beyond or outside of, the militant nativists of the Eastern Woodlands. His most recent biographer, Bil Gilbert, credits Tecumseh with having "conceived of a plan for uniting the red people," but Tecumseh was not the plan's sole creator; he drew upon traditions of nativism and networks of intertribal relations that had been vibrant throughout the trans-Appalachian borderlands, reaching back into the past beyond the time of Neolin and Pontiac. With Tecumseh, also drawing from this legacy, stood the prophets.[51]

The major northern religious leaders urged forms of intertribal unity between 1805 and 1812. Even Handsome Lake, whose Senecas were entirely surrounded by U.S. citizens, who had little direct contact with other militants, and who prudently drew back from military alliance as the War of 1812 erupted, nonetheless showed a certain solidarity with the more western Indians by demanding that his followers refuse to support the United States. Nor did Handsome Lake ignore other peoples; he sent his word to Sandusky in 1804 and visited the region in 1806.[52] But his influence remained largely confined to the reservations east of Lake Erie.

Tenskwatawa promoted pan-Indianism not with words alone, or only with the elaboration of separation theology, but with the time-honored if paradoxical political device of secession. Like the Susquehanna Delawares and Shawnees who had fled Anglo-Iroquois authority by both removing to Ohio and settling in polyglot villages in the early eighteenth century, like the Chickamaugas who had broken with the Cherokees to settle the Tennessee with their militant Shawnee allies during the American Revolution, Tenskwatawa broke from his hosts, invited Indians of all nations to join him, and settled new towns. He did so first at Greenville (1806–8), in symbolic defiance of the Treaty of Greenville, and later at Tippecanoe (1808–12), in outright defiance of Little Turtle's claim to authority over that land. The prophet warned Little Turtle that plans for the Tippecanoe settlement had been "layed by all the Indians in America and had been sanctioned by the Great Spirit." He then informed the Miami leader that Indian unity alone would end Indian poverty and defend Indian land.[53]

One band of Wyandots, joining the prophet in 1810, bound the movement to earlier decades by bringing with them "the Great Belt which was the Symbol of Union between the Tribes in their late war with the United States." Consciously reviving the pan-Indianism of their recent past, these Wyandots, in the prophet's words, could not "sit still and see the property of all the Indians usurped."[54]

Drawing upon the same tradition of resistance and adhering to Tenskwatawa, the Trout also advocated Indian unity. In the spring of 1807, before Tecumseh gained notice, this Ottawa addressed Ottawas and Chippewas, requesting that each of their villages send at least two deputies to his village, L'arbre Croche, to carry out the will of the Great Spirit. And he specifically demanded, in the voice of the Great Spirit, an end to intertribal hostilities: "You are, however, never to go to War against each other. But to cultivate peace between your different Tribes, that they may become one great people." The following spring, in the turbulent wake of a large land sale by Ottawas, Chippewas, Wyandots, and Potawatomis to the United States, militants of all four tribes declared it "a crime punishable by Death for any Indian to put his name on paper for the perpose of parting with any of their lands."[55]

The third prophet, Main Poc of the Potawatomis, stood for northern Indian solidarity, but limited his vision to what Americans would call the Old Northwest. He waged sporadic war on the trans-Mississippi Osage Indians, a war fought also by northern refugees who had already fled across that great river. Main Poc deviated in other ways: even after donning the prophetic mantle, he accepted a bribe from Wells, though it does not seem to have changed his behavior. Further, he continued to drink, advocating only temperance, while other nativists, as a rule, advocated abstinence. But Main Poc did think beyond the boundaries of his "tribe." This Potawatomi, in fact, recommended Tippecanoe to Tenskwatawa as a good site for a town. As hostilities neared in the fall of 1811, Main Poc actively sought recruits beyond his people, among the Ottawas and Chippewas.[56]

It might be argued that Tecumseh's southern journey in the late summer and fall of 1811 demonstrates a vision grander than all others, but even here Tecumseh traveled with others and in others' footsteps. Seventeenth- and eighteenth-century Shawnees had previously established relations with the Cherokees and Creeks. At least one of Tecumseh's own parents must have been widely traveled, for Tecumseh's mother was a Creek. Tecumseh himself had likely journeyed as a youth to the Chickamauga country, probably in the late 1780s, to join the Shawnees who fought beside Creeks and Cherokees during the long war of 1775–95. Apart from these historic links between the southeasterners and Shawnees, there is also evidence that

Shawnees and other northern Indians carried the Shawnee Prophet's message to the Creeks *before* Tecumseh's famous southward journey.

As early as July 1807, Harrison informed his superiors that, on the basis of "information which cannot be doubted," he knew "that war belts have been passing through all the Tribes from the Gulf of Florida to the lakes. The Shawnees are the bearers of these belts and they have never been our friends." Harrison understood that "a general combination of the Indians for a war against the United States is the object of all these messages." In June 1810, a Potawatomi government chief informed Harrison that the Shawnee Prophet "will now endeavor to raise the southern Indians, the Choctaws and the Creeks particularly (the Prophet's mother was a Creek)." One year later, Tecumseh fulfilled the Potawatomi's predictions. Historian John Sudgen has recently argued that Tecumseh probably made "preliminary overtures to the various tribes" as he prepared to journey southward. These findings confirm Sudgen's suspicion, although they give credit to the prophet as well.[57]

Visits in the other direction, from south to north, also prepared Tecumseh's way. In 1807, while the secretary of war, Henry Dearborn, worried about Tenskwatawa's movement, he recommended that a "banditti of Creeks" should "be driven out of" Indiana territory. In 1810, twenty to thirty Creeks joined the prophet at Tippecanoe. One of these may have been the Creek warrior Tuskenea, who, according to a memoir written much later, had journeyed to the Wabash "some few years before the war [of 1812]."[58]

Dissident Cherokees also maintained their presence in the Northwest. In July 1805, a Cherokee family that maintained contact with its southeastern kin purposefully disrupted the Moravian mission to the Delawares at White River, Indiana. They prepared "a heathen sacrificial feast . . . and invited to it a large number." This event may have had no direct connection with the prophet's similar activities toward the end of the year, but it does indicate an anti-Christian Cherokee presence in his very neighborhood. In 1810 a Cherokee at Black Hoof's Shawnee town informed John Norton, a Mohawk who was at the time returning from a visit to the Cherokee Nation, that "many" Cherokees "were at the Village of the Prophet."[59] Cherokees, then, had joined the militant followers of the Shawnee Prophet before Tecumseh's renowned tour; both Cherokees and Creeks were certainly acquainted with the northern movement.

Tecumseh departed for the South from Vincennes, where he had been holding talks with Harrison, in early August 1811. He planned, according to Harrison, to visit the Creeks, the Choctaws, and the Osages, and to encourage those peoples to unite with the militant northwesterners. Although Tecumseh reassured Harrison that he meant only peace, Harrison disbelieved, and with reason, for Tecumseh's plan of a defensive alliance against American expansion meant war with the acquisitive United States, a nation that could not accept the status quo in the West.[60]

Scholars wishing to distinguish between the pragmatic Tecumseh and his religious brother have dwelt on diplomacy. Tecumseh's journey had another, inextricably related object, however: he sought to spread the call for a restoration of sacred power. To that end, he traveled with another Shawnee prophet, Seekaboo. Little is known of Seekaboo. Thomas S. Woodward, an American officer in the Creek War, much later recalled that Seekaboo was a "Warpicanata chief and prophet." This probably identifies the visionary as a Mequashake Shawnee, a dissident from Black Hoof's town of Wapakoneta. Woodward further recounted both that Seekaboo remained with the Creeks when Tecumseh returned north and that Seekaboo shortly thereafter took up arms with the Creek nativists. Early historians of the Creek War (1813–14) describe him as about forty years of age in 1811, with skills as an interpreter and orator. Woodward also recalled that other Shawnee prophets, either from the northwest or from the Southern Shawnee confederates of the Creeks, joined Seekaboo in raising militant Creek spirits.[61]

One of the closest reports of Tecumseh's address to the Creeks, Benjamin Hawkins' speech to the Lower Creek chiefs on June 16, 1814, paraphrases a speech attributed to Tecumseh. This record comes two and one half years after the fact and two years into the war with Britain. It is written by one who did not hear the speech. In short it is a most doubtful form of evidence, as are all of our records of Tecumseh's speeches in the South. If it can be accepted at all, it demonstrates Tecumseh's affinity with nativism far more than it isolates him as a secular diplomat: "Kill the old chiefs, friends to peace; kill the cattle, the hogs, and fouls; do not work, destroy the wheels and looms, throw away your ploughs, and every thing used by the Americans. Sing 'the song of the Indians of the northern lakes and dance their dance.' Shake your war clubs, shake yourselves; you will frighten the Americans." But we need not accept the speech to see Tecumseh's southern mission as prophetic; it is enough to note that well-placed Creeks and Americans in the Southeast thought of him as a shaman. Indeed, Hawkins and one of his Creek allies, Alexander Cornells, thought that Tecumseh was the Shawnee Prophet.[62]

The precise language of the message spread by Tecumseh and the Shawnee prophets who accompanied him has yet to be discovered, but we do know that it took hold among a faction of the Creeks. The militant Creeks became known, after their war clubs, as the Red Sticks. Like the militants in the North, the Red Sticks sought to form a pan-Indian movement against American territorial expansion, political intrusion, and economic domination. As in the North, intertribal cooperation came at the cost of internal division, for the Red Stick militants met strong Creek opposition. The pressures straining the Creek confederacy were wrought by the very forces, although building up beneath a different landscape, that thrust up obstacles between nativists against their so-called chiefs. The brittle nature of the Creek political landscape meant that the pressures would be more violently felt; they would erupt into a devastating civil war in 1813, a war that would in turn become an American war of conquest. The neighboring Cherokees, surrounded by the turmoil, would avoid such intense division, though only for a time.

>>>>>>><<<<<<<

EIGHT

Conflict in the South

Villagers from across the ethnically diverse Creek confederacy came to hear the nineteen Indians from the North. Visiting Cherokees and Choctaws attended the meeting in the important Creek town of Tuckabatchee to listen to what the northerners, thirteen of them Shawnees, had to say. Tecumseh and Seekaboo understood, as they faced this crowd, that mighty obstacles rose before them. The majority of Cherokee and Choctaw emissaries stood against the proceedings; the Creeks stood against one another.

The Creek divisions fell along lines that the northerners could recognize: lines separating government chiefs from advocates of a pan-Indian nativist movement, lines separating open supporters of the "civilizing mission" from advocates of a native-directed economy. Tecumseh and the northern emissaries sought to give strength to nativists among the peoples of the South. They sought to revive the defensive confederacies of the past. In large measure, it must be said, they would fail. Tecumseh and his followers would never win deep support in the South. Their movement would not approach the dimensions achieved by their militant forebears. Only among the Creeks and their Seminole kin did the thirteen Shawnee emissaries discover willing bodies of allies, soon to be known as the Red Sticks.

"The Plan of Civilization" and the Creeks

The U.S. inroads into Creek government went much deeper than did federal influence anywhere in the Old Northwest. In 1799, American agent Benjamin Hawkins claimed credit for establishing the first Creek "National Council." Hawkins declared that "the Creeks never had, till this year, a national government and law," and some historians have taken him at his word. Hawkins exaggerated. The Creeks had in fact met in regular national council under the late McGillivray. But Hawkins could honestly boast that the new council represented a departure. Never before had the Creeks agreed that national law superceeded clan law in internal matters. Never before, moreover, had the Creeks given an outsider the authority, as they now gave Hawkins, to bring American troops into the Creek nation to reinforce Creek patrols.[1] Never before had the Creeks publicly administered punishment for crimes committed against foreigners.

The power of the new arrangement became manifest in May 1801. That year, at Hawkins's request, the council's patrol arrested a party of Creeks found guilty of raiding the Spanish. With apparent satisfaction, Hawkins recorded in his journal that seventy-two "warriors under the directions of their great chiefs" publicly "cropped" the ringleader's ears, whipped his back, destroyed his property and whipped "his associates."[2] Although Creeks had punished other Creeks for involving the nation in foreign-affairs crises, they had not previously done so in full view, by announced national authority, at the request of a resident foreign agent. The rite of punishment dramatized the advances of both federal authority and Creek accommodation to it. The advances would not go unchallenged. An angry reaction to less popular, and less ritualized exercises of cooperative Creek-American authority would trigger the Creek Civil War in 1813.

As in the North, the successful American infiltration of Indian government rested, in part, upon the annuity system, which its opponents charged was a system of bribery clothed in the mantle of payments for lands. Treaties promised annuities both to the entire Creek nation and to individual chiefs, but the even broader distribution benefited some Creeks greatly and others not at all. For Americans paid the stipends only to Creek "agents" appointed by each town. These Creek leaders, who were not expected to distribute the goods evenly, gained a control over the annuity that would permit them "to do justice to those who faithfully exerted themselves for the honour and interest of their country."[3] In other words, federally recognized leaders, the government chiefs, were to reward their followers. Indian annuities throughout the borderlands did not simply pay for land (a task for which they were woefully inadequate); they advanced American interests among factions of Indian leadership.

If this was bribery, however, it does not sufficiently explain Indian cooperation with the United States; other very powerful reasons compelled many to advocate cooperation with the Americans. Among the Creeks, as in the North, the local presence of well-armed American garrisons gave strong argument to Creek advocates of accommodation. Between 1794 and 1803, Americans flew their colors over three forts near the eastern reaches of the confederacy and one near the western reaches. These forts did not simply threaten the opponents of the United States with violence. They also provided an inducement: "factories," where a peaceful, if sometimes ill-managed, trade could be had at regulated prices. The avowed purpose of these government factories was to increase American influence over the Indians at the expense of the Spanish and British, and in this they were partly successful.[4]

Federal success in creating a Creek clientele stemmed too, as in the North, from the federal advocacy of a "civilizing mission," whose apparent promise of peaceful coexistence offered an opportunity to those Indians who sought peaceful development. In this endeavor, as with the reformation of Creek national government, federal success among the Creeks exceeded northern accomplishments. But in the South as well as in the North, Indian opposition to the mission grew partly out of Indian conceptions of gender.

Among all Eastern Woodlands peoples, women were the primary agriculturalists, although with the introduction of pastoralism in the colonial period, men, as well as women, had taken to the raising of livestock. Benjamin Hawkins attributed Creek stock-rearing to "the failure of supplies from hunting."[5] Without a livelihood from the peltry trade, Creek men with access to livestock could easily take to cattle herding and hog droving without violating traditional gender roles. But unlike herding, planting had an ancient and meaningful place in the Indian construction of gender.

Hawkins wrote more about the relationship between gender and the "plan of civilization" than did any of the government agents of his day. He perceived the profound division of Indian society into male and female spheres. Neglecting consideration of Indian thought, he maintained, as did all early advocates of the civilizing mission, that the Indians' social organization consisted simply of a division of labor between female agriculturalists and male hunters. And like most American observers, he thought of Indian women as the men's slaves, "destined to every office of labour and fatigue." The men he thought "too proud to labour."[6]

Hawkins portrayed his plan of civilization as a program for female

insurgency. Indian men, he wrote, feared that if women took up the spinning of cloth and were "able to cloathe themselves, they will attempt to
break the chains which degrade them." Women, on the other hand, appeared "capable of and willing to become instrumental in civilizing the
men." As he attempted to instigate a gender revolution, Hawkins achieved
a measure of success in the first step: encouraging women to spin cloth. He
reported in 1801 that "spinning and weaving had increased, had spread into
the several towns, and begun to be the theme of conversation among the
women." With the initial success, he grew enthusiastic about his prospects
for effecting a conversion of the Indian labor system. But Creeks molded
spinning around their customary arrangements. Creek men did not rush to
take up the plow, much less to work fields between the planting and the
harvest. In 1802, the powerful Mad Dog politely told Hawkins that men
might someday farm, but as long as they had some game, they would hunt.
Although Creek men would not "throw away" the idea of farming, their
hunting would continue.[7]

Nor did women fully comply with Hawkins's designs. Intent upon
destroying Creek gender roles as he understood them, Hawkins miscalcu-
lated the degree to which women would support him. Hawkins assumed
that Indian women would hurry to liberate themselves from what he saw
as oppression. When they did not, he teetered between his fabricated role
of the amused parent and his actual part, the confused outsider. In one
incident, a Creek grandmother offered Hawkins her daughter, as a mate
apparently. Hawkins, though a bachelor, treated the offer as an opportunity
to vaunt the virtues of Anglo-American marriage.[8] Ever careful, he jotted
down a reply before reading it to the elderly woman. He opened by
praising the daughter's beauty and family, noting with a trace of sarcasm,
that she had "some fine children, which I shant be pleased with." And here
began his critique of Creek gender roles. Americans make "companions"
of their wives, he argued, while Indians make "slaves of theirs." American
husbands provide for and "govern their families," while "red men take
little care of theirs, and the mothers have the sole direction of the children." It failed to impress the agent that the mother's "sole direction" in
a matrilineal society meant that she had support from her siblings and
clanspeople, which gave her a measure of independence from her husband
unknown among most married women of the republic. If, Hawkins continued, he ever did accept a Creek woman, and she had children, "I shall
look upon them as my own children . . . and no one of her family shall
oppose my doing so." Women should be proud of their husbands, he
concluded, "should always take part with them and obey them," and
"should make the children obey them." In the interest of "civilization,"

Hawkins sought at once to relieve women from their supposed enslavement to their husbands and to put them under their husbands' rule. He did not notice that what he offered was to replace the communal drudgery of the fields for the isolated drudgery of the home, at the cost, to women, of both their "absolute rule" over the children and the outside support of their matrilineal families.

Hawkins recorded that his opening compliments pleased the older woman, but that during his critique of Creek practices "she remained silent, and could not be prevailed on to acquiesce in the conditions proposed." In particular, "she would not consent that the woman and children should be under the direction of the father, and the negotiation ended there." Creek women would not easily exchange their "slavery" for Hawkins's patriarchy. As late as the 1840s, after most Creeks had been forced across the Mississippi, an officer in the United States Army reported that Creek women, by "a Creek rule . . . hold the children in case of separation of man and wife."[9] Such was not then the legal practice among Anglo-Americans.

The revolution in gender toward which Hawkins and others worked faced another barrier as formidable as those posed by cosmology, by the dislike of Anglo-Americans, by the love for tradition, or by the defense against the loss of power. It was what we might call a practical consideration: women knew the soil. They, not the men, knew how to cultivate crops and how to work their particular fields. Nothing in the hunters' training could prepare them for the task the Americans now outlined for them. A revolution in gender would mean the loss of knowledge that Indians, whether male or female, would not casually risk despite the republic's pressure.

Slavery

While the Indians' conceptions of gender threatened to frustrate the U.S. plan of civilization, their conceptions of race were developing along lines similar to, but not identical with, those of the southern citizens. The American agents found southern Indians already engaged in the ugly business of chattel slavery. While the Northwest Ordinance of 1787 prohibited slavery's expansion in the North, thus prohibiting the American cultural missionaries to the northern region from promoting the peculiar institution, no such restriction blocked southern cultural missionaries. Whereas the Quakers, in 1800 among the most prominent of American anti-slavery groups, provided the northern Indians with their example of a yeoman civilization, in the South it was provided by men like Benjamin Hawkins, a slaveholder, by Moravian missionaries who also owned and employed slaves, and by Return Jonathan Meigs and Gideon Blackburn, who did not interfere with the Indian adoption of a form of the institution.[10]

More important, Southern Indians had long been exposed to black slavery. Indian slaveholding changed over time and varied from place to place, but its basic chronology has been established. In the late seventeenth and early eighteenth centuries, South Carolina's neighboring Indians, including Cherokees, Southern Shawnees, and Creeks, raided other peoples, took captives, and sold them as slaves to the English settlers. In later years, Indians captured black slaves from southern whites. These captive African-Americans were sometimes adopted, but they were increasingly enslaved in the course of the late eighteenth century, and were often carried great distances to be sold to other Euro-Americans.[11]

During the Revolutionary War, Creeks amassed slaves both in raids upon American settlements and as rewards for their services to the British. Benjamin Hawkins noted in 1801 that Creek slaves called themselves "King's gifts." Many of the British traders to the Creeks and Cherokees had remained loyal to the crown and escaped with their slaves from the revolutionary states into Creek territory.[12] Some Indians, particularly—but not exclusively—those related by blood to these traders, took up the practice of employing black slaves as an agricultural labor force in the 1780s.

By the early 1790s, when the invention of the cotton gin provided for the survival of the South's peculiar institution until the Civil War, black slavery had become established among the Creeks and Cherokees. Slaveholding Indians tended to form the rising elites with whom the republic had to negotiate land cessions, and through whom the government hoped to implement its "plan of civilization." A few members of these elites, meanwhile, had already begun to experiment with full-blown plantation slavery. The Creek elite had even obtained vassalage in the aggressively expanding kingdom of cotton, processing the crop at traders' gins along the Alabama River.[13]

Slavery and Indian "civilization" became intimately related in the South, not only because the Euro-American models and missionaries promoted it, but also because slavery permitted the new southern Indian elites to take on selected accoutrements of "civilization," of Anglo-American culture, without violating their conceptions of gender. This was no simple or wholesale borrowing of an odious Anglo-American practice. Rather, the adaptation required a reformulation of Indian notions of the slaves' genders, a reformulation that produced a social pattern strikingly different from that which prevailed in the southern states.

Hawkins, like other agents of civilization, sought to remove Indian women from the fields, but he had no problem with their replacement by an African-American slave force that included female field hands. For Hawkins, Indian women had to quit farming, but black women could, with the sanction of the Anglo-American model, be forced to work crops. Historian Deborah Gray White points out that slaveholders in the United States accepted the "defeminization of black women." One visitor to the Old South went so far as to claim that white southerners did not consider black women "to belong to the weaker sex."[14] As far as those who directed the plantations were concerned, black women and white women were differently gendered. Among slaveholding Indians, conversely, it was enslaved men and kinsmen, that is, men of the people, who were differently gendered. Adopted men, whatever their perceived color, stood with their new kinsmen as real people, but enslaved men, however male, and increasingly of African descent, had a place in the fields with women both slave and free. Not adopted, not members of a clan, they were not conceived of as real men, they were not warriors or hunters, and they could therefore not threaten the fields.

Creek Divisions

Southern Indian "civilization," then, did not accord with the Anglo-American model. American agents achieved only limited successes as they attempted to control the direction of change in Creek government and culture, and those successes met either adaptation or opposition. Slavery may even have provided opponents of the mission with argument, for Creeks, no less than the Shawnees and other northerners, suspected American missionaries of abetting an American plan to enslave Indians; on those grounds some plotted to drive Hawkins from the nation. Others objected more directly to the "plan of civilization" itself. Hawkins noted a "spirit or party of opposition" that prevailed in "more or less every town in the nation." Each of his proposals to the Creeks was "immediately opposed." One town even divided formally in halves: "the ill-disposed" to Hawkins's plan "remained in the town, and the others moved across the river and fenced their fields." Another village kept whites at a distance and attempted to avoid contamination: "As soon as a white person has eaten of any dish and left it, the remains are thrown away, and everything used by the guest immediately washed." In 1803, Indians of the Lower Creek town of Oositche anticipated the Shawnee Prophet by insulting their accommodating leaders, and they went much further: "They would adhere to old times," they declared, for " they preferred the old bow and arrow to the gun." But it was American influence in the Creek National Council that provided the most fundamental and persistent source of discontent within the Creek confederacy in the years before the arrival of Tecumseh and Seekaboo. Particularly repugnant to dissident Creeks were the council's land sales to the Americans, most negotiated with the careful Benjamin Hawkins. Hawkins, with more influence than any other Anglo-American in Creek affairs, portrayed himself as the defender of Creek lands against the unjust encroachments of Georgia, and that is how his Georgian enemies saw him. Seaborn Jones lashed out at Hawkins for his "partiality to savages." Criticizing Hawkins's promise to remove white settlers from Creek lands, Jones disputed Creek possession and objected to "yielding up part of a well settled country."[15]

Whatever his critics said of him, Hawkins favored American expansion, although he thought it should advance honorably. He lamented the plight of the targeted white settlers, "a poor decent, orderly and industrious set of people," who had fallen on the Indian side of the line that he ran in 1798 to settle the Treaty of Coleraine (1796). Although he willingly presided over this setback to American expansion, he later worked with the federal government to obtain U.S. title to the contested lands. This the government accomplished, with a little of what Reginald Horsman calls "judicious bribery," in the Treaty of Fort Wilkinson (1802) and the Treaty of Washington (1805). The very text of the 1802 treaty displays the U.S. promise to pay off the government chiefs, granting one thousand dollars in personal annuities "for the term of ten years, to the chiefs who administer the government, agreeably to a certificate under the hands and seals of the commissioners of the United States."[16]

Such proceedings combined with the cessions themselves to precipitate rebellion. Mad Dog, while speaking for Creek negotiators at the 1802 treaty, informed Hawkins of fissures in the nation. "Many of the old chiefs," he said, "are opposed to us" and to the council's cooperation with the United States. An 1805 treaty fed even greater opposition, for it ceded the finest remaining hunting ground in the nation. What was more, it allowed the United States to construct and to use regularly a "horse path" across the heart of the nation, from the Ocmulgee River (near present Athens, Georgia) to Fort Stoddert in the Mobile region. The "path" quickly became a twenty-foot wide road that aroused the anger of the very chiefs who signed the treaty permitting it. The road encouraged the Anglo-American settlement of the Tensaw region near Mobile, settlements that destroyed the hunting ground of the Creeks' Alabama confederates. The Alabamas, not surprisingly, would provide militant nativists with hearty support in 1813.[17]

According to one report, Hawkins, the supposed defender of Indian land, even advocated Creek removal west of the Mississippi, though he did so carefully and quietly. George Stiggins, a Creek who deeply admired Hawkins and who wrote on the basis of hearsay evidence almost twenty years after the fact, recalled that in 1808 a principal chief, the Singer, had agreed to explore lands west of the Mississippi. The Singer had promised Hawkins that if he found suitable land he would work among the Creeks for removal, but he was killed before he could carry out the task.[18]

So strong did internal opposition to land cessions, road building, and removal become that even Hawkins's usual ally, the Creek National Council, temporarily held out against intense American pressure for a treaty that would allow the United States to build a new road from the Tennessee River to Fort Stoddert. In September 1811, under orders from Secretary of War William Eustis and President James Madison, Hawkins informed the body that the United States would build the road regardless of the Creeks' wishes.[19] Hawkins, who had claimed credit for creating the Creek National Council with its rule of law, thus overruled it unilaterally by American fiat. By finally caving in to the American demand, the accommodationists suffered a stunning blow, and Creek independence lay deeply in question.

At this critical turn, the annuity chiefs, prostrate before American authority, met two more challenges: one from the north, the other from their southeast. From the Great Lakes Country, Tecumseh and Seekaboo arrived with the familiar message of pan-Indian unity, a message now joined, at least implicitly, to a call for the overthrow of government chiefs. The road issue, central to the Creeks' own understanding of their loss of power, gave weight to these northerners' militant message. From the Seminole country to the Southeast, meanwhile, came news that drove the northerners' point home. The United States had invaded Seminole lands, claimed also by Spain, and the Seminoles were bound by ties of language and lineage to the Creeks. The invasion was termed by Americans the "Patriot's War."

The Americans met unexpected resistance. Hard fighting and well-laid defenses by Seminoles, among them many escaped slaves whom the Seminoles did not treat as chattels, sapped the invaders' strength while Spanish protests embarrassed the federal government, caught in an act of aggression. As other issues forced war with Britain to loom, Washington abandoned the expedition.[20] But the attack could only add to militant arguments, now supported by northern visitors. Neither the United States nor its client chiefs could be trusted, and Creek militancy swelled.

Hawkins had long considered it imperative to peace between the Americans and the Creeks that Creek murderers of whites be executed by order of the National Council. Between the springs of 1812 and 1813 a series of killings of whites by Creeks, perhaps planned by militants as a rebellious challenge to the Creek National Council, provoked that body to violence. By April 1813, the council had slaughtered over ten of its countrymen and had dutifully reported the killings to Hawkins.[21] The killings were hardly executions. Far from being ritualized affairs designed to awe the public, performances dramatizing state power and justice, the council's executions were actually surprise attacks, affairs whose very lack of ritual or order revealed the council's weakness more than its strength. The council could assassinate, but it could not "perform" its authority.

The council's victims included an admired militant, Little Warrior, who had joined Tecumseh in his travels back north. Little Warrior's assassination—he was hunted down in a swamp, attempting to resist the council's gunmen with his bow and arrows—outraged Creek nativists and triggered an internal Creek war. Militants now determined, at all odds, to kill the accommodating leaders Big Warrior, Alexander Cornells, William McIntosh, and a few others. American General James Wilkinson, stationed in the Creek nation, wrote in June 1813 that the nativists had besieged Big Warrior's fortified town of Tuckabatchee, intent upon slaughtering the chief "and all who have been concerned in the execution of the murderers." The government chiefs of the Creeks reaped what their cooperation with the Americans had sown, a bitter harvest of internal discord. They turned to the United States for military assistance.[22] The appeal brought about the lifting of the siege but did nothing to reduce the intensifying ferocity of what was now a civil war.

Cherokee Divisions

As the Creek Civil War escalated, the militants, who came to be called the Red Sticks, followed the strategy of their forebears and appealed to the Cherokees.[23] Although since the mid-1750s militant Creek emissaries had found allies among Cherokee factions, most notably the Chickamaugas from 1776 to 1794, in 1812 the militants failed. Cherokees, it is true, had been reported among the Shawnee nativists in the North, and some Cherokees now attended kindly to the Red Sticks, but no known Cherokee militants allied with the militant Creeks. In fact, the Red Sticks met with severe Cherokee opposition; as many as eight hundred Cherokees took up arms against the southern militants, playing decisive roles in at least two major battles.[24] What had happened to Cherokee militancy?

One thing is certain. The Cherokee rebuff to the Red Sticks cannot be attributed to "traditional" intertribal animosities. Although the Cherokees had fought the Creeks throughout much of the early eighteenth century, by 1813 it had been some sixty years—a period of considerable cooperation among militants of both nations—since the last serious conflict between the two peoples. During the Creek War, moreover, American-allied Creeks fought side by side with Cherokees, Cherokee villagers gave shelter to Creek refugees, and Cherokees attempted to protect captured Red Stick women and children from American troops.[25] The conflict was neither tribal nor ethnic.

The Red Stick failure to recruit Cherokees stemmed instead from a peculiar cluster of circumstances that had both drained some one thousand opponents of the civilizing mission from the Cherokee nation and had united the remaining Cherokees in what William G. McLoughlin aptly labels a common, "nationalist" struggle against an American policy. What had encouraged both the emigration of a large body of traditionalists and the development of Cherokee unity was the American plan to "remove" the Cherokees across the Mississippi.[26] Federal agents had more quietly raised such a plan among the Creeks, but only among the Cherokees had they pushed it with blind determination. This first removal crisis, as it is called, created divisions among the Cherokees that were unfamiliar to the Creeks, Shawnees, and Delawares. The threat of removal subdivided both nativists and accommodationists, and new factions emerged. But the old differences in outlook did not evaporate, even in the heat of so burning an issue. The differences ran at levels too deep for that.

The willingness to accommodate to American power had developed among the Cherokees in much the same manner as it had among other peoples in the years following the defeat of pan-Indianism in 1794. But it had done so with still greater strength. The United States dominated them with forts, wooed them with the civilizing mission, and enticed their leaders with bribes. In 1794, Fort Southwest Point and Fort Tellico Blockhouse, both with ready access to reinforcements, stood guard over Cherokee villages. In 1806, Tellico fell out of use and Americans replaced it with a stockade near the town of Hiwassee.[27] Even without the forts Cherokee militants had to consider their new geography. The Cherokee nation sat between the American pincers of Tennessee and Georgia; potential militants had to confront the overwhelming likelihood of defeat in the event of war.

Accompanying the American forts and coinciding with the near surrounding of the nation by American states was the civilizing mission. Although the phrase "Five Civilized Tribes" had yet to enter American parlance on the eve of the War of 1812, the Cherokees had earned a degree of recognition from Americans for their interest in adopting elements of

Anglo-American culture. Most of these early reports recklessly exaggerated the Cherokee developments. As early as 1801 Benjamin Hawkins praised what he called the "total change" that his "plan for their civilization" had wrought. In 1808, crediting churchmen rather than federal agents, the Cherokees' Presbyterian missionary, Gideon Blackburn, wrote optimistically of his five-year-old mission that "My Indian experiment has in no instance fallen below my expectation—its effects are apparent not only on the pupils but on the Nation."[28] Hawkins and Blackburn overestimated; the civilizing mission had actually reached only a small segment of Cherokee society. But that segment, to be sure, was politically influential.

Both religious missionaries and federal agents worked to promote "civilization" among the Cherokees. The Moravians Abraham Steiner and Gottlieb Bryhan settled with the Cherokees in 1801 as the first missionaries to work extensively among them. Moravian missionaries, on the whole, were an undeniably patient lot, willing to wait years for the satisfying taste of spiritual victory. Among the Cherokees, the Moravians would enjoy that taste very, very rarely.[29] By 1811, their success was still negligible. Close on the Moravians' heels, in 1805, came the Presbyterian Blackburn. Unlike the Moravians, who thought an understanding of Christianity could precede reading knowledge of the Bible and who cared far less about the trappings of Euro-American civility, Blackburn, in fine step with British and American Calvinist mission history, sought to convert the Indians to civility before attending seriously to their souls. This suited Cherokee leaders, who sought not the Americans' religion but rather the skills they needed to interact successfully with Americans.[30] In converting souls, consequently, Blackburn achieved no more success than had the Moravians before his mission ended in 1810. The Cherokees were in no way a Christian people on the eve of the War of 1812. Their traditional beliefs remained too strong.

The war department's more secular effort to alter Cherokee culture, an effort promised in the Treaty of Hopewell (1791), did not really get under way until after the true end of war in 1794. The Tellico Blockhouse Treaty of that year, which ended, for the most part, Cherokee hostilities, also promised the standard annuities. By 1795 a significant feature of the mission was under way, as blacksmiths employed by the federal government worked among the Cherokees. Soon thereafter, visiting Moravian missionaries learned from the federal agent that the Cherokee nation possessed herds of cattle, droves of hogs, and three hundred plows and cotton cards.[31]

Among the Cherokees as among the Creeks, African-American slaves may have been the most important agents of cultural change. Cherokee neighborhoods with more slaves were identified by American agents as places where the "desire for individual property was very prevalent." And through the curious agency of the recent war, no region had more slaves than the one that had recently been the most militant section of the country, the section that had raided the republic most actively: the Chickamauga region, now more commonly called the Lower Towns.³² These Lower Towns differed markedly from the Upper Towns, the older villages in the eastern half of the Cherokee nation.

In part, the Chickamauga leaders embraced both slavery and the civilizing mission following their defeats in 1794 precisely because they had amassed slaves during their raids on the American settlements of the South. Two reports from 1808 and 1809 agree that Cherokees (population 12,400) held 583 blacks in bondage, most of them in the Chickamauga regions of northern Georgia and northern Alabama. It is not clear just how many of these slaves might have been held by the 341 reported whites in the nation, including the 113 white men with Indian wives, though the number is likely to have been substantial. We do know that, at least in later years, European ancestry correlated closely, but not exactly, with slaveholding: while only a fifth of Cherokees claimed some European ancestry in 1835, over three-quarters of Cherokee slaveholders did. It was this group, according to Meigs in 1805, that stood "in favor of improvements & have very much thrown off the savage manners and habits of their ancestors."³³

The Chickamauga region did not entirely shed its militant past, however. It had not become a solid bastion of assimilation. Despite the higher incidence of slavery and the more widespread acceptance of the "civilizing" mission, *most* Chickamaugas were slaveless and ambivalent toward Anglo-American ways. Not many Chickamaugas possessed the resources to adopt the slave-based commercial agricultural practices of their government chiefs even had they wanted to do so. Most Cherokees, including most Chickamaugas, therefore stuck with the old economy, modified in many cases by the herding of cattle or the droving of hogs. Some Chickamauga men ventured across the distant Mississippi to find game; others substituted horse stealing and trading for hunting and war. Similarly, of the "civilizing" minority, some lived outside the Lower Towns. James Vann, for example, one of the wealthiest Cherokees, lived in the Upper Towns. Least influenced by the mission was a subsection of the Upper Towns, known as the Valley.³⁴

The 3,000 or so Valley Cherokees lived in that portion of the Upper Towns that constituted what was left of the original homeland. The Valley people held the fewest slaves, only 5 of the 583 held by the Cherokee nation as a whole. Just as the regions worked by slaves and most thickly freckled with Euro-American inhabitants supported the civilizing mission, so the Valley Cherokees, with the fewest slaves and lowest incidence of European ancestry and influence, rejected the attempts by cultural missionaries to direct their ways.

On one level, then, the Cherokees resembled Indians across the borderlands. An emerging elite, backed by agents of the "plan of civilization," supported by its ability to distribute annuities, and desperate to avoid a recurrence of the terrible wars of the past, began to consolidate power in national affairs. Many of these Cherokee leaders—Chickamaugas Doublehead, Dick Justice, and the Glass, for example—carried with them reputations as brave opponents of the United States in earlier wars. They shared this reputation with the leaders of accommodation in other nations: the Shawnee Black Hoof, the Potawatomi Five Medals, the Miami Little Turtle, and the Creek Mad Dog. But the Cherokee elite would become more resilient than these others, and what would make it so, in addition to its greater wealth and its greater military vulnerability, would be a grave internal political struggle, followed rapidly by the first removal crisis.

Elite Cherokee Factionalism and the First Removal Crisis

In October 1805, under pressure from the American agent, Return Jonathan Meigs—pressure that included the threat of withholding annuities—Cherokee leaders agreed to cede about ten million acres of land north of the Tennessee River, allowing the unification of eastern and middle Tennessee. Further, they sanctioned the presence of two new roads that had been illegally built through their country, despite the objections of several important leaders in the Upper Towns. For both concessions the United States provided the Cherokees with annuities, and it reserved small tracts of land, privately, for leaders Doublehead and Toluntuskee. Even for those who did not know that an additional secret clause granted yet another large tract to Doublehead, the deal reeked of bribery and boded ill for the unity of the Cherokee elite.[35]

The federal government allowed the Cherokee leaders very little rest after the 1805 treaty. To gain new cessions, it supported a Cherokee embassy to Washington in the winter of 1805–6. While there, Cherokee negotiators learned not only of Doublehead's acceptance of a secret American bribe, but of yet another gift, worth one thousand dollars, given to the Chickamauga hero "in consideration of his active influence in forwarding the views of Government."[36]

A violent political struggle followed the disclosures. The Upper Towns, whose councils met at Oostenali in April 1806, immediately objected, sending word to Thomas Jefferson that they supported all previous land sales to the United States, except the grants to Doublehead and members of his party. Reminding the United States of Cherokee conceptions of land ownership, they declared that "lands & reservations shall belong to the whole nation & not to individuals." They also pointed out that Double-head, as a speaker alone and not a Beloved Man, had no authority to accept such gifts.[37] In September 1806, a faction under elite leader James Vann, which included dissidents from the Lower as well as the Upper Towns, seized the initiative at the National Council, declaring that future cessions fell under the authority of the council alone; federal agents could no longer select chiefs who would pretend to speak for the nation. The council also claimed control of all annuities. But Doublehead, absent from the meeting and supported by the principal chief, Black Fox, convinced the federal agents to overlook the council's demands. Boldly ignoring the council's declarations, he and his faction entered into negotiations for yet another cession to the United States. Two factions of Cherokees, each friendly to the civilizing mission, began consolidating into mutually hostile camps.

Over the summer and fall of 1807, Doublehead's faction flouted the council and yielded thirty-six square miles to an American citizen in-volved in a federally sponsored mining project. In addition to the two thousand dollars that the United States agreed to pay the Cherokee nation, the compliant chiefs, members of the Doublehead faction, received a thousand dollars and two rifles each. Doublehead himself, no longer among the living, was not among the bribed. By the time this last agree-ment over lands between the Cherokees and the Americans had been reached, a party of angry and determined National Council members had called Doublehead "to an account," assassinating him at the national ball play on August 9, 1807.

Doublehead's murder did not heal the fractured Cherokee elite, nor did it immediately consolidate the ascendancy of the victim's opponents, with whom the federal government continued to talk. But Vann's faction was able deftly to unseat its opponents in the fall of 1808. That is when it discovered that several of the late Doublehead's allies, again on their way to Washington, planned, with agent Meigs's concurrence, to discuss Cher-okee removal across the Mississippi.[38]

Until this point, the pattern of Cherokee politics—which displayed an emerging elite caught in its own internecine struggle between two fac-tions, each seeking support from the United States—did not differ dra-matically from the politics of Indian nations to the north and south. But when it became widely known that one of the elite factions, the faction most favored by the United States, was actively cooperating in a plan to deprive the Cherokees of their *entire* homeland, Cherokee politics departed from the pattern, as Vann's elite faction joined with militant opponents of the civilizing mission to stop the planned removal.

Meigs, the American agent, had favored the idea of Cherokee removal almost since the Louisiana Purchase had made it possible, in the arrogance of Euro-American "international law," for the United States to lay claim to Indian country west of the Mississippi. Throughout 1808, Meigs pushed the government chiefs, among whom representatives of the Lower Towns predominated, to "exchange" their lands for trans-Mississippi lands. The federal government supported his efforts. Meigs confidently believed that he could, with the proper proposal, "produce a general sentiment amongst them in favor of an exchange."[39]

His arguments in support of the "exchange," both before the Cherokees and before the secretary of war, laid bare his ambivalence for the Cherokees. On the one hand, Meigs lauded the Cherokees for their embrace of the civilizing mission; on the other hand, he made it clear that their accomplishments were not yet enough to qualify them for citizenship in the United States. With one breath, he could praise those who had "become good farmers." But in the next breath, he could argue that "the greatest number still love the hunting life better than farming." In one sentence, he could explain to the secretary of war that, because of the Cherokees' love for their land, "they must have strong excitements to leave the place of their nativity & graves of their fathers." But in another, he could recommend that the Cherokees be given, in the "exchange," western lands amounting to only one-half the area of the Cherokees' then-current holdings.[40]

His entire endeavor was paradoxical. While it would perhaps meet the unstated aim of the civilizing mission—the appropriation of Indian land in a manner that would not tarnish the image of the United States—it would work against the mission's ostensible aim, the assimilation of Indians with the Anglo-American yeomanry. The expressed goal of the civilizing mission had hitherto been the assimilation of the Cherokees, as smallholding, individual farmers, into the republic's body politic. While learning the ways of whites, the Cherokees were to trade their "surplus" lands for education in white ways. Thus both peoples would benefit by their eventual, peaceable, union. But Meigs had become dissatisfied by the Cherokees' mounting resistance to cessions, disappointed by their progress in education, and distressed by their turbulent government. As he abandoned the idea of a union with Americans in the near future, a union unwanted by most Cherokees and most Americans in any case, he began to argue against it. He spoke of removal as a way to "lengthen out their existence as a distinct people." Their "existence as a distinct people depends on their migrating."[41] Meigs had given up on assimilation; the civilizing mission's mooring had slipped within its most promising deep harbor.

Meigs did not speculate about the possibility that the Indians who already possessed the lands beyond the Mississippi might resent an invasion by tens of thousands of Cherokees, but the thought must have occurred to the Cherokees, who knew of those lands from hunting forays. Perhaps this consideration, along with the widespread determination to remain in their own country, encouraged a core of important Cherokee leaders—all opponents of the late Doublehead—to act quickly when news leaked that several allies of Doublehead were on their way to Washington to talk with the president about Meigs's proposal for an "exchange."

The leaked news proved highly combustible. The insurgent National Council met in Hiwassee, not far from the guns of a federal fort. It defiantly denounced as illegitimate the delegation to Washington, it deposed Black Fox, the Cherokees' principal chief and a member of the delegation, and it sent its own delegates to Washington. On their arrival, these insurgents displayed their tact, opening their speeches with thanks to the United States for the civilizing mission and stressing their faith in the republic's continued "magnanimity." After a full week of cordiality, they announced that they had thrown out their old leaders, Black Fox, Toluntuskee, and the Glass, all members of the Doublehead faction. They claimed the support of forty-two towns. The coup was justified, they argued, because the Lower Town's chiefs "had already made up their minds to move us out of our houses before we knew any thing of it." These old chiefs had also, the insurgents claimed, retarded Cherokee progress in gaining knowledge of white ways and had stood against the civilizing mission: "Father those men that wants to move . . . throw away the plow and pick up the gun and also throw away the wimmin Spinning wheles." The new Cherokee government promised to adhere to the civilizing mission, and asked the president to recognize Path Killer as the new headman.[42]

While two elite factions—each of which supported the civilizing mission and stood for accommodation—struggled over removal in 1808 and 1809, Cherokee opponents of the civilizing mission also divided. As historian John Finger has pointed out, some of these traditionalists favored removal. Particularly in the Chickamauga region, traditionalists felt the promising twin pulls of better hunting and isolation from white settlers. The Chickamaugas had some history of migration: three decades before they had left their natal villages for familiar hunting lands lower down the Tennessee River, and many of them regularly hunted beyond the Mississippi early in the decade. A minority of Chickamaugas decided to go west.

By the end of 1809, about a thousand Cherokees emigrated to Arkansas. Most left from the Chickamauga country, but some were from the Valley towns. Together the emigrants constituted perhaps a twelfth of the nation. At the head of one party stood Toluntuskee, an ally of Doublehead's who had also been bribed in the treaty of 1805 and who, now in ill favor, had every reason for wishing to leave. He was supported by others of the Lower Towns who opposed the recent coup and who continued to look upon the "old chiefs" as legitimate. Despite Meigs's encouragement, the emigrants received very little material assistance from the United States. This large party, a traditionalist majority headed by an elite, accommodating minority, settled on the Arkansas River by June 1810.

Other Cherokees, little touched by the civilizing mission, who lived in every corner of the nation but particularly those who clung to the original homeland in the Valley, stoutly opposed removal. The Valley people shared in what Meigs called in 1809 the "predilection for the hunters state." The towns of the Valley remained the region least influenced by the civilizing mission, and it is not surprising that many among them would obstinately refuse to emigrate even during the forced removal of the age of Jackson, three decades later.[43]

Elite factionalism, common among all borderland peoples, thus combined with traditional factionalism and the removal issue, intense only among the Cherokees, to separate the Cherokees out of the general Eastern Woodlands pattern on the eve of the War of 1812. While a struggle over the issue of accommodation—over how to treat the influence of Meigs, the civilizing mission, and the republic—still tugged at Cherokee loyalties, Cherokees of radically different cultural and political outlooks united to kill the federal project for the nation's removal. Most traditionalists across the Cherokee nation, with their religious attachment to their lands, joined with those elite government chiefs who felt strong attachment to their farms, herds, and commercial networks.

By September 1809, under the pressure of a general antipathy toward removal, several allies of the federal government, including Black Fox and the Glass, closed their ears to talk of an "exchange" of lands and reentered Cherokee politics, joining their opponents with the understanding that removal would require a decision in the full National Council. American agents never gave up the plan, but not for another decade would they find support for removal in Cherokee councils. On the eve of Tecumseh's visit southward, then, a significant, indeed a controlling portion of the Cherokee elite had consolidated power through a strong stand against removal, that most ambitious form of American expansion. This stand had won an elite Cherokee faction the loyalty of even those Cherokees who otherwise opposed government chiefs on such issues as the legitimacy of earlier cessions and the civilizing mission.

The Cherokee government chiefs had proved to their people that they could thwart dramatic and dangerous American plans. Unlike their counterparts to the north and south, who seemed ready to yield to American demands for lands and for road rights, a faction of the Cherokee elite had stood firm against removal and had seized control of the National Council. The accommodationists of this faction had shown that while they called for interdependence with the republic, they did not mean to be dominated by it. Cherokees who disagreed with them over the civilizing mission found agreement with them on this more perilous matter.

The Cherokees would consequently escape civil conflict on the scale of the disorders that soon shattered the Creeks to the south and the majority of still-independent peoples in the Old Northwest. The Cherokees would not face civil war. But the issue of the civilizing mission and the attendant rising influence of the United States in Cherokee affairs would survive the removal crisis, as would the memory of recent land sales. While the government chiefs of the Cherokees would not come under actual fire for their role in these issues, they would, like their counterparts to the north and to the south, meet challenging criticism in the form of a religious revival.

>>>>>>>>><<<<<<<<<<

NINE

Renewing Sacred Power
in the South

Creek and Cherokee politics were, as we have seen, deeply involved with the issues of land and dependence upon the United States. But if Tecumseh's visit to the South meant anything, it meant that Indian politics was also a matter of religion. This was particularly true for the Creeks, where the Red Stick challenge to the Creek National Council sprang largely from a quest for sacred as well as political power. Messianic dreams would stir Cherokees too; but more united in the wake of the removal crisis, the Cherokees would not, like the Creeks, be swept into the maelstrom.

Despite two and a half centuries of contact with Europeans, the Creeks who greeted Tecumseh in 1811 warmly held their religious traditions. Even accommodationist Alexander Cornells, born to a British father, invoked the doctrine of the separate creation in reply to Moravian missionaries. In 1811, Cornells told visitors that although Indians had no Bible, they knew God "without a book; they dream much of God, therefore they know it." Creek religion displayed less Christian influence at the turn of the nineteenth century than did its counterparts in the North. The old conjurer and great leader Mad Dog held views of the afterlife more ancient among Indians than those of the Shawnee Prophet: "Those who behaved well" headed west, where they joined their family and the Great Spirit, whereas those who "behaved ill, are left . . . to shift for themselves, and . . . there is no other punishment." But the understanding in the two regions of the importance of ritual to the securing of power was similar. To behave well

TECUMTHA

Tecumseh, the most famous participant in the struggle for Indian unity. No reliable portrait exists. This, widely regarded as the best, appeared in Benjamin Lossing's *Pictorial Field Book of the War of 1812* (New York, 1869). It is a post-1858 composite of two sketches made between 1810 and 1812: one, showing the head and headgear, by Pierre Le Dru, who met Tecumseh at Vincennes; the other, showing the bust, by an unknown British officer. (*Source:* National Anthropological Archives, Negative No. 770, Smithsonian Institution, Washington, D.C.)

meant in part to honor the central ceremonies. "It is our opinion," Mad Dog told Hawkins, "that the Boosketau and our physics proceeds from the goodness of [the Master of Breath]." Both the celebration of the Green Corn Ceremony and the ritual drinking of Black Drink remained central to Creek religious life in the early nineteenth century.[1]

Tecumseh and his visionary Shawnee companions thus entered a world in which it was still common to hear that proper rituals, prescribed for Indians by the Great Spirit, brought power. The northerners carried new rituals with them, rituals that were "intermixed with warlike sports," such as "wielding the war club." This item would mark the militant movement among the Creeks, as the militants became known for the symbolic weapon as the Red Sticks. Tecumseh's religious message, spoken and performed in ceremony, was integrally related to politics and diplomacy. It inspired others to take up the prophetic mantle.[2] It provided not only the movement's name but the language of resistance and the promise of victory.

Creek Prophets of War, 1811–1814 and Beyond

The Red Sticks performed the new war dances and war songs taught them by the northwesterners and attended to their own prophets, who devised rituals of their own. One of these may have been expressly designed as a ritual of rejection, directed against supporters of accommodation. Sam Moniac, a Creek and a trader, reported it. He met one of several Creek prophets, High Head Jim, on the path from the Upper Creek Towns to Pensacola in July 1813. Moniac shook hands with the nativist, who, dramatizing the danger of accommodation, "immediately began to tremble and jerk in every part of his frame, and the very calves of his legs would be convulsed, and he would get entirely out of breath with the agitation."[3] The most famous of Creek prophets, Hillis Hadjo, or Josiah Francis, like most American Indian nativists, opposed the growing influence of the Federal Government in Creek affairs, but he sought no total rejection of the technological and social transformations that Creeks had seen over the past century. He intended the Creek material inventory to retain many items of trans-Atlantic origin. Shortly after the American intervention in the Creek Civil War, he asked the Spanish for material assistance: "Our gunlocks have grown feeble with age, we need new ones, also clothes to cover our naked bodies, gunpowder, ball, and knives."[4]

Creek nativists, like their contemporaries and forebears in the North, did not oppose all things European, but they did seek to control cultural change. Their Creek opponent George Stiggins recalled that they forbade the salting of meats. They exhibited ambivalence about the adoption of herding. Many records indicate the widespread killing of cattle and hogs. The records are unclear as to the significance of the act; a portion point only to the destruction of the government faction's herds and say nothing of the nativists' stock. At the battle of Holy Ground and at a failed attack on Fort Sinquefield (September 2, 1813), the Red Stick prophets waved enigmatic banners: red cows' tails, some fastened to staffs, others tied along their arms.[5] These may have symbolized the Red Stick destruction of cattle, beasts that themselves represented accommodation, private property, and ties to the United States.

The clearest nativistic attack on accommodation had not to do with technological or material innovation, which Red Sticks often tolerated, but with faith and politics. It came in a religious assault with definite political overtones. The Red Sticks, perhaps following the example of their northern allies, accused the friends of the United States of witchcraft. The Creek prophets shared with Tenskwatawa the power, through ritual, to "be assured of such as were witches." These they seized and burned. As in the North, the accused frequently bore marks of accommodation. Many "of the most inlightened and well disposed to peace and good order," according to the accommodating Stiggins, met fiery ends. One of the accused, Captain Isaacs, participated in the National Council's killing of the nativist Little Warrior in April 1813. Isaacs, himself a noted conjurer, claimed to spend long periods at the bottoms of rivers conversing and learning from Great Horned Serpents. Because these mythological beasts embodied pure malevolence, it seems likely that Isaacs's own claims to sacred power gave substance to the nativists' suspicions. When the Creek National Council's gunmen under Big Warrior rescued Isaacs from an attempted assassination, the nativists drew their own conclusions.[6] From their point of view, the accommodating Isaacs, killer of a nativist leader, protected by the National Council, stood as the embodiment of evil. Nativists laid siege to Big Warrior's town of Tuckabatchee, and what had been a series of desultory assaults and retaliations became the Creek Civil War.

Creek Pan-Indianism

The Creek Civil War became the perverse consummation of the pan-Indian movement. Resounding with a chorus of ideas largely generated in the North, inspired by a historic spirit of intertribal militant cooperation, Red Sticks embarked on a path of mutual destruction with the government faction. Creeks entered the War of 1812 through the tempestuous passage of genuine civil war. The United States, though clearly provocative early on, came to actual blows with the Red Sticks only after a considerable escalation of internal Creek violence. The militants' endeavors to cooperate with northern militants against accommodationists in both regions brought the movement for Indian unity to a tragically divisive end.

But if the level of internal conflict among the Creeks exceeded levels elsewhere, the Creeks nonetheless conformed to the broad and paradoxical pattern of internal division over the idea of union. In their bid to defeat both the government chiefs within and, once war with the United States began, the Americans invading from without, the Red Sticks, themselves so affected by the Shawnees, appealed to militants in other tribes. Seeking help abroad, the militant Creeks hoped to draw on a widely shared militant sense of Indian identity. While their movement was itself in part a triumph of militant Shawnee diplomacy, their own efforts among other peoples would yield them little.

Reports circulated throughout the North in January 1812 that two hundred Creeks had gathered around the Shawnee Prophet. Some, with Little Warrior, had joined Tecumseh on the Shawnee's return to the North. Others had gone northward separately, some in advance of the great Shawnee. After Little Warrior came homeward, to meet his death at the hands of the Creek National Council, Red Sticks intensified their efforts to revive the old alliances. One report intimates that news of the killing sent some members of Little Warrior's party racing again to the northern Shawnees. As late as October 1812, another party also traveled northward "to Join the Prophet."[7]

But in 1812 the calls for Eastern Woodlands pan-Indianism sounded against the powerful baffles of an American presence in the West, stronger than any previously known. Throughout the War of 1812 the United States would tighten its already firm grip on the Tennessee, Ohio, and Mississippi rivers, shortly choking off the avenues of communication between the Indian north and south. The states of Tennessee, Kentucky, and Ohio stood as prodigious bulwarks against infiltration by the woefully outnumbered Indians, and additional American settlements spread and thickened along the riverbanks of Indiana, Illinois, and Missouri. The immigration of citizens would soon be decisive. Conflict in the Old Northwest during the War of 1812 would become quickly confined to the Great Lakes region, and in the South it only rarely would erupt north of the Tennessee River. Once the western states and territories had mobilized for war, they effectively severed the old Indian networks of northern and southern communication. The Indians' movement for unity did not collapse during the War of 1812, it was split to bits.

The militant Creeks, not perceiving the mounting odds in this manner,

tried to raise allies in the Southeast. They even sent unsuccessful delegations to peoples across the Mississippi. But their only notable success came
in securing the alliance of a people only recently regarded as separate: the
Seminoles. Hawkins once reported that the Seminoles "are Creeks," but
he quickly added that they had "left their old towns and made irregular
settlements" in east Florida. He noted that the very word Seminole meant
"wild" in Creek. The accommodationist Stiggins, no friend to the militants, wrote that the word referred to "any beast that is strayed from the
original stock."[8]

In August 1812, Hawkins discovered both that the Seminoles knew of
the Creek Prophet, Francis, and, more remarkably, that "they have a
prophet there also." Hawkins later learned that the Seminoles adhered
closely to their prophet. Increasingly nativistic, the Seminoles stood
against the Creek National Council. This they demonstrated when they
coolly informed a party of would-be assassins, sent by the National Council and Hawkins to "execute" Seminoles who had killed whites, that it
must give up its mission and declare support for the Seminole Prophet, or
its members would not return home alive.[9] Seminole support for nativistic
militancy later played a major role in the Red Sticks' survival, when
following Andrew Jackson's ferocious defeat of the militants, Francis and
the nativists fled from Alabama to Florida. Other migrant Red Sticks,
among them Osceola, lent their aid to the Seminoles in succeeding wars
with the United States.[10]

While appealing southeastward to the Seminoles, Red Sticks also appealed westward to the Choctaws, but here they drew a discouraging
response, although it was lined with some hope. Officially, the Choctaws
rejected the Red Sticks as they had previously rejected Tecumseh. Choctaw leaders later harmed the Creek militants by communicating Red Stick
intentions to the Americans. The Choctaw leader Pushmataha adopted the
strongest posture of accommodation, raising 135 warriors for the United
States in August 1813.[11]

But Choctaws, like others, were divided. Some did join the militants, as
we know from various sources. General F. L. Claiborne notified the secretary of war that parties of Choctaws fought beside the Creek militants, and
the Creek prophet Francis sent word to the Spanish requesting arms not
only for his own people but also for Choctaws and Seminoles, implying
that he had Seminole and Choctaw allies.[12] While isolated parties of Choctaw militants, who may not have numbered as many as thirty or forty,
could contribute little to the militant cause, their willingness to join the
Red Sticks against the will of their own leaders does suggest that the

strains tearing at Creek and northern Indian tribes pulled at the Choctaws as well. So too did they tear at the Cherokees.

Cherokee Visions

We have seen that by the end of 1810 the emerging Cherokee elite and the poorer, traditionalist Cherokee majority had shared in a common struggle against a most ambitious federal design on their homeland, while many of their Cherokee opponents had migrated west. The Cherokees' defeat of American plans gave ordinary Cherokees a measure of confidence in their National Council and may well, as William G. McLoughlin has argued, have given rise to a new, "national," Cherokee identity.[13] But the common struggle, while it strengthened and lent respect to an elite party that favored accommodation, did not eliminate all sources of nativistic opposition. Beginning in 1811, the strain between nativism and accommodation manifested itself, as among the other tribes, in a religious movement.

Contemporary reporters found the Cherokees very much attached to their religious beliefs in this period. In 1799 the Moravian, Abraham Steiner, wrote with alarm about the "many deceivers among the Cherokees, who go by the name of sorcerers." Return Jonathan Meigs, the federal agent, recorded in 1801 that Cherokees still strictly adhered to the Green Corn Ceremony. Despite the claims of some historians that the ceremony had lost its meaning, Meigs noticed how solemn an affair it was: "In dancing their motions are slow, decent, graceful, & regular, keeping perfect time with the music, hardly a smile to be seen on their faces. The appearance suggests the Idea of a religious dance." Meigs found the sincerity disturbing, wondering how the plan of civilization could succeed "while the ancient usages are so much ensconced." Even the accommodating rulers mixed politics with religion, as did their counterparts to the north and south. Before treating with Meigs in 1805, they scheduled the Green Corn Ceremony "to prepare their minds."[14]

As with all the borderland peoples, those individuals who adhered most closely to the "ancient usages" found themselves confronting both Cherokee and federal proponents of the civilizing mission. The strongest defenders of the traditional religion did not oppose change, but they rallied against change under American direction. The Cherokee revival constituted a revolt, expressed in religious rhetoric, against the influence of Americans in Cherokee affairs. For this reason, powerful Cherokees, who both supported the civilizing mission and who had negotiated earlier land cessions, chose to bring their popularity to bear against the religious move-

ment. It should be clear by now, but it bears emphasis, that these accommodationists were not federal tools. They had stood with the majority of
Cherokees against removal. Nor were they assimilationists. They still
attended Green Corn Ceremonies and ball plays. But they did seek the
assistance of the United States in economic development, and they did fear
that the Cherokee prophets might force them onto the losing side in yet
another lost cause.

The revival is better understood as a fully religious expression of social
and political conflict than, as one analyst suggests, as the cathartic reformation of Cherokee culture in the face of psychic stress. In its opposition
to direct American influence in Cherokee affairs, the movement can be
understood, moreover, as springing from the same sources that produced
the northern and Creek movements. The extensive contacts among
Creeks, Shawnees, and Cherokees since the mid-eighteenth century do
more to explain similarities in the movements than do psychological
profiles drawn by twentieth-century scholars.[15]

The nativists plainly expressed their objections to American influence.
Meigs, writing in the midst of the revival, noted a generalized hostility
toward the civilizing mission. The Cherokee visionaries, he wrote, "tell
them that the great spirit is angry with them for adopting the manners,
customs, and habits of the white people who they think are very wicked."
The prophets' followers tossed "off their clothing to the fire & burned
them up." Nativists targeted the fine muslin dresses, popular among young
women, as "causes of the displeasure of the great spirit." The struggle
against Anglo-American influence was remembered by Cherokees over
thirty years later, in an article unsympathetic to the revival printed in the
Cherokee Advocate. After a vision forecasting the end of the present world,
the article recalled, nativists headed for a designated sanctuary, abandoning "everything about them that came from, or savored of the *pale-faces*."[16]
These reports, though hostile to the revival, though perhaps extravagant,
do not miss its militant spirit.

Without lessening that spirit, the closest record of the visions, the
Springplace Moravian Mission Diary, reveals the greater complexity of the
revival.[17] The first two of a cluster of prophecies received by Cherokees
between the early months of 1811 and the spring of 1812 demanded that the
Indians throw out *specific* items of Anglo-American culture; they did not
mount a generalized assault on whites or white culture. They did, however, demand both the elimination of the American voice in the Cherokee
nation's political affairs, and the return, from the Americans, of sacred
places that had been ceded by the Cherokee National Council, a body that
felt strongly the influence of American agent Meigs.

During the first vision, received by "a man and two women," on Rock (also Rocky) Mountain in northwest Georgia, a messenger from the sky told the Indians that "God was dissatisfied that you are receiving the white people into your land without any distinction." The Cherokees should, in other words, take control of American influence. The messenger further chastised the Indians for planting "the corn of the white people"—barley, oats, and wheat—and for grinding Indian corn in mills instead of pounding it in mortars. Recalling ancient myths, the messenger invoked the corn goddess, widely revered by the borderland Indians and called *Selu* by the Cherokees. "The Mother of the Nation has forsaken you because all her bones are being broken through the grinding of the mills."

The messenger also spoke in the language of the separate creation of whites and Indians, the language that had been circulating throughout the Eastern Woodlands since at least the 1750s: "You yourselves can see that the white people are entirely different beings from us; we are made from red clay; they, out of white sand." This was not a new revelation to the Cherokees; Moravian Abraham Steiner reported a similar discussion of inherent differences in 1799, and late in the colonial period British agents had heard Cherokees speak of being under the charge of a different "Great Being" from that of the "white people." In 1805 Meigs repeated the widely held belief among Cherokees that "they are not derived from the same stock as the whites, that they are favorites of the Great Spirit, & that he never intended this people to live the laborious lives of the whites." Cherokees may have received the notion from other Eastern Woodlands peoples during the long wars of the mid to late eighteenth century, when militant Cherokees cooperated with militants from other peoples. But though the messenger used the theology of separation to justify his order to "put the white people out of the land," he modified that order by allowing Cherokees to build "four white houses" as dwellings for "white men who can be useful to the Nation with writing." Again, the prescription was not for a total purge of white influence, but for Cherokee control over that influence. The white people were to be treated well, but they were to live where the Great Spirit ordained them to live. And most significant, the United States was to yield back the "old Beloved Towns."[18]

Implied in this last point was criticism of the National Council for its extensive land cessions to the United States. These cessions had been made, to be sure, before the removal crisis of 1808–9, but in the years of the revival that was still the recent past, and the people still felt acutely the loss. The second prophecy, received in December 1811 (well after Tecumseh's visit to the nearby Creeks), more strongly directed the Cherokees to regain control over the beloved towns. The vision accompanied the series of earthquakes that radiated throughout the Mississippi and upper gulf drainages in 1811, adding eschatological urgency to the spiritual commands. A spiritual messenger revealed that the Great Spirit might soon "destroy the earth," for "God is not pleased that the Indians have sold so much land to the white people." The messenger repeated the Creator's special distress over the loss of the town of Tugaloo, which the government chiefs had sold in 1798, and which was "the first place which God created." He demanded that the Americans remove all buildings from Tugaloo's sacred hill; "on that hill there should be grass growing, only then will there be peace."[19]

The displeasure of the sacred powers at the cessions of land to the whites translated into a censure of the leaders who had negotiated those cessions. Such a censure was muted by the fact that Cherokee leaders had, unlike northern and Creek leaders, successfully resisted all efforts on the part of the United States to obtain land since 1807. But anger remained directed both at those cessions that had been made before the removal crisis and at the government chiefs responsible. Some of these leaders still occupied positions of conspicuous power.

The nativists' dislike for the Cherokee leaders, among the strongest advocates of the civilizing mission in the Eastern Woodlands, surfaced in the revival's early strictures against both milling and the raising of wheat and barley, "the corn of the white people." But the opposition to the elite is most clear in a commandment against the Cherokee National Council's developing legal system. In the first vision the messenger warned that Selu "is not pleased that you punish each other so hard, you even whip until [you draw] blood," a clear condemnation of the newly created patrols.[20]

Elite Reaction

If historians have recently underestimated the danger that the nativists posed to Cherokee elite rule, the elite itself did not. Ridge, a prominent government chief and friend of the Americans, denounced the first prophecy as soon as the visionaries reported it to the Oostenali council. Ridge would long stand against the nativistic delegates from Coosawatie, where the inhabitants maintained communal fields and stood against borrowing Anglo-American concepts of property. The Springplace Diary notes that Ridge's challenge to prophecy provoked the nativists to anger. Nineteenth-century historians Thomas L. McKenny and James Hall, who cite Ridge as their informant, write that the nativists "rushed upon" Ridge, who was rescued from a severe beating by the wealthy son of the late James Vann, among others.[21]

MAJOR RIDGE, A CHEROKEE CHIEF

Major Ridge stood against the Cherokee prophets and raised a force of Cherokees
to fight against the Red Stick Creeks. The lithograph, published by Thomas L.
McKenney in *History of the Indian Tribes of North America* [Plates] (Philadelphia,
187–?), was adapted from a painting done in Washington, D.C., in 1834, by an
unknown artist, probably Charles Bird King. (*Source:* National Anthropological
Archives, Negative No. 45-113-B, Smithsonian Institution, Washington, D.C.)

Early in the revival the Oostenali council sought a compromise with the nativists. By May 1811, it agreed to order all whites out of the nation, except for Meigs, the Moravian missionaries, four smiths, and "some school teachers." These, particularly the Moravians, the council deemed "very useful." At the council's request, Meigs sent federal troops to force illegal white settlers off the land. But beyond this level of support, the council yielded nothing to prophecy. In fact, it explicitly allowed those whites "who are building mills for us," to remain, in obvious defiance of the revival's strictures against milling.[22]

Elite opposition to prophecy intensified in 1812, as did the nativist objection to American influence. A new series of visions more directly challenged the adoption of white ways. One prophet ordered the Cherokees to "put aside everything that is similar to the white people and that which they had learned from them," particularly "any clothing or household articles of the white man's kind, together with all their cattle." Those who refused would be "snatched away," along with "all the white people," during a three-day period of darkness. James Vann's Christian widow embodied the elite response; she not only stood up to the prophets, she also purchased the disposed goods "just to show them that she did not pay any attention to the lies."[23]

"Mother Vann" did not stand alone. Charles Hicks, then the Cherokees' only other practicing Christian, called the prophets "liars" and advised the leading men to disavow them. In April 1812, the leaders united against the movement. One of them, the old counselor Sour Mush, spoke against nativism at Oostenali, employing acute accommodating logic. Cherokees, he argued, had to respect American power, regardless of what they thought of sacred power, for the Americans could kill with far greater certainty than could the earthquakes frequently invoked as spiritual chastisement by the nativists.[24]

Ritual, an integral part of the other revivals, lay at the center of the Cherokee movement. The first of the recorded visions of 1812 dwelt, like the Creek and northwestern prophecies, on the need for good ritual. A messenger from the sky world criticized the Indians because they had not properly observed the Green Corn Ceremony, because they had failed to "thank God before they enjoy the first fruits." Meigs reported that spring that the Cherokees now performed "the religious dances of ancient origin with as much apparent solemnity as ever was seen in worship in our churches." The Cherokees endeavored by these rituals "to appease the Anger of the Great Spirit occasioned by the late shocks of the earth." Records indicate that the Cherokees attributed recent earthquakes to the Great Spirit's anger over land sales, suggesting that the intensification of

ritual may have been more an attempt to purify the people of the abomination brought on by particular dealings with Americans than an attempt
to reverse serious prerevival religious declension. Meigs further noted that
the revivalists sought to wash away their spiritual "defilement" by ritual
bathing in the rivers.[25]

In its concern with both the disappearance of the game and the loss of
power occasioned by abomination, the Cherokee prophecy resonated with
Creek and northern prophecy. Even the form of the Cherokees' spiritual
encounters invites comparison with those of the northerners and Creeks.
Just before one vision, a Cherokee prophet sat "in his house deep in
thought, and his children were lying sick in front of the fire." Neolin and
Handsome Lake both experienced their visions as they contemplated the
sinfulness of their people by their fires; Tenskwatawa's first vision came
while he was tending the sick among the Delawares. Much as fabulously
clad celestial visitors entered the doorways of Handsome Lake and Neolin,
a Cherokee prophet, sitting by the fire, confronted "a tall man, clothed
entirely in the foliage of the trees, . . . who was carrying a small child in
his arm." The small child, the Great Spirit, may have been of Christian
influence, but it is noteworthy that both a Delaware visionary of the 1760s
and a Shawnee medicine society of the 1780s confronted diminutive deities.
In another sign of Cherokee participation in the wider movement, a participant in the Cherokee revival burned his hat at a public council and
called upon others to do the same. Like the Delaware Prophet of the 1760s,
the Shawnees and Delawares of the 1780s, and the contemporary Ottawa,
the Trout, this Cherokee saw in the hat a symbol of Anglo-America.[26]

The Cherokee revival, then, did not stand in complete isolation from
other movements. It drew on a common heritage of Indian ideas, sprang
from similar social conditions, and precipitated familiar political conflict.
Although with a different outcome, Cherokee conflict over the revival
followed patterns established among northerners and Creeks. The Cherokee revival resembled the northern and Creek revivals in its criticism of
the land cessions made by the government chiefs, in its rejection of certain
Anglo-American cultural forms, and in its objections to the reach of
American power into Indian government. Like followers of the Seneca
Prophet, Cherokee nativists did not go to arms in 1812, but they meditated
on prophecy in consonance with Creek and northwestern militants. A
corollary to the similarity is also worth considering: Creek and Cherokee
opponents of nativism recognized common goals. The Cherokee elite may
well have rushed to support the Creek National Council in order to
prevent Cherokee militants from rushing into what it saw as a hopeless
cause.

When fratricidal killings among the Creeks brought that nation civil war in 1812, Creek government chiefs felt compelled to explain the killings to the Cherokees. By the time the Creek Civil War had actually broken out, accommodating Cherokees raised a force "to go to the relief of the Government party" among the Creeks, but the Red Sticks had dispersed before the Cherokees entered Creek territory. The Creek civil conflict drew in the United States in late July 1813. After that, Americans joined the Creek government chiefs in seeking Cherokee assistance against the rebellious Red Sticks.[27]

Tied to the Americans by their interests as well as by their belief that the best way to survive American power was to cooperate discriminately with it, the opponents of the Cherokee revival—Ridge included—would openly support the Americans and Creek government chiefs in a war against the Red Stick Creek militants. The Cherokee opponents of the Cherokee revival, therefore, also opposed the Creek revival, but they did so on their own. There is no evidence that they enrolled Cherokee nativists in their war parties. They could not persuade the entire nation, or even its American-oriented National Council, to unite in a declaration of war on the Red Sticks. When they called for a Cherokee war on the Red Sticks, the council "concluded to lye still." Cherokees plainly disagreed with one another over what actions to take in the war. Their disagreements reflected concern over many of the same issues that divided all Eastern Woodlands peoples in these years.[28]

The first of Cherokee visions had occurred before Tecumseh's 1811 visit to the Chickasaws, Choctaws, and Creeks, but the Cherokee revival clearly accelerated after the Red Stick Creeks had adopted nativism with zeal. These later Cherokee visions called for a more militant posture toward the Anglo-Americans. This was no coincidence; it came about because of Cherokee-Creek contacts. Major centers of the Cherokee revival, Etowah and Coosawatie, lay on tributaries of the nearby Coosa River that flowed west and south into the neighboring Upper Creek country, a region thick with Red Sticks. The towns' proximity to Creek militancy allowed them to trade more easily with the Creeks in ideas than could much of the rest of the Cherokee nation; in any case Cherokee contacts with the Creeks were common. As recently as 1807 Meigs had discovered that Creeks resided "amongst the Cherokees" on the Tennessee River.[29] When Tecumseh addressed the Creeks in October 1811, he did so in the presence of Cherokees. Meigs noted of Tecumseh's address that there were Cherokees attending to the northern "Shawanoe Chief," who, accompanied by nineteen other northerners, counseled peace with the United States but admonished his listeners to "keep your lands."[30] The Cherokees, although almost surrounded by Anglo-American settlements, were not hermetically sealed from their old Creek and Shawnee allies. They counseled, renewed acquaintances, and exchanged ideas. Still, to the Red Sticks' dismay, they did not wage war on the United States.

Anticlimax: The War of 1812

Without the Cherokees and without the once-dissident Chickamaugas to occupy the critical territory separating the Indian North from the Indian South, and with much of that territory now occupied by American states that effectively sliced old networks of interregional Indian communication, the military and diplomatic accomplishments of the nativists who bore arms in the War of 1812 would not approach those of their militant predecessors in the revolutionary era. The odds against pan-Indian success had increased sharply since the early 1790s. By 1812 American citizens outnumbered Indians in the region between the Appalachians and the Mississippi by a margin of seven-to-one. The new states of Kentucky, Tennessee, and Ohio formed a pounding wedge that split the Indian quest for unity, already rotten with civil conflict, into two deteriorating blocs. Meanwhile Louisiana, admitted to statehood in 1812, and Missouri, established as a territory the same year, applied additional pressure from the west, disrupting Indian travel on the Mississippi River. The lower portion of the Ohio River had become similarly dominated not only by Kentucky but by the organized territories of Indiana and Illinois. The Upper Ohio, of course, had been finally lost by the independent peoples in 1795. This weighty American presence, combined with the loss of Cherokees as military allies, meant that the pan-Indian effort associated with Tecumseh would be more a severe aftershock than a seismic rift, a mere reminder of greater deeds done long ago.

While some Creeks would fight beside their northern allies, and while some Shawnees would do the same among the Red Sticks, the frequency of such exchanges would not compare with those of the recent past, nor would the War of 1812 see Indians mount any interregional strategic, or even tactical, deployments. The Native American North and the Native American South drew apart.

The increasing regionalization was serious enough, but further weakening pan-Indianism in this period was the failure of the militant nativists to come to terms with those, among each of their own peoples, who now cooperated with the United States, those who were now—more than ever—enemies at home. Prior to the American Revolution, it is true, Indian communities had divided between nativist and accommodationist, and often with violence. But with the Revolution had come the opportunity for Indian friends of the British to regain authority over, or at least co-operation from, the nativists. This was because the alliance with Britain meant, for Indians of both minds, war with the nativists' greatest enemies: the Anglo-American settlers. Indeed the mutual desire to stem American expansion muted nativism in the revolutionary era. The agreement among most accommodationists and nativists during the Revolution inaugurated the twenty-year period of the greatest pan-Indian triumphs.

That period had ended with the defeats of 1794. From that year forward, accommodating Indians within the claimed boundaries of the United States, seeking peace and goods, turned their attentions increasingly toward federal agents and Christian missionaries. Many of the warriors who had previously attained fame in their struggles against the states, men like the Miami Little Turtle, the Delaware Buckongahelas, the Cherokee Glass, the Shawnee Black Hoof, and the Creek Mad Dog, now signed treaties with federal representatives and welcomed the civilizing mission. The United States, not Britain, controlled the annuities that leavened the authority of these "government" chiefs and counselors. Even had these men wished to follow the nativist prophets, a break with the United States in 1812 would have been far more difficult than had been the much earlier decision, on the part of many colonial-era Indian brokers of British power, to remain with Britain while joining nativists against the United States in the Revolutionary War.

The refusal of the government chiefs of the early nineteenth century to break with the United States and resume a British alliance was no sign of inertia; it stemmed from clear tactical considerations. For one thing, these leaders remembered with clarity Britain's abandonment of them in 1783 and 1794, and the memory promoted reasoned distrust. But even more striking was the diminishing British presence. This was particularly true in the South, where the British had no official base closer than the Bahamas, and where the most active British trading company found it expedient to cooperate with the United States. Nor was Florida's Spanish king an able substitute for King George, as he had been in the decade that followed the Treaty of Paris (1783). Beset by colonial turbulence, Napoleonic occupation, the peninsular campaigns, and civil war, Spain had virtually nothing to offer its Indian allies in America. Andrew Jackson and the British both disregarded the recognized Spanish territorial bounds in the late years of the War of 1812. That they got cleanly away with it tells the story of Spanish colonial vulnerability. But even in the North, where the British had increased their presence in Ontario and the Upper Mississippi, it was not at all clear that they, devoured also by the Napoleonic conflict, possessed the supplies that accommodation-minded leaders required for a war against the United States. Upper Canada, largely neglected by Britain, was more parsimonious in the early nineteenth century than British agents had been in the 1770s and 1780s. Evidence of the British condition did not escape the Indians, and they chose to consider it carefully, recalling also that King George had, after all, lost the last war. Not before April 1814 would Britain, released briefly from the French grip, flatter Native North America with much attention—but by then the Red Sticks would be crushed, the northern militants dispersed, and Tecumseh dead.[31]

This all meant that in 1812, accommodating Indians in the North as well as in the South would stick with the United States, even to the point, for some, of firing upon their nativistic relatives.[32] The age of Tecumseh created little room for a joint alliance of nativist and accommodationist with Britain. Not only, then, did the War of 1812 bring an end to any serious military cooperation between northern and southern Indians, it also thrust peoples of both regions into the maelstrom of civil war.

In a narrow sense, however paradoxically, these years of devastating internal conflict and pan-Indian failure saw nativism's greatest triumph, for what unity was achieved owed itself, in the largest measure, to the spread of emphatically religious nativist thought along the networks that had for years brought warriors together from across the wide trans-Appalachian borderlands. While in the late eighteenth century multiple readings of opportunities brought into the same camp Indians of various persuasions—accommodationists who saw chances for Spanish or British alliance and nativists who sought to fight the Americans at all costs—in the first decades of the nineteenth century the United States fought against groups often wholly influenced by nativism. But however much the period saw nativism's greatest success among the Indians who bordered the states, it was not pan-Indianism's greatest triumph, as it is often portrayed in studies of Tecumseh. Instead, the War of 1812 stands as pan-Indianism's most thorough failure, its crushing defeat, its disappointing anticlimax.

The Northern Theater, 1811–1815

This was true both north and south of the Kentucky-Tennessee wedge. In the North, the renewal of Indian warfare in 1811 spread fear among the western citizens, but Indians descended upon only a handful of settlements. They killed relatively few noncombatants not attached to armies. Their main objectives were to throw back invading American forces and to rid their country of American garrisons. Theirs was a limited, defensive strategy, as limited in its successes as in its aims.

Even during the brief period of the northern militants' victories, they had no reason for confidence. This was in the first months after the British entry into the war, when American garrisons in Indian country fell swiftly. First to go was Fort Mackinac, whose bewildered commander learned of the war from the mouths of Indians and British traders compelling his surrender on July 27, 1812. On August 15 Indians wiped out most of the garrison retreating from Fort Dearborn in what is now Chicago. The next day Indians and Britons seized their most stunning victory: the capture of American Detroit.

The victories were soon nullified. The nativists and their allies failed to take several posts: Fort Wayne and Fort Harrison in Indiana, and Fort Madison, under Zachary Taylor, on the Upper Mississippi in what is now Missouri. What's more, although they had secured Michigan, the allies of Tecumseh and the Shawnee Prophet had been effectively driven from the southern and central portions of Illinois and Indiana, and from almost all that had remained to them of Ohio. Tippecanoe itself, which nativists had reoccupied after Harrison's 1811 attack, lay outside of the prophet's grasp by the end of 1812, and as American troops destroyed cornfields in the region throughout the fall they inflicted serious damage on the Indian war effort. The soldiers did not destroy the nativists' will to fight, but they pushed the nativists into a greater reliance upon the British. The British, for their part, encountered greater difficulties provisioning Indians in 1812 and 1813 than had their counterrevolutionary forebears. They could not be supplied from anti-Napoleonic Britain, and much local Canadian labor had been diverted to the defenses against repeated American invasions.

Far from possessing the military initiative, a position often enjoyed in the revolutionary era, Indians from the Ohio-Indiana-Illinois-Michigan heartland of the Old Northwest, even when supported by Britain, mounted few offensives in their occupied homeland, and none of any success after April 1813. About thirty of the forty-odd attacks made by forces composed at least partially of Indians in the North occurred before the decisive American naval seizure, under Oliver Hazard Perry, of Lake Erie in September 1813. After the close of that year *none* of the actions that bear names as battles east of Lake Michigan could be in any way construed as an Indian attack upon Americans; Indians decreasingly participated in the northern theater even as British armies augmented in 1814, and when Indians fought, they did so largely on Canadian soil.[33]

Perry's victory on Lake Erie was strategically the decisive battle in the Old Northwestern theater. The symbolically decisive battle for nativists was the rearguard action fought at Moraviantown, deep in Upper Canada, on October 5, 1813, as they retreated farther from their homeland. In a dim recollection of earlier glories, a few Creek Indians accompanied the 1,000 Shawnees, Ottawas, Chippewas, Delawares, Wyandots, Sauks, Foxes, Kickapoos, Winnebagoes, and Potawatomis in the battle, at which both Tecumseh and Tenskwatawa carried great influence. But the militants were clearly in retreat. They were far from their homeland, now under firm American control. And among their pursuers, beside the Americans, were some 260 Delawares, Shawnees, Wyandots, and Iroquois.[34]

Tecumseh dramatized the importance of nativism by choosing to fight the battle clad in skins and feathers, dropping cloth gifts of British manufacture. Later accounts amplify his spirituality by claiming that he predicted his death. But such marks of the sacred did not rally enough power for victory, and the Indians were driven from the field; among those they left dead was Tecumseh.[35] Tenskwatawa maintained a smaller force for the remainder of the war, and other Indians from the Old Northwest also continued to fight beside the British. But neither at Moraviantown, nor at any time in the War of 1812, did the Indians of the Old Northwest approach the degree of unity that they had seen at the height of their successes in the late eighteenth century.

The Southern Theater, 1813–1818

Far more brutal and far more immediately costly to Indians of all persuasions was the war in the South. As in the homeland of Tecumseh and Tenskwatawa, militants in the South were characterized by nativism, and indeed, during their war's most violent phase they had little else on which to rely than sacred power, although there had always been hopes for more. An attempt to fulfill those hopes brought on the first American intervention in the conflict, as Red Sticks returning from Pensacola with disappointing gifts of arms from Spain came under American fire at Burnt Corn Creek on July 27, 1813. About 180 American militia—some of them of Creek heritage—from the Tensaw and Tombigbee region, not far from Mobile, had surprised the 60 to 100 Red Sticks, most of whom were without firearms. Driven off at the first fire, the nativists counterattacked the unsuspecting militia, which believed it had already secured victory. The battle killed a handful of men on each side, enough to transform the Creek Civil War into a Red Stick war with the United States.[36]

For the next terrifying year the Red Sticks suffered multiple disabilities. They were isolated and divided against members of their own people. They were tremendously outnumbered and outgunned by their enemies. What hopes they had of obtaining arms from Spain or Britain went unfulfilled until it was far too late. Many among their enemies wanted to destroy them utterly, and their enemies had the firepower to do so. The Red Sticks' greatest success, in the end, would be the mere survival of some of their number.

Congress had ordered Georgia and Tennessee to raise troops before Burnt Corn; these were quickly deployed in its wake, with the support of Cherokee, Choctaw, and Creek accommodationist parties. The expeditions entered Creek country from three directions, in columns as malevolent to the Red Sticks as the great serpents of their myths. Georgia sent in Major General John Floyd at the command of some 1,500, including several hundred Creeks and Cherokees. Floyd succeeded by February 1814, despite delays and illness, in building a chain of posts from Georgia into the Creek heartland, engaging the Red Sticks in two major actions that strained their meager supplies and killed some 250 of their men, wounding many more.[37]

Meanwhile General Ferdinand L. Claiborne with 800 militia and the Third Regiment of Regulars, perhaps 1,200 men in all, ascended the Alabama River, building forts, burning towns, and clearing the region of poorly armed Red Sticks. The major engagement, the battle of Holy Ground (or Autosse) on December 23, 1813, deserves some attention. The role of ritual and sacred power in the Creek War has been most dramatically celebrated by historians in their treatment of this battle. In the standard interpretation, the prophet Francis had drawn a spiritual line around his settlement, promising that the area enclosed would "never be sullied by the footsteps of the real white man"; that any white who attempted to cross into it "would fall lifeless to earth." The spiritual wall failed; the American army captured and destroyed the village, leaving the nativists "badly shaken" in their faith.[38]

Red Sticks did lose the battle and they would lose the war, and it is easy to portray them as fanatics tempting fate and reaping disaster. But the American reporters of the battle sought to ridicule their enemies. Moreover, the distinction between the sacred and the profane, between the hopes for deliverance and the need for strategy, has been too starkly drawn in discussions of Creek nativism. However much they praised God, nativists knew to keep their powder dry—when they could get it, that is. It is worth pointing out that they had seen rituals fail before, and even at Holy Ground, in keeping with general Indian strategy, the warriors' women and children had fled at the news of the American advance into the earthly cover of the forest across the river from the village.[39] The nativists employed rituals taught them by their prophets, but they did not leave their families open to attack. Nor did the apparent failure of the ritual earn its alleged designer, Francis, the enmity of his followers; he was not aban-

doned after the loss, he did not wander friendless. He remained an impor-
tant leader of Indian resistance until his assassination by Americans in 1818.
The Red Stick will to fight, however "shaken" it may have been by Holy
Ground, would continue to withstand awful and awesome casualties.

Already by the end of the battle, Red Stick casualties in the Creek War
had mounted to a level proportionally comparable with that of any force
in American history, including Confederate soldiers in the Civil War. By
November, 750 militant warriors out of a warrior population that might
have reached 4,000 lay dead. At the time of the battle of Holy Ground, in
other words, less than six months after the American intervention, guns
under American control had killed, at a low estimate, 1 of 5 Red Stick men.
Figures for the wounded are unknown. Yet the Red Sticks fought on.[40]

Most of the casualties had been inflicted by armies under Andrew
Jackson, who had turned much of Upper Creek country into a charnel
house, destroying towns, killing men, sparing some women and children
but forcibly relocating them. The climax of the Tennessean incursion into
Creek country came at the battle of Horseshoe Bend, or Tohopeka, on
March 27, 1814. Jackson, with 3,000 men, including about 500 Cherokees
and Creeks, won a dreadful victory. One thousand nativists, clearly inferi-
or in number and firepower to their approaching enemy, dug in behind impressive fortifications across the peninsula formed by a bend in the Tallapoosa River, which looped around their backs, offering protection, drink,
and, they hoped, an opportunity for a quick downriver escape by dugout
canoe. Jackson directed the frontal bombardment and assault, while General John Coffee with Indians and mounted troops cut off the retreat along
the opposite side of the bend in the river. In a critical maneuver, the Indians with Coffee crossed the river, seized canoes that might have been
used for escape, and prepared the way for an invasion of Tohopeka from
the rear. Early in the battle Jackson informed the Red Sticks that no
quarter would be given without immediate surrender. The Red Sticks
refused. When he breached their lines, he had none spared. Two hundred
of the thousand nativists may have escaped, among these many must have
been wounded. The attackers killed the rest; they found 557 bodies on the
field, and they estimated that 250 or so of the Red Sticks who attempted to
escape by swimming the river were fired on and killed. Thus 8 of 10
defenders perished.[41] Between July 1813 and April 1814 close to half of all
Red Stick men had met violent deaths. Some of the survivors later gave up
to the government faction. Most regrouped and, incredibly, kept fighting.

Red Sticks fled Upper Creek and Alabama country for Spanish Florida,
where they met up with their Seminole relatives. Francis, the prophet,
who had hastened to Florida following the earlier disaster at Holy Ground,

found himself joined not only by Seminoles and refugee Red Sticks—among them the Shawnee Seekaboo—but also by black slaves seeking freedom. The combined force numbered about a thousand.[42]

The first British truly to attempt to coordinate plans with the Red Sticks arrived at the Apalachicola River on May 10, 1814, little over a month after Horseshoe Bend. These were only a few, under the command of Captain George Woodbine, but they carried with them impressive supplies of firearms and ammunition. Woodbine built a fort at Prospect Bluff, and awaited the British troops. About two hundred redcoats arrived in August, under the command of Major (he carried the highly irregular rank of acting lieutenant colonel) Edward Nicolls. For most of the next year, Nicolls attempted to keep the Indians fed and supplied, and he engaged them in several actions with the Americans. Between August 14 and November 17 the Red Sticks and Redcoats had taken Pensacola bloodlessly from the Spanish, had attempted but failed to take Mobile from the Americans, and had lost Pensacola, more bloodily, to Americans under Jackson. Britons, Red Sticks, Seminoles, and blacks took part in each action, with Indians forming the majority of the forces arrayed on that side, and with the number of African-Americans among the Red Sticks and Seminoles increasing.[43]

Blacks arrived both voluntarily and involuntarily, after fleeing from American plantations or after surviving capture by Seminoles and Red Sticks. In either case and either free or "with the expectation of being free," blacks fought alongside Creek Indians as early as the battle of Holy Ground, and probably earlier in the Seminole War of 1811. By the spring of 1815, a British reporter counted about 60 blacks on the Apalachicola River and noted that the Seminoles and Mikasukeys had another 170 male slaves, both groups whom he listed as warriors.[44] A black-Indian alliance of course, was anathema to all the enemies of the Red Sticks, and early on in the war one American commander carried orders to kill all blacks among the Indians who could not be captured or easily carried off. Blacks thus constituted a liability as well as an asset for the Red Sticks; their American enemies would not tolerate a southern sanctuary from slavery. By 1815, southern citizens of the United States faced the presence of a "Negro Fort" on the Apalachicola. It was the center, according to historian J. Leitch Wright, of "the largest and most heavily armed Maroon community ever to appear in the Southeast." A threat to the peculiar institution, it was destroyed with many of its defenders in an American invasion of 1816.[45]

Red Stick persistence after Horseshoe Bend must, then, be understood in the context of Seminole, African, and British support. The British supplies, however late, were real enough, and while not always plentiful, as long as Britain remained in the conflict they could be had. The Red Sticks therefore hoped to win back their recently lost lands, but short of a British victory, the hope was forlorn. They had neither the numbers nor the arms to effect such a reconquest. As if to underline Red Stick reliance on Britain in the years after Horseshoe Bend—and it is important to remember that British assistance was negligible throughout the Creek War proper—the prophet Francis became in these later years of Red Stick resistance, a resistance that would fade seamlessly into the First Seminole War, a major broker not only between the sacred and the mortal but also between the British and the Indians.[46]

He would be thrice disappointed. Invited to observe the anticipated British victory at New Orleans, he instead saw the British veterans of Wellington's campaigns cut down by Jackson, his greatest enemy. Sailing to England and the Bahamas between June 1815 and June 1817 in efforts to gain promised British support for the restoration of Creek lands, he received nothing but presents for his person. Finally, paddling out to an American gunboat deceptively flying a British flag in 1818, he was kidnapped and killed, with Jackson's approval and without trial. Hoping, like Francis, for British assistance but fighting on without it, the Red Sticks and Seminoles—Indian and African—defended their villages against the American assaults that followed the British evacuation in June 1815. They retreated deeper into Florida when their defenses failed. They signed no document agreeing to peace with the United States at the alleged end of what is now called the First Seminole War.[47]

Red Stick persistence in the face of repeated disappointments and astonishing losses can be explained by a final contingency: Jackson's unjust treatment of his own Indian allies. In a strange repetition of past American actions, Jackson drove some erstwhile accommodationists and peace-seekers into the nativist camp. Jackson's contempt for the Creek party of accommodation emerged with stark clarity during the negotiations that supposedly ended the Creek War, the Treaty of Fort Jackson on August 9, 1814. By this treaty, the United States did not so much make peace with its enemies as take land from its allies. According to its provisions, the Lower Creeks, by and large opponents of the Red Sticks, lost the southern third of their lands. Few Upper Creek Red Sticks and only one known Red Stick leader signed the document. The accommodationist leaders of the Lower Creeks, forced into drastic cessions by an overpowering American army, petitioned the federal government for redress on the very day they signed the treaty. These Creek leaders, reminding the Americans that "we have adhered faithfully in peace and war to our treaty stipulations with the

United States," described the Fort Jackson agreement as unfair: "We do not deem the exchange as equivalent." They acquiesced to it under Jackson's insistence, and they hoped, vainly, for "the justice of the United States to cause justice to be done us."[48]

After the decisive defeats of the northern and southern militants during the War of 1812 and in its immediate aftermath, no Indians, not even the determined Seminoles, seriously imperiled the republic.[49] The war dismembered the pan-Indian movement that had, for some seventy years, shaped Indian conceptions of themselves. The war demonstrated the Indians' weaknesses in the face of the United States. These disabilities did not stem from traditional intertribal enmities. None of the borderland peoples examined in this work entered the war in a spirit of internal unity, and none of them fought the war in order to settle old debts with traditional Indian enemies. Tribal identity had little to do with the war.

Instead, the Native Americans' loss of power grew out of several developments: their growing material dependence on colonial powers, their declining population in the region relative to that of the expansionist Anglo-Americans, their disappearing peltry trade and the consequent economic stress, and, most decisively, their violent internal divisions over the issue of federal interference in their societies. On the eve of the War of 1812 Cherokee leaders had managed this issue most adeptly, proving that they would, when pushed, stand up to federal authorities. But even they did not escape criticism and local hostility. Creek leaders, collapsing under federal pressure in 1811, suffered the most bitter penalty. But all peoples faced the tension, and it proved both to frustrate the nativists' hopes and to dissipate the most striking accomplishments of the pan-Indian movement. Oddly, the divisiveness also proved to be the lifeblood of nativist thought, which lived on beyond the disasters of 1813 and 1814.

>>>>>>><<<<<<<

A Conflict of Memory

The nativists failed. Measured by their own goals, the failure was complete. The union of all Indians, the rescue by sacred power, and the demise or containment of the Anglo-Americans did not come about. We might expect the failure to have led to repudiation; instead the ideas continued to animate isolated groups of believers on both sides of the Mississippi. Notions of Indian unity, of separation from Americans, and of the possible rescue by the sacred powers inspired resisters of removal under Black Hawk in Illinois as well as the far more powerful Seminoles of Florida, but the notions also lived on in the memory of people who would never again bear arms against the United States. As nativistic notions persisted, so did their Native American antitheses.

Nativism lived on in large measure because its opposition had failed just as bitterly. Within a generation of the murder of Francis and the battle death of Tecumseh, the United States had driven most of its Indian allies as well as its Indian enemies west of the Mississippi. There, and in scattered hollows throughout the East, the debates of the ages of Pontiac and Tecumseh found resonance: some continued to seek an accommodation with the United States, others argued for the irreconcilable differences separating all Indians, whatever their particular people, from the nation that stole their lands.

The strongest remnant of militant nativism continued to resist the United States in the Seminole country, as we have seen. The Red Stick influx had strengthened the Seminoles, providing them, among other

OSCEOLA

Osceola, the most famous of participants in the Second Seminole War, had been a young member of the Red Stick faction during the Creek Civil War. Painted by George Catlin, 1837. (*Source:* National Portrait Gallery, NPG 7.70, Smithsonian Institution, Washington, D.C.)

assets, with a youth who would come to be known as Osceola, one of the several leaders of the Seminoles during their war against removal (1835–42).[1] Far weaker than the Seminoles, though equally linked to the militancy of the age of Tecumseh, was the nativistic effort of the "Winnebago Prophet," Wabokieshiek, once described as "the efficient man" behind the movement that the United States crushed in the Black Hawk War (1832). In the late 1820s Wabokieshiek gathered some two hundred people from several tribes "into one body on the Rock River," in Illinois. In a muted echo of Old Northwestern militancy, the Winnebago preached that Americans who attempted to force the polyglot inhabitants of his village across the Mississippi would find themselves under fierce attack by the combined Sauk, Fox, Winnebago, Potawatomi, and Kickapoo peoples as well as by the British. Wabokieshiek, however, overboasted. Even more than his spiritual forebears, he met determined resistance among the great part of all the tribes he claimed were behind him. Of both Sauk and Winnebago ancestry, he could convince neither people to render him much support, but he did attract militants from several of the former peoples of Indiana and Illinois, peoples who had once rallied to the Shawnee Prophet. While Sauk, Fox, Potawatomi, and Kickapoo government chiefs watched dissident members of their communities join Wabokieshiek, his emissaries traveled southward among still independent Indian peoples, soliciting assistance that never came. Wabokieshiek was the central figure around which the weak movement arose, but, like Tenskwatawa before him, he drew upon a well-developed tradition; he did not create a new religion solely out of his own ecstatic visions. Black Hawk, who had once followed Tecumseh and Tenskwatawa, eventually became known to Americans as the leader of these nativists, but this was true only after military experience had become paramount, that is, after Black Hawk and his band had returned from Iowa to Illinois, crossing the Mississippi River in violation of removal to join the Winnebago Prophet. This brought on an American expedition, armed clashes, and what Americans call the Black Hawk War: ten weeks of dire suffering among vastly outnumbered, outgunned, and starving Native American families fleeing for their lives.[2]

Tenskwatawa himself, the symbol of religious nativism in the Northwest, weathered the War of 1812 and lived out his natural life. Had nativism depended solely upon this prophet it would have had a slim chance for survival, for in his later years, richly narrated by historian R. David Edmunds, Tenskwatawa did little to honor his own memory. He gave up the armed struggle with the end of the war, and he lost most of his followers, living first as a dependent of the British and later of the Americans. But he had not lost all authority with the escape of victory. He headed a small camp of Shawnee, Kickapoo, Sauk, and Fox refugees in Ontario until about 1825, when he returned to Black Hoof's town in Ohio. There his influence increased briefly; he may even have played a leading role in a Shawnee witch scare. But in contrast to his earlier years as a defender of the northern Indians against American expansion, he collaborated in these years in American plans for removal; he turned accommodationist. He led a large Shawnee contingent on a poorly supplied, starvation-ridden, two-year migration to Kansas between 1826 and 1828. Having given up the fight, Tenskwatawa gradually lost his remaining sway among the Shawnees. He managed to display in the West some vestigial religious authority, establishing a "Prophetstown" in his new Kansan land, but with few followers to inhabit the village, it could only have stood as a humiliating reminder of his earlier triumphs and failures.[3]

Tenskwatawa, however, had never been the single font from which all nativism had sprung. A player in a crowded field, his end was obscure and unknown to most. Among Indians throughout the era of removal, the memory of militant nativism ran a course that diverged from the downward personal trajectory of the Shawnee Prophet's career. Militant nativism survived, occasionally gaining strength, but always turning its main energies against its Indian opposition.

If nativists failed to secure for the Indians their homelands, so too, for the most part, did those who had tried to accommodate the American expansionists. In the Northwest, this was despite the best efforts of Tenskwatawa's old adversary, Black Hoof, to prevent Shawnee removal. The postwar era twisted Black Hoof into what he had been in his youth, an opponent of the United States; he discovered that his studied neutrality during the War of 1812 had not won his people the protection of their remaining lands. In their villages in northwestern Ohio, Shawnee supporters of accommodation under Black Hoof met with unyielding American pressure, and in 1817 the Treaty of the Miami Rapids limited their holdings to a small reserve around Black Hoof's village of Wapakoneta. Over the two decades following the war, the Americans forced most Shawnees to yield their land and to seek refuge across the Mississippi. By the late 1820s and early 1830s, against Black Hoof's wishes but with Tenskwatawa's blessing, most Shawnees had begun the trip to the Kansas River valley. Some were lucky enough to complete it.[4]

The Cherokees' failure to accommodate the United States and win its protection is even more bold. Cherokees had demonstrated their desire to remain at peace with the United States during the War of 1812. Hundreds, in fact, had done much more, taking up arms in the Americans' service.

This proved no more effective a means of appeasing the Americans than had the Shawnee Black Hoof's careful strategy. American pressure for Cherokee removal mounted steadily after the war and became particularly strong after the 1828 presidential election of Andrew Jackson, who had relied on Cherokee warriors at the battle of Horseshoe Bend.

By 1831 John Ross, a leading Cherokee who had joined Jackson's forces against the Red Sticks but who opposed Jackson's views on removal, wrote with evident dismay to a Tennessean friend in the U.S. Congress. His subject was the Jackson administration's hostile policy toward the Cherokees. Ross's letter conveys both his desire to live beside Americans in peace and his despair at the failure of his people's cooperation with the United States to produce a favorable American attitude toward the Cherokee nation. Ross pointed out that he had known Jackson "from my boyhood," that he had joined Jackson's forces in the Creek War, and that he counted among his "earliest and warmest friends" some of Jackson's Tennessean supporters. As far, he concluded, as Jackson's "measures are correct & just I should be Among the last to oppose them—but it is with deep regret, I say, that his policy towards the aborigines, in my opinion, has been unrelenting and in effect ruinous."[5]

Under Jackson and Van Buren, Indian removal was relentless indeed. In 1832, the Creeks ceded their remaining homelands in "exchange" for lands in Oklahoma. The Americans obtained the Cherokee "cession," against the wishes of a clear tribal majority, in 1835. So firmly did most Cherokees object to removal that it took federal troops to oust the stalwarts, driving them down the "Trail of Tears" toward Arkansas and Oklahoma, along which almost a quarter of the dispossessed people perished. A small band of Valley Cherokees took refuge in the Smoky Mountains of North Carolina, where many of their descendants remain as the Eastern Cherokees.

That band may represent the major exception to the nativists' record of failure among Delawares, Shawnees, Cherokees, and Creeks, for one of its leaders was Yonaguska. Yonaguska opposed removal, Christian missionaries, and Anglo-American control. Yonaguska led a nonviolent religious "reformation." His followers fled, they did not fight, the federal troops. As with the later phases of Handsome Lake's Seneca movement in the North, Yonaguska's revival constructed a limited form of Eastern Cherokee autonomy within the context of Anglo-American encirclement. And as with the early phase of Handsome Lake's revival, the early phase of Yonaguska's reform drew upon the widespread traditions of prophecy, or at least that was how it was remembered: "He was taken sick and to all appearance died was laid in State and his people assembled to attend his funeral—when they were about to berry him he revived—sat up on his bier and told them he had been to the spirit land." He stood against missionaries as well as against alcohol, and not until after his death in 1839 did Christian missionaries have much success in Yonaguska's village.[6]

By the end of the 1830s, however, despite the best efforts of nativists and their accommodating opponents, most Delawares, Shawnees, Cherokees, and Creeks had been forced across the Mississippi. Some families remained to labor among the Americans; small reserves lay scattered throughout the Old Northwest; Yonaguska's fellow Eastern Cherokees held out in the mountains of North Carolina and Seminoles in the swamplands and plains of Florida. For the most part, notwithstanding these important exceptions, the trans-Appalachian Indians had become trans-Mississippi Indians. The policy of accommodation, like that of nativism, had failed to arrest the American expropriation of Indian land. With no clear victor, no antithesis to replace the thesis, debate continued, and stretched into the realm of memory, of history, as Indians interpreted their past.

The memory of the nativists' struggle for unity has been fittingly contentious. Some Indians have recalled the nativists' dreams as embarrassing disasters, others have seen in them reason for pride and hope. Spiritual descendants of the nativists have at times admitted that the nativists lost their battles, but this has not led them to conclude that their forebears misunderstood the workings of power. Though unable to accomplish a watertight Indian alliance, though unable to win over entire tribal councils, though so apparently abandoned by the very sacred powers on whom they had counted for aid, though defeated, starved, murdered, and maligned, nativists did not make enemies of their progeny.

Among Indians whose ancestors once ruled the American Midwest, Tecumseh has been almost uniformly honored and exalted; Tenskwatawa, less popular, has often been disparaged and vilified. Well into the twentieth century some Shawnees of the two militant brothers' own Kispoko division paid respect to the warrior and spoke ill of the prophet, whom they accused of having been a witch and of commanding his people through fear. But there has never been a single Indian point of view, and the memory of Tenskwatawa has been as contested as was his message in his own day. Shawnees have dissented from the condemnations of the prophet, in spite of his behavior after the war. A family among Tenskwatawa's descendants honored his memory by taking the surname, "Prophet," a generation or two after his death. Among the Winnebagoes in the early twentieth century, whose ancestors provided Black Hawk with his prophet and Tenskwatawa with many ardent supporters, Paul Radin found the Shawnee Prophet's memory celebrated by a member of the Peyote movement: "Now, it is four generations since the Shawnee Prophet prophe-

sied. . . . The Shawnee Prophet was good. . . . The Peyote people claim
that their ceremony is the fulfillment of this prophecy and that it is true."[7]

The northern Indians' memory of Tecumseh, while favorable overall,
has been, in its meaning, as contested as that of his visionary brother.
Among Indians who once peopled the Midwest, some have seen him as a
secular leader untouched by religious nativism. These have recounted his
"war feats" and his impressive diplomacy. But others, even in very recent
years according to one student of the Shawnees, James Howard, have
raised him "to the level of a demigod" and have referred to him as a
"saint." Ohio's early twentieth-century antiquarian, James Galloway, reported millennial legends about the Shawnee leader's death and probable
return. According to these stories, Tecumseh had planned to return from
the dead as an immortal during the battle of Moraviantown; but when that
event failed, it was argued that he would return again "when it pleases the
Great Spirit." In the nineteenth century, a host of stories surrounding
Tecumseh's death were collected by those seeking to confirm or reject
Vice-President Richard Johnson's claim to having killed the Shawnee;
embedded within some of the Indian reports are references to Tecumseh's
miraculous prescience at Moraviantown—his forecasting of both his own
death and the defeat of the Indians—and his identification among Indians
with supernatural forces. Black Hawk himself is reported to have said of
that fatal shot at Moraviantown, "As soon as the Indians discovered he was
killed, a sudden fear came over them; and thinking the Great Spirit was
angry, they fought no longer, and were quickly put to flight."[8]

Creeks, with far more consistency than the northern Indians, remembered Tecumseh as a prophet, not as the secular leader of a purely political
movement. Tustenuckochee, an old Creek-become-Seminole making his
recollections in 1883, saw Tecumseh as a powerful shaman to whom the
Creeks paid inadequate attention. Tecumseh had immense "power to deal
with the evil spirit." His rites were so potent and dangerous that "he
warned the Muscogees not to attempt anything they had seen lest thereby
they bring illfate to themselves, for he himself was only able to do that
which they saw him do." The memory of that warning explained to Creek
and Seminole nativists the ultimate Red Stick defeat: the sacred powers
were real, but had not been handled correctly. Tustenuckochee's opinions
were largely confirmed by Colonel John Juniper, once a "Seminole
Chief."[9]

Creek accommodationists agreed with militants about Tecumseh's nature, but they ridiculed his spirituality. In the 1830s and 1840s George
Stiggins, an opponent of the Red Sticks who described himself as a Creek,
had little respect for Tecumseh's "mad notions" and remembered the

Shawnee militant largely for his claims to "great supernatural power."
According to Stiggins, Tecumseh had claimed that his mission "was afore
dictated to him by the great spirit, of whose will and mandates he acted as
a mere organ." Stiggins saw Tecumseh as inaugurating an "age and time
of prophecy in the creek nation," and in Stiggins's memory, it was an age
and time of foolishness. He blamed Creek misfortune on the prophets who
arose in the wake of Tecumseh's visit.[10]

Stiggins's dismissive views, however, did not represent the views of the
Creeks as a whole. It is worth pointing out that the name Tecumseh
enjoyed a vogue among nineteenth-century Creeks. Nor were his Red
Stick allies consigned to be buffeted with disdain in Muskogean memory.
Tustenuckochee, who as a young Creek boy had known Francis, recalled
in the 1880s that the Creek Prophet had first come "forward to restore
peace and harmony but he was ridiculed and made the victim of a most
unmerciful and base slander." Clearly Tustenuckochee would have disputed Stiggins's hostile assessment. In the 1930s Angie Debo met Creeks who
spoke not of Red Stick losses but of their "miraculous escapes." The Red
Sticks, one Creek told her, "knew how to make a bullet from a gun go
around them or glance from them." When wounded, her source continued, the Red Sticks only "blamed themselves for neglecting their medicine, although they were never wounded much."[11]

Cherokees, like the Creeks who took on Tecumseh's name, found elaborate ways of claiming the Shawnee as one of their own. One investigator
found of Tecumseh's mother "that all the Cherokees say she was a Cherokee." Several other stories about him also emerged: his name was actually
"Te kuh wa ser," a Cherokee word; the Shawnees had captured him from
the Cherokees when he was a boy; he had married into the Cherokees and
left children. In the 1880s, a Cherokee Christian, the Reverend A. N.
Chamberlin, reported the belief that one family, the Proctors, were descended from *both* Tecumseh and Tenskwatawa: "The fair skin Proctors of
the Nation (Cherokee) are his [Tecumseh's] grandchildren—the dark skin
Proctors are the descendants of his brother, the Prophet." The latter, the
minister recorded, as he overlaid the imagined dimensions of race and
religion, "still believe in conjurers and Prophets." While the validity of
each claim should be left to an unusually credulous genealogist, the lesson
for historians is that the Cherokees' memories of the Shawnee brothers
were contentious: the memories reflected Cherokee divisions over traditional religion, imported racism, and cooperation with Anglo-America. It
made sense to some "progressives" among the nineteenth-century Cherokees to claim a pragmatic Tecumseh as their own while identifying the
"traditionalists" and the "full bloods" with the Shawnee Prophet. Other

Cherokees hostile to nativism, however, placed Tecumseh with the prophet. William Ross did so, and in the 1880s he recalled hearing that the Shawnee Prophet had visited the Cherokees and had come close to winning over the "portion of this Tribe . . . dissatisfied and inclined to hostility."[12]

Cherokees recalled their own prophetic movement with similar ambivalence and contention. In the 1840s the *Cherokee Advocate*, an elite organ published among the Western Cherokees, lampooned the revival of 1811–13 in an effort to discredit the Millerites. In 1891 James Wafford, an Eastern Cherokee who had little more respect for the Cherokee revival than did the *Advocate*, nonetheless admitted that not all Cherokees were convinced by its most spectacular failure, which he described for James Mooney. Wafford, a child during the revival, recalled that a Cherokee conjurer in northern Georgia had predicted that on a "day near at hand there would be a terrible storm . . . which would destroy from the face of the earth all but the true believers who had previously taken refuge on the highest summits of the Great Smoky mountains." Convinced by the visionary, many Cherokees left their homes and possessions to climb to the safety of the high country, where "they waited until the appointed day arrived, only to find themselves disappointed." Wafford ended the recollection with the pilgrims' embarrassed return to their home villages. But in a point that emphasizes the resilience of religious nativism, he noted that they continued to believe "in their hearts that the glorious coming was only postponed for a time."[13] He does not tell us when, if ever, the nativists were totally disillusioned. If nativist prophecy never convinced all members of any Indian people, neither did the failure of prophecy, so apparently manifest, convince all nativists of the inadequacy of sacred powers. Rather, nativists could still assert that the Indians had failed to appeal to the powers correctly, as a united people.

In the decades following the collapse of the Indian quest for unity, a Cherokee named Shield Eater told the Protestant missionary Daniel Buttrick a tale set in very ancient days before the Cherokee migration to this continent, but one that conforms in certain particulars with Wafford's relation of the revival. According to Shield Eater, the ancient Cherokees, distraught at their military weakness and in great danger of destruction, appealed to the Great Spirit for aid. The Creator "told them to march to the top of a certain mountain, and He would come down and afford them relief. They ascended far up the mountain, and thought they saw something coming down from above which they supposed was for their aid." But the climbers were not of a single mind. One of their number did not share his fellows' singleness of purpose, and "began to talk about women." His horrified companions reproached him, "but instantly a sound like thunder struck the mountain, and God told them to go back, as he would do nothing for them." Still seeking to appease the Great Spirit the party "killed the offending warrior, but notwithstanding, God would not forgive, and had not blessed them since, as he had done before."[14]

That the improper behavior of one could mean disaster for the whole was a Native American corollary to the well-worn notion that proper ritual delivered power. Abominable actions were antirituals. Buttrick noted this in the context of Shield Eater's story: "Though different Cherokees ascribe different reasons for their decline, yet all, so far as I know, ascribe it ultimately to the displeasure of God towards them." Charles Hudson writes of the southeastern Indians that they explained misfortune "as having come about because people in their communities broke rules of ritual separation or propriety." The punishment was corporate; the individual wrongdoer brought spiritual wrath down upon the community. No Noahs escaped the flood; no Lots were spared destruction for their individual goodness. Those individuals who survived punishment could thank their good fortune alone, not their good behavior. Cherokee nativists, seeking that deliverance in 1812, had wondered openly about the consequences of the government chiefs' embrace of the corrupting American influences.[15] But though the nativists had so challenged the Cherokee National Council, they had been unable to alter the general course of Cherokee politics. Their failure, they could believe, was in their inability to win over their own people.

The nativists' failure, in other words, could be laid to other Indians' violations. In the nativists' view, their failure was not one of their prophets' misunderstandings, but of the Indians' seduction by the Anglo-Americans. The nativists could see that they had not been rescued by the sacred powers, but they could also maintain that the ways of their Indian opponents had proved no more effective in preserving their lands and people. The United States, by driving its friends as well as its enemies across the Mississippi, gave force to nativistic arguments that Indians would never be welcome either in the neighborhood of whites or in the Christian heaven. It is not surprising, therefore, that Shawnees west of the Mississippi, despite the disastrous failure of their forebears' nativism, continued to speak of separate heavens for Indians and whites. It is not surprising that they spoke of an "anti-christian sage," unnamed in our record, who had just a "few years" before Josiah Gregg took his notes in the 1830s opposed the work of missionaries.

In the manner of the earlier prophets, the sage had collapsed with all the appearance of death, "and became stiff and cold, except a spot upon his breast, which still retained the heat of life." Awakening, he told his friends

A CONFLICT OF MEMORY

and family that he "had ascended to the Indian's heaven." There his grandfather gave him a warning, a warning flushed with the memory of numerous Shawnee "removals." As Anglo-America had forced them repeatedly from their homes and had failed to honor promises made even to its Indian allies, so, the grandfather warned the new prophet, would Christian promises yield no salvation, no heavenly mansion: "Beware of the religion of the white man: . . . every Indian who embraces it is obliged to take the road to the white man's heaven; and yet no red man is permitted to enter there, but will have to wander about forever without a resting place."[16]

Abbreviations

ASPIA   Walter Lowrie and Matthew St. Clair, eds., *American State Papers, Documents, Legislative and Executive of the Congress of the United States (1789–1815), Class II, Indian Affairs* (Washington, D.C., 1832)

Ayer MSS   Edward E. Ayer Manuscripts, Newberry Library, Chicago

CO   Colonial Office Papers, British Public Record Office, Kew, Great Britain

CO (DLC)   Colonial Office Papers, British Public Record Office, microfilms in the Library of Congress, Washington, D.C.

Draper MSS   Lyman Copeland Draper Manuscripts, State Historical Society of Wisconsin, Microfilm at Firestone Library, Princeton University

DRCHSNY   E. B. O'Callaghan and Berthold Fernow, eds., *Documents Relative to the Colonial History of the State of New York . . . ,* 15 vols. (Albany, N.Y., 1853–87)

ETHSP   East Tennessee Historical Society Publications

Ethnohistory Ohio Valley–Great Lakes Ethnohistory Archive, Glenn A.
Archive   Black Archaeological Laboratory, Indiana University, Bloomington, Indiana

HSP   Historical Society of Pennsylvania, Philadelphia

Ill. Hist. Coll. — Clarence Walworth Alvord et al., eds., *Collections of the Illinois State Historical Library,* 26 vols. (Springfield, Ill., 1905–34)

Kappler, Treaties — Charles J. Kappler, ed., *Indian Affairs, Laws and Treaties,* vol. 2 (Washington, D.C., 1904)

MAB — Carl John Fliegel, Vernon H. Nelson, et al., eds., *Records of the Moravian Mission among the Indians of North America from the Archives of the Moravian Church, Bethlehem, Pennsylvania,* trans. William N. Schwarze, et al., 40 microfilm reels (New Haven, 1970), located at the American Philosophical Society, Philadelphia

Michigan Pioneer — *Historical Collections of the Michigan Pioneer and Historical Society,* 40 vols. (1874–1929)

MLB — George Mogan Letter Books, Carnegie Library, Pittsburgh, typescript copy at the Ethnohistory Archive

MVHR — Mississippi Valley Historical Review

NA — U.S. National Archives, Washington, D.C.

Penn. Archives — Samuel Hazard, ed., *Pennsylvania Archives . . . ,* 1st ser., 12 vols. (Philadelphia, 1852–56)

PMHB — *Pennsylvania Magazine of History and Biography*

PRO — British Public Record Office, Kew, Great Britain

TPUS — Clarence Edwin Carter, ed., *The Territorial Papers of the United States,* 28 vols. (Washington, D.C., 1934–75)

Notes

Preface

1. James Mooney, "The Ghost Dance Religion and the Sioux Outbreak of 1890," in *Fourteenth Annual Report of the Bureau of American Ethnology*, pt. 2 (Washington, D.C., 1896).

2. Francis Parkman, *The Conspiracy of Pontiac and the Indian Uprising of 1763*, 2 vols. (1851; Boston, 1898).

3. For fine examples bearing on colonial and revolutionary history, see David Corkran, *The Cherokee Frontier: Conflict and Survival, 1740–1762* (Norman, Okla., 1966); Verner W. Crane, *The Southern Frontier: 1670–1732* (Durham, N.C., 1928); Barbara Graymont, *The Iroquois in the American Revolution* (Syracuse, 1972); Theda Perdue, *Slavery and the Evolution of Cherokee Society, 1540–1866* (Knoxville, Tenn., 1973); Neal Salisbury, *Manitou and Providence: Indians, Europeans, and the Making of New England, 1500–1643* (New York, 1982); Allen W. Trealease, *Indian Affairs in Colonial New York: The Seventeenth Century* (Ithaca, N.Y., 1960); Bruce G. Trigger, *The Children of Aataentsic: A History of the Huron People to 1660*, 2 vols. (Montreal, 1976).

4. For good early American examples see John Richard Alden, *John Stuart and the Southern Colonial Frontier: A Study of Indian Relations, War, Trade and Land Problems in the Southern Wilderness, 1754–1775* (Ann Arbor, Mich., 1944); Robert F. Berkhofer, Jr., *Salvation and the Savage: An Analysis of Protestant Missions and American Indian Response, 1787–1862* (Lexington, Ky., 1965); Henry Warner Bowden, *American Indians and Christian Missions: Studies in Cultural Conflict* (Chicago, 1981); Collin G. Calloway, *Crown and Calumet: British-Indian Relations, 1783–1815* (Norman, Okla., 1987); Reginald Horsman, *Expansion and American Indian Policy* (East Lansing, Mich., 1967); Wilbur R. Jacobs, *Diplomacy and Indian Gifts: Anglo-French Rivalry along the Ohio and Northwest Frontier, 1748–1763* (Stanford, Calif., 1950); Dorothy Jones, *License for*

Empire: Colonialism by Treaty in Early America (Chicago, 1982); Yasuhide Kawashima, *Puritan Justice and the Indian: White Man's Law in Massachusetts, 1630–1763* (Middletown, Conn., 1982); James H. O'Donnell, *Southern Indians in the American Revolution* (Knoxville, Tenn., 1973); Francis Paul Prucha, *American Indian Policy in the Formative Years: The Indian Trade and Intercourse Acts, 1780–1834* (Cambridge, Mass., 1962).

5. R. David Edmunds, *The Shawnee Prophet* (Lincoln, Neb., 1983); Isabel Thompson Kelsay, *Joseph Brant, 1743–1807: Man of Two Worlds* (Syracuse, 1984); Howard H. Peckham, *Pontiac and the Indian Uprising* (Chicago, 1961).

6. See, for example, Robert F. Berkhofer, Jr., *The White Man's Indian: Images of the American Indian from Columbus to the Present* (New York, 1978); Olive Patricia Dickason, *The Myth of the Savage and the Beginnings of French Colonialism in the Americas* (Edmonton, 1984); Reginald Horsman, *Race and Manifest Destiny: The Origins of American Racial Anglo-Saxonism* (Cambridge, Mass., 1981); Cornelius J. Jaenen, *Friend and Foe: Aspects of French-Amerindian Cultural Contact in the Sixteenth and Seventeenth Centuries* (New York, 1976); Karen Ordahl Kupperman, *Settling with the Indians: The Meeting of English and Indian Cultures in America, 1580–1640* (Totowa, N.J., 1980); Roy Harvey Pearce, *The Savages of America: A Study of the Indian and the Idea of Civilization* (Baltimore, 1953); Bernard W. Sheehan, *Savagism and Civility: Indians and Englishmen in Colonial Virginia* (Cambridge, Mass., 1980); Richard Slotkin, *Regeneration through Violence: The Mythology of the American Frontier, 1600–1860* (Middletown, Conn., 1973).

7. Gary B. Nash, *Red, White, and Black: The Peoples of Early America* (Englewood Cliffs, N.J., 1974); Edmund S. Morgan, *American Slavery, American Freedom: The Ordeal of Colonial Virginia* (New York, 1975). See also Wilcomb E. Washburn, *The Governor and the Rebel: A History of Bacon's Rebellion in Virginia* (Chapel Hill, N.C., 1957). For a contrasting assessment of the problem discussed in these paragraphs, one that argues for further local study, see James H. Merrell, "Some Thoughts on Colonial Historians and American Indians," *William and Mary Quarterly*, 3rd ser., 46 (1989): 94–119.

8. For examples see James Axtell, *The Invasion Within: The Contest of Cultures in Colonial North America* (New York, 1985); Francis Jennings, *The Ambiguous Iroquois Empire: The Covenant Chain Confederation of Indian Tribes with the English Colonies from Its Beginnings to the Lancaster Treaty of 1744* (New York, 1984); James H. Merrell, *The Indians' New World: Catawbas and Their Neighbors from European Contact through the Era of Removal* (Chapel Hill, N.C., 1989); Daniel K. Richter, "War and Culture: The Iroquois Experience," *William and Mary Quarterly*, 3rd. ser., 40 (1983): 528–59; Daniel K. Richter and James H. Merrell, eds., *Beyond the Covenant Chain: The Iroquois and Their Neighbors in Indian North America* (Syracuse, 1987); Richard White, *The Roots of Dependency: Subsistence, Environment, and Social Change among the Choctaws, Pawnees, and Navajos* (Lincoln, Neb., 1983); J. Leitch Wright, *Creeks and Seminoles: The Destruction and Regeneration of the Muscogulge People* (Lincoln, Neb., 1986).

9. Henry Adams, *History of the United States of America during the Administrations of Thomas Jefferson and James Madison*, 2 vols. (1889–90; New York, 1986) 2:342–58.

TES TO PAGES xiv–xxii207

10. Parkman arranged the figures in what has since become the conventional scheme. Parkman, *Conspiracy of Pontiac* 1:186–91; see also Helen Hornbeck Tanner, ed., *Atlas of Great Lakes Indian History* (Norman, Okla., 1986), 103.

11. William Henry Harrison to Secretary of War, June 14, 1810, in *Governor's Messages and Letters of William Henry Harrison, 1800–1811,* ed. Logan Esarey, 2 vols. (Indianapolis, 1922), 1:425.

12. James T. Adams, ed., *Atlas of American History* (New York, 1943); Lester J. Cappon, *Atlas of Early American History: The Revolutionary Era, 1760–1790* (Princeton, 1976); Tanner, *Atlas of Great Lakes Indian History.*

Introduction

1. "John Hays' Diary and Journal of 1760," ed. William A. Hunter, *Pennsylvania Archaeologist* 24 (1954): 76–77.

2. For an early report of the inchoate state of Delaware tribal identity, see William Franklin's classification, which lists, in addition to the Munsees and Unamis (who are included in virtually every list), the "Chihohoki," "Mawhicon," and "Wapinger," in Governor Franklin to Board of Trade, Burlington, N.J., October 28, 1764, CO 323/20, f. 57, PRO. For a survey of the inadequacy of the term *tribe,* see Raymond D. Fogelson, "The Context of American Indian Political History: An Overview and Critique," in *The Struggle for Political Autonomy: Papers and Comments from the Second Newberry Library Conference on Themes in American Indian History,* ed. Frederick E. Hoxie, D'Arcy McNickle Center for the History of the American Indian Occasional Papers in Curriculum Series, no. 11 (Chicago, 1989), 14–18.

3. For the Tiogans as French allies, see M. De Vaudreuil to M. de Moras, Montreal, July 13, 1757, in *DRCHSNY,* 10:588–90.

4. See, for example, Anthony F. C. Wallace, *The Death and Rebirth of the Seneca* (New York, 1969); R. David Edmunds, *The Shawnee Prophet* (Lincoln, Neb., 1983); and William G. McLoughlin, "The Cherokee Ghost Dance Movement," in *The Cherokee Ghost Dance: Essays on the Southeastern Indians, 1789–1861,* ed. William G. McLoughlin (Macon, Ga., 1984).

5. Wallace does note the relationships, but they do not form part of his analysis. See Wallace, *Death and Rebirth,* 115, 117, 121. Anthony F. C. Wallace, "Revitalization Movements," *American Anthropologist* 58 (1956): 264–81; Max Weber, *The Theory of Social and Economic Organization,* ed. Talcott Parsons (New York, 1964), 358–92.

6. Peter Worsley discovers the same process at work in his study of Melanesia, *The Trumpet Shall Sound: A Study of the "Cargo" Cults in Melanesia* (London, 1957), 271–72.

7. See, for example, James H. Merrell, "Declarations of Independence: Indian-White Relations in the New Nation," in *The American Revolution: Its Character and Limits,* ed. Jack P. Greene (New York, 1987), 203.

8. Ralph Linton, "Nativistic Movements," *American Anthropologist* 45 (1943): 230; Peter Worsley, "Millenarian Movements in Melanesia," *Rhodes-Livingston Journal* 21 (1957): 18–37.

9. James Mooney, "Myths of the Cherokee," in *Nineteenth Annual Report of the Bureau of American Ethnology* (Washington, D.C., 1900), 336.

One. Power

1. James Kenny, "Journal of James Kenny, 1761–1763," ed. John W. Jordan, *PMHB* 37 (1913): 153, 184, 191, 193.

2. For a study of "structured" innovation, conditioned by tradition, see Marshall Sahlins, *Islands of History* (Chicago, 1985); Raymond D. Fogelson, "The Ethnohistory of Events and Nonevents," *Ethnohistory* 36 (1989): 139.

3. Eva Horner, "Shawnee Stories Recorded in the Sperry and White Oak Communities of Oklahoma, 1934–1936," National Anthropological Archives of the Smithsonian Institution, National Museum of Natural History–Museum of Man, Washington, D.C., 206. For a Cherokee version, see John Witthoft, "Bird Lore of the Eastern Cherokees," *Journal of the Washington Academy of Sciences* 36 (1946): 372–84.

4. James Mooney, "Myths of the Cherokee," in *Nineteenth Annual Report of the Bureau of American Ethnology* (Washington, D.C., 1900), 255–56.

5. Josiah Gregg, *Commerce of the Prairies,* ed. Max L. Moorhead (1844; Norman, Okla., 1954), 387–88. Gregg wrote *Commerce* in the 1840s. For twentieth-century variants, see Horner, "Shawnee Stories," 312–13; and C. F. Voegelin, "The Shawnee Female Deity," *Yale University Publications in Anthropology* 10 (1936): 3–21.

6. Mooney, "Myths of the Cherokee," 261, 327–29.

7. C. C. Trowbridge, "Shawnese Traditions," ed. Vernon Kenietz and Ermine W. Voegelin, *Occasional Contributions from the Museum of Anthropology of the University of Michigan* 9 (1939): 2–3; James Adair, *Adair's History of the American Indians, 1775,* ed. Samuel Cole Williams (New York, 1966), 140.

8. Ruth M. Underhill, *Red Man's Religion: Beliefs and Practices of the Indians North of Mexico* (Chicago, 1965), 42. See also Calvin Martin, "Subarctic Indians and Wildlife," in *Old Trails and New Directions: Papers of the Third North American Fur Trade Conference,* ed. Carol M. Judd and Arthur J. Ray (Toronto, 1980), 73–80; Martin, *Keepers of the Game: Indian-Animal Relationships and the Fur Trade* (Berkeley, 1978), 18, 35–39, 71; Ake Hultkrantz, "The Owner of the Animals in the Religion of the American Indians," in Ake Hultkrantz, *Belief and Worship in Native North America,* ed. Christopher Vecsey (Syracuse, 1981), 142–43; and Charles Hudson, *The Southeastern Indians* (Knoxville, Tenn., 1976), 172.

9. Mooney, "Myths of the Cherokee," 262.

10. Frank G. Speck, Leonard Broom, and Will West Long, *Cherokee Dance and Drama* (1951; Norman, Okla., 1981), 84.

11. *Adair's History,* 124; Hudson, *The Southeastern Indians,* 173; James Howard, *Shawnee! The Ceremonialism of a Native Tribe and Its Cultural Background* (Athens, Ohio, 1981), 270; William Schutz, Jr., "The Study of Shawnee Myth in an Ethnographic and Ethnohistorical Perspective" (Ph.D. diss., Indiana University, 1975), 23.

12. Underhill, *Red Man's Religion,* 49; *Adair's History,* 130; Horner, "Shawnee Stories," 304.

13. John R. Swanton, "Myths and Tales of the Southeastern Indians," *Bulletin of the Bureau of American Ethnology* 88 (1929): 15-16.

14. Albert S. Gatschet, "Shawnee Texts, Myths, with Interlinear English Translation," c. 1878-79, National Anthropological Archives of the Smithsonian Institution, Washington, D.C. For a Cherokee parallel see Raymond D. Fogelson, "Windigo Goes South: Stone Clad among the Cherokees," in *Manlike Monsters on Trial: Early Records and Modern Evidence,* ed. Marjorie M. Haplin and Michael M. Ames (Vancouver, 1980), 134-35.

15. Jack F. Kilpatrick and Anna G. Kilpatrick, *Friends of Thunder: Folktales of the Oklahoma Cherokees* (Dallas, 1964), 46.

16. Ake Hultkrantz, *The Religions of the American Indians,* trans. Monica Setterwall (1967; Berkeley, 1979), 53.

17. John Howard Payne, "Papers concerning the Cherokee Indians," 14 vols. (1789-1839), 1:26-31, Ayer MSS; Mooney, "Myths of the Cherokees," 244-45; Swanton, "Myths and Tales," 15. For a list of the Corn Woman's traits in North America, see Gudmund Hatt, "The Corn Mother in America and Indonesia," *Anthropos* 46 (1951): 853-914.

18. Henry Timberlake, *Lieutenant Henry Timberlake: Memoirs, 1756-1765,* ed. Samuel Cole Williams (Johnson City, Tenn., 1927), 68; *Adair's History,* 276, 435; Bruce G. Trigger, *The Children of Aataentsic: A History of the Huron People to 1660* (Montreal, 1976), 1:41; James P. Pate, "The Chickamauga: A Forgotten Segment of the Indian Resistance on the Southern Frontier" (Ph.D. diss., University of Mississippi, 1969), 11; J. Leitch Wright, Jr., *The Only Land They Knew: The Tragic Story of the American Indians in the Old South* (New York, 1981), 8.

19. O. M. Spencer, *The Captivity of O. M. Spencer,* ed. Milo Milton Quaife (Chicago, 1917), 75; James Smith, "A Narrative of the Most Remarkable Occurrences in the Life and Travels of Col. James Smith, During His Captivity among the Indians from the Year 1755 until 1759," in *A Collection of Some of the Most Interesting Narratives of Indian Warfare in the West,* ed. Samuel Metcalf (1821; New York, 1977), 203-4.

20. For a full discussion of alternative gender roles among the American Indians, see Walter L. Williams, *The Spirit and the Flesh: Sexual Diversity in American Indian Culture* (Boston, 1986); Jonathan Katz, *Gay American History: Lesbians and Gay Men in the U.S.A.* (New York, 1973), 285, 288-89, 291; Raymond E. Hauser, "The Berdache of the Illinois Indian Tribe during the Last Half of the Seventeenth Century," *Ethnohistory* 37 (1990): 45-65.

21. Payne, "Papers concerning the Cherokee Indians," 1, 28-31.

22. Horner, "Shawnee Stories," 312-13, 316.

23. Benjamin Hawkins, "A Sketch of the Creek Country in the Years 1798 and 1799," *Collections of the Georgia Historical Society* 3, pt. 1 (1848): 80.

24. One example of a "new" ceremony of diplomacy appears in the use by non-

Iroquois of a "shortened form" of the Iroquois condolence ceremony when treating with the English in the eighteenth century. See Dorothy Jones, *License for Empire: Colonialism by Treaty in Early America* (Chicago, 1982), 30.

25. *Adair's History*, 168–72; Payne, "Papers concerning the Cherokee Indians," 3:60; Hawkins, "A Sketch of the Creek Country," 79; Louis Le Clerc de Milford, *Memoir or a Cursory Glance at My Different Travels & My Sojourn in the Creek Nation [1802]*, trans. Geraldine de Courcy (Chicago, 1956), 171–72; Trowbridge, "Shawnese Traditions," 20; "J.C.B.," *Travels in New France by J.C.B.*, ed. Sylvester K. Stevens (Harrisburg, Penn., 1941), 69; Henry Rowe Schoolcraft, *Historical and Statistical Information Respecting the History, Condition, and Prospects of the Indian Tribes of the United States*, 6 vols. (Philadelphia, 1851–57), 6:661; James Axtell, "The White Indians of Colonial America," in *The European and the Indian: Essays in the Ethnohistory of Colonial North America*, ed. James Axtell (New York, 1981), 181–82.

26. George Stiggins, "A Historical Narration of the Genealogy Traditions and Downfall of the Ispocaga or Creek Tribe of Indians," Draper MSS, 1 U 66, 35.

27. Lieutenant Governor William Bull to General Jeffrey Amherst, Charles Town, January 24, 1761, *Letters and Diaries Relating to Major General Amherst*, microfilm, 1 reel, 61:187, Princeton University Library.

28. Pate, "The Chickamauga," 69; Payne, "Papers Concerning the Cherokee Indians," 3:60; Howard, *Shawnee!*, 116–17; Trowbridge, "Shawnese Traditions," 22. For a similar ceremony among the Chippewas see Louis Antoine de Bougainville, *Adventure in the Wilderness: The American Journals of Louis Antoine de Bougainville, 1756–1760*, trans. and ed. Edward P. Hamilton (Norman, Okla., 1964), 117.

29. Hawkins, "A Sketch of the Creek Country," 79–80. Kilpatrick and Kilpatrick, *Friends of Thunder*, 46; Speck, Broom, and Long, *Cherokee Dance*, 62–63; Howard, *Shawnee!*, 119.

30. Trowbridge, "Shawnese Traditions," 18.

31. James Mooney, "Sacred Formulas of the Cherokees," in *Seventh Annual Report of the Bureau of American Ethnology* (Washington, D.C., 1891), 388–91.

32. Payne "Papers concerning the Cherokee Indians," 3:175; Christian Frederick Post, "Journal," in *Early Western Travels*, ed. Reuben Gold Thwaites (Cleveland, 1904), 1:254.

33. *Adair's History*, 416; see also William Harlen Gilbert, *Eastern Cherokee Social Organization* (Chicago, 1935), 1.

34. Marian W. Smith, "American Indian Warfare," *New York Academy of Science, Transactions*, 2nd ser., 13 (1951): 353–54; Daniel K. Richter, "War and Culture: The Iroquois Experience," *William and Mary Quarterly*, 3rd. ser., 40 (1983): 528–59.

35. Jean Bernard Bossu, *Travels in the Interior of North America, 1751–1762*, ed. Seymour Feiler (Norman, Okla., 1962), 144.

36. John M'Cullough, "A Narrative of the Captivity of John M'Cullough," in *Selection of Some of the Most Interesting Narratives of the Outrages Committed by the Indians*, ed. Archibald Loudon (Carlisle, Penn., 1808–11), 293–94.

37. John Heckewelder, *History, Manners, and Customs of the Indian Nations Who Once Inhabited Pennsylvania, and the Neighboring States* (1819; Philadelphia, 1876), 136;

David Zeisberger, *Diary of David Zeisberger, A Moravian Missionary among the Indians of Ohio*, trans. and ed. Eugene F. Bliss (St. Clair Shores, Mich., 1972), 1:25.

38. Howard, *Shawnee!*, 119; Antoine Bonnefoy describes similar ties among the Cherokees in his "Journal" [1741–42] in *Early Travels in the Tennessee Country, 1540–1800*, ed. Samuel Cole Williams (Johnston City, Tenn., 1927), 150.

39. Thomas Ridout, "Narrative of the Captivity among the Shawanese Indians, in 1788, of Thomas Ridout, Afterwards Surveyor-General of Upper Canada, from the Original Manuscript in Possession of the Family," in *Ten Years of Upper Canada in Peace and War, 1805–1815*, ed. Matilda Edgar (Toronto, 1890), 354.

40. Smith, "A Narrative of the Most Remarkable Occurrences," 173–74. Bonnefoy, "Journal," 149–53.

41. John Slover, "The Narrative of John Slover," in Metcalf, *A Collection of Some of the Most Interesting Narratives*, 59; Ridout, "Narrative of the Captivity," 346–47; James Adair noted that before burning a captive, southeastern Indians gave him a pair of black moccasins (*Adair's History*, 418).

42. *Adair's History*, 418–19; Bossu, *Travels*, 145.

43. See for example, *Adair's History*, 418–19; Slover, "Narrative," 59–60; Ridout, "Narrative of the Captivity," 362–64; Trowbridge, "Shawnese Traditions," 21.

44. Knight, "The Narrative of Dr. Knight," in Metcalf, *A Collection of Some of the Most Interesting Narratives*, 46–49.

45. Mooney, "Myths of the Cherokee," 373.

46. Martin, *Keepers of the Game*, 52, 53, 57, 61; Hultkrantz, "Feeling for Nature among the North American Indians," in *Belief and Worship*, 133; James H. Merrell, "The Indians' New World: The Catawba Experience," *William and Mary Quarterly*, 3rd ser., 41 (1984): 543; Merrell has since modified the event in *The Indians' New World: Catawbas and Their Neighbors from European Contact through the Era of Removal* (Chapel Hill, N.C., 1989), 21–22, 44–45, demonstrating that critical elements of the native world view and ritual practice survived epidemics.

47. James Axtell, *The Invasion Within: The Contest of Cultures in Colonial North America* (New York, 1985), 282. Charles Bishop has also put it well. Adaptive change in religion, he writes, "is not necessarily apostatization." Charles A. Bishop, "Northeastern Indian Concepts of Conservation and the Fur Trade: A Critique of Calvin Martin's Thesis," in *Indians, Animals, and the Fur Trade: A Critique of "Keepers of the Game,"* ed. Shepard Krech III (Athens, Ga., 1981), 239–40.

48. *Adair's History*, 115; Gavin Cochrane, "Treatise on the Indians of North America Written in the Year 1764," chap. 6, Ayer MSS; Heckewelder, *History, Manners, and Customs of the Indian Nations*, 293.

49. Richard White, *The Roots of Dependency: Subsistence, Environment, and Social Change among the Choctaws, Pawnees, and Navajos* (Lincoln, Neb., 1983), 42–43, 46.

50. William G. McLoughlin, "Thomas Jefferson and the Beginning of Cherokee Nationalism, 1806–1809," *William and Mary Quarterly*, 3rd ser., 32 (1975): 547–80; and William G. McLoughlin, *Cherokee Renascence in the New Republic* (Princeton, 1986).

51. Kenny, "Journal," 193.

Two. The Indians' Great Awakening, 1745–1775

1. Captain Raymond to La Jonquière, Fort Miami, January 5, 1750, *Ill. Hist. Coll.* 19: 155–56. It is noteworthy that the more famous lead plates were buried and hidden from view.

2. Jean Pierre Joseph de Céloron, "Journal of Captain Celoron," in *Fort Pitt and Letters from the Frontier,* 2nd ed., ed. Mary C. Darlington (New York, 1971), 35, 42–45.

3. Helen Hornbeck Tanner, "Cherokees in the Ohio Country," *Journal of Cherokee Studies* 3 (1978): 95. William Trent, *Journal of Captain William Trent from Logstown to Pickawillany, A.D. 1752,* ed. Alfred T. Goodman (New York, 1971), 103; George Croghan to James Hamilton, Shippensburg, November 12, 1755, in *Penn. Archives,* 1st ser., 2:483–85.

4. James Bennet Griffin, *The Fort Ancient Aspect* (Ann Arbor, Mich., 1943), 207, 308; Helen Hornbeck Tanner, "The Greenville Treaty," in *Indians of Ohio and Indiana Prior to 1795,* ed. Helen Hornbeck Tanner and Erminie Wheeler-Voegelin (New York, 1974), 1:65–67; Erminie Wheeler-Voegelin, "Ethnohistory of Indian Use and Occupancy in Ohio and Indiana Prior to 1795," in ibid., 1:173–76; Jerry Eugene Clark, "Shawnee Indian Migration: A System Analysis" (Ph.D. diss., University of Kentucky, Lexington, 1974), 22. Charles Callender, "Shawnee," in *Northeast: Handbook of North American Indians,* ed. William C. Sturtevant (gen. ed.) and Bruce Trigger (Washington, D.C., 1978), 15:622–35, is more tentative about centering the Shawnees in Ohio.

5. George Henry Loskiel, *History of the Mission of the United Brethren among the Indians in North America* (London, 1794), 127; Callender, "Shawnee," 622; [Charles Thomson,] *An Enquiry into the Causes of the Alienation of the Delaware and Shawanese Indians from the British Interest* (London, 1759), 25; Tanner, "The Greenville Treaty," 65.

6. [M. Roucher,] "Account," Fort Duquesne, July 6, 1755, excerpted and translated in Paul E. Kopperman, *Braddock at the Monongahela* (Pittsburgh, 1977), 266–72; "Abstract of Dispatches from Canada," in *DRCHSNY,* 10:423.

7. Howard H. Peckham, ed., "Thomas Gist's Indian Captivity," *PMHB* 80 (1956): 293–94.

8. Louis Antoine de Bougainville, *Adventure in the Wilderness: The American Journals of Louis Antoine de Bougainville, 1756–1760* (Norman, Okla., 1964), 117–21; M. De Vaudreuil to M. de Moras, Montreal, July 13, 1757, in *DRCHSNY,* 10:588–90.

9. Four works examine the prophets of the mid-eighteenth century: James Mooney, "The Ghost Dance Religion and the Sioux Outbreak of 1890," in *Fourteenth Annual Report of the Bureau of American Ethnology,* pt. 2 (Washington, D.C., 1896), which suggests that the Delaware Prophet's movement may have been directly related to the Shawnee Prophet's movement of the nineteenth century; Melburn Delano Thurman, "The Algonquian Prophetic Tradition," chapter 7 of his "The Delaware Indians: A Study in Ethnohistory" (Ph.D. diss., University of California, Santa Barbara, 1973), and Charles Hunter, "The Delaware Nativist

Revival of the Mid-Eighteenth Century," *Ethnohistory* 18 (1971): 39–49, both of which push Mooney's suggestion further by bringing to light several of the Delaware prophets who surrounded Neolin between 1760 and 1775; and Anthony F. C. Wallace, "New Religions among the Delaware," *Southwestern Journal of Anthropology* 12 (1956): 1–21, which, unlike the other works, emphasizes discontinuity.

10. Bruce G. Trigger, *Children of Aataentsic: A History of the Huron People to 1660* (Montreal, 1976), 2:592–94; James P. Ronda, "Black Robes and Boston Men: Indian-White Relations in New France and New England, 1524–1701," in *The American Indian Experience: A Profile,* ed. Philip Weeks (Arlington Heights, Ill., 1988), 16.

11. Paul A. W. Wallace, *Conrad Weiser, 1696–1760, Friend of Colonist and Mohawk* (Philadelphia, 1945), 88.

12. David Brainerd, *The Life of David Brainerd,* ed. Jonathan Edwards and Philip E. Howard, Jr. (1749; Chicago, 1949), 233–34, 236–38.

13. Francis Jennings, *The Ambiguous Iroquois Empire* (New York, 1984), 309–46; and his *Empire of Fortune: Crowns, Colonies, and Tribes in the Seven Years War in America* (New York, 1988), 262–67, 271–80.

14. The Reverend John Brainerd to Ebenezar Pemberton, 1751, in *Life of John Brainerd,* ed. Thomas Brainerd (Philadelphia, 1865), 233–34.

15. John Brainerd to Pemberton, 1751, in *Life of John Brainerd,* 234–35.

16. Contrast with William G. McLoughlin, "A Note on African Sources of American Indian Racial Myths," in *Cherokee Ghost Dance: Essays on the Southeastern Indians, 1789–1861,* ed. William G. McLoughlin (Macon, Ga., 1984), 253–60.

17. "Remarks made by a Person [Anthony Benezet?] who accompanied Papoonhoal and other Indians on their way home as far as Bethlehem, July, 1760," Huntington MSS, 8249, Henry E. Huntington Library, San Marino, California; [Anthony Benezet,] *Some Observations on the Situation, Disposition, and Character of the Indian Natives of This Continent* (Philadelphia, 1784), 24; "Relation by Frederick Post of Conversation with Indians, 1760" *Penn. Archives,* 1st ser., 3:743; Edmund A. De Schweinitz, *The Life and Times of David Zeisberger* (Philadelphia, 1871), 427.

18. "Council at the State House in Philadelphia, Friday, July 11, 1760," Pennsylvania Council Minutes, Huntington MSS, 8249, Huntington Library; Christian Frederick Post, "Journal, 1760," May 19, on microfilm at American Philosophical Society, Philadelphia.

19. "Relation by Christian Frederick Post," 743; Wallace, "New Religions among the Delaware," 8–9; "Journal Kept at Fort Augusta, 1763," *Penn. Archives,* 2nd ser., 7:439; John Heckewelder, *Narrative of the Mission of the United Brethren* (Philadelphia, 1820), 90–92.

20. Hunter, "The Delaware Nativist Revival," 42–43, argues convincingly that Wangomend and the Assinsink Prophet were one and the same; Zeisberger supplies the 1752 dating: David Zeisberger, "1769 Diary," 79, translated typescript in Miscellaneous File, Ethnohistory Archive; "John Hays' Diary and Journal of 1760," ed. William A. Hunter, *Pennsylvania Archaeologist* 24 (1954): 76–77, also quoted in Wallace, "New Religions among the Delaware," 9.

21. Post, "Journal, 1760," May 23, May 24; "John Hays Diary," 77; Hunter, "The Delaware Nativist Revival," 43; Zeisberger, "1769 Diary," 79.

22. Charles Beatty, *Journals of Charles Beatty, 1762–1769*, ed. Guy Soulliard Klett (University Park, Penn., 1962), 65; see also Charles Beatty, *The Journal of a Two Months Tour with a View of Promoting Religion* (Edinburgh, 1798), for a fairly faithful, though polished, revision of the original journals; James Kenny, "Journal of James Kenny, 1761–1763," *PMHB* 37 (1913): 171.

23. Kenny, "Journal," 171; Wallace, "New Religions among the Delaware," 9. "John Hays Diary," 77, suggests the similarity between the two charts in n. III. On abstention from alcohol, see John Heckewelder, *History, Manners, and Customs of the Indian Nations Who Once Inhabited Pennsylvania, and the Neighboring States* (1819; Philadelphia, 1876), 292–93; [Robert Navarre,] "Journal of Pontiac's Conspiracy," in *The Siege of Detroit in 1763, the Journal of Pontiac's Conspiracy and John Rutherford's Narrative of a Captivity,* ed. Milo Quaife (Chicago, 1958), 14; Neyon de Villiers to d'Abbadie, Fort Chartres, December 1, 1763, in *Ill. Hist. Coll.,* 10:51.

24. That Neolin preached a gradual abandonment, a point missed by scholars, is implied in his suggestion that boys be trained "to ye use of the Bow & Arrow for Seven Years," and that the people were, "at ye Expiration of ye Seven Years, to quit all Commerce with ye White People & Clothe themselves with Skins." See Kenny, "Journal," 188.

25. De Schweinitz, *Life and Times of Zeisberger,* 383; Heckewelder, *Narrative of the Mission,* 104–5, refers to Wangomend's advocacy of "purging the body"; Zeisberger, "1767 Diary," translated typescript in Miscellaneous File, Ethnohistory Archive, 608–609a; Zeisberger, "1769 Diary," 6; John Ettwein, "Some remarks and annotations concerning the Traditions, Customs, languages &c. of the Indians in North America, from the memoirs of the Rev. David Zeisberger and other Missionaries of the United Brethren. Sent to General Washington by Rev. John Ettwein, Bethlehem, March 28, 1788," Miscellaneous Papers, Historical and Philosophical Society of Ohio, on microfilm in Ethnohistory Archive; William L. Merrill, "The Beloved Tree, *Ilex Vomitoria* among the Indians of the Southeast and Adjacent Regions," in *Black Drink: A Native American Tea,* ed. Charles Hudson (Athens, Ga., 1979), 40–82. For early use of emetics among the New England Peoples, close cultural cousins of the Delawares, see William S. Simmons, *Spirit of the New England Tribes: Indian History and Folklore, 1620–1984* (Hanover, N.H., 1986), 40.

26. Reuben Gold Thwaites and Louise Phelps Kellogg, *Documentary History of Dunmore's War, 1774* (Madison, Wis., 1905), 153n; Bouquet to Lieut. Francis and Col. Clayton, Fort Pitt, September 23, 1764, in *The Papers of Colonel Henry Bouquet,* ed. Sylvester K. Stevens and Donald H. Kent (Harrisburg, Penn., 1943), 13, pt. 2:142.

27. Kenny, "Journal," 171; Randolph Downes, *Council Fires on the Upper Ohio* (Pittsburgh, 1949), 105–6; Wilbur Jacobs, *Wilderness Politics: Diplomacy and Indian Gifts* (Lincoln, Neb., 1950), 183–85; [Navarre,] "Journal of Pontiac's Conspiracy," 14–15; De Villiers to D'Abbadie, December 1, 1763, in *Ill. Hist. Coll.,* 10:51.

28. *Ill. Hist. Coll.,* 10:51–52.

29. Major Gladwyn to Johnson, Detroit, June 9–11, 1764, in *The Papers of Sir William Johnson*, ed. James Sullivan, Alexander C. Flick, Almon W. Lauber, Milton W. Hamilton, 14 vols. (Albany, 1921–1965), 11:228; "Indian Conference," May 25, 1764, ibid., 11:206, hereafter cited as *Johnson Papers*.

30. Kenny, "Journal," 173; "Journal of Captain Thomas Morris of His Majesty's XVII Regiment of Infantry," in *Early Western Travels*, ed. Reuben Gold Thwaites (Cleveland, 1904), 1:309–10; Indian Conference, Johnson Hall, September 8–10, 1762, in *Johnson Papers*, 10:505–6.

31. Francis Parkman, *The Conspiracy of Pontiac and the Indian Uprising of 1763* (1851; Boston, 1898), 1:180–84.

32. Howard Peckham, *Pontiac and the Indian Uprising* (Chicago, 1961), 98, 116; Thurman, "The Delaware Indians," 160, also sees Pontiac as an "empirical" leader.

33. See Gregory E. Dowd, "The French King Wakes Up in Detroit: 'Pontiac's War' in Rumor and History," *Ethnohistory* 34 (1990): 254–78.

34. "A council in Illinois, Pontiac addresses Mons. Neyon de Villiers, April 15, 17, 1764," enclosed in Farmer to Gage, December 21, 1764, Thomas Gage Papers [selected], William Clements Library, on microfilm at the Ethnohistory Archive.

35. [Navarre,] "Journal of Pontiac's Conspiracy," 8; Ecuyer to Bouquet, May 29, 1763, quoted in Parkman, *The Conspiracy of Pontiac*, 2:7.

36. "Journal of Transactions with the Indians at Fort Pitt," in *Pennsylvania Colonial Records* (Harrisburg, Penn., 1852), 9:254–56; Croghan to Gage, Pittsburgh, May 12, 1765, Gage Papers, on microfilm at the Ethnohistory Archive.

37. [Navarre,] "Journal of Pontiac's Conspiracy," 63.

38. Johnson to Lords of Trade, May 11, 1764, in *DRCHSNY*, 7:624–26; entry for June 16, 1763, in "William Trent's Journal at Fort Pitt, 1763," ed. Albert T. Volwiler, *MVHR* 11 (1924–25): 399.

39. Loskiel, *History of the Mission*, 38.

40. David Zeisberger, "The Diaries of David Zeisberger Relating to the First Missions in the Ohio Basin," ed. Archer Butler Hulbert and William Nathaniel Schwarze, *Ohio Archaeological and Historical Quarterly* 21 (1912): 28. Quotations from Zeisberger's 1767 material derive from this translation, which is more accessible to the researcher. This translation and the 1767 material in the Ethnohistory Archive are substantively quite similar. See also Zeisberger, "1767 Diary," 610 a; and Zeisberger, "1769 Diary," 23.

41. Heckewelder, *Narrative of the Mission*, 102–3; De Schweinitz, *Life and Times of Zeisberger*, 340.

42. Zeisberger, "Diaries . . . Relating to the First Missions in the Ohio Basin," 24–25; Zeisberger, "1767 Diary," 608–9.

43. Heckewelder, *History, Manners, and Customs of the Indian Nations*, 293–95; Heckewelder, *Narrative of the Mission*, 108, 112, 135–36; Jungmann, "Diaries of Brother Jungmann, 1771," 202–4, typescript in Miscellaneous File, Ethnohistory Archive; Zeisberger, "1769 Diary," 62–63, 74, 125, 172; David Zeisberger Diary, 1772–81, in MAB, reel 8, box 141, 15:11.

44. Zeisberger, "1769 Diary," 22, 144, 150; Heckewelder, *Narrative of the Mission*, 116.

45. Zeisberger, "1769 Diary," 167–70.

46. Zeisberger, "1769 Diary," 81, 132; Beatty, *The Journal of a Two Months Tour*, 23–30; Kenny, "Journal," 188.

47. Zeisberger, "1767 Diary," 603; Zeisberger, "1769 Diary," 28, 81; John George Jungmann, "Diaries," 217. Thurman, "The Delaware Indians," 150, points to similarities between the witch-hunts of the 1760s and 1770s and those of the Shawnee Prophet.

48. De Schweinitz, *Life and Times of Zeisberger*, 416–18; Dunmore to Dartmouth, Williamsburg, December 24, 1774, Draper MSS, 15 J 48.

49. David Zeisberger, Diary, 1772–81, in MAB, reel 8, box 141, May 7, 1772, 12:3, January 1, 1773, 13:7–8.

50. Ibid., reel 8, box 141, January 1, 1773, 13:7–8.

51. David Jones, *A Journal of Two Visits Made to Some Nations of Indians on the West Side of the River Ohio in the Years 1772 and 1773* (Burlington, N.J., 1774), 64, and viii.

52. Ibid., 72, 78; Zeisberger, Diary, MAB, reel 8, box 141, October 7, 1772, 12:4.

53. Zeisberger, Diary, MAB, reel 8, box 141, September 19, 1773, 13:17–18.

54. Zeisberger, "Diaries . . . Relating to the First Missions in the Ohio Basin," 14–15; Zeisberger, "1767 Diary," 601–2.

55. McKee to Croghan, Fort Pitt, February 20, 1770, in *Johnson Papers*, 7:404–8; Thomas Gage to Earl of Shelburn, New York, October 10, 1767, CO 5/85, f. 205, PRO.

56. "Journal of Alexander McKee," enclosed in McKee to Johnson, Ostega, September 18, 1769, in *Johnson Papers*, 7:184. The famous Mingo, Logan, lived near the Shawnees in a Mingo settlement at the mouth of the Scioto River. He was apparently married to a Shawnee woman. Draper MSS, 14 J 10–11.

57. "Journal of Alexander McKee," in *Johnson Papers*, 7:184–85; Thomas Gage to William Johnson, April 1, 1771, in *Johnson Papers*, 8:58; Gage to Earl of Hillsborough, New York, September 9, 1769, CO 5/87, f. 157; John Stuart to Governor Botetourt, Charleston, January 13, 1770, CO 5/71, f. 61; Croghan to Gage, Philadelphia, January 1, 1770, CO 5/88, f. 44, PRO.

58. John Stuart to Earl of Hillsborough, Charleston, May 2, 1770, CO 5/71, f. 105; Gage to Hillsborough, New York, August 18, 1770, CO 5/88, f. 122, PRO.

59. For the peace with the Cherokees, see George Croghan to Thomas Gage, September 20, 1770; Gage to John Stuart, New York, October 16, 1770; Gage to Stuart, New York, November 20, 1770, all in the Papers of General Thomas Gage, William Clements Library, University of Michigan, Ann Arbor (hereafter cited as Gage MSS). See also John Stuart to George Germain, Pensacola, August 23, 1776, CO 5/77, f. 126; Croghan to Gage, Philadelphia, January 1, 1770, CO 5/88, f. 44; Gage to Hillsborough, New York, November 12, 1770, ibid., f. 174, PRO. For Shawnee messengers to Creeks, see Stuart, "Talk to the Headman and Warriors of the Upper Creek Nation," Charleston, November 25, 1770, Gage MSS; for mes-

sengers to Cherokees, see Croghan to Gage, September 20, 1770, and John Stuart to Gage, Charleston, December 12, 1770, Gage MSS.

60. Stuart to Gage, March 12, 1771, Charleston; Gage to Stuart, New York, October 16, 1770; Gage to Stuart, New York, May 17, 1771; Stuart to Gage, Charleston, December 12, 1770; Stuart to Gage, Charleston, February 8, 1771; Gage to Stuart, New York, September 19, 1770, Gage MSS; copy of the Report of the General Meeting with the Principal Chiefs and Warriors of the Cherokee Nation with John Stuart, Lochaber, October 18–20, 1770, CO 5/72, f. 22, PRO.

61. George Galphin to John Stuart, February 19, 1771; "Convention of the Overhill Cherokee Chiefs and Beloved Men . . . at Taquah . . . March 3, 1771; Alexander Cameron to Stuart, March 19, 1771 (abstract); Stuart to Gage, Charleston, April 29, 1771; Gage to Stuart, New York, June 11, 1771; Stuart to Gage, Pensacola, August 31, 1771; Stuart to Gage, Mobile, December 14, 1771; Gage to Stuart, New York, February 17, 1772, Gage MSS; Governor Wright to Hillsborough, Savannah, February 28, 1771, CO 5/661, f. 25; John Stuart to Hillsborough, Charleston, March 5, 1771, CO 5/72, f. 165, PRO.

62. Alexander Cameron to John Stuart, Lochaber, August 9, 1772; Stephen Forester to Stuart, Tuccabatchies, September 7, 1772; Stuart to Gage, Charleston, September 7, 1772; Gage to Stuart, New York, September 30, 1772; David Taitt to Stuart, Little Tallassies, October 19, 1772; Gage to Stuart, New York, December 20, 1772, Gage MSS.

63. Gage to Johnson, New York, April 1, 1771, in *Johnson Papers,* 8:58; Gage to Frederick Haldimand, New York, June 3, 1773, in Haldimand Papers, British Museum Additional Manuscripts, 21665, pt. 3, ff. 141–42, photostats in the Library of Congress, Washington, D.C.

64. Croghan to Johnson, September 18, 1769, in *Johnson Papers,* 7:182.

65. Major Arthur Campbell to Colonel William Preston, July 9, 1774, Draper MSS, 3 QQ 58; "Colonel Fleming's Orderly Book," Draper MSS 2 ZZ 72; "Conference at Fort Pitt," Draper MSS, 4 J 103.

66. Zeisberger, Diary, MAB, reel 8, file 141, October 11, 1774, 15:3; David Zeisberger, "History of the Northern American Indians," ed. Archer Butler Hulbert and Nathaniel Schwarze, *Ohio Archaeological and Historical Society Publications* 19 (1910): 127; "Extract from the Journal of Alexander McKee," March 8, 1774, CO 5/75, f. 142, PRO.

67. "Extract from the Journal of Alexander McKee, Sir William Johnson's Resident on the Ohio, March 8, 1774," CO 5/75, ff. 142–47; John Stuart to Earl of Dartmouth, Charleston, August 2, 1774, ibid., f. 165; Alexander Cameron to John Stuart, Lochaber, February 23, 1775, CO 5/76, f. 91.

Three. Revolutionary Alliances, 1775–1783

1. Henry Stuart to John Stuart, Pensacola, August 25, 1776, in *Documents of the American Revolution,* ed. K. G. Davies (Shannon, Ireland, 1976), 12:202–3. The following paragraphs rely on the same source.

2. "Deposition of Charles Robertson, October 3, 1777," in *The Calendar of Virginia State Papers, 1652–1781,* ed. William P. Palmer (1875; New York, 1968), 1:291–92; "Deposition of Thomas Houghton, October 3, 1777," in ibid., 290; John P. Brown, *Old Frontiers: The Story of the Cherokee Indians from Earliest Times to the Date of Their Removal West, 1838* (Kingsport, Tenn., 1938), 4–13; and James P. Pate, "The Chickamauga: A Forgotten Segment of the Indian Resistance on the Southern Frontier" (Ph.D. diss., University of Mississippi, 1969), 53; *Pennsylvania Packet,* August 13–27, 1776, HSP.

3. Pate, "The Chickamauga," 56; William Christian to Patrick Henry, Island Town, October 23, 1776, in "Virginia Legislative Papers," *Virginia Magazine of History and Biography* 17 (1909): 62–63.

4. For Shawnee promotions of alliance among the Cherokees, Creeks, and Chickasaws, see John Stuart to Frederick Haldimand, Charleston, January 23, 1771, Haldimand Papers, British Museum Additional Manuscripts, 21672, pt. 1, ff. 10–11, photostats in the Library of Congress, hereafter B.M. Add. MSS (DLC); John Stuart to Frederick Haldimand, Charleston, January 5, 1774, ibid., pt. 4, ff. 156–57; Charles Stuart to Haldimand, Mobile, July 22, 1774, ibid., pt. 6, ff. 272–74; John Stuart to Haldimand, Charleston, September 13, 1774, ibid., pt. 6, ff. 274–75; David Taitt, "Journal of a Journey through the Creek Country, 1772," in *Travels in the American Colonies,* ed. Newton D. Mereness (New York, 1916), 495, 559.

5. Haldimand to Stuart, New York, March 13, 1774, B. M. Add. MSS (DLC), 21672, pt. 6, ff. 238–39; John Stuart to Haldimand, Charleston, September 13, 1774, ibid., 274–75. Creek efforts are more fully described by David Corkran in *The Creek Frontier, 1540–1783* (Norman, Okla., 1967), 273–87.

6. James Wood's journal is copied into the text of treaty negotiations at Pittsburgh, 1775. See "Treaty at Pittsburgh [minutes, September 12–October 17], 1775," in *The Revolution on the Upper Ohio, 1775–1777,* ed. Reuben Gold Thwaites and Louise Phelps Kellogg, (Madison, Wis., 1908), 57–58.

7. "Information from James Rogers," Pittsburgh, September, 1775, and "James Wood's Journal," both in Thwaites and Kellogg, *Revolution on the Upper Ohio,* 72 and 62–63.

8. David Taitt to John Stuart, Little Tallassee, July 7–10, 1776, CO 5/77, f. 163a; John Stuart to General Howe, Pensacola, August 30, 1776, CO 5/94; f. 43, PRO; "Information of William Wilson, Pittsburgh, September 26, 1776," in Papers from the Yeates Collection relating to the 1776 Treaty of Pittsburgh, HSP; "A letter to the Committee of Congress for Indian Affairs, Pittsburgh, August 2, 1776," and "Information from John Hamilton and John Bradley to the Commissioners," MLB 2; "Captain Matthew Arbuckle to Colonel William Fleming," Fort Randolph, August 15, 1776, in Thwaites and Kellogg, *Revolution on the Upper Ohio,* 186–87.

9. James Mooney, "Myths of the Cherokees," in *Nineteenth Annual Report of the Bureau of American Ethnology* (Washington, D.C., 1900), 370–71.

10. Captain William McClenechan to Colonel William Flemming, Hands Meadows, July 24, 1776, in Thwaites and Kellogg, *Revolution on the Upper Ohio,* 170.

11. Pate, "The Chickamauga," 64–65; "Deposition of Jaret Williams, Fincastle

County," *Pennsylvania Packet,* August 13, 1776, HSP; Governor Chester to George Germain, Pensacola, September 1, 1776, CO 5/592, f. 395, PRO.

12. *Maryland Journal,* November 29, 1776, extract in Draper MSS, 2 JJ, 265–67; William Christian to Patrick Henry, October 23, 1776, ibid., 13 S 207–12; Brown, *Old Frontiers,* 154–61; Pate, "The Chickamauga," 70; Emmet Starr, *History of the Cherokee Indians and Their Legends and Folklore* (Oklahoma City, 1921), 32–33; Theodore Roosevelt, *The Winning of the West* (New York, 1889), 1:294–305.

13. David Taitt to Governor Patrick Tonyn, May, 23, 1777, Upper Creek Nation, British Public Record Office, Colonial Office, CO 5/ 557: ff. 299–302, PRO.

14. John Stuart to Germain, Pensacola, January 23, 1777, CO 5 (DLC) 78: f. 77.

15. Brown, *Old Frontiers,* 165–71, 551; Starr, *History of the Cherokees,* 33; Pate, "The Chickamauga," 73; Randolph C. Downes, "Cherokee-American Relations in the Upper Tennessee Valley, 1776–1791," *ETHSP* 8 (1936): 35–36

16. Brown, *Old Frontiers,* 163; Pate, "The Chickamauga," 80–81; John Stuart to George Germain, Pensacola, December 4, 1778, CO 5/80, f. 20, PRO.

17. Brown, *Old Frontiers,* 163, 257 (map); Starr, *History of the Cherokees,* 33; Pate, "The Chickamauga," 80–81.

18. John Stuart to Germain, Pensacola, March 5, 1778, CO 5 (DLC), 79: ff. 112–15.

19. Indian Agents to George Germain, Pensacola, July 12, 1779, CO 5 (DLC), 81: ff. 73–79; Brown, *Old Frontiers,* 172–75; Pate, "The Chickamauga," 80–81, 91–102.

20. Anthony Wayne to Arthur St. Clair, Greenville, August 19, 1795, Ayer MSS, Governor William Blount to Secretary of War, Knoxville, May 15, 1793, in *TPUS,* 4:258; Brown, *Old Frontiers,* 205.

21. John Stuart to General Howe, Pensacola, August 30, 1776, Davies, *Documents,* 13:21; Emistisiguo to John Stuart, Little Tallassee, November 19, 1776, Davies, *Documents,* 12:250; John Richard Alden, *John Stuart and the Southern Colonial Frontier* (Ann Arbor, Mich., 1944), 182–83, n 21.

22. James Howlett O'Donnell III, "The Southern Indians in the War for American Independence, 1775–1783," in *Four Centuries of Southern Indians,* ed. Charles M. Hudson (Athens, Ga., 1975), 52–53; Alexander McGillivray to John Stuart, Little Tallassee, September 21, 1777, CO 5 (DLC) 79: ff. 33–34.

23. Stuart to Germain, Pensacola, May 19, 1778, CO 5/79, 160–61; same to same, Pensacola, January 23, 1778, ibid, 64–67; quotation from David Taitt to Governor Patrick Tonyn, Upper Creek Nation, May 23, 1777, CO 5/557, 299–302, PRO; O'Donnell, "The Southern Indians," 50–51. For a very different interpretation, which stresses ethnic conflict within the Creek confederacy, see J. Leitch Wright, *Creeks and Seminoles: The Destruction and Regeneration of the Muscogulge People,* 113–15. Wright unconvincingly identifies the American faction as "predominantly non-Muskogee." This may or may not be true of the two pro-American leaders, the Tallassee King of Tallassee and (although it is even less likely) the Fat King of Cusseta. The latter's followers, however, were Muskogees, as were the Oakfus-kies—certainly pro-American. The Southern Shawnees, among the least Muskogean of the non-Muskogees, opposed the United States, as did one of the most

important of the Creeks, the non-Muskogean Emistisiguo. See Wright, *Creeks and Seminoles*, 5, 17, 113–15, 118, 334–35

24. Copy of a talk from the Seminollie Indians dated Flint River, September 3, 1777, CO 5 (DLC) 79: f. 37; Corkran, *The Creek Frontier*, 301.

25. John Stuart to George Germain, Pensacola, January 23, 1778, CO 5/79, 64–66, PRO; Alexander McGillivray to John Stuart, Little Tallassee, September 21, 1777, ibid., 33.

26. Alexander Cameron to John Stuart, July 13, 1777, Little Tallassee, CO 5 (DLC) 78: ff. 199–200; John Stuart to George Germain, Pensacola, January 23, 1778, CO 5/79, ff. 64–66, PRO; and same to same, Pensacola, August 10, 1778, CO (DLC) 5/79: 67, 184–85; Pate, "The Chickamauga," 91.

27. Henry Hamilton, "Substance of a Conference with the Indians," St. Vincennes, January 26, 1779, CO 42/39, f. 115; Hamilton to Haldimand, St. Vincennes, (copy) January 24, 1779, ibid., f. 109, PRO.

28. Henry Hamilton, "Account of the Expedition of Lieut. Gov. Hamilton," in "The Haldimand Papers," *Michigan Pioneer* 9 (1886): 497. Henry Hamilton to Commandant at Natchez, Vincennes, January 13, 1779, CO 5/97, f. 235; Hamilton to Stuart, December 25, 1778, Ft. Sackville, Vincennes, CO 5/80, f. 163; Board of Commissioners for the Indian Department to Germain, July 12, 1779, Pensacola, CO 5/81, ff. 73–79; Hamilton to Frederick Haldimand, Ft. Vincennes, January 24, 1779, CO 42/39, f. 109, PRO.

29. Clark to Henry, February 3, 1779, Kaskaskias, Ill., in *Ill. Hist. Coll.*, 8:97–100. For a critical look at Clark's raid, see Randolph Downes, *Council Fires on the Upper Ohio* (Pittsburgh, 1949), 237–39.

30. R. David Edmunds, *The Potawatomis: Keepers of the Fire* (Norman, Okla., 1978), 105.

31. Brown, *Old Frontiers*, 205; Pate, "The Chickamauga," 96, 129; Draper MSS; Arthur V. Goodpasture, "Indian Wars and Warriors of the Old Southwest," *Tennessee Historical Magazine* 4 (1918): 39–40; Evarts B. Greene and Virginia Harrington, *American Population before the Federal Census of 1790* (New York, 1932), 192.

32. Detroit Council, April 5, 1781, *Michigan Pioneer* 10 (1886): 462–64.

33. Downes, *Council Fires*, 277–78; Barbara Graymont, *The Iroquois in the American Revolution* (Syracuse, 1972), 240–41; Brown, *Old Frontiers*, 198; James Howlett O'Donnell III, *Southern Indians in the American Revolution* (Knoxville, Tenn., 1973), 124.

34. See, for example, Bernard W. Sheehan, "'The Famous Hair Buyer General': Henry Hamilton, George Rogers Clark, and the American Indian," *Indiana Magazine of History* 79 (1983): 9.

35. Michael D. Green, *The Politics of Indian Removal: Creek Government and Society in Crisis* (Lincoln, Neb., 1982), 15–16; Wright, *Creeks and Seminoles*, 22; John Stuart to Germain, Pensacola, August 10, 1778, CO 5 (DLC) 79: ff. 184–85; David Holms, "Journal of an Expedition against the Rebels," 1778, in ibid., 80: 34–43; Indian agents to George Germain, Pensacola, July 12, 1779, ibid., 81:73–79.

36. Taitt, "Journal of a Journey," 538–39. W. C. Sturtevant, "Cherokee Fron-

tiers, the French Revolution, and W. A. Bowles," in *The Cherokee Nation: A Trouble of History*, ed. D. King (Knoxville, Tenn., 1978); A. S. Gatschet, *A Migration Legend of the Creek Indians* (St. Louis, 1881), 90; J. N. B. Hewitt, "Notes on the Creek Indians," ed. J. R. Swanton, *Bureau of American Ethnology Bulletin* 123 (1939): 142.

37. William Bartram, *The Travels of William Bartram*, ed. Mark Van Doren (New York, 1940), 215–17, 390.

38. Raymond David Fogelson, "The Cherokee Ball Game: A Study in Southeastern Ethnology" (Ph.D. diss., University of Pennsylvania, 1962), 2, 157–58, 166.

39. Alexander Cameron to [John Stuart,] Keowee, Cherokee Nation, April 12, 1774, B.M. Add. MSS (DLC) 21672, pt. 6, ff. 246–49.

40. Starr, *History of the Cherokee*, 32; for captive burning as a divinatory rite, see Chapter One.

41. Quoted in Brown, *Old Frontiers*, 166–67, 276–78.

42. Corkran, *The Creek Frontier*, 97–98; Samuel Cole Williams, ed., "An Account of the Presbyterian Mission to the Cherokees, 1757–1759," *Tennessee Historical Magazine*, 2nd ser., 1 (1930–31): 125–38; "Bro. Martin Schneider's Report of His Journey to the Upper Cherokee Towns," in *Early Travels in the Tennessee Country, 1540–1800*, ed. Samuel Cole Williams (Johnson City, Tenn., 1928), 251–57.

43. James Axtell, *The Invasion Within: The Contest of Cultures in Colonial North America* (New York, 1985), 43–127; Trigger, *The Children of Aataentsic: A History of the Huron People to 1660* (Montreal, 1976), 2:699–850; "Indian Speech at Sandusky," *Michigan Pioneer* 20 (1892): 392; "Indian Villages in Ohio, Pennsylvania, and New York," in *Atlas of Early American History: The Revolutionary Era, 1670–1720*, ed. Lester J. Cappon (Princeton, 1976), 21.

44. David Zeisberger, Diary, March and April, 1777, MAB, reel 8, box 141, 17:8–11; David Zeisberger, *Diary of David Zeisberger*, trans. and ed. Eugene F. Bliss (1885; St. Clair Shores, Mich., 1972), 1:27.

45. Zeisberger, *Diary*, 1:7.

Four. Neutrality, A World Too Narrow, 1775–1781

1. Gage to Stuart, New York, September 19, 1770, The Papers of General Thomas Gage, William Clements Library, University of Michigan, Ann Arbor.

2. Message sent to the inhabitants of Kentucky by Commissioners of Indians, October 12, 1775, in *The Revolution on the Upper Ohio, 1775–1777*, ed. Reuben Gold Thwaites and Louise Phelps Kellogg (Madison, Wis., 1908), 111; Richard Butler, "On the Tour of the Delawares Yendots Mingoes and Shawnies" September 12, 1775, 25, Manuscript Journal, HSP; and "Information from James Rogers," and "James Wood's Journal," both in *Revolution on the Upper Ohio*, 70–71, and 57–58.

3. Captain William Russell to Colonel William Fleming, Fort Blair, June 12, 1775, in Thwaites and Kellogg, *Revolution on the Upper Ohio*, 14–15; Butler, "Tour," September 12, 1775, 25; General Edward Hand to Jasper Yeates, Fort Pitt, July 12, 1777, in *Frontier Defense on the Upper Ohio*, State Historical Society of Wisconsin, Collections, vol. 22, ed. Louise Phelps Kellogg (Madison, 1915), 19–20; Helen

Hornbeck Tanner, ed., *Atlas of Great Lakes Indian History* (Norman, Okla., 1987), 81.

4. Randolph Downes, *Council Fires on the Upper Ohio* (Pittsburgh, 1949), 183–86; "Treaty at Pittsburgh" [minutes, September 12–October 17, 1775], in Thwaites and Kellogg, *Revolution on the Upper Ohio*, 84–86.

5. Thwaites and Kellogg, *Revolution on the Upper Ohio*, 103–4.

6. Ibid., 116–17, 118–19, 121.

7. Zeisberger, Diary, August 17, 1774, MAB, reel 8, box 141, 14:22–23; March 1775, ibid., 17:4–8. Killbuck should not be confused with his forebear, also known as Killbuck. This younger Killbuck, or Gelelemend, is the better known of the two. See "Appendix," *Michigan Pioneer* 19 (1891): 685.

8. John Parrish, "Extracts from the Journal of John Parish (1773)," ed. T[homas] S[hoemaker], *PMHB* 16 (1892): 448.

9. Zeisberger, Diary, August 12, 1775, MAB, reel 8, box 141, 15:5; November 5, 1774, ibid., 15:11; February 11, 1776, ibid., 15:15.

10. David Zeisberger, *Diary of David Zeisberger,* trans. and ed. Eugene F. Bliss (St. Clair Shores, Mich., 1972) 1:27–28; see also Zeisberger, Diary, November, 1774, MAB, reel 8, box 141, 15:12.

11. "James Wood's Journal," July 10, 1775, in Thwaites and Kellogg, *Revolution on the Upper Ohio*, 40–41; "Treaty at Pittsburgh," in ibid., 85–86.

12. Reginald Horsman, *Expansion and American Indian Policy, 1783–1812* (East Lansing, Mich., 1967), 10–12, 17–23. For Six Nations' claims over Shawnees, see Butler, "Tour," August 30, 1775, 3; over Delawares, see George Morgan to John Hancock, Fort Pitt, February 12, 1777, MLB, 1.

13. "Negotiations with the Delawares," Fort Pitt, September 12, 1778, in *Frontier Advance on the Upper Ohio,* State Historical Society of Wisconsin, Collections, vol. 23, ed. Louise Phelps Kellogg (Madison, 1916), 143.

14. Kappler, *Treaties,* 2:4–5; Kellogg, "Introduction," *Frontier Advance,* 20–21; Annie H. Abel, "Proposals for an Indian State, 1778–1878," *Annual Report of the American Historical Association* (1907): 89–104; C. Hale Sipe, *The Indian Chiefs of Pennsylvania* (Butler, Penn., 1927), 413–14.

15. *Frontier Advance,* 319, editor's note 1; Varnum Lansing Collins, "Indian Wards at Princeton," *Princeton University Bulletin* 13 (1901): 101–6; Draper MSS, 11 YY 30, 9 S 175, 16 S 288.

16. "Negotiations with the Delawares," Fort Pitt, September 12, 1778, in Kellogg, *Frontier Advance,* 143; "Message from the Delaware Council to Colonel George Morgan," Coochocking, February 26, 1777, MLB, 1.

17. Quoted in Downes, *Council Fires,* 217.

18. Killbuck to Colonel George Morgan, January 20, 1779, in Kellogg, *Frontier Advance,* 203–4.

19. Downes, *Council Fires,* 217–19; General Lachlan McIntosh's speech to the Delawares, Camp at Tuscorawas, November 22, 1778, in Kellogg, *Frontier Advance,* 178–79.

20. Morgan to Committee of Congress for Indian Affairs, July 30, 1776, Pitts-

burgh, MLB, 2; General Hand to Richard Peters, July 10, 1778, in Kellogg, *Frontier Advance*, 107.

21. Speech of Delawares to Washington and Congress, May 10, 1779, in Kellogg, *Frontier Advance*, 318-19.

22. Ibid., 318-21; Joseph Reed to Colonel Broadhead, n.p. [Philadelphia?], n.d. [c. July, 1779], in *Penn. Archives*, 1st ser., 7:569; Broadhead to Washington, Pittsburgh, November 22, 1779, ibid., 12:189; Morgan to John Jay, May 16, 1779, MLB, 3; Downes, *Council Fires*, 242-43; George Washington to Deputies from the Delaware Nation, May 12, 1779, *Publications of the Colonial Society of Massachusetts, Transactions* 13 (1910-11): 262-64; Broadhead to Joseph Reed, Fort Pitt, May 13, 1780, and Broadhead to Richard Peters, May 14, 1780, in *Frontier Retreat on the Upper Ohio*, State Historical Society of Wisconsin, Collections, vol. 24, ed. Louise Phelps Kellogg (Madison, 1917), 180-81.

23. Council, Detroit, June 14, 1778, with Ottawa, Chippewa, Huron, Potawatomi, Delaware, Shawnee, Miami, Mingo, Mohawk . . . , *Michigan Pioneer* 9 (1886): 447; Major de Peyster to Captain McKee, Detroit, November 2, 1779, ibid., 10 (1886): 371; Haldimand to De Peyster, Quebec, August 10, 1780, ibid., 9 (1886): 639.

24. Major de Peyster to General Haldimand, Detroit, November 3, 1781, ibid., 10 (1886): 536-37.

25. Barbara Graymont, *The Iroquois in the American Revolution* (Syracuse, 1972), 192-222; Downes, *Council Fires*, 253, 278-79; Broadhead to Timothy Pickering, November 3, 1779, in Kellogg, *Frontier Retreat*, 109; Speech of Shawnees to de Peyster, August 22, 1780, *Michigan Pioneer* 10 (1886): 420-21; de Peyster to Haldimand, Detroit, August 31, 1780, ibid., 10 (1886): 423; de Peyster to Brigadier General H. Watson Powell, Detroit, March 20, 1782, ibid., 20 (1892): 4; de Peyster to Brigadier General Allan Maclean, Detroit, January 7, 1783, ibid., 20 (1892): 87; Zeisberger, *Diary*, 1:107-8, 124.

26. Morgan to Hancock, Fort Pitt, March 15, 1777, MLB, 1.

27. John Page to General Edward Hand, Williamsburg, September 17, 1777; in Kellogg, *Frontier Defense*, 85-86, editor's note 53; General Edward Hand to Jasper Yeates, Fort Pitt, December 24, 1777, in ibid., 188.

28. Matthew Arbuckle to Edward Hand, Fort Randolph, October 6, 1777, November 7, 1777, in ibid., 125-28, 149-50; Zeisberger to Hand, November 16, 1777, in ibid., 167; General Edward Hand to Jasper Yeates, Fort Pitt, December 24, 1777, in ibid., 188; Hand to Morgan, Fort Pitt, December 24, 1777, in ibid., 188; Thwaites and Kellogg, *Revolution on the Upper Ohio*, 41, n. 67.

29. Hand to Patrick Henry, Stauton, December 9, 1777, and editor's note 43, in Kellogg, *Frontier Defense*, 176-77. For the few extraordinary cases in the late eighteenth century in which a British subject or an American citizen was executed for killing an Indian, see Alden Vaughan, "Frontier Banditti and the Indians: The Paxton Boys' Legacy, 1763-1775," *Pennsylvania History* 51 (1984): 16; John Richard Alden, *John Stuart and the Southern Colonial Frontier* (Ann Arbor, Mich., 1944), 298.

30. Morgan to Shawnee Chiefs, Pittsburgh, March 25, 1778, in Kellogg, *Frontier*

Defense, 234–36; William Preston and William Fleming to Shawnees, April 3, 1778, in ibid., 258–61.

31. White Eyes and John Killbuck to Colonel Morgan and the Commissioners, Cochocking, April 6, 1778, MLB, 3; Downes, *Council Fires,* 211.

32. Message to Delawares from Ottawas, Chippewas, Hurons, Potowatomis, and Miamis, Detroit, June 18, 1778, MLB, 3; Message from the Delawares, May, 1779, MLB, 3; Colonel Daniel Broadhead to Delawares, Pittsburgh, June 20, 1779, in Kellogg, *Frontier Advance,* 365–66, and "Recollections of Samuel Murphy," in Kellogg, *Frontier Defense,* 218–19; "Council Held at Detroit . . . " June 14–June 20, 1778, *Michigan Pioneer* 9 (1886): 446, 451–52; Lieutenant Governor Hamilton to Haldimand, Detroit, September 5, 1778, ibid., 9 (1886): 465.

33. White Eyes and Killbuck to George Morgan, Coshocton, March 14, 1778, MLB, 3; H. C. Shetrone, "The Indian in Ohio," *Ohio Archaeological and Historical Society Publications* 27 (1919), inserted map; Downes, *Council Fires,* 218–20.

34. Killbuck to Colonel Morgan, January 20, 1779, in Kellogg, *Frontier Advance,* 203–4. Ibid., 156–57, editor's note 3; Taimenend [Morgan] to Delawares, Fort Pitt, January 5, 1779, MLB, 3; Downes, *Council Fires,* 217; Sipe, *The Indian Chiefs of Pennsylvania,* 418.

35. "Estate of White Eyes," in Kellogg, *Frontier Advance,* 168.

36. Broadhead to Delawares, Pittsburgh, June 22, 1779, ibid., 368; Joseph Reed to Colonel Broadhead, n.d., 1779, n.p., in *Penn. Archives,* 1st ser., 7:569.

37. William Wilson's Report, copied in 1778 by George Morgan, in David I. Bushnell, "The Virginia Frontier in History," *Virginia Magazine of History and Biography* 23 (1915): 344–46; for the Mequashake-Coshocton arrangement, see White Eyes and Killbuck to Morgan, June 9, 1778, in Kellogg, *Frontier Advance,* 83–84, George Morgan to Delaware Chiefs, March 27, 1778, in Kellogg, *Frontier Defense,* 241–42, and Killbuck to Daniel Broadhead, September 21, 1779, in Kellogg, *Frontier Retreat,* 73–75. For Shawnee disputes see entry for November 4, 1776, Yeates Collection relating to the 1776 Treaty of Pittsburgh, HSP; General Edward Hand to Jasper Yeates, Fort Pitt, July 12, 1777, in Kellogg, *Frontier Defense,* 19–20.

38. Morgan to Jay, Philadelphia, May 28, 1779, in Kellogg, *Frontier Advance,* 344; John Heckewelder to Colonel John Gibson, February, in ibid., 222; George Morgan to John Jay, Philadelphia, May 28, 1779, in ibid., 343; John Heckewelder to Colonel Daniel Broadhead, Coochocking, March 12, 1779, in ibid., 242–45; Zeisberger to Morgan, Lichtenau, January 20, 1779, MLB, 3. It should be noted that the forces withdrew only after killing at least eighteen of the garrison's defenders. See Downes, *Council Fires,* 221–23.

39. Council at Detroit, June 20, 1778, *Michigan Pioneer* 9 (1886): 448; Killbuck to General Lachlan McIntosh, Cooshocking, March 15, 1779, in Kellogg, *Frontier Advance,* 254.

40. Broadhead to Heckewelder, Pittsburgh, May 13, 1779, in *Penn. Archives,* 1st ser., 12:111–12.

41. Daniel Broadhead to General Washington, Pittsburgh, June 25, 1779, in *Penn. Archives,* 1st ser., 12:131–32; Zeisberger, *Diary,* 2:357–58.

42. Council of Delawares with Colonel Daniel Broadhead, Pittsburgh, July 12, 1779, in Kellogg, *Frontier Advance,* 388; Broadhead to General Washington, Fort Pitt, July 31, 1779, in *Penn. Archives,* 1st ser., 12:146–48; same to same, September 16, 1779, in ibid.., 12:155–58; Downes, *Council Fires,* 251–53; Graymont, *The Iroquois in the American Revolution,* 214–15, 222; Kellogg, "Introduction," *Frontier Retreat,* 14–15.

43. The Chiefs . . . to . . . Captain Lernoult, Upper Shawnee Village, October 20, 1779, *Michigan Pioneer* 10 (1886): 364–65.

44. Broadhead to Washington, Pittsburgh, September 16, 1779, in *Penn. Archives,* 1st ser., 12:189. Mequashakes remained an integral part of Coshocton. Delawares and Mequochoke-Shawnees to Broadhead, Pittsburgh, February 17, 1780, in Kellogg, *Frontier Retreat,* 139.

45. Downes, *Council Fires,* 263–64.

46. Zeisberger, Diary, February 16, 1781, MAB, reel 8, box 141, 17:15; Killbuck to Broadhead, Salem, January 15, 1781, in Kellogg, *Frontier Retreat,* 316–17; Killbuck to Broadhead, Salem, February 26, 1781, in ibid., 340; Heckewelder to Broadhead, February 26, 1781, in ibid., 337–39.

47. Broadhead to Colonel David Shepherd, Fort Pitt, March 8, 1781, in Kellogg, *Frontier Retreat,* 342–43; Broadhead to Washington, Fort Pitt, March 8, 1781, in ibid., 342–43; Alexander Fowler to Joseph Reed, Pittsburgh, March 29, 1781, in ibid., 356–57.

48. Kellogg, "Introduction," *Frontier Retreat,* and C. W. Butterfield, "Narrative of Broadhead's Expedition," in ibid., 33–35, 376–81; Downes, *Council Fires,* 265–66, and Broadhead to Joseph Reed, Philadelphia, May 22, 1781, in Kellogg, *Frontier Retreat,* 399; Arrent De Peyster, "Memorandum," April 26, 1781, *Michigan Pioneer* 10 (1886): 476.

49. Colonel Archibald Lochry to Joseph Reed, Twelve Mile Run, July 4, 1781, in Kellogg, *Frontier Retreat,* 415–16; Isaac Mason to Joseph Reed, July 1, 1781, in ibid., 413–14; Indian Council, Detroit, December 8, 1781, *Michigan Pioneer* 10 (1886): 542.

50. Zeisberger, *Diary,* 1:1–4, 9. For Pipe's defection, see "Captain Pipe & Win, gi, nam . . . , in Council," Detroit, November 9, 1781, *Michigan Pioneer* 10 (1886): 538–39.

51. Zeisberger to Morgan, Cuchochunk, July 19, 1778, in Kellogg, *Frontier Advance,* 119–20.

52. Zeisberger to General Edward Hand, Cuchochunk, July 29, 1777, in Kellogg, *Frontier Defense,* 29; Zeisberger to Morgan, Cuchochunk, August 25, 1778, in Kellogg, *Frontier Advance,* 132–33; Heckewelder to Colonel Daniel Broadhead, June 30, 1779, in ibid., 383.

53. Zeisberger to Colonel John Gibson, Ochi Town, January 19, 1779, in *Ill. Hist. Coll.,* 1:381–82; Colonel Daniel Broadhead to David Zeisberger, Pittsburgh, December 12, 1779, in Kellogg, *Frontier Retreat,* 119; Major De Peyster to Captain McKee, Detroit, February 1, 1781, *Michigan Pioneer* 10 (1886): 452.

54. Morgan to Zeisberger, Fort Pitt, January 30, 1779, in Kellogg, *Frontier Advance,* 216; Broadhead to General George Washington, Pittsburgh, December 13, 1779, in Kellogg, *Frontier Retreat,* 120.

55. Zeisberger, Diary, March, 1777, MAB, reel 8, box 141, 17:4–7.

56. Zeisberger, Diary, October 23, 1780, MAB, ibid., 17:5–6.

57. Theodore Roosevelt, *The Winning of the West* (New York, 1889), 2:156.

58. Colonel John Gibson to Governor Thomas Jefferson, Fort Pitt, May 30, 1781, in Kellogg, *Frontier Retreat,* 400.

59. Zeisberger, *Diary,* 1:85–86; 419–20.

60. Lawrence Henry Gipson, "Introduction," in *Moravian Indian Mission on White River: Diaries and Letters, May 5, 1799, to November 12, 1806,* ed. L. H. Gipson (Indianapolis, 1938), 10–11.

61. Zeisberger, *Diary,* 1:85–86, 419–20, 2:8–9, 357–58.

62. Zeisberger, *Diary,* 1:86, 124, 127; de Peyster to Haldimand, Detroit, May 13, 1782, *Michigan Pioneer* 10 (1886): 573–74.

63. De Peyster to Haldimand, Detroit, June 23, 1782, *Michigan Pioneer* 10 (1886): 594–95.

64. Lieutenant Governor Sinclair to Haldimand, Michilimackinac, June 25, 1782, *Michigan Pioneer* 10 (1886): 595; Major de Peyster to Haldimand, Detroit, June 23, 1782, ibid., 594–95; Major de Peyster to Haldimand, Detroit, August 18, 1782, ibid., 628–29.

65. McKee to de Peyster, Shawnee Country, August 28, 1782, *Michigan Pioneer* 20 (1892): 50–51; de Peyster to McKee, Detroit, August 6, 1782, ibid., 10 (1886): 623–24; Downes, *Council Fires,* 274; Zeisberger, *Diary,* 1:133.

Five. A Spirit of Unity, 1783–1794

1. James H. Merrell treats the two as similar culture brokers in "Declarations of Independence: Indian-White Relations in the New Nation," in *The American Revolution: Its Character and Limits,* ed. Jack P. Greene (New York, 1987), 202; Reginald Horsman attributes the leading role in the organization of the Northwest confederacy to Joseph Brant in *Expansion and American Indian Policy* (East Lansing, Mich., 1967), 31, 39; Isabel Kelsay goes so far as to argue that Brant himself germinated the idea of a confederacy in *Joseph Brant, 1743–1807: Man of Two Worlds* (Syracuse, 1984), 346, 398; similarly, Arthur Preston Whitaker suggests that McGillivray formulated a notion of intertribal union in "Alexander McGillivray, 1783–1789," *North Carolina Historical Review* 5 (1928): 198.

2. Frederick Haldimand to Thomas Townshend, Quebec, October 30, 1782, *Michigan Pioneer* 10 (1886): 662–63; Maclean to Haldimand, Niagara, May 18, 1783, ibid., 20 (1892): 119; Thomas Brown to Thomas Townshend, St. Augustine, June 1, 1783, CO 5/82, f. 367; "McGillivray for the Chiefs," July 10, 1785, in *McGillivray of the Creeks,* ed. John W. Caughey (Norman, Okla., 1938), 90–92.

3. De Peyster to Maclean, Detroit, March 5, 1783, *Michigan Pioneer* 20 (1892): 96; Captain Alexander McKee to de Peyster, Shawnee Town, May 24, 1783, ibid., 122–23; "Papers of the Continental Congress," item 150, "Letters from Major General Henry Knox, Secy. at War, 1785–1788," 1:155–56, NA, microfilm M-247, reel 164, at the University of Pennsylvania; David Zeisberger, *Diary of David Zeisberger,* trans.

and ed. Eugene F. Bliss (St. Clair Shores, Mich., 1972), 1:233; Josiah Harmar to Thomas Mifflin, Fort McIntosh, June 25, 1785, in *Journal of Captain Jonathan Heart, 1785,* ed. C. W. Butterfield (Albany, 1885), 75–76; Samuel Montgomery, "A Journey Through the Indian Country beyond the Ohio in 1785," ed. David I. Bushnell, Jr., *MVHR* 2 (1915): 272: Information of Captain Tunis [also Teunise], a Delaware Indian Addressed to Colonel Harmar, July 6, 1786, Harmar Papers, Draper MSS, 1 W 155–58; John F. Hamtramck to Harmar, May 21, 1788, in *Outpost on the Wabash,* Indiana Historical Society Publications, vol. 19, ed. Gayle Thornbrough (Indianapolis, 1957), 80.

4. Colonel Joseph Martin to Governor Alexander Martin, Sittico, January 11, 1784, in *The State Records of North Carolina,* ed. Walter Clark (Goldsboro, N.C., 1899), 16:924, Alexander McKee to Sir John Johnson, Detroit, June 2, 1784, *Michigan Pioneer* 20 (1892): 229–30.

5. "Report of Benjamin Hawkins . . . to Congress in 1785, in *ASPIA,* 1:39; McGillivray to O'Neil, Little Tallassee, November 8, 1785, *ETHSP* 9 (1937): 136; O'Neil to Bernardo Galvez, Pensacola, September 4, 1785, ibid., 133; "Treaty of Pensacola, June 1, 1784," in Caughey, *McGillivray,* 75–76; McGillivray to O'Neil, Little Tallassee, January 1, 1784, in ibid., 72–73; McGillivray to Miró, Little Tallassee, March 28, 1784, in ibid., 73–74; James P. Pate, "The Chickamauga: A Forgotten Segment of the Indian Resistance on the Southern Frontier" (Ph.D. diss., University of Mississippi, 1969), 148, 159; Jack D. L. Holmes, "Spanish Policy toward the Southern Indians in the 1790s," in *Four Centuries of Southern Indians,* ed. Charles M. Hudson (Athens, Ga., 1975), 68, 70; Whitaker, "McGillivray," 181–203; R. S. Cotterill, *The Southern Indians: The Story of the Civilized Tribes before Removal* (Norman, Okla., 1954), 63.

6. Andrew Pickens, Benjamin Hawkins, Joshua Martin to Richard Casswell, June 10, 1785, Andrew Pickens Papers, Henry E. Huntington Library, San Marino, California; Benjamin Hawkins, Andrew Pickens, Joshua Martin, Lachlan McIntosh to Congress, Keowee, November 17, 1785, in *ASPIA,* 1:16.

7. For a critical look at the Treaty of the Mouth of the Miami, see Randolph Downes, *Council Fires on the Upper Ohio* (Pittsburgh, 1949), 289–98, esp. 297–98; Obadiah Robins to Captain Fergeuson, New Coshocton, September 29, 1786, Harmar Papers, Draper MSS, 1 W 249; George Brickell's deposition, September 13, 1786, ibid., 214; General Henry Lee of Mason Co., Kentucky, to Lyman Copland Draper, July 1843, Draper MSS, 9 BB 60–60(5); J. P. M. La Gras to General G. R. Clark, Post Vincennes, July 22, 1786, in Lawrence Kinnaird, ed., *Spain in the Mississippi Valley 1765–1794,* Annual Report of the American Historical Association, 1945, 4 vols. (New York, 1946–49), 3:178.

8. William Albert Galloway, *Old Chillicothe: Shawnee and Pioneer History* (Xenia, Ohio, 1934), 90–91; Harmar to the Secretary of War, Fort Harmar, November 15, 1786, in *St. Clair Papers,* ed. William Henry Smith (Cincinnati, 1882), 2:18–19; General Henry Lee to Lyman Copland Draper, Mason County, Kentucky, July, 1843, Draper MSS, 9 BB 60–60(5); Henry Alder, *The Captivity of Jonathan Alder and*

His Life with the Indians as Dictated by Him and Transcribed by His Son Henry, ed. Orley E. Brown (Alliance, Ohio, 1965), 39–40.

9. Speech of the United Indian Nations, . . . November 28– December 18, 1786, in *ASPIA,* 1:8–9.

10. "Br. Martin Schneider's Report of His Journey to Long Island on Holston River, & From thence farther to the Upper Cherokee Towns on Tenassee River from the Middle of Dec. 1783 till Jan. 24th 1784," MAB, reel 24, box 192, folder 1: not paginated, date: January 4, 1784.

11. Samuel Cole Williams, *History of the Lost State of Franklin,* Perspectives in American History, vol. 23 (1933; Cambridge, Mass., 1974), 39–45, 99–121, 212, 249–54; Randolph C. Downes, "Cherokee-American Relations in the Upper Tennessee Valley, 1776–1791," *ETHSP* 8 (1936): 40–43; Hopewell Treaty Council, November 26–29, 1785, in *ASPIA,* 1:42–43; Joshua Martin to Governor Henry, Long Island [Holston], August 14, 1786, in *Calendar of Virginia State Papers,* ed. William P. Palmer (Richmond, 1884), 4:164, "A Treaty between Whites and Indians," in Clark, *State Records,* 22:655–59; Thomas Hutchings to Colonel Joseph Martin, Hawkins County, July 11, 1788, ibid., 22:695; John P. Brown, *Old Frontiers: The Story of the Cherokee Indians from Earliest Times to the Date of Their Removal West, 1838* (Kingsport, Tenn., 1938), 277–78.

12. M.A.H., "The Captivity of Jane Brown and Her Family," in *The Garland Library of Narratives of North American Indian Captivities,* vol. 64 (New York, 1977), 7.

13. David Corkran, *The Creek Frontier, 1540–1783* (Norman, Okla., 1967), 316; Mary Jane McDaniel, "Relations between the Creek Indians, Georgia, and the United States, 1783–1797" (Ph.D. diss., State College, Mississippi, 1971), 60–84; Caughey, "Introduction," in Caughey, *McGillivray,* 27–29; McGillivray to Miró, Little Tallassee, May 1, 1786, *ETHSP* 10 (1938): 131.

14. Alexander McGillivray to James White, Little Tallassee, April 8, 1787, in *ASPIA,* 1:18–19; Angie Debo, *The Road to Disappearance* (Norman, Okla., 1941), 40; McGillivray to Miró, Little Tallassee, May 1, 1786, *ETHSP* 10 (1939), 132–33; Talk of Part of the Creek Indians to the Georgia Legislature, August 3, 1786, in Caughey, *McGillivray,* 123–24.

15. O'Neil to Miró, Pensacola, September 18, 1786, *ETHSP* 10 (1938): 147; McGillivray to Fauvrot, Little Tallassee, November 8, 1786, in Caughey, *McGillivray,* 135–36; [John] Linder to Fauvrot, Tensa, November 13, 1786, in ibid., 137.

16. McGillivray to Zespuedes, Little Tallassee, November 15, 1786, in Caughey, *McGillivray,* 138–39; Caughey, "Introduction," in ibid., 32–33.

17. McLatchy to John Leslie, Cabanny, May 14, 1787, in ibid., 151.

18. McGillivray to Pickens and Mathews, Little Tallassee, June 4, 1788, in ibid., 180–83; Caughey, n. 93, in ibid., 152; McGillivray to O'Neil, Little Tallassee, March 4, 1787, in ibid., 144–45; Mathews to the Lower Creeks, June 29, 1787, in *ASPIA,* 1:32–33; Fat King to Mathews, July 27, 1787, in *ASPIA,* 1:33.

19. Butler to Knox, Carlisle, March 28, 1787, in Papers of the Continental Congress, Item 150, Letters from Major General Henry Knox, Secretary of War, 1785–1788, National Archives Microfilm Publication, M-247, reel 164, 2:288.

20. Minutes of Transactions with the Indians at Sandusky, Tuesday, August 26 [1783], *Michigan Pioneer* 20 (1892): 176; Hopewell on Keowee, November 23, 1785, in *ASPIA*, 1:41.

21. David Taitt, "Journal of a Journey through Creek Country, 1772," in *Travels in the American Colonies*, ed. Newton D. Mereness (New York, 1916), 538–39; McGillivray to Miró, Little Tallassee, May 1, 1786, in Caughey, *McGillivray*, 108–9; McGillivray to Panton, Apalachy, December 19, 1785, in ibid., 100.

22. O'Neil to Gálvez, Pensacola, May 30, 1786, *ETHSP* 10 (1938): 139–40.

23. William Bartram, "Observations on the Creek and Cherokee Indians (1789)," *American Ethnological Society Transactions* 3 (1853): 27.

24. John Pope, *A Tour through the Southern and Western Territories of the United States of America; the Spanish Dominions of the River Mississippi and the Floridas; the Countries of the Creek Nations; and Many Uninhabited Parts* (Richmond, Va., 1792), 62; Louis Le Clerc de Milford, *Memoir or a Cursory Glance at My Different Travels & My Sojourn in the Creek Nation [1802]*, trans. Geraldine de Courcy, ed. John Francis McDermott (Chicago, 1956), 152–53. For descriptions of the ceremony, see John R. Swanton, *Social Organization and Social Usages of the Indians of the Creek Confederacy* (Washington, D.C., 1928), 546–614; William W. Willett, ed., *A Narrative of the Military Actions of Colonel Marinus Willett* (1831; New York, 1969), 103.

25. McGillivray to O'Neil, July 10, 1787, Little Tallassee, in Caughey, *McGillivray*, 155; McGillivray to Panton, August 10, 1789, Little Tallassee, in ibid., 245–49; Benjamin Fishbourne to ——, Augusta, June 25, 1787, Ayer MSS.

26. McGillivray to Miró, June 2, 1790, in Caughey, *McGillivray*, 265–67; Caughey, "Introduction," ibid., 40–52; J. Leitch Wright, Jr., *Creeks and Seminoles: The Destruction and Regeneration of the Muscogulge People* (Lincoln, Neb., 1986), 137–40.

27. Alder, *The Captivity of Jonathan Alder*, 45; O. M. Spencer, *The Captivity of O. M. Spencer* (Chicago, 1917), 102–7.

28. James Moore Brown, *The Captives of Abbs Valley: A Legend of Frontier Life, By a Son of Mary Moore* (1853; New York, 1978), 41–53, 58–59.

29. "Indian Council at the Glaize, [September 30–October 9,] 1792," in *The Correspondence of John Graves Simcoe*, ed. E. A. Cruikshank, 5 vols. (Toronto, 1923), 1:218–19.

30. Helen Hornbeck Tanner, "The Glaize in 1792: A Composite Indian Community," *Ethnohistory* 25 (1978): 15–16; Helen Hornbeck Tanner and Ermine Wheeler-Voegelin, *Indians of Northwestern Ohio* (New York, 1974), fig. 9; Henry Knox to Anthony Wayne, War Department, June 22, 1792, Anthony Wayne Papers, 20:33, HSP.

31. "Council," in Cruikshank, *Simcoe Correspondence*, 1:218–20, 226.

32. McGillivray thought the meeting important enough to write three letters about it on June 20, 1787, from Little Tallassee: to Miró, *ETHSP* 11 (1939): 83; to "a Person in New Providence," Little Tallassee, June 30, 1787, ibid., 14 (1942): 96; to O'Neil, in Caughey, *McGillivray*, 153–54.

33. Williams, *Lost State*, 172–73; McGillivray to Miró, Pensacola, October 4, 1787, in Caughey, *McGillivray*, 160–61; n. 162, in ibid., 206–7; Downes, "Cherokee-

American Relations," 48; M.A.H., "The Captivity of Jane Brown," 5; John Doughty, "Up the Tennessee in 1790, the Report of Major Doughty to the Secretary of War," ed. Colton Storm, *ETHSP* 17 (1945): 121–23; McGillivray to Miró, Little Tallassee, May 8, 1790, *ETHSP* 23 (1951): 83–84.

34. Knox to Harmar, War Office, May 23, 1789, Harmar Papers, Draper MSS, 1 W 43–44; Hamtramck to Harmar, Post Vincennes, May 18, 1788, in Thornbrough, *Outpost on the Wabash,* 80; Hamtramck to Harmar, Post Vincennes, August 12, 1788, in ibid., 105–7; Charles Johnston, *Incidents Attending the Capture, Detention, and Ransom of Charles Johnston of Virginia* (1827; Cleveland, 1905), 31–44; Thomas Ridout, "Narrative of a Captivity among the Shawnese Indians . . . ," in *Ten Years of Upper Canada in Peace and War, 1805–1815,* ed. Matilda Edgar (Toronto, 1890), 344–50.

35. David Craig, "Description of Five Cherokee Towns Lying Northwest of Chatanuga Mountain," in *ASPIA,* 1:264; "Information by James Leonard, to James Seagrove," Rock Landing, July 24, 1792, in ibid., 1:308; "William Blount's Information," October 7, 1792, Draper MSS, 3 YY 32.

36. "Report of David Craig, March 15, 1792, in *ASPIA,* 1:264–65; Leonard to Seagrove, Rock Landing, July 10, 1792, in ibid., 308; Blount to Knox, Knoxville, March 20, 1792, in ibid., 263; James Seagrove to McGillivray, May 21, 1792, in ibid., 298–99; Blount to Secretary of War, Knoxville, September 26, 1792, in ibid., 288; Blount to Robertson, Knoxville, April 1, 1792, in "Correspondence of James Robertson," *American Historical Magazine* 1 (1896): 290; Carondelet to McGillivray, New Orleans, December 14, 1792, in Caughey, *McGillivray,* 349–50; Carondelet to Aranda, New Orleans, November 28, 1792, *ETHSP* 28 (1956): 140.

37. Report of David Craig, March 15, 1792, in *ASPIA,* 1:264–65; Blount to Knox, Knoxville, March 20, 1792, in ibid., 263; Secretary of War to Blount, War Department, August 15, 1792, in *TPUS,* 4:163.

38. Information given by Red Bird to Major David Craig, September 4, 1792, in *ASPIA,* 1:282; Knox to Wayne, War Department, October 12, 1792, in *Anthony Wayne: A Name in Arms,* ed. Richard C. Knopf (1959; Westport, Conn., 1975), 115; Andrew Pickens to Governor of South Carolina, Hopewell, September 13, 1792, in *ASPIA,* 1:316; see also Draper's notes in Draper MSS, 1 YY 14–15.

39. "Council," in Cruikshank, *Simcoe Correspondence,* 1:227.

40. Major Smith, 5th Regiment, the Glaize, October 16, 1790, *Michigan Pioneer* 24 (1894): 103; Wiley Sword, *President Washington's Indian War* (Norman, Okla., 1985), 101–16; John Cleves Symmes to Jonathan Dayton, Cincinnati, November 4, 1790, in *The Correspondence of John Cleves Symmes,* ed. Beverly W. Bond, Jr. (New York, 1926), 132–38.

41. Knox, "Instructions to St. Clair," March 21, 1791, in *ASPIA,* 1:173; Thomas P. Slaughter, "Liberty, Order, and the Excise: The Origins and Contexts of Frontier Unrest in Early America" (Ph.D. diss., Princeton University, 1982), 255, 291.

42. St. Clair to Knox, Fort Washington, November 9, 1791, in *ASPIA,* 1:137; Arthur St. Clair, *A Narrative of the Campaign against the Indians, under the Command of Major General St. Clair* (Philadelphia, 1812), in the Library Company of Philadelphia.

43. Sword, *Indian War,* 191, 195. I accept Sword's estimates of forces and casual-

ties on each side. For other estimates see Knox, "Statement relative to the Frontiers," December 26, 1791, in *ASPIA*, 1:198–99; St. Clair to Knox, Fort Washington, November 9, 1791, in ibid., 137–38; Glenn Tucker, *Tecumseh: Vision of Glory* (Indianapolis, 1956), 58–59; St. Clair, *Narrative*, 71, 101–6.

44. Winthrop Sargent to St. Clair, Fort Washington, January 8, 1792, Massachusetts Historical Society, Sargent Papers, typed transcript in the Shawnee File, 1792, Ethnohistory Archive. For a similar description, see Paul Wallace, *Thirty Thousand Miles with John Heckewelder* (Pittsburgh, 1958), 261.

45. See Helen Hornbeck Tanner, "Coocoochee: Mohawk Medicine Woman," *American Indian Culture and Research Journal* 3 (1979): 23–41; Spencer, *The Captivity*, 78, 86, 116, 127.

46. Spencer, *The Captivity*, 103–4.

47. Captain Hendrick Aupaumut, "A Short Narrative of My Last Journey to the Western Country," ed. Dr. B. H. Coates, *Memoirs of the Historical Society of Pennsylvania* 2 (1827): 104, 115–22, 126–27.

48. Journal of the Grand Cherokee Council, Tuesday, June 26, 1792, in *ASPIA*, 1:272.

49. Craig to Blount, Knoxville, March 15, 1792, in *ASPIA*, 1:264

50. Pope, *Tour*, 55; Willett, *Narrative*, 102–5; Milford, *Memoir*, 139–41. The prohibition of steel and flint became a widespread feature of Indian ceremonialism. See, for example, Mark Harrington, *Religion and Ceremonies of the Lenape*, Indian Notes and Monographs (New York, 1921), 86.

51. Milford, *Memoir*, 171–72; Pope, *Tour*, 63–64.

52. Information by Richard Finnelson, to Richard Peters, November 1, 1792, in *ASPIA*, 1:289–90; Information by James Leonard, to James Seagrove, Rock Landing, July 10, 1792, in ibid., 1:308.

53. Information by James Carey to Blount, Knoxville, November 3, 1742, in ibid., 1:327–29.

54. Information by Richard Finnelson, November 1, 1792, in ibid., 1:290–91.

55. William Blount, "A Return of Persons Killed," Knoxville, November 3, 1792, in ibid., 1:329–31; Blount to Knox, Knoxville, October 7, 1792, in *TPUS*, 4:193; Blount to Knox, Knoxville, October 10, 1792, in ibid., 4:197.

56. General Blount to General Robertson, Knoxville, October 17, 1792, in "Correspondence of James Robertson," 80–82; Campbell to Governor, November 1, 1792, in Palmer, *Virginia State Papers*, 6:121–22; Pate, "The Chickamauga," 222; Blount, "A Return of Persons Killed, . . ." Knoxville, November 5, 1792, in *ASPIA*, 1:329–31; Draper MSS, 1 YY 13.

There is confusion about Tecumseh's presence in these actions. According to Benjamin Drake, *Life of Tecumseh and His Brother the Prophet with a Historical Sketch of the Shawanoe Indians* (Cincinnati, 1852), 66–71, Tecumseh and his older brother accompanied Chickamaugas in battle for a time between 1787 and 1790, and the brother met his end in an assault on a post. Drake carefully employed three memoirs now in the Draper MSS: W. A. Thomas, 2 YY 21–22; Stephen Ruddell's Narrative, Draper 2YY 137; Anthony Shane's "Statement," 12 YY 35–36. None of

these convincingly pinpoints the post at which the brother was killed or the date
of the battle. There is therefore no evidence to date or place Tecumseh's early
travels, and unlike other historians, Drake left out the details. Cf. R. David
Edmunds, *Tecumseh: The Quest for Indian Leadership* (Boston, 1984), 28–29; R. David
Edmunds, *The Shawnee Prophet* (Lincoln, Neb., 1983), 30–31, 198, n. 6; Tucker, *Vision
of Glory*, 62, 64–65; Brown, *Old Frontiers*, 271.

57. Welbank to McKee, Coweta Old Town, Creek Nation, February 6, 1793, in
"British in Canada and the Southern Indians," ed. Philip Hamer *ETHSP* 2 (1930):
118–19; James Seagrove to Alexander Cornell, St. Mary's, February 20, 1793, in
ASPIA, 1:375–79. For other reports of Northern Shawnees among the Creeks, see
Coweta Indians to McKee, Coweta Old Town, April 12, 1793, in Hamer, "British
in Canada," 120; Simcoe to Allured Clark, Navy Hall, July 29, 1793, ibid., 125;
Simcoe to McKee, Navy Hall, July 23, 1793, ibid., 123, also in Cruikshank, *Simcoe
Correspondence*, 5:63; Information by James Carey, Cherokee Nation, March 20, 1793,
in *ASPIA*, 1:438–39; Timothy Barnard to James Seagrove, March 26, 1793, in ibid,
1:381–82; Knox to Anthony Wayne, War Department, June 28, 1793, in Knopf,
Anthony Wayne, 249–50.

58. Western Indians to J. G. Simcoe, June 16, 1793, Foot of the Rapids in Cruikshank, *Simcoe Correspondence*, 5:59–60; Council held at Buffalo Creek, October 10,
1793, in *ASPIA*, 1:477–78, also in *Simcoe Correspondence* 2:85–86.

59. Speech of the Western Nations, August 22, 1793, in Cruikshank, *Simcoe
Correspondence*, 2:35–36. For other indications of a Southern presence in the North,
see Tanner, "Cherokees in the Ohio Country," *Journal of Cherokee Studies* 3 (1978):
100; Jacob Lindley, Joseph Moore, and Oliver Paxson, "Expedition to Detroit,
1793," *Michigan Pioneer* 17 (1890): 611, 614; Wayne to Knox, Hobsons Choice, July 10,
1793, in Knopf, *Anthony Wayne*, 255; Wayne to Knox, August 8, 1793, in ibid., 263;
Benjamin Lincoln, Beverly Randolph, and Timothy Pickering to Knox, on Lake
Erie, August 21, 1793, in *ASPIA*, 1:359; Benjamin Lincoln's Journal, August 14, 1793,
in *Simcoe Correspondence*, 2:33; Speech of the Confederated Nations, the Glaize,
February 27, 1793, in ibid., 5:34; Simcoe to McKee, Niagara, June 2, 1793, in ibid.,
5:47; McKee to Simcoe, Foot of the Rapids, July 15, 1793, ibid., 5:58; Simcoe to
George Hammond, Navy Hall, July 24, 1793, in ibid., 5:65; Brant's Journal, August
7, August 9, 1793, in ibid., 2:12–13.

60. Baron de Carondelet to Cherokees, New Orleans, July 4, 1794, in *ASPIA*,
1:540–41; Arthur Preston Whitaker, *The Spanish-American Frontier, 1783–1795* (1927;
Lincoln, Neb., 1969), 171–84.

61. Panton to Carondelet, February 20, 1793, Pensacola, in Caughey, *McGillivray*,
354; Panton to Lachlan McGillivray, Pensacola, April 10, 1794, in ibid., 362–63;
[Louis Le Clerc de] Milfort to Carondelet, Tuquebatchet, May 26, 1793, in ibid.,
357–58. Milford signed his name De Milford, but his publisher employed the spell-
ing Milfort. Caughey thus chooses to use Milfort. I follow the Lakeside edition of
Milford's *Memoir*, cited previously, and use Milford. Colonel Melton to Governor
Telfair, Greene County, September 26, 1793, in *ASPIA*, 1:373; Blount to Robertson,

Knoxville, October 20, 1793, "Correspondence of James Robertson," *American Historical Magazine* 3 (1898): 77–79.

62. Holmes, "Spanish Policy," 74. For divisions within the Chickasaws themselves that limited the scope of the conflict, see Doughty, "Up the Tennessee in 1790," 124, 130; D. Manuel Gayoso to Barón de Carondelet, Natchez, March 14, 1795, in *Documentos Relativos a la Independencia de Nortéamerica Existentes en Archivos Españoles, Archivo General de Indias: Seccion Papeles de Cuba . . . (años 1778–1817)*, ed. Rosario Parra Cala (Madrid, 1981), 7:32, item 87.

63. For continued Creek resistance, see Gayoso to Carondelet, February 8, 1795, in ibid., 7:31, item 85. For the Creek peace, see the Treaty of Coleraine, June 29, 1796, in Kappler, *Treaties,* 2:46–50.

64. M.A.H. "The Captivity of Jane Brown," 10–12; Pate, "The Chickamauga," 247–55, Brown, *Old Frontiers,* 424–27; Carondelet to Cherokees, New Orleans, July 4, 1794, in *ASPIA* 1:540–41; Tellico Blockhouse Conference, November 7–8, 1794, "Correspondence of James Robertson," 67–72.

65. For the lowest estimate of the Indian forces, see McKee to Joseph Chew, Fort Miami, September 20, 1794, in Cruikshank, *Simcoe Correspondence,* 3:7. See also McKee to Chew, Fort Miami, August 27, 1794, *Michigan Pioneer* 20 (1892): 370–72; Deposition of Thomas Stephens, Miami Villages, October, 1794, Anthony Wayne Papers, 37:85, HSP; for fasting, see Isaac Weld, Jr., *Travels through the States of North America and the Provinces of Upper and Lower Canada, During the Years 1795, 1796, and 1797* (London, 1799), 367–68; Sword, *Indian War,* 297–98.

66. Figures vary. Reliable figures hover at around forty dead on each side. See Sword, *Indian War,* 312, 306, and Reginald Horsman, *Matthew Elliot, British Indian Agent* (Detroit, 1964), 104, for informed estimates.

67. McKee to Chew, Fort Miami, August 27, 1794, *Michigan Pioneer* 20 (1892): 370–72; Wayne to Knox, Grand Glaize, August 28, 1794, in Knopf, *Anthony Wayne,* 355; J. F. Hamtramck to Wayne, Fort Wayne, April 26, 1795, Anthony Wayne Papers, 40:67, HSP.

68. Deposition of Thomas Stephens, Miami Villages, October, 1794, Anthony Wayne Papers, 37:85, HSP. Stephens, a released captive of the Ottawas, claims that the volunteers drew arms from the British garrison. The British denied this. Sword, *Indian War,* 306; McKee to Chew, Fort Miami, August 27, 1794, *Michigan Pioneer* 20 (1892): 370–72.

69. Treaty of Greenville, *Michigan Pioneer* 20 (1892): 413–17; Sword, *Indian War,* 330.

Six. Republican Interlude

1. Robert F. Berkhofer, Jr., *Salvation and the Savage: An Analysis of Protestant Missions and American Indian Response, 1787–1862* (Lexington, Ky., 1965), 157–60; Bernard W. Sheehan, *Seeds of Extinction: Jeffersonian Philanthropy and the American Indian* (Chapel Hill, N.C., 1973), 180, for quotation, and see also 10, 122, 123, 137, 149, 172–73, 212.

2. Reginald Horsman, *Expansion and American Indian Policy* (East Lansing, Mich., 1967), 110.

3. Henry Adams, *History of the United States during the Administrations of Thomas Jefferson and James Madison* (1889–90; New York, 1986) 2:343–44.

4. Francis Paul Prucha, *American Indian Policy in the Formative Years* (Cambridge, Mass., 1962), 143, 158–63.

5. Thomas Jefferson to John Adams, Monticello, April 20, 1812, in *The Adams-Jefferson Letters: The Complete Correspondence Between Thomas Jefferson and Abigail and John Adams*, ed. Lester J. Cappon (Chapel Hill, N.C., 1959), 2:299; Thomas Jefferson to Henry Dearborn, August 12, 1807, Monticello, Daniel Parker Papers, HSP.

6. Harrison to Dearborn, Vincennes, July 11, 1807, in *Governor's Messages and Letters of William Henry Harrison, 1800–1811*, ed. Logan Esarey (Indianapolis, 1922), 1:223; "Annual Message, November 12, 1810," ibid., 490. See this volume for scores of similar declarations.

7. Andrew Jackson to Rachel Jackson, Nashville, January 8, 1813, in *The Papers of Andrew Jackson,* ed. Harold D. Moser and Sharon Macpherson (Knoxville, Tenn., 1984), 2:354; Jackson to Governor William Blount, Hermitage, June 5, 1813, ibid., 2:301; Frank Lawrence Owsley, Jr., *Struggle for the Gulf Borderlands: The Creek War and the Battle of New Orleans, 1812–1815* (Gainsville, Fla., 1981), 26–27, 107.

8. For discussions of these problems, see Royal B. Way, "The United States Factory System for Trading with the Indians, 1796–1822," MVHR 6 (1919): 224; R. S. Cotterill, "Federal Indian Management in the South, 1789–1825," ibid., 20 (1933–34): 337–38; Marshall Smelser, *The Democratic Republic, 1801–1815* (New York, 1968), 164, 173. For evidence among the Creeks, see "Letters from the Creek Factory, 1795–1816," NA, roll M-4, 47, 91, 92, 97–98, 99, 100. See also "Letters from the Creek Trading House, 1795–1816," a typescript of the National Archives materials, in the Edward Ayer collection at the Newberry Library, Chicago, in particular letters from Jonathan Halsted to George Ingels, Philadelphia, November 9, 1802; to Abraham D. Abrams, Fort Wilkinson, March 1805; to John Mason, Ocmulgee Old Fields, August 5, 1808; to William Davy, Fort Wilkinson, July 30, 1805; and to John Mason, Fort Hawkins, August 14, 1809. For northern complaints, see Alexander Henry to John Askin, Montreal, January 25, 1799; January 18, 1800; and March 1807; and "James & McGill & Co.: Indebtedness of John Askin," Montreal, April 21, 1801; all in *The John Askin Papers*, ed. Milo Milton Quaife (Detroit, 1931), 2:181, 274–75, 543–44, 334.

9. John Shee, Superintendent of Indian Trade, to Thomas M. Linnard, Factor at Natchitoches, May 29, 1807, in Rhees Collection, Indian Affairs, 1796–1858, Henry E. Huntington Library, San Marino, California; Benjamin Hawkins to Secretary of War, Coweta, January 6, 1797, in Benjamin Hawkins, *Letters of Benjamin Hawkins,* Collections of the Georgia Historical Society, vol. 9 (Savannah, 1916), 57; Speech of General James Wilkinson to the Creeks, May 29, 1802, in Benjamin Hawkins, Journal of a Treaty with the Creek Indians, 1802, manuscript, Library Company of Philadelphia, in HSP; Richard White, *The Roots of Dependency: Subsistence, Environment, and Social Change among the Choctaws, Pawnees, and Navajos* (Lincoln, Neb.,

1983), 92–101; R. Dickinson, Merchant, to Robert Hamilton, Legislative Counselor, Michilmackinac, July 14, 1793, in *The Correspondence of John Graves Simcoe*, ed. E. A. Cruikshank (Toronto, 1923), 1:388; Harold Innis, *The Fur Trade in Canada: An Introduction to Canadian Economic History*, rev. and ed. S. D. Clark and W. T. Easterbrook (Toronto, 1956), 187–88; Bert Griswold, ed., *Fort Wayne, Gateway of the West, 1802–1813;* Garrison Orderly Books, Indian Agency Account Book, Indiana Historical Collections, vol. 15 (Indianapolis, 1927), 480–82, 499; Ida Amanda Johnson, *The Michigan Fur Trade* (Lansing, Mich., 1919), 115–16; Paul Chrisler Phillips, *The Fur Trade* (Menasha, Wis., 1961), 2:148.

10. Peter Jones, Secretary to Governor Harrison, "Journal of the Proceedings at the Indian Treaty at Fort Wayne," 1809, in *Messages and Letters of Harrison*, 1:365; Horsman, *Expansion*, 126; Benjamin Hawkins to Secretary of War, James McHenry, Cussetah, November 19, 1797 and Hawkins to Henry Dearborn, Fort Wilkinson, May 2, 1802, in *Letters of Hawkins*, 239, 414–15; Entry for June 8, 1802, Hawkins's Journal, HSP.

11. Kappler, *Treaties*, 2:70–71.

12. Harrison to William Eustis, Vincennes, July 25, 1810, *Presidential Papers Microfilm: The James Madison Papers* (Washington, D.C., 1965), series 1, reel 12, located at the Library of Congress. An unfortunately misprinted copy of this letter, in *Messages and Letters of Harrison*, 1:451, has Harrison seeking "the extinguishment of the Indian Tribe," but Harrison wrote not "Tribe," but "title." Harrison did not advocate Indian extermination.

13. Ibid.

Seven. Renewing Sacred Power in the North

1. David Zeisberger, *Diary of David Zeisberger*, trans. and ed. Eugene F. Bliss (St. Clair Shores, Mich., 1972), 2:447; Seneca quoted in Anthony F. C. Wallace, *Death and Rebirth of the Seneca* (New York, 1969), 230.

2. Wallace, *Death and Rebirth*, 207; Elizabeth Tooker, "The Iroquois White Dog Sacrifice in the Latter Part of the Eighteenth Century," *Ethnohistory* 12 (1965): 132–34. For Seneca performances see Halliday Jackson, "Halliday Jackson's Journal to the Seneca Indians, 1798-1800," ed. Anthony F. C. Wallace, *Pennsylvania History*, 19 (1952): 135, 142.

3. Wallace, *Death and Rebirth*, 239–302.

4. Charles Beatty, *Journals of Charles Beatty, 1762–1769*, ed. Gary Soulliard Klett (University Park, Penn., 1962), 65; "Halliday Jackson's Journal," 146–147; Wallace, *Death and Rebirth*, 239–40; Richard McNemar, *The Kentucky Revival* (1846; New York, reprinted 1974), 125–26. Edmunds places Tenskwatawa in his dwelling, by the fire, at the time of the vision; if true, the visionary process is even more similar among the three men. R. David Edmunds, *The Shawnee Prophet* (Lincoln, Neb., 1983), 28–29.

5. Beatty, *Journals*, 65; "Halliday Jackson's Journal," 146–47; Wallace, *Death and Rebirth*, 239–44; McNemar, *Kentucky Revival*, 125–26; Arthur C. Parker, "The Code

of Handsome Lake, the Seneca Prophet," in *Parker on the Iroquois*, ed. William N. Fenton (Syracuse, 1968), book two, 69; [Robert Navarre,] "Journal of Pontiac's Conspiracy," in *The Siege of Detroit in 1763, the Journal of Pontiac's Conspiracy and John Rutherford's Narrative of a Captivity*, ed. Milo Quaife (Chicago, 1958), 10–13; Melburn Delano Thurman, The Delaware Indians: A Study in Ethnohistory" (Ph.D. diss., University of California, Santa Barbara, 1973), 155.

6. McNemar, *Kentucky Revival*, 126; Anthony Shane, "Statement," 12 YY 11; Parker, "Code," 71; Wallace, *Death and Rebirth*, 245. For the same punishment among Arkansas Cherokees in the early nineteenth century, see Cephas Washburn, *Reminiscences of the Indians by Cephas Washburn*, ed. Hugh Park (Van Buren, Ark., 1955), 162.

7. "Substance of a Talk delivered at La Maiouitinong, entrance of Lake Michigan, by the Indian Chief *Le Maigouis* or the 'Trout's Talk,' May 4, 1807," NA M222, roll 2, L-1807 (hereafter cited as "Trout's Talk"). For the Trout's alliance with Tenskwatawa, see Edmunds, *The Shawnee Prophet*, 51–52.

8. See Ake Hultkrantz, "The Problem of Christian Influence on Northern Algonkian Eschatology," in *Belief and Worship in Native North America*, ed. Christopher Vecsey (Syracuse, 1981), 187–211, for a discussion of "hell" among Native Americans. David Brainerd's "reformer," whom we encountered in Chapter Two and who preached along the Susquehanna River in the mid-1740s, held a view similar to that of the Trout; see David Brainerd, *The Life of David Brainerd*, ed. Jonathan Edwards and Philip E. Howard, Jr. (1749; Chicago, 1949), 238.

9. James Axtell, "Early Indian Views of Europeans," in *After Columbus: Essays in the Ethnohistory of Colonial North America*, ed. James Axtell (New York, 1988), 136–38.

10. [Navarre,] "Journal of Pontiac's Conspiracy," 12–13; J. P. M. La Gras to General G. R. Clark, Post Vincennes, July 22, 1786, in Lawrence Kinnaird, ed., *Spain in the Mississippi Valley, 1765–1794* (New York, 1946), 3:178. During the Cherokee revival of 1811–13, hats were singled out by a nativist as objects of ritual destruction; see "Some Reflection on Cherokee Concerns, manners, state &c., not a letter," in Return Jonathan Meigs to William Eustis, March 19, 1812, NA M208, roll 5.

11. Wallace, *Death and Rebirth*, 243; Parker, "Code," 74–75; "Halliday Jackson's Journal," 146–47, 342; McNemar, *Kentucky Revival*, 126.

12. James Kenny, "Journal of James Kenny, 1761–1763," *PMHB* 37 (1913): 188; Parker, "Code," 75; "Halliday Jackson's Journal," 343; Wallace, *Death and Rebirth*, 247–48, 252–53; McNemar, *Kentucky Revival*, 123–27; Christian Frederick Post, "Journal, 1760," May 23–24, on microfilm at American Philosophical Society, Philadelphia.

13. *Moravian Mission on White River*, ed. L. H. Gipson (Indianapolis, 1938), 392, 402; "Trout's Talk"; "Halliday Jackson's Journal," 343; Wallace, *Death and Rebirth*, 243–44, 249–50; Wells to Harrison, Fort Wayne, August 20, 1807, *Governor's Messages and Letters of William Henry Harrison, 1800–1811*, ed. Logan Esarey (Indianapolis, 1922), 1:239; Richard McNemar, quoted in J. P. McLean, "Shaker Mission to the

Shawnee Indians," *Ohio Archaeological and Historical Publications* 11 (1903): 221–28; William Wells to Henry Dearborn, Fort Wayne, August 14, 1807, NA M221, 15, W-340 (3).

14. Wallace, *Death and Rebirth*, 251.

15. [Navarre,] "Journal of Pontiac's Conspiracy," 15; "Trout's Talk."

16. "Trout's Talk"; entry for December, 3, 1805, Gipson, *Moravian Mission on White River*, 392.

17. "Trout's Talk"; William Wells to Henry Dearborn, Fort Wayne, April 22, 1808, in *TPUS*, 7:558.

18. Secretary of War Dearborn to Governor Harrison, War Department, February 23, 1802, in *TPUS*, 7:50. My assessments of Little Turtle and William Wells differ markedly from those, more favorable, of Paul Hutton, "William Wells: Frontier Scout and Indian Agent," *Indiana Magazine of History* 74 (1978): 183–222; and Harvey Lewis Carter, *The Life and Times of Little Turtle: First Sagamore of the Wabash* (Chicago, 1987), 197–208. They emphasize the laudatory goals of peaceful development.

19. C. F. Volney, *A View of the Soil and Climate of the United States of America: With Supplemental Remarks,* trans. C. B. Brown (Philadelphia, 1804), 378; Secretary of War Dearborn to Governor Harrison, War Department, February 23, 1802, in *TPUS*, 7: 48–50.

20. William Kirk to Dearborn, Black Hoof's Town, July 20, 1807, NA, M221, roll 9, K-46 (3); Dearborn to Wells, August 5, 1807, in *TPUS*, 7:467; John Johnson to Secretary of War William Eustis, Fort Wayne, July 1, 1809, NA, M221, roll 24, J-263 (4); Hutton, "William Wells," 210–13.

21. Harrison to Dearborn, Vincennes, February 14, 1809, NA, M221, roll 23, H-347 (4); Wells to Eustis, Fort Wayne, December 20, 1811, NA, M221, roll 49.

22. Harrison to Secretary of War, Vincennes, November 9, 1808, in *Messages and Letters of Harrison*, 1:322; Benjamin Drake, *Life of Tecumseh and His Brother the Prophet* (Cincinnati, 1852), 41–45; William Albert Galloway, *Old Chillicothe: Shawnee and Pioneer History* (Xenia, Ohio, 1934), 71–75.

23. William Schutz, "The Study of Shawnee Myth in an Ethnographic and Ethnohistorical Perspective," (Ph.D. diss., Indiana University, 1975), 42.

24. George Ellicott and Gerard T. Hopkins, "A Visit to the Delaware, Miami and Eel River Indians [September 23, 1802–May 27, 1803], Reported to the Baltimore Yearly Meeting, 1803," 3–5, 12–13, Ayer MSS; Philip Thomas, "Brief Account: Friends Committee for the Improvement and Civilization of the Indians," *The Massachusetts Missionary Magazine* 5 (1807): 267–70.

25. Edmunds, *Shawnee Prophet*, 18–19; Kirk to Dearborn, Black Hoof's Town, July 20, 1807, NA, M221, roll 9, K-46 (3); Kirk to Dearborn, Kirk's Settlement, April 12, 1808, ibid., M221, roll 25, K-16 (4); John Johnson to Dearborn, Fort Wayne, April 15, 1809, in *TPUS*, 7:648.

26. *TPUS*, 7:647; F. Duchoquet to Secretary of War, Kirk's Settlement, December 4, 1808, NA M221, roll 25, K-54 (4); Shawnee Chiefs to President and Secretary of War, December 1, 1808, ibid.

27. Thomas, "Brief Account," 267–70; Ellicott and Hopkins, "A Visit," 8.

28. Ellicott and Hopkins, "A Visit," 9.

29. Wells to Dearborn, Fort Wayne, April 23, 1808, in *TPUS,* 7:560.

30. McNemar, *Kentucky Revival,* 126–27.

31. Shane, "Statement," 8–10; David Zeisberger, "1769 Diary," 81, Ethnohistory Archive; David Zeisberger, Diary, MAB, reel 8, box 141, 15:11; John Heckewelder, *Narrative of the Mission of the United Brethren* (Philadelphia, 1920), 108, 135–36. See also Handsome Lake's accusations against Red Jacket, in Wallace, *Death and Rebirth,* 254–62; Parker, "Code," 68.

32. Gipson, *Moravian Mission on White River,* 413–16, 556–65, 624; McLean, *Kentucky Revival,* 224; Shane "Statement," 13–14; Edmunds, *The Shawnee Prophet,* 43–46; Kappler, *Treaties,* 2:44–45, 70–71. The names read "Tetabokshke" and "Hawkinpumiska" on the 1795 treaty and "Jeta Buxika" and "Hoking Pomskann" on the 1804 treaty. "Hocking Pomskan" also signed a treaty with the United States in 1805, Kappler, *Treaties,* 2:81. "Topethteboxie," a Delaware speaker, supported the Quakers' proposed reforms in 1804; see Thomas, "Brief Account," 268.

33. Gipson, *Moravian Mission on White River,* 565.

34. Kirk to Dearborn, Fort Wayne, May 28, 1807, NA M229, roll 9, K-36 (3); Shawnee Chiefs to the President and the Secretary of War, December 1, 1808, NA M221, roll 25, K-54.

35. Thomas Jefferson to Dearborn, August 12, 1807, Monticello, Daniel Parker Papers, HSP.

36. "Trout's Talk"; John Askin, Jr., to John Askin, St. Josephs, September 1, 1807, in *The John Askin Papers,* ed. Milo Milton Quaife (Detroit, 1931), 2:568–69.

37. Wells to Dearborn, April 23, 1808, in *TPUS,* 7:560; Wells to Dearborn, April 2, 1808, in ibid., 7:541; Edmunds, *The Shawnee Prophet,* 69.

38. Horsman, *Expansion,* 146–55; Kappler, *Treaties,* 2:70, 72, 77, 80, 89, 93, 99.

39. Secretary of War to Harrison, June 5, 1809, *Messages and Letters of Harrison,* 1:347; Harrison to Secretary of War, October 1, 1809, in ibid. 1:358–59; Edmunds, *The Shawnee Prophet,* 80–81; Horsman, *Expansion,* 166; Kappler, *Treaties,* 2:101–5.

40. Edmunds, *The Shawnee Prophet,* 92–93; Horsman, *Expansion,* 152–53, 166–67; James H. Merrell, "Declarations of Independence: Indian-White Relations in the New Nation," in *The American Revolution: Its Character and Limits,* ed. Jack P. Greene (New York, 1987), 212; John Sudgen, "Early Pan-Indianism, Tecumseh's Tour of the Indian Country, 1811–1812," *American Indian Quarterly* 10 (1986): 273–304.

41. Michel Brouille to Harrison, June 30, 1810, *Messages and Letters of Harrison,* 1:436–37; Harrison to Secretary of War, June 14, 1810, in ibid., 1:425; Jared Mansfield to Albert Gallatin, September 18, September 28, and Gallatin to Mansfield, October 12, 1810, in *TPUS,* 8:47, 49, 52–53.

42. Speech by Tecumseh to Harrison, Vincennes, August 20, 1810, *Messages and Letters of Harrison* 1:465–66.

43. Ibid., 1:466, 469; Harrison to Secretary of War, June 15, 1810, in ibid., 1:426–27; Edmunds, *The Shawnee Prophet,* 91–92.

44. Harrison to Secretary of War, August 6, 1810, *Messages and Letters of Harrison,* 1:457; Harrison to Secretary of War, July 4, 1810, ibid., 1:439.

45. Drake, *Life of Tecumseh,* 21–22; James Smith to Charlotte Ludlow, Bourbon County, December 21, 1801, Historical and Philosophical Society of Ohio, on microfilm at Ethnohistory Archive.

46. James Hughes, "Letter to the General Assembly's Chairman of the Committee of Missions," *General Assembly's Missionary Magazine or Evangelical Intelligencer* 1 (1805): 401; C. C. Trowbridge, "Shawnese Traditions," *Occasional Contributions from the Museum of Anthropology of the University of Michigan* 9 (1939):3; Gipson, *Moravian Mission on White River,* 406, 419, 562; Harrison to Secretary of War, June 26, 1810, *Messages and Letters of Harrison,* 1:434; "Trout's Talk."

47. Gipson, *Moravian Mission on White River,* 438; Tecumseh's reply to Harrison, August 10, 1810, in *Messages and Letters of Harrison,* 1:467. See Chapter Two for a mid-eighteenth-century expression of this. See Wallace, *Death and Rebirth,* 244, 247; "Henry Simmons' Version of the Visions," in "Halliday Jackson's Journal," 349; and Parker, "Code," 67–68.

48. Harrison to Secretary of War, June 26, 1810, in *Messages and Letters of Harrison,* 1:435.

49. Alvin M. Josephy, *The Patriot Chiefs: A Chronicle of American Indian Leadership* (New York, 1961); James McCague, *Tecumseh: Shawnee Warrior-Statesman* (Champaign, Ill., 1970); Glenn Tucker, *Tecumseh: Vision of Glory* (Indianapolis, 1956), 93.

Richard Drinnon more narrowly argues that the "insistence upon racial solidarity and their angry refusal to consider land cessions were no doubt largely Tecumseh's contribution to the Code." Richard Drinnon, *Facing West: The Metaphysics of Indian Hating and Empire-Building* (New York, 1980), 92. The notion of racial solidarity is taken much further in the most recent work on Tecumseh, Bil Gilbert's *God Gave Us This Country: Tekamthi and the First American Civil War* (New York, 1989), 208. The term *racial,* however, is anachronistic. Tecumseh and others sought Indian unity, and they saw Indians as having spiritual differences with American citizens. Their relationship with Canadians is less clear, and they never moved against adopted "white Indians," Indian descendants of Europeans, or against white traders and agents who did not threaten to interfere with their plans.

50. Edmunds, *The Shawnee Prophet,* 189. See also John K. Mahon, "British Strategy and Southern Indians, War of 1812," *Florida Historical Quarterly* 44 (1965–66): 286.

51. Gilbert, *God Gave Us This Country,* 3.

52. Wallace, *Death and Rebirth,* 297–98, 294–95; Hughes, "Letter," 403; Parker, "Code," 65–66.

53. Wells to Dearborn, Fort Wayne, April 22, 1808, in *TPUS,* 7:558. At Greenville, Tenskwatawa hosted Chippewas, Ottawas, Potawatomis, Delawares, Shawnees and Wyandots. See, for example, Edmunds, *The Shawnee Prophet,* 59–60; Harrison to Secretary of War, September 5, 1807, in *Messages and Letters of Harrison,* 1:247; Wells to Dearborn, Fort Wayne, January 23, 1808, NA, M221, roll 15, W-457

(3); Gipson, *Moravian Mission on White River*, 392. At Tippecanoe, the list grew to include members of all the previously mentioned tribes, with members of the Kickapoos, Winnebagos, Miamis, Sauks, and Foxes. See, for example, Wells to Dearborn, Fort Wayne, March 6, 1808, NA M221, roll 15, W-520 (3); Harrison to Secretary of War, April 25, 1810, June 14, 1810, July 18, 1810, and July 25, 1810, in *Messages and Letters of Harrison*, 1:417–18, 424, 446–47, 449.

54. Harrison to Secretary of War, June 14, 1810, in *Messages and Letters of Harrison*, 1:423.

55. "Trout's Talk"; Wells to Dearborn, Fort Wayne, April 2, 1808, in *TPUS*, 7:540; Kappler, *Treaties*, 2:92–95.

56. Wells to Dearborn, Fort Wayne, April 20, 1808, in *TPUS*, 7:556; Edmunds, *The Shawnee Prophet*, 63–65, 68; Draper MSS, 7 BB 48; Ottawas to Secretary of War, October 5, 1811, in *ASPIA*, 1:804.

57. Harrison to Dearborn, Vincennes, July 11, 1807, in *Messages and Letters of Harrison*, 1:224; Harrison to Secretary of War, Vincennes, June 26, 1810, ibid., 1:434 (the parenthetical remark is Harrison's). Note that the Cherokees are not mentioned. Neither did Tecumseh visit the Cherokees in 1811; Sudgen, "Early Pan-Indianism," 278–79.

58. Secretary of War to Harrison, War Department, June 20, 1807, in *TPUS*, 7:462; Harrison to Secretary of War, Vincennes, May 15, 1810, *Messages and Letters of Harrison*, 1:420–21; Thomas Simpson Woodward, *Woodward's Reminiscences of the Creek, or Muskogee Indians* (Montgomery, Ala., 1859), 94–95.

59. Gipson, *Moravian Mission on White River*, 297–98, 371, 521, 539; Carl F. Klink and James J. Talman, eds., *The Journal of Major John Norton, 1816*, Publications of the Champlain Society, vol. 46 (Toronto, 1970), 175.

60. Harrison to Secretary of War, Vincennes, August 6, 1811, in *Messages and Letters of Harrison*, 1:545.

61. Woodward, *Reminiscences*, 36, 99; H. S. Halbert and T. H. Ball, *The Creek War of 1813 and 1814*, ed. Frank Lawrence Owsley, Jr. (1895; University, Ala., 1969), 40.

62. Colonel Hawkins to Big Warrior, Little Prince, and other Chiefs, Creek Agency, June, 16, 1814, in *ASPIA*, 1:845; Cornells to Hawkins, June 22, 1813, and Hawkins to General Armstrong, June 28, 1813, in ibid., 1:845–47.

Eight. Conflict in the South

1. Benjamin Hawkins, "A Sketch of the Creek Country in the Years 1798 and 1799," *Collections of the Georgia Historical Society* 3, pt. 1 (1848): 67–68; Merrit B. Pound, *Benjamin Hawkins—Indian Agent* (Athens, Ga., 1951), 163.

2. Entry for May 8, 1802, in Benjamin Hawkins, Journal of a Treaty with the Creek Indians, 1802, Manuscript, Library Company of Philadelphia, in HSP.

3. Hawkins to Secretary of War, Cusseta, November 19, 1797, in *Letters of Benjamin Hawkins* (Savannah, Ga., 1916), 241. Pound, *Hawkins*, 205–6.

4. R. S. Cotterill, "Federal Indian Management in the South, 1789–1825," *MVHR* 20 (1933–34): 336–37, 344; Pound, *Hawkins*, 198.

5. Benjamin Hawkins, *Copy of a Letter from Benjamin Hawkins* (Washington, D.C., 1801), 4–5, pamphlet in the Ayer MSS. Daniel H. Unser, Jr., "American Indians on the Cotton Frontier: Changing Economic Relations with the Citizens and Slaves in the Mississippi Territory," *Journal of American History* 72 (1985): 305; Richard White, *The Roots of Dependency: Subsistence, Environment, and Social Change among the Choctaws, Pawnees, and Navajos* (Lincoln, Neb., 1983), 110.

6. Hawkins to Mrs. Eliza Trist, Cussetah, in the Creek Nation, November 25, 1797, in *Letters of Hawkins,* 256; Hawkins to Secretary of War, James McHenry, Coweta, January 6, 1797, in ibid., 57; Hawkins to Secretary of War, Coweta, November 19, 1797, in ibid., 240.

7. Hawkins to Secretary of War, Coweta, January 6, 1797, in ibid., 57; Hawkins, Journal, entry for December 18, 1796, in ibid., 40; entry for January 24, 1802, Hawkins, Journal of a Treaty, HSP; "Journal of the Commissioners for the United States, for holding conferences with the Indian nations, south of the Ohio [1802]," ed. Thomas Cochran, in *The New American State Papers: Indian Affairs* (Wilmington, Del., 1972), 6:193.

8. Hawkins had not yet personally embraced the institution of marriage, though he had already found a lifelong companion in Lavinia Downs, with whom he had six or seven children and whom he married shortly before his death. See Florette Henri, *The Southern Indians and Benjamin Hawkins, 1796–1816* (Norman, Okla., 1986), 111, 334 n. 50, 317.

9. Hawkins, Journal, February 1, 1797, in *Letters of Hawkins,* 83–84; Ethan Allen Hitchcock, *A Traveller in Indian Territory: The Journal of Ethan Allen Hitchcock, Late Major-General in the United States Army,* ed. Grant Foreman (Cedar Rapids, Iowa, 1930), 162. Contrast with Alexander Spoehr, who finds that patterns had shifted decisively toward a conjugal family of an Anglo-American type, and who implies that the shift occurred before removal. Alexander Spoehr, *Changing Kinship Systems: A Study in the Acculturation of the Creeks, Cherokee, and Choctaw,* Anthropological Series, Field Museum of Natural History, vol. 33 (Chicago, 1947), 159–235, esp. 186, 196, 221. Spoehr conducted his fieldwork in 1938 and 1939.

10. Theda Perdue, *Slavery and the Evolution of Cherokee Society, 1540–1866* (Knoxville, Tenn., 1979), 124, 144.

11. Verner Crane, *The Southern Colonial Frontier, 1670–1732* (Ann Arbor, Mich., 1956), 139–40, 152; Theda Perdue, *Slavery,* 12–16; Charles Hudson, *The Southeastern Indians* (Knoxville, Tenn., 1976), 252–55; J. Leitch Wright, Jr., *The Only Land They Knew: The Tragic Story of the American Indians in the Old South* (New York, 1981), 127, 138; Henry Alder, *The Captivity of Jonathan Alder and His Life with the Indians,* ed. Orley E. Brown (Alliance, Ohio, 1965), 67; Thomas Ridout, "Narrative of the Captivity among the Shawanese Indians," in *Ten Years of Upper Canada in Peace and War, 1805–1815,* ed. Matilda Edgar (Toronto, 1890), 364.

12. Hawkins, "Sketch of the Creek Country," 66; J. Leitch Wright, Jr., *Creeks and Seminoles: The Destruction and Regeneration of the Muscogulge People* (Lincoln, Neb., 1986), 84.

13. Unser, "Indians on the Cotton Frontier," 306.

14. Deborah Gray White, *Ar'n't I a Woman? Female Slaves in the Plantation South* (New York, 1985), 120.

15. George Stiggins, "A Historical Narration of the Genology Traditions and Downfall of the Ispocaga or Creek Tribe of Indians," Draper MSS 1 U 66, 40; Methlogee to James Seagrove, Point Peter, June 14, 1799, enclosed in James Seagrove to James Jackson, Point Peter, June 17, 1799, Ayer MSS; Hawkins, "Sketch of Creek Country," 27, 32–33, 36–37; *Letters of Hawkins,* 438; Seaborn Jones to Benjamin Hawkins, February 3, 1798, in Hawkins, Journal of a Treaty, HSP.

16. Hawkins to Secretary of War McHenry, February 16, 1798, Hawkins, Journal of a Treaty, HSP; Kappler, *Treaties,* 2:59; Reginald Horsman, *Expansion and American Indian Policy* (East Lansing, Mich., 1967), 130–33.

17. Entry for March 27, 1802, Hawkins, Journal of a Treaty, HSP; John Innerarity, "The Creek Nation, Debtor to John Forbes & Co., Successor to Panton Leslie & Co., A Journal of John Innerarity," *Florida Historical Quarterly* 9 (1930): 79; Kappler, *Treaties,* 2:85; William McIntosh, J. Parker, Alexander Cunnelly to President James Madison, Tuckabache Square, January 6, 1810, Daniel Parker Papers, HSP; H. S. Halbert and T. H. Ball, *The Creek War of 1813 and 1814,* ed. Frank Lawrence Owsley, Jr. (1895; University, Ala., 1969), 98.

18. Stiggins, "Narration," 29–31. For a more sympathetic, though by no means uncritical, view of Hawkins, see Henri, *The Southern Indians and Benjamin Hawkins,* esp. xii, 242–43, 259.

19. Pound, *Hawkins,* 209–10; Horsman, *Expansion,* 163–64.

20. Roger H. Brown, *The Republic in Peril: 1812* (New York, 1971), 126–27; Marshall Smelser, *The Democratic Republic, 1801–1815* (New York, 1968), 108; J. H. Alexander, "The Ambush of Captain John Williams, U.S.M.C.: Failure of the East Florida Invasion, 1812–1813," *Florida Historical Quarterly* 56 (1977–78): 280–82.

21. Big Warrior to Hawkins, Tuckabatchee, April 26, 1813, in *ASPIA,* 1:843.

22. Ibid.; Harry Toulmin, "Deposition of Samuel Manac [Moniac], of lawful age, a Warrior of the Creek Nation," Mississippi Territory, August 2, 1813, in Halbert and Ball, *The Creek War,* 93; James Wilkinson to Judge Toulmin, Sam Manac's, Creek Nation, June 25, 1813, extracted in *The Creek War,* 89–90.

23. Meigs to John Armstrong, Hiwassee Garrison, August 23, 1813, NA, M222, M-200 (7); Meigs to Secretary of War, November 17, 1813, ibid., M-294 (7); Cussetah Micco to Hawkins, July 10, 1813, in *ASPIA,* 1:849

24. For Cherokee attention to Red Sticks, see Henry Thompson Malone, "Return Jonathan Meigs—Indian Agent Extraordinary," *ETHSP* 28 (1956): 20. For Cherokee warriors with the United States, see Gideon Morgan to Return Jonathan Meigs, November 23, 1813, NA, M222, M-200 (7); Robert Grierson to Andrew Jackson, Hillabee, November 13, 1813, in *The Papers of Andrew Jackson,* ed. Harold Moser and Sharon Macpherson (Knoxville, Tenn., 1984), 2:451–52; John Cocke to Jackson, Fort Armstrong, November 27, 1813, ibid., 2:462; and editor's comment, ibid., 2:461–62; Halbert and Ball, *The Creek War,* 271–72; Albert James Pickett, *History of Alabama and Incidentally of Georgia and Mississippi from the Earliest Period* (Sheffield, Ala., 1896), 556; Emmet Starr, *History of the Cherokee Indians and*

Their Legend and Folklore (Oklahoma City, 1921), 42; Frank Lawrence Owsley, Jr., *Struggle for the Gulf Borderlands: The Creek War and the Battle of New Orleans, 1812–1815* (Gainesville, Fla., 1981), 62, 66–67, 73. Henry Thompson Malone, *Cherokees of the Old South: A People in Transition* (Athens, Ga., 1956), 71.

25. Meigs to John Armstrong, Hiwassee Garrison, August 23, 1813, NA, M222, M-200 (7); John Lowry to Andrew Jackson and John Strother, November 7, Turkey Town, in Moser and Macpherson, *Jackson Papers*, 2:445–46.

26. See the following three works by William G. McLoughlin: "Thomas Jefferson and the Beginning of Cherokee Nationalism, 1806–1809," *Cherokee Ghost Dance: Essays on the Southeastern Indians, 1789–1861*, ed. William G. McLoughlin (Macon, Ga., 1984), 73–110; *Cherokees and Missionaries, 1789–1839* (New Haven, 1984); *Cherokee Renascence in the New Republic* (Princeton, 1986), 128–67.

27. Cotterill, "Federal Indian Management," 336–37, 344.

28. Hawkins, Journal, entry for August 7, 1801, in *Letters of Hawkins*, 360; Gideon Blackburn to Jedediah Morse, December 17, 1808, Ayer MSS.

29. Starr, *History of the Cherokee*, 247; McLoughlin, *Cherokees and Missionaries*, 81, 101. They had only two converts by the outbreak of the War of 1812.

30. John Manford Carselowey, *Cherokee Notes* (Fayetteville, Ark., 1960), 25; Starr, *History of the Cherokee*, 247–48; James Axtell, *The Invasion Within: The Contest of Cultures in Colonial North America* (New York, 1985), 133, 273; William G. McLoughlin, "James Vann, Intemperate Patriot, 1768–1809," in *Cherokee Ghost Dance*, 47; McLoughlin, *Cherokees and Missionaries*, 35–39.

31. Silas Dinsmoor to the Cherokees, April 30, 1795, Ayer MSS; Abraham Steiner and Frederick Christian de Schweinitz, "A Short Account of a Visiting Journey . . . among the Cherokee Indians (1799)," in MAB, on microfilm at the American Philosophical Society, reel 24, box 192, 4:13.

32. Hawkins, Journal, entry for August 7, 1801, in *Letters of Hawkins*, 360; McLoughlin, *Cherokee Renascence*, 58–60.

33. Perdue, *Slavery*, 46–49, 60; Gideon Blackburn to Jedediah Morse, January 5, 1810, Huntington MSS, 13469, Henry E. Huntington Library, San Marino, California; "Letter from Return Jonathan Meigs, esq., to Secretary of War," *The Globe* 1 (Richmond, Ky., January 22, 1810), on microfilm at Princeton University; Meigs to Secretary of War, Southwest Point, July 27, 1805, NA, M208, roll 3; William G. McLoughlin, "Cherokee Anomie," in McLoughlin, *Cherokee Ghost Dance*, 22, n. 30.

34. McLoughlin, *Cherokee Renascence*, 57, 60, 68; McLoughlin, "Anomie," 18–19; George B. Davies to Meigs, Lovies, October 17, 1808, NA, M208, roll 4; William G. McLoughlin and Walter H. Conser, "The Cherokee Censuses of 1809, 1825 and 1835," in McLoughlin, *Cherokee Ghost Dance*, 224–25; Perdue, *Slavery*, 69; John R. Finger, *The Eastern Band of the Cherokees, 1819–1900* (Knoxville, 1984), 3; entry November 8, 1799, in Steiner and de Schweinitz, "Short Account," 21; McLoughlin, "James Vann," 62.

35. Horsman, *Expansion*, 127; McLoughlin, *Cherokee Renascence*, 104; McLoughlin, "James Vann," 57–59; Kappler, *Treaties*, 2:82–84; Council of Eustinale to Meigs, April 5, 1805 NA, M208, roll 3; Doublehead, Toluntuskee, Ketiguskee, The Seed,

Sequeechee to Black Fox, the Glass, Dick Justice, Turtle at Home, Chenouee, The Slave Boy Eustanalle, Toutchallee, Parched Corn Four & other Chiefs, Southwest Point, August 9, 1805, ibid.; Meigs, "Address to the Cherokee council to be held at Willstown," April 2, 1806, ibid.

36. Quoted in Horsman, *Expansion,* 128; McLoughlin, "James Vann," 59.

37. Cherokee Address to President, April 25, 1806, at Eustanalie, NA, M208 roll 3; Indian Concil to Agent Hicks, Eustanalie, April 25, 1806, ibid.

38. McLoughlin, *Cherokee Renascence,* 115–24, 134, 144–45; McLoughlin, "James Vann," 59–64. I follow McLoughlin's interpretation of the fracturing of the Cherokee elite. For the details of the cession and the bribes, see also Horsman, *Expansion,* 139.

39. Meigs to Secretary of War, Hiwassee Garrison, February 9, 1808, M208, roll 4; for the full story, see McLoughlin, *Cherokee Renascence,* 128–67; and his "Thomas Jefferson and the Beginning of Cherokee Nationalism, 1806–1809," *William and Mary Quarterly,* 3rd ser., 32 (1975): 547–80.

40. Meigs to Dearborn, Hiwassee Garrison, June 3, 1808, NA, M208, roll 4; Meigs to Cherokee Council at Brooms Town, August 29, 1808, ibid.

41. Meigs to Secretary of War, Hiwassee Garrison, July 11, 1808, ibid.; Meigs to Secretary of War, Hiwassee Garrison, June 3, 1808, ibid.

42. John McIntosh, Ridge, Seed, Toutchallee, John Walker, Skiukee, Samuel Riley Interpreter, to Thomas Jefferson, President, Washington D.C., December 21, 1808, Daniel Parker Papers, in HSP; John McIntosh, John Walker, Ridge, to the President, Washington, D.C., December 28, 1808, ibid.; John Walker, John Meentush, Ridge, to the President, Washington, D.C., January 5, 1809, in ibid.; McLoughlin, "James Vann," 68–69.

43. Finger, *The Eastern Band,* 3, 10; McLoughlin, *Cherokee Renascence,* 159–60; Tew chale, or Flute, to the President, Washington D.C., January 4, 1809, in Daniel Parker Papers, HSP; Meigs to Secretary of War, Southwest Point, May 31, 1805, NA, M208, roll 3; George B. Davies to Meigs, Lovies, October 17, 1808, NA, M208, roll 4; Meigs to Chiefs of the Cherokee Nation, Hiwassee Garrison, September 16, 1809, ibid.; Meigs to Cherokee Council at Willstown, Hiwassee Garrison, November 2, 1809, ibid.; Meigs to Secretary of War, Hiwassee Garrison, December 1, 1809, ibid.; Meigs to Secretary of War, Hiwassee Garrison, January 22, 1810, NA, M208, roll 5; Toloteskie to Meigs, Arkansas River, June 23, 1810, ibid.; Meigs to Secretary of War, Hiwassee Garrison, December 15, 1810, ibid.

Nine. Renewing Sacred Power in the South

1. J. C. Burckhard, *Partners in the Lord's Work: The Diary of Two Moravian Missionaries in the Creek Indian Country, 1807–1813,* trans. and ed. Carl Mauelshagen and Gerard H. Davis (Atlanta, 1969), 53; Benjamin Hawkins, "Sketch of the Creek Country in the Years 1798 and 1799," *Collections of the Georgia Historical Society* 3, pt. 1 (1848): 80–81; George Stiggins, "A Historical Narration of the Genealogy Traditions and Downfall of the Ispocaga or Creek Tribe of Indians," Draper MSS 1 U

66, 26; John Innerarity, "The Creek Nation, Debtor to John Forbes & Co. . . . ," *Florida Historical Quarterly* 9 (1930): 73.

2. Harrison to Dearborn, May 19, 1808, in *Governor's Messages and Letters of William Henry Harrison, 1800–1811*, ed. Logan Esarey (Indianapolis, 1922), 1:291; Theron A. Nunez, Jr., "Creek Nativism and the Creek War of 1813–1814," *Ethnohistory* 5 (1958): 8, 13.

3. Harry Toulmin, "Deposition of Samuel Manac [Moniac]," quoted in H. S. Halbert and T. H. Ball, *The Creek War of 1813 and 1814*, ed. Frank Lawrence Owsley, Jr. (1895; University, Ala., 1969), 91–93; Stiggins, "Narration," 43.

4. Extract of Josiah Francis to Gonzales Manrique, Mouganweihche, Interpreter from Creek to Spanish, enclosed in Don Mateo Gonzalez to Don Ruiz de Apodaca, Pensacola, October 28, 1813, Papeles Procedentes de Cuba, Papers from the Archivo General des Indias, Seville, Legajo 1794: 61, Spanish typescript at the Newberry Library, Chicago.

5. Halbert and Ball, *The Creek War*, 184, 187–91, 251.

6. Stiggins, "Narration," 45–49; Big Warrior to Hawkins, April 26, 1813, in *ASPIA* 1:843.

7. Acting Governor Attwater to Secretary of War, Detroit, January 21, 1812, in *TPUS*, 10:376–77; T. S. Woodward, *Woodward's Reminiscences of the Creek, or Muskogee Indians* (Montgomery, Ala., 1859), 36–37; William Blount to Andrew Jackson, Knoxville, July 21, 1812, *The Papers of Andrew Jackson*, ed. Harold Moser and Sharon Macpherson (Knoxville, Tenn., 1984), 2:316; Jackson to George Washington Campbell, Hermitage, October 15, 1812, in ibid. 2:335.

8. W. C. C. Claiborne to L. B. Macarty, Nachitoches, October 16, 1813, in *Official Letter Book of W. C. C. Claiborne*, ed. Dunbar Rowland (Jackson, Miss., 1917) 6:274; Claiborne to Caddo Nation, Nachitoches, October 18, 1813, ibid., 275–77; Claiborne to John Armstrong, County of Rapides, Louisiana, Oct. 25, 1813, ibid., 277–78; Hawkins, "Sketch of the Creek Country," 25–26; Stiggins, "Narration," 13. For a fascinating discussion of the word "Seminole," as well as of the development of the Seminoles into an independent people, see William C. Sturtevant, "Creek into Seminole," in *North American Indians in Historical Perspective*, ed. Eleanor Burke Leacock and Nancy Oesteich Lurie (New York, 1971), 105.

9. Benjamin Hawkins to Judge [Toulmin], Creek Agency, [September 16,] 1812, Ayer MSS; Hawkins to Georgia Governor Mitchell, Creek Agency, September 13, 1812, quoted in Merrit B. Pound, *Benjamin Hawkins—Indian Agent* (Athens, Ga., 1951), 217–18.

10. Stiggins, "Narration," 72; Sturtevant, "Creek into Seminole," 106; John Quincy Adams to George William Erving, Department of State, Washington, D.C., November 28, 1818, *Writings of John Quincy Adams*, ed. Worthington Chauncey Ford (New York, 1916), 6:474–502, esp, 478–84, 490–95, 499.

11. Richard White, *The Roots of Dependency: Subsistence, Environment, and Social Change among the Choctaws, Pawnees, and Navajos* (Lincoln, Neb., 1988), 112; Halbert and Ball, *The Creek War*, 44, 120–24, 211–22.

12. Frank Lawrence Owsley, Jr., *Struggle for the Gulf Borderlands: The Creek War and*

the Battle of New Orleans, 1812–1815 (Gainesville, Fla., 1981), 33; Josiah Francis to Gonzales Manrique, August, 1813, Papeles Procedentes de Cuba, Legajo 1794: 62. Return Jonathan Meigs, agent to the Cherokees, also had information that "some of the Choctaws were in favor of the rebellious Creeks." Meigs to John Armstrong, Highwassee Garrison, August 23, 1813, NA M222: M- 200 (7). See also H. S. Halbert, "A Correction of a statement in regard to the Choctaw Renegades of the Creek War of 1813–14 [1884]," Draper MSS, 10 yy 49–50.

13. McLoughlin, "Thomas Jefferson and the Rise of Cherokee Nationalism, 1806–1809," *William and Mary Quarterly*, 3rd ser., 32 (1975): 77–78.

14. R. J. Meigs, "Journal of Occurrences in the Cherokee Nation," n.d., in the Meigs Family Papers, United States Library of Congress, Manuscripts Division, Madison Building, Washington, D.C.; Meigs to General Smith, August 19, 1805, NA, M208, roll 3; Abraham Steiner and Frederic K. Christian de Schweinitz, November 19, 1799, in "A Short Account of a Visiting Journey . . . among the Cherokee Indians (1799)," in MAB, on microfilm, APS, reel 24, box 192, 4:55.

15. Here I depart from William McLoughlin's interpretation of Cherokee religion and politics, which ties the Cherokee revival to rising Cherokee nationalism, both against a background of religious and cultural decline. See "Cherokee Anomie," and "The Cherokee Ghost Dance Movement," both in *The Cherokee Ghost Dance: Essays on the Southeastern Indians, 1789–1861* (Macon, Ga., 1984); also see *Cherokee Missionaries, 1789–1839* (New Haven, 1984). I also take issue with Anthony Wallace's emphasis upon psychic stress and religious collapse in his widely applied work, "Revitalization Movements," *American Anthropologist* 58 (1956): 264–81.

16. Contrast with James H. Merrell's assertion that the Cherokee reform "stopped short of condemning whites. These people were not . . . necessarily evil," in "Declarations of Independence: Indian-White Relations in the New Nation," in *The American Revolution: Its Character and Limits*, ed. Jack P. Green (New York, 1987), 213; Meigs, "Some reflections on Cherokee Concerns, manners, state &c., not a letter," in Meigs to Eustis, March 19, 1812, NA, M208, roll 5; also excerpted in Meigs, "Some Reflections on Cherokee Concerns . . . ," McLoughlin, ed., *Cherokee Ghost Dance*, 148; excerpt from "Parson Miller Thirty Years Behind the Indians," *Cherokee Advocate* (Tallequah, Cherokee Nation, November 16, 1844), in McLoughlin, *Cherokee Ghost Dance*, 141.

17. The Springplace Diary, first employed to treat the Cherokee revival by Thurman Wilkins, *Cherokee Tragedy: The Story of the Ridge Family and the Decimation of a People* (London, 1970), is more fully analyzed by William McLoughlin in "The Cherokee Ghost Dance Movement." For excerpts of the diary see "The Springplace Diary, 1811–1812," ed. William G. McLoughlin, trans. Elizabeth Marx, appendix to "The Cherokee Ghost Dance Movement," 142–47.

18. "Springplace Diary, 1811–1812," entry February 10, 1811, 142–43; Meigs to Hawkins, Southwest Point, February 13, 1805, NA M208, roll 3; Steiner and de Schweinitz, entry for November 19, 1799, 54; "Copy of a Report of the General Meeting with the Principal Chiefs and Warriors of the Cherokee Nation with John Stuart," October 18–20, 1770, Lochaber, CO 5/72, f. 22, PRO. For a different

interpretation of the doctrine of separate creations, see William G. McLoughlin, "A Note on African Sources of American Indian Creation Myths," in McLoughlin, *Cherokee Ghost Dance*, 253–60.

19. "Springplace Diary, 1811–1812," entry for February 17, 1812, 145; Kappler, *Treaties*, 2:53, for Tugaloo cession.

20. "Springplace Diary, 1811–1812," entry for February 10, 1811, 142. See also McLoughlin, *Cherokee Missionaries*, 89.

21. "Springplace Diary, 1811–1812," entry for February 10, 1811, 143; Thomas L. McKenny and James Hall, *The Indian Tribes of North America* (Edinburgh, 1933), 388–89; William C. Sturtevant, ed., "John Ridge on Cherokee Civilization in 1826," *Journal of Cherokee Studies* 6 (1981): 81; Wilkins, *Cherokee Tragedy*, 57.

22. "Springplace Diary, 1811–1812," entry for May 10, 1811, 143; McLoughlin, "Cherokee Ghost Dance Movement," 122–23; Cherokee Chiefs to Meigs, Eustanalie, May 5, 1811, NA M208, roll 5.

23. "Springplace Diary, 1811–1812," entry for March 8, 1812, 146–47.

24. "Springplace Diary, 1811–1812," entry for April 30, 1812, 147. See also Meigs, "Some reflections."

25. "Springplace Diary, 1811–1812," entry for February 17, 1812, 145; Meigs, "Some reflections."

26. "Springplace Diary, 1811–1812," entry for February 17, 1812, 145; Meigs, "Some reflections," Handsome Lake's sky messengers of one vision carried green branches; see Halliday Jackson, "Halliday Jackson's Journal, to the Seneca Indians, 1798–1800," ed. Anthony F. C. Wallace, *Pennsylvania History* 19 (1952): 146–47.

27. The Bark a Creek Chief to the Cherokees, September 1812, NA M208, roll 5; Meigs to Sec. of War, July 30, 1813, NA M208, roll 6.

28. Copy of Charles Hicks to Return Jonathan Meigs, Fortville, August 19, 1813, enclosed in Meigs to Armstrong, Hiwassee Garrison, August 23, 1813, NA M222, M, 200 (7); McLoughlin, *Cherokee Missionaries*, 99–101.

29. Meigs to Dearborn, May 1, 1807, Southwest Point, NA M208, roll 3. In 1804 and 1805, important Cherokees were present at Creek Councils. See Opoyomico to Governor Vicente Folch, May 6, 1804, Papeles Procedentes de Cuba, 1573, Packet C, Correspondence of the Governors of the Floridas, Photostat in the Library of Congress; and Meigs to the Secretary of War, Southwest Point, August 4, 1805, NA, M208, roll 3. For Etowah, see McLoughlin, *Cherokee Missionaries*, 98.

30. Meigs to Secretary of War, Hiwassee Garrison, December 4, 1811, NA M208, roll 5.

31. Harry L. Coles, *The War of 1812* (Chicago, 1965), 256; Reginald Horsman, *The War of 1812* (New York, 1969), 25, 42, 102.

32. For allies of the United States in the North, see John Sudgen, *Tecumseh's Last Stand* (Norman, Okla., 1985), 34, 97, 110, 119.

33. See "Chronology of Hostile Actions, 1811–1815," in *Atlas of Great Lakes Indian History*, ed. Helen Hornbeck Tanner (Norman, Okla., 1986), 108–15.

34. Sudgen, *Tecumseh's Last Stand*, 34, 110, 113, 119.

35. Ibid., 133.

36. Albert James Pickett, *History of Alabama and Incidentally of Georgia and Mississippi from the Earliest Period* (Sheffield, Ala., 1896), 521–27; Stiggins, "Narration," 52–54; Owsley, *Borderlands*, 30–31; J. Leitch Wright, *Creeks and Seminoles: The Destruction and Regeneration of the Muscogulge People* (Lincoln, Neb., 1986), 172.

37. Daniel F. Littlefield, *Africans and Creeks from the Colonial Period to the Civil War* (Westport, Conn., 1979), 64; Owsley, *Borderlands*, 51–60.

38. Owsley, *Borderlands*, 42–50; Stiggins, "Narration," 67; Halbert and Ball, *The Creek War*, 241–48.

39. Halbert and Ball, after calling the Red Sticks "credulous . . . ignorant and fanatical," mention the "good sense" they had in securing their families in the woods; see *The Creek War*, 248–49.

40. Horsman, *The War of 1812*, 221–24.

41. Pickett, *History of Alabama*, 589; Owsley, *Borderlands*, 79–83; Wright, *Creeks and Seminoles*, 176–77; Littlefield, *Africans and Creeks*, 64.

42. Pickett, *History of Alabama*, 593; Littlefield, *Africans and Creeks*, 69; Wright, *Creeks and Seminoles*, 177, 179; Stiggins "Narration," 72.

43. Coles, *The War of 1812*, 203–6; Owsley, *Borderlands*, 69, 107–18; Pickett, *History of Alabama*, 602; Horsman, *The War of 1812*, 234–35; Littlefield, *Africans and Creeks*, 69; Wright, *Creeks and Seminoles*, 180.

44. "Return of the Muscogee or Creek Indians under the command of Lieut. Colonel Nicolls" (1815), Great Britain, War Office, 1/43, Letters Miscellaneous, Part Two, Folio 161, Photostat, Library of Congress; Owsley, *Borderlands*, 47; Stiggins, "Narration," 70; Littlefield, *Africans and Creeks*, 68; Wright, *Creeks and Seminoles*, 181.

45. Wright's coverage of this maroon settlement is engrossing. Wright, *Creeks and Seminoles*, 183; Owsley, *Borderlands*, 184; Pickett, *History of Alabama*, 560.

46. Wright, *Creeks and Seminoles*, 191, 202; Owsley, *Borderlands*, 178–85.

47. Stiggins, "Narration," 72; Owsley, *Borderlands*, 181–84; Wright, *Creeks and Seminoles*, 190, 197, 205, 207–8.

48. Minutes of the Treaty of Fort Jackson, August 9, 1814, Ayer MSS; Kappler, *Treaties*, 2:110; Pound, *Hawkins*, 238; Wright, *Creeks and Seminoles*, 180.

49. R. S. Cotterill, "Federal Indian Management in the South, 1789–1825," *MVHR* 20 (1933–34): 346.

Afterword. A Conflict of Memory

1. Richard Drinnon, *Facing West: The Metaphysics of Indian Hating and Empire-Building* (New York, 1980), 104–8; Frank Lawrence Owsley, Jr., *Struggle for the Gulf Borderlands: The Creek War and the Battle of New Orleans, 1812–1815* (Gainesville, Fla., 1981), 87–94; "Extract of a Letter from David B. Mitchel, Indian agent, to the Secretary of War, Milledgeville, Georgia, March 30, 1817," in *Message from the President of the United States . . . March 25, 1815* (Washington, D.C., 1818), 12, pamphlet at the Library Company of Philadelphia; William Hartley and Ellen Hartley,

Osceola, the Unconquered Indian (New York, 1973), 33–44; Edwin C. McReynolds, *The Seminoles* (Norman, Okla., 1957), 137–242, esp. 146.

2. Winfield Scott to Lewis Cass, Fort Armstrong, August 19 [–21st], 1832, in *The Black Hawk War, 1831–1832: Letters and Papers*, Collections of the Illinois State Historical Library, vols. 36 and 37, ed. Ellen M. Whitney (Springfield, 1973–75), 37:1026; Minutes of an Examination of Indian Prisoners, Fort Armstrong, August 27, 1832, in ibid., 37:1056; Joseph M. Street to William Clark, Prairie du Chien, Wisconsin, July 6, 1831, in ibid., 36:104; William Clark to Secretary of War, St. Louis, August 12, 1831, in ibid., 36:136; Henry Gratiot to William Clark, Gratiot Grove, October 15, 18[31], in ibid., 36:164; Caleb Atwater, *Remarks on a Tour of Prairie du Chien; Thence to Washington City, in 1829* (Columbus, Ohio, 1831), 134. See especially Anthony F. C. Wallace, *Prelude to Disaster: The Course of Indian-White Relations Which Led to the Black Hawk War of 1832* (Springfield, Ill., 1970), 2, 44–46; William T. Hagan, "The Black Hawk War," in *An Anthology of Western Great Lakes Indian History*, ed. Donald L. Fixico (Milwaukee, 1987), 271–91.

3. R. David Edmunds, *The Shawnee Prophet* (Lincoln, Neb., 1983), 143–90; Henry Harvey, *History of the Shawnee Indians, from the Year 1681 to 1854, Inclusive* (1855; New York, 1971), 169–81.

4. Edmunds, *The Shawnee Prophet*, 165–83; Kappler, *Treaties*, 2:145–51.

5. John Ross to David Crockett, Head of Coosa, Cherokee Nation, January 13, 1831, Ayer MSS.

6. James Terrell to L. C. Draper, Qualla Town, N.C., September 27, 1893, Draper MSS, 10 U 16; John R. Finger, *The Eastern Band of Cherokees, 1819–1900* (Knoxville, Tenn., 1984), 11, 18, 63, 65–66.

7. Vernon Kinietz and Ermine W. Voegelin, eds., "Shawanese Traditions," *Occasional Contributions from the Museum of Anthropology of the University of Michigan* 9 (1939): xv–xvi; James Howard, *Shawnee! The Ceremonialism of a Native Tribe and Its Cultural Background* (Athens, Ohio, 1981), 198–99; Paul Radin, *The Winnebago Tribe* (1923; Lincoln, Neb., 1971), 25.

8. Howard, *Shawnee!*, 198; Atwater, *Remarks on a Tour*, 119; William Albert Galloway, *Old Chillicothe: Shawnee and Pioneer History* (Xenia, Ohio, 1934), 162–63. Galloway's informant may have been the Shawnee scholar, Thomas Wildcat Alford, who contributed essays to Galloway's volume. For the issue of Tecumseh's death, see W. [Anon.], "From the Baltimore American: Black Hawk—Tecumseh," *Army and Navy Chronicle* 7 (1838): 296; Colin C. Ironside to L. C. Draper, Vinita, Indian Territory, May 4, 1885, Draper MSS, 7 YY, 76; "From Joseph N. Bournassa, born March 19, 1810, near Bertraud, Michigan, resides near Topeka, Kansas," in Draper, MSS, 23 S, 185; and esp. John Sudgen, *Tecumseh's Last Stand* (Norman, Okla., 1985), 136–81.

9. Statement of Tustenuckochee, August 22, 1883, enclosed in I. G. Vore to L. C. Draper, Webbers Falls, Indian Territory, August 16, 1886, and A. W. Crain to L. C. Draper, Sasakwa, Seminole Nation, Indian Territory, January 11, 1882, Draper MSS, 4 YY, 2–3, 16.

10. George Stiggins, "A Historical Narration of the Genealogy Traditions and Downfall of the Ispocaga or Creek Tribe of Indians," Draper MSS, 1 U 66, 42–45.

11. A. E. W. Robertson to Draper, Tallahassee, Indian Territory, December 2, 1881, Draper MSS, 4 YY, 43; "Statement of Tustenuckochee," ibid., 2–3. Angie Debo, *The Road to Disappearance* (Norman, Okla., 1941), 81.

12. A. N. Chamberlin [Cherokee] to L. C. Draper, Vinita, Cherokee Nation, Indian Territory, February 4, 1882, and April 22, 1882; J. T. Adair to Draper, Oak Grove, Cherokee Nation, May 1882, and John G. Harnage to [illeg.], Kilgore Texas, February 7, 1881, all in Draper MSS, 4 YY, 28, 29, 31, 36, 39; Charles Tucker to Draper, Vinita, Indian Territory, August 16, 1889, Draper MSS, 1 YY; William Ross to Draper, Fort Gipson, Indian Territory, February 1, 1882, Draper MSS, 4 YY 61.

13. James Mooney, "Ghost Dance Religion and the Sioux Outbreak of 1890," in *Fourteenth Annual Report of the Bureau of American Ethnology*, pt. 2 (Washington, D.C., 1896), 676–77.

14. Daniel Sabin Buttrick, *Antiquities of the Cherokee Indians* (Vinita, Cherokee Nation, 1884), 15.

15. Ibid.; Charles Hudson, *The Southeastern Indians* (Knoxville, Tenn., 1976), 173; Meigs, "Some Reflections on Cherokee Concerns . . . ," in Meigs to Eustis, March 19, 1812, NA, M208, roll 5.

16. Josiah Gregg, *Commerce of the Prairies,* ed. Max L. Moorhead (1844; Norman, Okla., 1954), 388–89.

Index

>>>>>>><<<<<<<

Prophets (cont.)
"traditional" religion and, xvii, xviii, 2,
9, 32, 128, 129; visions of, compared, 124,
126, 127. See also Annuities; individual names;
Red Sticks; Trade; Tribal denominations
Providential thought, among Indians, 5, 200
Pushmataha, 172

Quakers, 31, 152; and Delawares, 69; mission
in Old Northwest, 134; nativists' attitudes
toward, 138; prophets' attitudes toward,
36, 69, 124

Radin, Paul, 196
Raven (of Hiwassee), 48, 49, 53
Red Hawk, 41, 42; murder of, 76
Red Sticks, 93, 147, 148, 157, 158, 169, 170,
180, 198; acculturation and, 169, 170;
attacked by Americans, Cherokees,
Choctaws, and Creeks, 186; Cherokee
relations with, 157, 158, 180, 181; Choctaw
relations with, 172; disadvantages of, 185;
nativism of, 167; pan-Indianism among,
171–72; persistence of, after 1814, 188, 189;
remembered, 197, 198; rituals of, 169;
Seminoles and, 191, 193; Shawnee rela-
tions with, 171, 181; Spanish aid and, 185
Religion: "despiritualization" in, 17; resilience of, 17–19, 60–64, 101, 102, 167, 173;
shared traditions, xviii, 3–18. See also
Nativism; Prophets; Sacred power; tribal
names
Removal crisis, among Cherokees, 158, 161–66
Republicanism, 90; and Indian dependence,
118–21
Revitalization movements, xvii, 129. See also
Wallace, Anthony F. C.
Richter, Daniel K., x, xi
Ridge, 176, 177, 180
Ridout, Thomas, 13
Ritual: anti-ritual and, 200; Cherokee nativ-
ism and, 178; as gift, 3, 4, 9, 169; origins
of, 3; pan-Indianism and, 52; role of, 3, 5,
32, 35, 39, 45, 60, 123; sacred power and, 9
Roads: issue among Cherokees, 161; issue
among Creeks, 155, 156
Rogers, James, 37, 51
Roman Catholicism, 37, 64
Roosevelt, Theodore, 86
Ross, John, 195
Running Water, 104, 105, 112

Sacred power, xviii, 3, 4, 9, 10, 19, 35, 36, 61,
128, 167, 185; definition of, 3; ritual and,
16, 19; war and, 16
Salem, 64
Sandusky, 34, 83, 88, 134
Sauks, 26, 120, 185, 193–94
Savannah, 55
Scattameck, 40
Schönbrunn, 64
Schoolcraft, Henry Rowe, 10
Scioto Conferences, 42–44
Seekaboo, 134, 146, 148, 155, 156; joins
Seminoles, 188
Selu. See Corn Woman, among Cherokees
Seminoles, 191, 196, 197; African-Americans
and, 156, 188; American Revolution and,
56; conjurers among, 62; Creek National
Council challenged by, 172; Josiah Francis
among, 172; nativism among, 172;
prophets among, 172; Red Stick relations,
172; religion among, 62; U.S. invades
(1811), 156
Seminole War: first (1812–c.1820), 188, 189;
second (1835–42), 193
Senecas, 35, 53, 57, 75, 76, 142, 143; delegates
attacked at Pittsburgh, 75; divided by
Pontiac's War, 37; prophets among, 34, 41,
42, 124–28; suffer invasions (1779), 53, 74–
75, 80, 81; war rituals of, 13
Senecas, Genessee, 37
Separate creation, 21, 30, 31, 41, 42, 44, 141,
142, 167, 200; among Cherokees, 63, 100,
108, 175; among Creeks, 167; among Delawares, 30; Indian identity and, xi, 30, 31,
42; among Mingos, 41–42; among Shawnees, 141, among Wyandots, 141
Separatism, 32, 33, 35, 37, 38, 40, 63, 83, 108,
142, 178, 200; Cherokee, 174, 175. See also
Separate creation
Seven Years' War (1754–63), xvi, xix, 30, 36;
Cherokee-Shawnee relations during, 51;
religious diffusion in, 25, 26
Shawnee Prophet. See Tenskwatawa
Shawnees, xx, 2, 13–15, 23, 25, 34, 36, 53, 59,
81, 102, 114, 118, 120, 181, 198; agricultural
rituals of, 8; at Battle of Moraviantown,
185; Cherokee relations, 67, 102, 109, 110,
112; Chickamauga relations, 58, 59, 91, 93,
94, 99, 104, 105, 109; Chillicothe division
of, 66, 67; Creek relations, 94, 102, 104,
105, 109–11, 145, 146, 148, 171, 181; Dun-

A Spirited Resistance

Designed by Ann Walston

Composed by Blue Heron, Inc.
in Bembo text and display

Printed by Princeton University Press
on 50-lb. Glatfelter Offset Vellum